Mike Ashley was born in 1948 and has spent all his working life in Local Government. He has been writing since 1965 and has published nearly fifty books and some five hundred articles and reviews, including many contributions to encyclopedias on fantasy and science fiction. He has published the definitive bibliography of Algernon Blackwood, on whose biography he is working, and has written a major survey of the early days of science fiction. He has edited the previous Arthurian anthologies, *The Pendragon Chronicles, The Camelot Chronicles, The Merlin Chronicles* and *The Chronicles of the Holy Grail*, and has compiled *The Mammoth Book of Historical Whodunnits* and *The Mammoth Book of Historical Detectives*. He has compiled two anthologies of classical stories, including *Classical Whodunnits*, and has also edited *The Mammoth Book of New Sherlock Holmes Stories*.

In the same series

THE PENDRAGON CHRONICLES
THE CAMELOT CHRONICLES
THE MERLIN CHRONICLES
THE CHRONICLES OF THE HOLY GRAIL

The Chronicles of the Round Table

Edited by

Mike Ashley

RAVEN BOOKS
London

Robinson Publishing Ltd
7 Kensington Church Court
London W8 4SP

First published by Raven Books, an imprint of
Robinson Publishing Ltd 1997

A copy of the British Library Cataloguing in Publication Data is available from the British Library.

ISBN 1-85487-953-7

Printed and bound in the EC

10 9 8 7 6 5 4 3 2 1

CONTENTS

Acknowledgements

The editor would like to thank Larry Mendelsburg for his help and encouragement throughout the compilation of this and earlier volumes. He acknowledges the following authors or their representatives for granting the right to use the stories in this volume. Every effort has been made to identify the copyright holder. The editor would be pleased to hear from anyone if there has been any inadvertent infringement of copyright.

"A Figure in Faerie Time" © 1997 by John T. Aquino. First publication, original to this anthology. Printed by permission of the author.
"The Trial of Sir Kay" © 1997 by Cherith Baldry. First publication, original to this anthology. Printed by permission of the author.
"Arthur, the Demigod?" © 1989 by Vera Chapman. First published in *The Once and Future Arthur*, edited by Edmund R. Meskys (Center Harbor: Niekas Publications, 1989). Reprinted by permission of Laurence Pollinger Ltd.
"The Hand of Fair Lysette" © 1997 by Michael Coney. First publication, original to this anthology. Printed by permission of the author and the author's agent, Virginia Kidd Literary Agency.
"Meraugis and Medwina" © 1997 by Seamus Cullen. First publication, original to this anthology. Printed by permission of the author and the author's agent, Virginia Kidd Literary Agency.
"My Lady of the Ashes" © 1997 by Paul Finch. First publication, original to this anthology. Printed by permission of the author.
"Dieu et Mon Droit!" © 1997 by Eliot Fintushel. First publication, original to this anthology. Printed by permission of the author and his agent Linn Prentis.
"A Tribute of Ferns" © 1997 by Peter T. Garratt. First publication, original to this anthology. Printed by permission of the author.
"The Road to Camelot" © 1984 by Parke Godwin. First published in *Fantasy Review*, April 1984. Reprinted by permission of the author.
"Uallanach" © 1988 by Parke Godwin. First published in *Invitation to Camelot* (New York: Ace Books, 1988). Reprinted by permission of the author.
"The Knight of Good Heart" © 1997 by Liz Holliday. First publication, original to this anthology. Printed by permission of the author.
"Clarissant" © 1997 by Phyllis Ann Karr. First publication, original to this anthology. Printed by permission of the author.
"Twice Knightly" © 1936 by Alan Kennington. Published in the

Evening Standard (London), 28 September 1936. Unable to trace copyright holder.
"The Fight for the Queen" by Leonora Lang first published in *The Book of Romance* edited by Andrew Lang (London: Longmans, Green, 1902). Copyright expired in 1962.
"Earthworks" © 1997 by Patrick McCormack. First publication, original to this anthology. Printed by permission of the author.
"The Goose Girl" by Theodore Goodridge Roberts © 1951 by McCall Corporation. First published in *Blue Book Magazine*, August 1951. Copyright expired in 1977. No record of copyright renewal.
"The Gest of Sir Brandiles" © 1997 by Kurt Roth. First publication, original to this anthology. Printed by permission of the author.
"Just Cause" © 1997 by Fay Sampson. First publication, original to this anthology. Printed by permission of the author.
"Belleus's Demon" © 1997 by Lawrence Schimel. First publication, original to this anthology. Printed by permission of the author.
"The Dragon of Camlann" © 1997 by Darrell Schweitzer. First publication, original to this anthology. Published by permission of the author, and the author's agent Dorian Literary Agency.
"My Mother, the Hag" © 1997 by Brian Stableford. First publication, original to this anthology. Printed by permission of the author.
"The Perfect Stranger" © 1997 by R.H. Stewart. First printing, original to this anthology. Printed by permission of the author and the author's agent, Laurence Pollinger Ltd.
"Tournament of Rogues" © 1997 by Keith Taylor. First publication, original to this anthology. Printed by permission of the author.
"The Hedge of Mist" © 1997 by Peter Valentine Timlett. First publication, original to this anthology. Printed by permission of the author.
"Knight of the Golden Collar" © 1997 by Peter Tremayne. First publication, original to this anthology. Printed by permission of the author and the author's agent, A.M. Heath & Co. Ltd.

Foreword: ARTHUR, THE DEMIGOD?

Vera Chapman

I have always been attracted by the romantic figure of King Arthur, as well as his Knights and Ladies. I remember as a child being presented by my teacher with a tidy list, with dates, of the Kings and Queens of England from William the Conqueror, 1066, down to Edward VII, and asking, "But where does King Arthur come in?" Needless to say, there was no answer.

As I went through life I picked up scraps of information here and there, but all inconclusive. Arthur seemed to have no date. I stood on the battlements of Tintagel, and by the hallowed spot in the ruins of Glastonbury where two bodies, supposedly Arthur and Guinevere, had long rested in a shrine. Of course, I read Malory and (later) Geoffrey of Monmouth. Arthur and his knights seemed to be dispersed over the centuries and over the British Isles.

I was greatly stimulated by a charming book written by the late (alas!) Edith Ditmas, treating the Arthurian characters as real people – also by T.H. White, who brought Arthur's world into a new dimension. But it was the Ancient Order of Druids (and subsequently the Order of Bards, Orates and Druids) that gave me the clue that linked all these scattered and contradictory pieces – Arthur was a god, no less. It is possible to see him as a great traditional archetype of the British people. In fact, it can be said, with some conviction, that the mysterious and elusive St George of England is Arthur, or that Arthur is St George. The armour, the horse, the spear, the pursuit of evil powers, the great aim and object of restoring and maintaining the peace, liberty and all things good, fit the picture entirely. His sword and spear, shield and magical cup or stone, and his Round Table and band of faithful followers, bring him into relation with the Parsifal knight. He is born in obscurity and is miraculously manifested. With his band (who sometimes are twelve or twenty-four) he goes through his land and subdues it. In the end of the story he does not die, but is carried away into "the West", and is to come again. All these things proclaim him as the Archetype of Britain who is everywhere and nowhere, was born many times and yet never died – he lies somewhere in Britain, in a cave, asleep with all his knights around him.

When William Shakespeare makes Mistress Quickly, in reporting the death of Falstaff, say: "Nay, he's in Arthur's bosom if ever a man went to Arthur's bosom", she is not making a malapropism of Abraham and Arthur; I am sure she is not making any error. "Arthur's bosom" would, of course, be more congenial to Falstaff than Abraham's, but I am sure the archetypal Arthur lived on and took his chosen knights into his own peculiar paradise.

So when the hawthorn is in bloom and Guinevere goes a-Maying, let us lift our hearts to Britain's great defender, Arthur or St George.

Vera Chapman

Introduction: THE REALM OF THE ROUND TABLE

Mike Ashley

Few names can conjure up such images of chivalry and knightly valour as those of the Knights of the Round Table. The idea of a table where all could sit as equals before their king was so powerful that it influenced the actions of two of England's greatest kings of the Middle Ages. In June 1284, following his conquest of Wales, Edward I set up a Round Table court at Nefyn in celebration. Apparently the festivities were so well attended that the floor of the court gave way under the strain. It may be this Round Table, or a later one made for Edward I's marriage celebrations to Margaret, the daughter of the King of France in 1299, that is now on display at Winchester. Sixty years later, Edward III's court at Windsor Castle was modelled on the concept of the Round Table. He had a Round Table made some 200 feet in diameter. He called for the greatest knights in Christendom to attend his realm and take part in contests and tournaments. As a reward he established the Most Noble Order of the Garter in 1348 as the highest order of chivalry. He was originally going to call this the Most Noble Order of King Arthur. Arthur was Edward's hero, and there is no doubt that the world of Edward and of his son, the Black Prince, was the closest England came to the legendary world of King Arthur. This was the world that Thomas Malory wrote about in his *Le Morte D'Arthur* in the 1460s. By then the Arthurian tales and the legend of the Round

Table had been around for over three centuries. But where did it come from? What was the Round Table? And who were the knights honoured with the right to sit alongside their king?

The very first reference to the Round Table is in the narrative ballad *Roman de Brut*, or the *Romance of Brutus*, completed about the year 1155 by the Norman poet Wace, who lived from about 1110 to 1175. Wace was born on the island of Jersey but travelled around Brittany and south-west England and resided for some time at the court of the Dukes of Normandy at Caen. The Dukes of Normandy were also the Kings of England, and Wace's *Roman de Brut* was dedicated to the remarkable Eleanor of Aquitaine, the wife of Henry II.

Wace introduced the Round Table as follows:

> *On account of his noble barons, each of whom thought himself the best and none of whom accounted himself the worst, Arthur made the Round Table, of which the Britons tell many fabulous tales. There sat his vassals, all noble and all equal; they sat equally at table and were equally served. No one of them could boast of sitting higher than his peer.*

Apparently Wace's source for the Round Table came from the Breton storytellers who drew their own tales from their Celtic past. Celtic warriors would often sit in a circle around their king, both when he held court and when they celebrated victories. Sometimes the bravest warrior would sit alongside the king as a reward for his achievements.

An English monk called Layamon, who lived in Worcestershire, translated Wace's *Roman de Brut* into English some time around the year 1190. Layamon's *Brut* is a less romantic account of the history of Britain. He also drew upon Celtic tradition and embellishes the story of the Round Table by telling how a fight broke out one Christmas at Arthur's court over which knight had precedence. Arthur ordered a local carpenter to create the table which could seat up to 1,600 knights. This size is unlikely, for even if we allow the knights to sit shoulder to shoulder and allow them about 3 feet each the table would need to be about 1,500 feet across, or a quarter of a mile! This conjures up images more of an Olympic arena, or perhaps a Roman amphitheatre. It is entirely possible that the Celtic kings used Roman amphitheatres for their courts, especially in the days soon after the passing of Roman authority from Britain in the fifth century, when the amphitheatres would still have been in good condition. There were at least seven amphitheatres in Britain: at Dorchester, Silchester, Chichester, Cirencester, Carmarthen, Caerleon and Chester – the last two being military bases strongly associated with King Arthur. There may also have been amphitheatres at Verulamium (St Albans), London, Canterbury and York.

However, the attraction remains strong for a genuine physical table. By the time Robert de Boron, a poet at the French court in Burgundy, came to complete his *Merlin*, around the year 1200, the Round Table had started to take on mystical proportions. According to Robert, the Table was created by Merlin for Uther Pendragon as a commemoration of the table of the Last Supper at which Jesus drank from the Holy Grail. This Table, which could seat fifty knights, kept one seat empty in memory of the traitor Judas. That seat could only be filled by the knight who had sufficient virtue to achieve the quest for the Grail. After Uther's death the Table was inherited by King Leodegrance of Cameliard and from him it passed to Arthur as a wedding gift when Arthur married Leodegrance's daughter Guinevere. Arthur retained the empty seat, which became known as the Siege Perilous, although on a couple of occasions knights overcome with their vanity chose to sit at it. Sir Perceval, having defeated all the other knights in a tournament, regarded himself as the most valorous of knights and requested Arthur's permission to sit at the vacant seat. This led to an earthquake which rent the land, which would only be repaired following the success of the Grail Quest. Sir Brumart, a nephew of the French King Claudas, also believed he had the right to sit at the empty seat, but died in the attempt. It was not until Sir Galahad came to Arthur's Court that the seat revealed itself as his rightful place because he was the most holy of all knights.

More than its physical appearance, the Round Table came to signify an order of chivalry. It was this group of the bravest knights in Christendom who would undertake quests at the command of the king to right wrongs throughout the land. The order came to an end when the war broke out between Arthur and Lancelot over Queen Guinevere. Nevertheless for the period of its existence the Round Table was symbolic of the government of Britain ruled by a strong and chivalrous king who despatched his knights to keep law and order.

Both Wace's and Layamon's works were based on an earlier book, the popular *Historia Regum Britanniae* or *The History of the Kings of Britain*, written by the Oxford scholar and canon Geoffrey of Monmouth in 1136. It was Geoffrey who more or less created the legend of King Arthur. He did not specifically refer to the Round Table but he did refer to Arthur's court in a section that is remarkably prophetic of Edward III's court two centuries later. Geoffrey recounts that after Arthur's conquests "he established the whole of his kingdom in a state of lasting peace," and goes on to say that he "began to increase his personal entourage by inviting very distinguished men from far-distant kingdoms to join it. In this way he developed such a code of courtliness in his household that he inspired peoples living far away to imitate him. The result was that even the man of noblest birth, once he was roused to rivalry, thought nothing at all of himself unless he wore his arms and dressed in the same way as Arthur's knights."

Geoffrey names very few of Arthur's knights. He refers to Bedivere, his Cup-Bearer, whom he made Duke of Normandy, and to his Seneschal, Kay, whom he made Duke of Anjou. He also names all the leading kings and earls of Britain whom he summons to a special court, amongst whom are Peredur, Urien of Moray and Cador of Cornwall. There is also a brief reference to the young Gawain, twelve-year-old son of King Lot. Clearly, though, there was a tradition of Arthur and his most famous companions. In "Culhwch and Olwen", one of the stories in the noted Welsh collection of tales and legends *The Mabinogion*, which survives in manuscript from the fourteenth century, but was certainly in oral tradition long before, there is a list of over 200 champions at Arthur's court. Most of these names are now long forgotten, but amongst them, in addition to the ever-present Kay and Bedivere (or Cai and Bedwyr), were heroes capable of remarkable feats. These include Clust the Big-Boned, who could hear an ant move from fifty miles even if buried forty feet under the earth; Medyr, who could cast a stone from Wales and hit a wren in Ireland, and Ol the Tracker who found his father's cattle even though they had been stolen seven years before he was born.

The list of knights grew with each story told, but the most famous came from the works of the French romancist Chrétien de Troyes. At the outset of his adventure *Erec and Enide*, completed about the year 1170, he lists several of Arthur's court, not all by name. He regarded the three greatest knights as Gawain, Erec and Lancelot – Chrétien was the first to name Lancelot. He then went on to list Gornemant of Gohort, Meliant of Liz, Mauduit the Wise, Dodinel the Wild, Karadués the Short-Armed, Yder of the Dolorous Mount, Gales the Bald, Sagremor the Impetuous, Labigodés the Courtly, and many more including Gandelu, Eslit, Yvain, Tristan, Caveron, Gaheriet, Kay, Tor, Amauguin, Girflet, and Arthur's own son Loholt.

It is unlikely that these troubadors and tale-tellers invented these names. Many may have been the names of contemporary or near-contemporary knights included in tribute to the knights of the court. Little wonder that the lists became so long if the storytellers were trying to please everyone and not risk offence by leaving names out. But it is also likely that many of the names came from well-known tradition. The listing of names is suggestive of ancient genealogical tables and Welsh triads, where names are remembered by linking together three key events. The oldest of these names, certainly Kay, Bedivere and Gawain, are likely to have come from the same period as Arthur and to relate to real heroes, who were either vassal kings in their own right or the sons of kings. Their lands would have been scattered throughout Britain and northern France, and their most heroic exploits were probably against not only the Saxons but also the Irish and Picts, all of whom tried to plunder the rich pickings of southern Britain in the decades after the fall of Rome. Tradition has many of these related to Arthur. Gawain, Gaheris, Agravaine and Gareth, for instance, were all the sons of King Lot, who had married Arthur's half-sister (or in some accounts his aunt) Morgause. Lancelot's mother Viviane was another of Arthur's sisters or aunts. Yvain or Owain was the son of Urien, an historical king of Rheged, who was reputedly married to Morgaine (the Morgan le Fay of legend), Arthur's half-sister, whilst Perceval was the son of Pellinore whose brother Pelles was the father-in-law of Lancelot.

It is very likely that most of the knights of the Round Table are based on historical characters who had shown prowess in battle or had some remarkable gift or skill with which they became famed at court. Lancelot was almost certainly the high-born son of a king and might even have been a king himself. His castle, Joyeuse Gard, is usually acquainted with the fortress of Bamburgh in Northumbria. At the time Lancelot lived Northumbria was under invasion by the Angles, the start of centuries of conflict between the Germanic races, the Picts and the Irish (who settled in Argyll and became known as the Scots). Lancelot is sometimes regarded as the French version of Auguselus, whom Geoffrey of Monmouth recognized as the brother of Lot and king of Albany, the name given to the Dal Riatan kingdom of the Scots. If this has any grain of truth then Lancelot was probably related to the Scottish kings descended from Fergus and his brothers Angus and Loarn, who settled in Argyll and Moray in the early sixth century.

Some of these knights, especially Lancelot, Gawain, Galahad, and Perceval, are as well known as Arthur. But what were they really like? That is what this book is about. In twenty-four stories, this anthology explores the lives of these knights and discovers who they were, what drove them on their quests, and what pain and anguish they encountered and fought to conquer. Previous anthologies in this series have covered some of the knights and their more traditional adventures, including the Grail Quest, so this volume probes deeper. It deliberately shifts away from the better-known knights. This means that although you will still encounter Lancelot, Gawain, Tristram and others, you will also find the opportunity to discover some of the lesser-known knights and explore their worlds. In these stories you will find the adventures of Artegall, Balin, Belleus, Blamore, Brandiles, Breunis, Dinadan, Gereint, Lionel, Mador, Marrok, Melleas, Meraugis, Pelleas, Sagramor, Tor, Villiars and Yder, as well as the better-known Bedivere, Kay, Lancelot, Mordred and Owain. Most of the stories have been written specially for this anthology and the few reprints are mostly from rare sources, unlikely to be encountered by other than the most ardent collector.

I have also provided a special afterword in which the well-known Arthurian authors Marion Zimmer Bradley and Parke Godwin discuss their views of the Arthurian world.

Once again we peel back the curtains of time to explore that distant world of King Arthur. I hope you find it enjoyable.

Mike Ashley

Sir Gereint in
THE HEDGE OF MIST

Peter Valentine Timlett

There is little doubt that Gereint was an historical figure. He appears in the king lists of Dumnonia, which was a Celtic kingdom in south-west England roughly equal to Devon and Cornwall. He lived some time in the early-to-mid sixth century and was probably killed in battle against the Saxons. He is best remembered in the story "Gereint, son of Erbin" which is included amongst the collection of Welsh tales The Mabinogion. *The following story is based on that tale.*

Peter Valentine Timlett (b. 1933) is the author of the Seedbearers trilogy, The Seedbearers *(1974),* The Power of the Serpent *(1976) and* The Twilight of the Serpent *(1977), plus a handful of short horror stories. He is also a long-time student of the occult with a special interest in the Arthurian world.*

Arthur lolled forward, chin in hand, and scarcely heard the babble around him. Odyar the Frank was telling a tale so preposterous that scarcely anyone bothered to listen. Bedwyr, good Bedwyr, was trying to pay him heed but even his good nature was sorely tried. "There are times, Gwalchmei," he said softly, "when tournaments are not enough, nor the comeliness of maidens, even the finest." He gazed around the huge table. Gwrddnei Cat Eye was talking to Gwenhwyvar, trying to impress the Queen, but failing – as usual. He was a good man with a sword but the ladies found him uncouth. Glewlwyd Strong Grip was bloated with drink, though the day was still in its youth. Chief Gatekeeper he was supposed to be, though the only time he ever kept the gate was at the major festivals when he sought to justify his position. And as for the ladies – well, cast from nature's standard mould, most of them, no matter how their respective champions boasted their charm and wit.

Gwalchmei grunted. "A man who is tired of beauty is tired of life."

"It's not beauty I'm tired of," said Arthur sharply, "it's drabness praised beyond its worth. If I hear of just one more dull bawd being lauded as the most beautiful maiden in the land I shall . . . I shall . . ."

"You are bored, my liege."

"Oh yes. Merlin said I would be, once the novelty of kingship wore off."

Gwalchmei grunted but said nothing at first. The wizard had not been heard of for some years, and there were those who were not displeased with that. "Kei tells me that a minstrel-bard has arrived at court."

Arthur's eye brightened. "Do we know him?"

"No, never seen him before, nor heard of him."

"Excellent," said the King, rubbing his hands. "New stories and new songs. By all the gods, what would we do without bards? Let him be brought in."

He was a tall lad with hair like summer wheat, thin but well muscled with long legs that Arthur guessed would enable him to run like a startled hart if he had to. His eyes were a vivid blue, noticeably blue even amongst a people in whom blue eyes were common, and Arthur saw that he was handsome and would have little trouble finding a warm companion for his bed. "You are a minstrel bard, I hear," said the King.

The lad bowed gracefully and Arthur saw that he was well mannered and probably of noble birth. "I am Tygry of Kernow, my liege."

"Have you been given food and drink?"

The lad glanced at the huge knight who had brought him into hall. "Yes, my lord, Sir Kei has been most kind."

There was some laughter at that for the often surly Kei was not noted for compassion, though Arthur was aware that Kei often performed acts of kindness in secret, as though ashamed of a weakness. "Tygry? Isn't that 'kestrel' in your father's tongue?"

"Yes, my lord, and perhaps because of that I was led by the gods to bear witness to the tale of the Knight of the Kestrel," and Arthur's eye brightened still further, "and of Gereint son of Erbin."

"Gereint?" said Gwenhwyvar sharply.

"Yes, for indeed my tale begins with you, my lady," he said boldly.

Arthur frowned. "Take care, lad, even bards can be beaten for impertinence."

"I intend no disrespect to the Queen, my liege, it's just that the tale begins with your fine lady, and it is a true tale," and he glanced round at the assembled knights, "as all tales of Arthur's knights are true – though perhaps embroidered just a trifle."

"A little more than just a trifle," said Arthur, and some of the knights at table had the grace to look sheepish. "Begin, then."

The bard did not sit to tell his tale, but strode around the hall as he spoke, stopping, turning, retracing, gesticulating with his hands, and within moments the audience, King and knights all, and their ladies, were entranced, for the lad had a fine ringing voice, a dramatic voice, sonorous when needed, rising to crescendo when describing battles, sinking to quieter tones when love and maidens softened the tale. "Some little while ago," Tygry began, "here at Caer Llion ar Wysg, you, my king, and others here – my lord Gwalchmei, Sir Bedwyr and his son Amren, and many another fine knight, set forth to hunt the white hart."

"I remember it," said Arthur, "a fine hunt."

"You had given permission for the Queen to join the hunt but she slept beyond your departure."

"I did not like to call her," said Arthur, though in truth he did not like women on a hunt, they slowed everything down and were apt to complain when mud spattered their fine dresses.

"And when I did rise," said Gwenhwyvar, "the court was practically empty and only two spare horses in the stables fit for women to ride."

"And so you rode out with just one handmaiden," said Tygry, wishing they would not keep interrupting. "But you were not the last to rise that morning, for soon after your departure Gereint came galloping to join you."

"He had no doubt been late to bed," said the Queen, defending him.

"Late to sleep anyway," said Kei sourly, ever jealous of Gereint's success with women. "No doubt some wench robbed him of his sleep," and the knights roared with laughter, but Arthur noted where more than a few maidenly cheeks suddenly flushed, for Gereint was handsome, young, brave, and already renowned throughout the land.

Gwenhwyvar sighed. Ah Gereint, how handsome you looked that day, bare-legged astride that huge willow-grey colt, your auburn hair blowing in the forest breeze, Cordovan shoes upon your feet, that fine mantle of green purple around your broad shoulders, the one with a gold apple at each corner, and your gold-hilted sword upon your thigh. Even your horse had looked handsome that day, proud and high-stepping, swift and lively. I don't know which saucy *scowt* had kept you from your sleep but I hope her teeth fall out and she withers quickly to be an old hag.

"But then you spied a stranger knight approaching through the forest, with a beautiful maiden and a dwarf."

"By the gods, bard," said Arthur, "are there no ugly maids in my kingdom, are then all maidens beautiful?"

"Indeed not, my liege," said Tygry patiently, for one always needed to be patient with kings, "but in bardic tales all maidens are beautiful and all knights bold and handsome."

"I don't see why," said Arthur, "ugly people can be interesting, look at Kei there," and again the knights hooted with laughter.

"Sir Kei is renowned for his deeds," said Tygry carefully, "and has a noble bearing, and indeed is subject of many a tale told and retold in the many courts of your realm."

"Very well," sighed Arthur, "so this maiden was beautiful."

"But the dwarf was ugly and vicious," said Gwenhwyvar. "I sent my hand-maiden forward to inquire the identity of the knight, for he was fully armoured with his visor down, but the dwarf would not let him get near and when she persisted he cut her across her eyes with a whip." Several of the knights cried out in anger, and some called out as to what Gereint did. Tygry kept silent. Let the Queen have her moment. Soon now the tale would move on to matters of which none here had any knowledge. "I did indeed send Gereint forward," said the Queen hotly, "but again the dwarf would not let him near the knight and cut him with the whip as he had the girl."

The table grew quiet, for this was a matter of honour.

"And?" said Arthur quietly.

Gwenhwyvar looked around at the assembled knights and knew

that what she had to say now would not reflect well on Gereint. "I saw him put his hand to his sword and assumed that the cruel dwarf was moments away from death." She hesitated. "But Gereint was not armoured. Had he killed the dwarf the stranger knight would certainly have killed Gereint, and the insult to my hand-maiden, and hence to me personally, would not have been avenged, and so he turned away and rode back to me."

Cries rang out from around the table. "We would have avenged his death, *and* your insult! To turn away from battle was not the conduct of a knight of honour!"

"Oh you are so quick to condemn," said Gwenhwyvar hotly. "How many of you would have accused him thus to his face." The hubbub died down to an uneasy silence. "To have fought the knight unarmoured would have been an act of folly, and folly is not valour."

"So what did Gereint do?" said Arthur patiently.

The Queen took a deep breath. "Had he returned here for his armour the stranger knight would have long moved on, and so Gereint left me and followed him, still unarmoured, hoping to borrow armour and a lance and so challenge the man – and I have not heard of him since."

All eyes turned to the bard. "Well?" said Arthur.

The stranger knight crossed the River Wysg at the ford below Caer Llion, with the dwarf and the maid following, and Gereint hanging well back in the trees. The sounds of the King's hunt had long died away, and the sun was climbing to its zenith. Following the strangers through the forest had been easy enough, for he had been able to keep close, but across the Wysg the forest gave way to grasslands that rose and fell as a green gown on a young maid and Gereint had perforce to allow the strangers to draw well ahead, and could only hurry after them when a fold in the ground permitted. All that afternoon he followed them as they drew steadily northwards with the Black Mountains already beginning to loom in the distance. Rarely did Arthur or his knights venture in this direction, for there was no large game on the grasslands, the boar and stag were strictly forest dwellers, and already Gereint was beyond the farthest point that he had ever reached in this direction, and still the strangers led northwards.

Then the land rose steadily, no longer undulating, no longer giving Gereint cover, and he had to halt and watch in fury as the strangers climbed the foothills to skirt the mountains, not daring to advance across open country. Then at last the strangers passed round the shoulder of a low hill, and Gereint was once again able to take up the pursuit, but by now the sun was beginning to sink beyond the western mountains and the light to fade, and as he breasted the rise he caught his breath, for in the gloaming the land fell away again, sweeping down to a wide valley, and to a well-situated fortified town. Gereint spurred his horse down the slope, careless now of cover for he was but another traveller seeking to make the town before the gates closed for the night.

Slowing as he reached the town, Gereint passed through the gateway, his horse's hooves echoing on the split timbers of the roadway that crossed the dry moat into the town itself. Though dusk Gereint could see that the town was beautiful, the courts and houses seeming well maintained, the streets still thrumming with activity, the knights and ladies strolling through the market-place, the townspeople at the stalls and shops. As Gereint clip-clopped his way through the town he saw men feeding falcons and sparrowhawks while others were grooming tercels and sorrel-headed goshawks, and there a woman rolling cloth and lifting it onto a cart, and there a maid flirting with a gawky boy, and elsewhere men played dice and other games of chance, and two old men sat opposite each other across a low wooden table engrossed in chess.

The stranger knight was obviously well known for many greeted him with smiling faces, obviously glad to see him, calling out their good wishes, and the knight nodded and gave greeting but moved onwards to the castle where again he was made welcome and passed within. The light was fading fast and the town gates were closing and Gereint looked around for where he might stay. At the far end of the market, but set a little back, was an old court that had once been a handsome dwelling but was now run-down and badly in need of repair, and as Gereint moved towards it he saw an old man resting on top of a flight of stone steps to the upper storey. As Gereint edged his horse through the gate the old man rose and came down to meet him. "Greetings, noble sir, for so I judge you, if it is hospitality you seek my court is yours."

Gereint slid from the saddle and stroked his horse's neck reassuringly, for the court was strange to him. "You are kind, good sir, my horse and I certainly need shelter for the night."

The old man clapped his hands and an older woman appeared at the top of the stairs. "Prepare food for our guest, my dear, the best we have," and as she turned back into the chamber a young girl appeared. "Ah, there you are, make haste, my dear, for there is a good beast here that needs your care."

The girl came down the stairs stepping lightly and gracefully and began to lead his horse away. She was dressed in a white shift of fine but threadbare material, and over it a plain long-sleeved smock of white linen worn through at the elbows. But though the clothing was poor the maiden herself was achingly beautiful. Nature had surpassed herself and ne'er again would fashion any maid so fine. Hair of gold spun in hot sunshine, forehead as white and lovely as the finest lily, her complexion a fresh rosy hue, her lips red as the blush of modesty, eyes as blue as forget-me-nots in spring, and she moved with all the flowing grace of a young deer.

"My daughter," said the old man.

Gereint took a deep breath. "She is more fair than any maid I have ever seen, and I have come from Arthur's court where there are fair maids a-plenty."

The old man smiled and led the way up the stone stairs and into the hall where the good lady, his wife, was already bustling hither and thither to prepare a meal. "Pray be seated," said the old man, "let me take your sword, you are among friends here."

Gereint unbuckled his sword but kept it by his side, and the old man nodded his approval. Presently the maid appeared and bobbed in curtsy. "I have fed and watered your horse, good sir, fresh sweet hay and good new oats, and I have set the boy to brushing and grooming him."

He smiled and bowed to her. "You are kind and caring, and I thank you."

The girl blushed and bustled to help her mother. Behind her a tall thin young man had followed her into the chamber and bowed to the guest. "I am Tygry of Kernow," he said, "just a minstrel-bard travelling south."

"Forgive my bad manners," said the old man hastily, "I should have announced my name when first you entered. I am Earl Niwl. I built and owned the fine castle that you saw at the end of the town, but my nephew waged war on me and took it from me, and all else I had save this one poor court." He sighed. "And so my good wife and daughter are dressed no better than any common wench in the fields."

"But there are those, no doubt," said Gereint carefully, "who would clothe your daughter in fine gowns, and adorn her throat with jewels."

"Oh yes, any number, but I will not have her go to just any man."

The good wife brought meat and wheaten loaves to the table, and a jug of ale, and Gereint sat down with the earl and young Tygry, and the daughter served them, blushing when ere she passed near their guest. Gereint ate heartily for he had not eaten since the previous day, and praised the food which set the good wife blushing in her turn. He emptied the platter and drained the goblet and then stretched his legs and sighed.

"Normally," said the Earl, "I would now ask young Tygry here for a tale to brighten our evening, but I suspect that you, chieftain, have a tale of your own to tell."

The bard looked up, his eye bright. "A tale of honour, I suspect," he said quietly.

Gereint nodded. "Yes, honour and dishonour both," and he told them of the stranger knight and of the injury he had done Gwenhwyvar's hand-maiden, "and so I followed him here, and if I can borrow some armour I will fight him and so avenge the insult."

"Ah, you speak of Edern son of Nudd," said the Earl. "The dwarf does but ape his master, for Edern is an arrogant man, and none have been able to teach him good manners though many have tried."

"Then perhaps he will learn his lesson from me."

The Earl looked at him carefully. "As far as I know he has never been defeated. He is called the Knight of the Kestrel, for once a year the young earl, my wretched nephew, holds a tournament in the meadow beyond the gates. Two forked sticks are driven into the ground, and across the sticks is placed a silver rod, and on the rod a kestrel, the prize of the tournament. Only those who bring the lady they love best may take part. He who has no lady, or who is not prepared to declare his love publicly, may not joust. Edern has won the kestrel for the past two years. By the strict rules of the tournament Erden ought not to be called the Knight of the Kestrel until he has won it three years running, but there is none to defeat him."

"There is now," said Gereint quietly, "for I am Gereint son of Erdin of Kernow, and I will teach manners to that ill-mannered oaf."

The Earl gasped and young Tygry cried out. "Of course, Gereint, I know your father, I have sung and told tales at his court. I, too, am from Kernow."

The old Earl's hair was as grey-white as winter frost upon a hawthorn bush but his eyes were suddenly bright. "Ah, at last, perhaps this is the year when Edern will be sent sprawling in the dust. As for armour, you are welcome to borrow mine; I would be honoured. But hold, even so you may not take part for you have no lady."

The young maiden had drawn near, holding her breath waiting for his answer. Gereint looked at her, and saw in her eyes that a gentle and caring spirit dwelt within that lovely form. He was not given to hasty decisions but there are moments in life when good fortune should be taken at the flood and not questioned too deeply. "Earl Niwl," he said suddenly and formally, "if it is your will, pray present your daughter to me."

"Gladly," said the Earl, "for you are not just any man." He rose and fetched the maiden by the hand and brought her to Gereint. "Gereint son of Erbin, knight renowned of great King Arthur's court, I present to you with glad heart my daughter, Enid."

Gereint took her hand and drew her near. He gazed deep into her eyes and felt his very soul stir with love. "Enid, graceful and lovely, will you permit me to publicly profess my love for you so that I may take part in tomorrow's tournament?"

"She will, gladly," said the Earl.

Gereint held up his hand. "No, the decision shall be hers, and hers alone, and I vow that she shall be free to reject me if that is her will."

Then Enid knew that her heart did not lie, that already there was love for him in her very soul. "Gladly, Gereint of Kernow, gladly with all my heart."

Gwenhwyvar dabbed her eyes with a fine linen handkerchief, and many a maiden round Arthur's table sighed with thoughts of love, though chastened that the handsome Gereint was now no longer available. Kei and Bedwyr and other knights stirred and grunted for tales of love made them uneasy, but their eyes quickened for now it meant that Gereint would fight, and that was more to their taste than all this talk of love.

The bard spread his hands and his voice lowered. "They rose before dawn," he said dramatically, and all the knights leant forward to hear his words, "and prayed at the church where a monk sang mass, and then returned to the old Earl's poor court where Enid dressed Gereint in her father's armour."

He stared around the court, silent now, eager for his next words.

"No spell she sang, no charms, but girded him with love, laced up his iron greaves with a deerskin strap, dressed him in a coat of mail, placed a shining helmet upon his head, and hung his gold-hilted sword at his waist, and thus accoutred, shield and lance in hand, he sallied forth with Enid on a palfrey behind, and the Earl and myself on either side."

"Ah knights all, what a brave sight the tourney field, two score doughty knights and fine ladies, a soft breeze blowing across the meadow, banners streaming, pavilions gay with flags and bunting, a wooden stand bedecked with garlands whereon the nobility sat, the smell of leather and horses, the shouts of the commoners, the hawkers with their trays of pies and sweetmeats, the brewmasters with their barrels pierced and spigoted to slake the thirst – ah it was a sight to stir the blood of valorous men."

Then Arthur's knights thumped the table with their fists and shouted their excitement, for the joust was meat and drink to them.

"Then came Edern son of Nudd, clad in black armour, his helmet neath his arm, his vile dwarf trotting at his side, his lady upon a palfrey, and rode up to the forked sticks, scattering the commoners aside, and the knights cheered, ladies waved their scarves, and the young Earl sat in grandeur, clapped his hands and cried out: 'Good fortune, sir knight, may God guide your arm!'"

Tygry paused for effect, and as Arthur's knights craned forward, he suddenly raised his arm aloft and cried: "But then came Gereint son of Erbin, the old Earl and the lovely Enid, and all there could see that she far surpassed the black knight's lady in beauty."

The bard paused and lowered his head and began to whisper so low that all had to crane still further to hear his words. "And as I, Tygry of Kernow, drew near I heard the arrogant son of Nudd say to his lady 'Step forth and claim the bird, for none here are more beautiful than you, and I do here publicly proclaim my love for you' and the wretched wench was so bold as to stretch out her hand to obey her lord."

Then Tygry raised his hand, finger pointing to the ceiling, "But Gereint son of Erbin urged his horse forward and cried out: 'Stay, lady, the bird is not for you, for here is one who is lovelier than thou,' and Gereint took Enid by the hand and drew her forward. 'Behold the lovely Enid, daughter of Earl Niwl, and I proclaim my love for her, now and forever – the kestrel is hers by right!' and the commoners cheered and stamped their feet.

"Then the black knight's face grew dark with fury and he urged his own horse forward. 'Foolish youth!' he cried, 'You know not what you do. Persist in this folly and Death himself shall visit you today,' but Gereint answered him boldly. 'Aye, uncaring and brutal knight, Death shall come this day but not to me, for I am Gereint son of Erbin, a knight of Arthur's court, and I am here to seek redress for the injury your dwarf caused Queen Gwenhwyvar's hand-maiden, such behaviour being an insult to the Queen herself,' and the black knight shook his lance in fury."

The knights cheered and Gwenhwyvar smiled in satisfaction. "There, my lords, did I not tell you that you were over-hasty in your judgment of him."

"It was nobly done," said Arthur, "but what then of the fight?"

"A great space was cleared," said Tygry, "and each knight drew apart the full length of the tilt-yard and then charged, one upon the other. They rode full war-horses, great beasts whose hooves drummed the ground like thunder, their nostrils flaring, their eyes wild and staring. Each knight held his lance sure and steady, and they met with such force that both shields were pierced and cracked asunder by the lance-head of the other, and the lances themselves were shattered to splinters. Neither of them had withstood the charge, such was the force of that impact that the very cantles of their saddles were broken and both knights were flung backwards off their horses and crashed to the ground."

"Was he hurt?" cried Gwenhwyvar breathlessly, and several of the knights looked at her sourly. Of course he was hurt, there was not a knight there at Arthur's table who had not at one time been hurled backwards from his horse in that manner, and to crash to the ground from that height in full armour was a brutally painful business.

"Shaken, my lady, as were they both, but they struggled to their feet and drew their swords, but Edern son of Nudd was first to rise and swinging his sword high he dealt Gereint a tremendous blow that sent him sprawling again," and Gwenhwyvar's hand flew to her mouth, "but he staggered to his feet," Tygry went on, "and raised his own sword and taking a mighty swing he aimed for the sword-arm but hit him too high on the shoulder," and many a knight nodded for it was not an easy stroke to control in full armour.

"Again and again they slashed at each other, their swords ringing on armour, cutting through shields, slicing through the elbow joints and necks, always the weakest parts of armour, and soon their swords were red with blood," and several of the maidens there gasped with horror, "and such was the force of their blows that even their great strength began to fail and their strokes came more slowly until each stood before the other, sword-points in the ground, leaning on the hilts, gasping for breath."

"Oh that I would like to have seen," said Arthur. "Never have I ever seen any knight who could fight Gereint to a standstill."

"They rested awhile to regain their strength," Tygry went on, "and the fair Enid came to Gereint with love in her eyes and said to him 'My lord, for so you are, you have professed your love for me, and I await your victory so that I might profess my love to you,' and he took fresh courage from her words and joined the battle anew, but Edern son of Nudd was fighting for pride, there in his own town, in front of his friends and his earl and all the townspeople, and he too came out anew and struck Gereint so mighty a blow that it split his shield down to the buckle and the sword-blade on the downward stroke cut into his thigh even to the bone, and his blood ran down to the ground."

Gwenhwyvar gasped to think of that fair flesh mutilated thus, but then she reddened and controlled her voice. "God speed him home to us that we might nurse his wounds," and Arthur smiled sourly.

"But Gereint shook off the blow," cried Tygry, "and sprang at his opponent and smote him across the shoulder so fiercely that Edern's shield also gave way and the blade cut down to the bone, and *his* blood too ran red, even unto his waist. And both were proud men and neither would give way. Again and again they struck at each other, and as each weakened their defence grew feeble and more of the blows got through until each was able to cut the other freely. Then Gereint summoned up all his strength and struck Edern across the helmet so fiercely that the black knight became dizzy, and Gereint followed up his advantage and struck him three heavy blows in quick succession, and Edern son of Nudd staggered about as a drunken man, and Gereint pursued him and struck him one last time and the black knight fell onto his right side, and Gereint son of Erbin seized him by the helmet and ripped it from his head," and Arthur's knights cheered and banged the table in their excitement.

Tygry flung wide his arms. "And the black knight cried 'Mercy! Take thou my sword, I surrender it to you!' and I ask you all, knights of Arthur, King, what would you have done – death or mercy?"

"Death!" came the cry. "Death to avenge the insult to the Queen! Death!"

"And you, my Queen?" said Tygry softly.

Gwenhwyvar sighed. "Mercy, I would grant mercy. Agony and defeat has already been his lot, and public humiliation. It is enough, I am satisfied, more than satisfied."

"Well answered, my lady, and mercy it was. 'I grant your life,' said Gereint, 'but you shall go to Caer lion ar Wysg, and there you shall yield yourself, your dwarf, and your maiden to Queen Gwenhwyvar to do with as she wills,' and so my Queen I hastened away; an unbattled bard travels more swiftly than a sorely wounded knight."

The knights applauded, banging their fists on the table. It had been a good tale, a lady's honour impugned, and revenged. "So, the black knight is coming here," said Arthur. "No doubt Gwenhwyvar will forgive him, but he has me to answer to."

Tygry spread his hands. "Far be it from bards to advise kings," he said carefully, "but were I king I would remember that here is a knight who fought Gereint of Kernow to a standstill and very nearly won, and no other knight has ever been able to do that. I would consider him a worthy addition to my table, were I king," he added hastily.

It was three days before Edern son of Nudd presented himself at Arthur's court, and even then his wounds had scarcely begun to heal. There was at first a silent hostility to his presence, but he knelt before the Queen and begged forgiveness with such genuine fervour, as did the ill-mannered dwarf before the maiden he had wronged, that Gwenhwyvar forgave him with all her heart and bade the court make them welcome. Arthur reserved his judgment, for it would take more than pretty words to win his approval.

"So where is Gereint?" said Arthur.

"He has remained for a few days," said Edern, "to mediate a proper settlement between the old Earl and his nephew, one that is just to both sides, and then he will come."

"With Enid, I trust," said Gwenhwyvar.

"Oh yes, they now dote one upon the other, and I know not whose love is the greater, his or hers."

It was a further week before Gereint arrived at court, and Arthur himself went down to the courtyard to welcome them, and took Enid's hand and helped her down from her palfrey, and all were in wonder at her beauty. "Did I not say she was beautiful," Tygry whispered to the King. The whole court made them welcome, and Enid was taken in hand by Gwenhwyvar's hand-maidens and dressed in fine gowns with precious gems at her bosom, and no one at court had ever seen a greater love than Enid had for Gereint, and he for her.

Then Tygry of Kernow took his departure, ". . . for a bard must travel, my liege."

"So, your tale is done," said Arthur, "and a good tale it was." Tygry remained silent, and Arthur looked at him. "What is it?"

The bard sighed. "I don't know, I wish I did." They were in the courtyard and Tygry held the bridle of his horse in readiness to mount and depart. "I am a teller of tales, King Arthur, and such a one always knows when a tale is done: it has a rounded finish to it, complete and precious as sapphire or a diamond, but my dreams are stirred by strange thoughts that this tale is far from over."

"It seems complete to me," said Arthur.

Tygry put his foot in the stirrup and swung himself up on to the saddle. "But not to me. There is more, my liege, believe me, though I know not what it could be."

In the months that followed the fame of Gereint and Enid spread, and Tygry took particular pleasure in the thought that his tale of their love had been the first. Then came news of the wedding, a sumptuous affair at which all the nobility for leagues around attended, ". . . after which," a fellow-bard told him, "they retired to their bedroom with more eagerness than a hunted stag seeks a river to slake its thirst, and there they did sport themselves mightily, and never more enthusiastically did any maiden give up her maidenhood to become a woman."

"And how do you know that?" said Tygry.

The boy had shrugged. "As you know better than most, servants will listen more avidly at bedroom doors than any other."

Then months later came further news that Gereint had taken Enid home to Kernow to meet his father, and to rid his realm of robber-knights who had begun to plague the land now that his father was aged and nearing his time, and many knights went with him, all with Arthur's blessing.

"Who?" asked Tygry of the bard who had brought the news.

"Well, Kei and Bedwyr, and Gwalchmei of course, you could not keep *him* from such an adventure, oh and Gwynn son of Tringad, Howel son of Emhyr, Garanhon son of Glythvyr, Peredur son of Evrawg, and many more, some sixty or so I heard – oh yes, and Edern son of Nudd, the black knight himself."

"And when was this?"

"Four months ago."

Tygry cursed that he was this far north, two days south of Carlisle. "What else?"

"Gereint demanded that all the vassals and lordlings who had given their homage to Erbin, his father, should now renew that homage to him as the heir to the realm, and since Gereint was neither aged nor feeble those homages were hastily given. The entire campaign lasted no more than two weeks."

"Oh God's curse, and I have missed it all – the adventure, the tournaments, the feasts."

"You missed nothing," said the bard. "Oh we had a feast that first night when they all returned in triumph," he said, "but Gereint retired early to his bed and to his wife, and there has been no feasting since, nor any tournaments. Most of Arthur's knights have returned to Caer Llion. Gereint rewarded them well enough with gold and silver, new swords and armour, new lances, and the like, but you know what knights are like, they want feasts and revelry and merry-eyed wenches, and there it was as merry as a funeral pyre."

"Enid?"

"The fault lies not with Enid, for she is lovely and sweet natured. It is just that my lord Gereint is besotted with her. They retire early to bed and are late to rise, it's rare you see them before noon, and for most of the time they sport with each other mightily, or so the servants' gossip goes. When he was not seen out and about for a few weeks," the bard added, "and when there were no more tournaments, the people nudged each other and laughed, and talked of the pleasures of a young wife, but as the weeks rolled into months their mood has turned sour, and now they are angry and curse him as mightily as once they cheered."

Tygry sighed and turned his horse's head to the south. Now was the tale about to continue; he felt it in his bones.

Gradually his heaving chest began to subside, and his breathing eased. His hair fell damp across his forehead and his eyes were bright with pleasure. He slid alongside her and began to stroke her hair. "I was not alive until I met you," he said simply. "Oh I ate, I drank, I rode and fought, and slept, all the things that a young knight does, but I was not alive. I was but a statue of a man until you breathed life into me. Now, when I am with you I am alive, but when we have to be apart I die and become that statue again."

She smiled. Her skin was damp and the dawn air struck chill. She pulled the bedclothes more closely around them and snuggled into him. "Oh you'll go jousting again and leave your wife behind, as all knights do."

"Never," he said firmly.

She stroked his chin with her finger. "You need to go among your people. The day will come when you will be their king." She had heard through her hand-maiden that the people's mood had turned sour against him, and that some of his knights were already saying aloud that he was lost to honour at arms. "My father went among his people every day, even into the market and traded for goods like a peasant, and the people loved him for it."

"I am not your father."

"And there are things that I need to do, things that I cannot do with you."

His eyes narrowed. "What things?"

Her hand fluttered nervously. "Oh just things. I'd like to spend more time with my hand-maidens, and with the wives of your knights, just talking, women's talk. And I too would like to go among your people, to let them see me, to talk with the wives of the landowners and the market-stall holders, to let them know that we care about them."

"All I care about is you," he said simply.

She sighed and smiled slightly. "A king should love his people as well as his queen."

"I do, but I don't have to go jousting every day to prove it." She kept her peace but she remembered her father's words – uneasy lies the crown of an unloved king. But she had learnt from her mother when to hold her tongue. Gereint's brow was furrowed and dark clouds had appeared in his eyes. "Perhaps it is you who are tiring of me," he said.

She reached up and stroked his face and put her lips to his ear and nuzzled him. "Of course not. I love you, sometimes I think I will burst with love," and she caressed him and kissed him until they were once more on fire for each other, and the sun rose steadily until it was high in the heavens before they fell exhausted to sleep.

And he dreamed a foul dream. Crowds gathered around them, jostling them, jeering at them, and he felt Enid drawn away from him to dance among the people. Knights there were who danced with her, whirling her round and round, handsome knights, tall and strong, and woodsmen and blacksmiths with bulging muscles and strong white teeth, and she loving it, laughing gaily with never a thought for him. Again and again he pressed forward towards her but always the press of the people held him back. "You are king," they kept saying, "you are king." And then she was drawn still further away, towards the woods, and he remembered the old rites, the dark rites of mating in the old religion, and he strove frantically towards her, but even at this distance he could see that her eyes had turned smoky and did not resist.

She woke before him, also troubled with dark dreams, and she looked down at his sleeping face, seeing his eyes twitch and his mouth writhe with words she could not hear. Her heart was troubled and tears ran down her cheeks. She was a stranger here in this far-off land. How could the people learn to love her if she did not go among them as a loving queen should, and would they blame her, the Stranger Queen, if he had abandoned all deeds of chivalry for her sake? She turned from him, blind with tears, and stuffed a kerchief in her mouth to stifle the sobs.

At last he woke and saw her tears but his heart and mind were still full of the shadowy dream, and the nightmare oozed its dark way into his waking life and he saw her as a woman pining for another, and her earlier words took on another and more insidious meaning. A woman only ever cries for the man she desires, or her child, and as she was childless so it was some man for whom her tears fell. But who? As he was there with her then it could not be him.

He reached forward and grasped her arm. "Why do you weep?" he said harshly.

Startled she turned to him. "What?"

"Why do you weep? Is that why you want me to go jousting? You want me out of the way?"

Her mouth fell open in astonishment and her heart pounded. She had received none but fair words from him since ere they met, but this was a different Gereint to the one she knew. His eyes were as chips of black flint, and his tone was harsh and challenging. "I don't want you out of the way. It's just that you have shut yourself away from your people, with me, and it may be me that they will blame."

"You want to be free of me, is that it?"

"No, no!"

"You pine for another, that is clear."

"For another? Oh Gereint, I love only you, I want no other."

The darkness of his nightmare so overcame him that it was as if his face was suffused with dark blood so black did his expression become. For several long moments she watched as the turmoil within tore at him, the dark emotions seething and writhing in his soul, and then his will took command and the turbulence subsided to be replaced by an icy anger.

He leapt from the bed and drew on his tunic. "Get dressed," he commanded, "travelling clothes, and send your maid to have your best palfrey made ready," and he left her forthwith before she could utter another word.

The shock of it had bereft her of wit. Oh how foolish, how foolish she had been to have spoken to him thus. Would that she had remained silent. It was the King, his father, who should have spoken of the people's mood, not she, and her tears fell even more freely as she summoned her maid and began to dress.

Within minutes the news reached all parts of the castle that Gereint was arming and about to leave, and all the young knights came running, anxious to be included in whatever adventure he had in mind, but he was as brusque with them as he had been with Enid. "I travel only with my wife and no other, and where I go is my affair." Even to his father he would reveal nothing. "No, my father, I go alone, no knights, and no companions save only my wife."

"Then stand ready to defend your life again and again," said the King, "for over the years you have defeated too many men not to have made many enemies."

Gereint paused and looked at his ageing father. "I do ask one boon of you, Father. If I am to die on this journey, and if Enid returns here, will you vow to honour and cherish her as if she were your own daughter?"

The King nodded. "Gladly, for I already think of her as such."

Then Gereint sent a page to summon his wife and met her in the great courtyard, and all there saw the misery in her face and wondered what sick evil had suddenly become between them. Again knight after knight came to Gereint and offered to travel with him but he refused them all, and then to Enid he said coldly: "You ride out well ahead of me, and no matter what happens you are not to speak to me until I give you leave to do so," and he slapped her palfrey's rump and set her on her way, and the old King frowned and spread his hands helplessly, and the women of the castle began to cry to see the gracious Enid treated so.

It was high summer and the old god, Belenos, the shining one, still shed his light generously upon the land even though the day was well advanced. They travelled at a good pace and soon crossed the boundary of Kernow into the wild lands beyond. Here no strong king ruled but each valley, each stretch of wild forest, each river bend, was dominated by a robber-chieftain and his brigand-knights. "Now, my lady," thought Gereint grimly, "let's see who comes for you, for if your paramour holds you dear he will not see you suffer so."

Ahead of him Enid rode astride a full saddle, as do men, for on a long journey side-saddle was impractical, and her heart was full of grief and her mind full of unanswered questions – where were they going? – why? – and if she was not permitted to speak how could she convince her lord that no other held her heart? That he was deliberately setting himself up as a target by riding alone into the wild lands was obvious – but why?

Towards early evening, with the light still strong, they approached a dark forest and a sudden fear clutched Enid's heart as she saw four knights, fully armoured, lurking in the first line of trees, and as she drew near one of them called out to her: "Stay, maiden, sit with us awhile, for we are lonely men."

"I am no maid," she retorted, "for yonder rides my lord, and he has a cure for your loneliness – vie with him and he will send you to join your ancestors."

"Oh, wit as well as beauty, we are well rewarded today," said the elder, "a suit of armour, two fine horses, and a warm woman to grace our bed."

"It will take more than vain words to force me to your bed, brigand," she said tartly, and she wheeled her horse and galloped back to Gereint. "Prepare yourself, my lord, there are four brigand-knights in those trees yonder, all fully armed and intent on battle."

Gereint reined his horse. "I told you not to speak to me until I give you leave."

"But the knights would waylay you and . . ."

"You seem unable to understand plain words, madam," but he couched his lance and rode ahead, and as the first knight charged down upon him he side-stepped the rush, and thrust his lance so powerfully that it speared the man through, throwing him over the hind-quarters of his horse. The remaining three, who had thought this stranger easy prey, were enraged and charged down upon Gereint one upon the other, but he as easily disposed of them until all three lay dead, and the fair Enid was sickened at the sight of so much blood. Gereint dismounted and gathered all four of their horses and bade Enid drive the horses on ahead. ". . . And be silent, speak not until I give you leave."

Gereint then followed, a good distance behind as they entered the forest. Here it was dark for the sun could not peep through the thick foliage, but soon they realized that this was but a spur of the forest and soon the trees began to thin again and they came out into the grasslands beyond – and as they did so five knights bore down upon what they thought was a maid alone.

"Well, well," said their leader darkly. "Four horses, and your own, of course, my dear, and a lovely maid to share our lonely nights," and the others guffawed and roved their lustful eyes immodestly upon her form.

"I share the night with none but my lord," said Enid boldly, "and there he comes, and I am a woman who does not relish blood or death, so I entreat you, brigands, fly while you still can, or meet thy deaths here and now."

Then they saw Gereint emerge from the trees and they laughed. "What, that sorry knight, we'll soon dispose of him!"

But again Enid wheeled her horse and galloped back to Gereint. "Stand fast, my lord, for those knights yonder seek your death!"

"God's breath, madam, I told you not to speak to me. Why is it that you cannot understand plain words!" but he couched his lance and rode to meet the first of them, and soon three were dead, and the last two came cowardly together to attack him but soon they too were sent bloodily into the Otherworld. Gereint gathered up all the horses and strung them together and handed the halter to Enid. "Ride on ahead, as before, but do not speak to me for your words are vile to me," and Enid rode ahead, the tears streaming down her face and her heart heavy with sorrow.

They came then to the forest again and when they were deep within its canopy Gereint bade her halt. "There is no point in going farther tonight. We will rest here and go on at daybreak," and weary with combat he lay down and slept in his armour, bidding her to watch the horses.

Night came and the forest grew darker still, and the thickets rustled with unknown beasts. The queen of the night rose and shed her pale radiance. Hunting owls hooted dismally in the darkness and their snowy breasts were as dread spectres swooping through the forest seeking God knows what prey, and Enid sat against a tree, her cloak gathered around her, trying to still the fear within her.

Then came a soft voice from out the darkness. "Enid." Fear struck at her and she gasped aloud and rose to waken Gereint. "Stay," came the voice, "it is a friend."

She paused. "No friend of mine would creep upon me in a wild forest," she whispered.

"This one does, I have been following you all day. Don't waken Gereint else he will believe I am the one he's been waiting for."

"Is that you, Tygry?" she said, recognizing his voice. The bard came forward and the moonlight palely lit him as a ghost, but enough to recognize him.

He took her hand. "Come, we must talk," and he drew her a little way into the trees.

She looked back at the sleeping Gereint, uneasy at this new development. "What did you mean just now?" she whispered. "Who has he been waiting for?"

"Your paramour. Nothing else about all this makes sense."

"But I *have* no paramour," she wailed.

"Shhhhhhh. You and I know that, but he doesn't."

"But how did you know that this evil had come between us? Nobody knows, it only happened this morning."

Even in the moonlight she could see that he was suddenly embarrassed. "I arrived soon after you left, and your hand-maiden and the other servants told me."

"But how did they . . .?"

He shrugged. "Servants listen at doors; they always have and no doubt always will. They will have heard every word that passed between you."

Her hand flew to her mouth as she thought of what else they would have heard. She looked back at Gereint, sleeping there, the moonlight on his face. "Oh Tygry, how could he think that I would be untrue."

He shrugged. "Jealousy is a sickness that addles the brain. With this disease a man will believe what the sickness tells him to believe."

"And you think he's been waiting for my paramour to ride to the rescue."

"Yes, as I say, nothing else makes sense."

"But why?"

He looked down at her. "Oh Enid, to kill him, of course. Had I ridden up openly he would have thought that I was the one, and my horse would have been added to your string."

"But there *is* no paramour."

Gently he took her hands in his. "Enid, do try to understand. In his mind he *does* exist. He can him clearly as he sees you. He sees him take you in his arms, and sees you respond lovingly, and sees far beyond that to matters that should be private."

"But what can I do?" she wailed again. "How do I convince him that I am true?"

"I do not know, but there is someone who perhaps could help, which is why I am here."

"Who?"

He hesitated. "I will have to stand surety for several pieces of gold," he warned.

"Anything, anything!"

"And for your discretion."

"Of course, I promise, I promise!"

Again he hesitated. "Don't make that vow lightly," he said grimly, "for if you break your word you will pay a hideous price for your indiscretion."

She looked at him. "Who is it?" she said.

He took a deep breath. "It is a sorceress I know, one of the Elder faith."

She was silent for some time. "But I am of the Christian faith," she said, "as is my father and Gereint, and his father, and King Arthur and all his court. What would they say if they knew?"

"But they will not know, for you will say nothing – nothing."

She was not naive, she knew the old ones still existed and that the peasants sometimes consulted them for their love philtres and their powders and potions. Oh but there were dark tales about them, tales of magic and non-human beings from the Otherworld, though how much of that was owed to primitive peasant fear she did not know. "Who is she, this hag?"

"Oh she's no hag," said Tygry, "and I vouch for her. She lives near here which is why I hurried to catch you up. Ahead is a small town. My guess is that Gereint will take lodging there tomorrow night. Wait there for me. I will go ahead and arrange matters."

Gereint woke at dawn and Enid gathered the horses and they set off as before with she riding some way ahead. In the wild lands a woman seemingly alone is a tempting morsel for any brigand, as Gereint obviously knew, and it was not long before they were again accosted, but again their attackers knew not whom they fought and paid the price of their ignorance with their lives. Twice that morning, and again after noon, did brigand-knights come against them, but always Gereint slew them and took not a scratch himself. He was no doubt a mighty knight and though she hated the violence and blood nonetheless her heart leapt with love to see him charging to the fray, lance held steady, his stance noble and valorous.

Then they came to tilled fields and Enid knew they neared the town. A young lad sat by the field eating his noonday meal. "What have you there, lad?" called Gereint.

"Just some meat and bread, my lord, and a little wine."

Gereint pointed to the string of horses. "My lady and I have eaten nothing since yesterday. If you give us what food you have you may take whichever horse you wish and the armour to go with it in payment, but for that you must go to town and prepare lodgings for us."

The boy leapt to his feet. "Gladly, my lord," he said excitedly, for a horse and armour was worth more than he earned in a year.

When he had ridden off Gereint helped Enid down and they began their meal. "My lord . . ." she began, but he cut her short. "I have warned you again and again, do not speak to me without my leave," and she fell silent again.

When they reached the town they found that the lad had kept his vow and secured them fine lodgings. Gereint went with the ostler to ensure that his horse would be well cared for before he saw to his own needs, as a good knight should, and then he and Enid sat down to supper. Gereint was tired, as tired as he could ever remember. He had fought more times in the past two days than he had in the past two years. He ate and drank his fill but could scarce keep his eyes open, and soon they retired. The chamber was roomy and comfortable with plenty of straw and good warm coverings, and Gereint sent Enid to bed down at the far end of the room and he took the bed at this end – and soon was fast asleep.

Enid remained awake for she knew not when Tygry would come, but ere long, well before midnight, there came a scratching at the door, and when she opened it the bard beckoned her outside. She glanced at the sleeping Gereint but Tygry whispered: "He will not awaken, not until morning."

"Oh are you sure?"

"Oh yes. You would perhaps be surprised what a little gold in the right places will achieve."

She followed him down the stairs and out into the stableyard and there the sleepy ostler handed over two horses and returned to his billet yawning. Tygry helped Enid into the saddle, and then swung up onto his own horse. It was only a small town and the gate was a modest affair manned by only a single custodian who opened it for them and closed it behind them. "More gold, Tygry?" she said as they cantered away.

He led the way at first along the well-used road, but then turned off up the hill where the trees were sparse. They rode in silence, their horses snuffling in the night air, their hooves soft on the turf. At the crown of the hill the path led round the shoulder and then upwards into the rocky higher slopes. At length he stopped and helped her down. "We leave the horses here and go on by foot, but it is not far."

He tethered the horses to a stunted bush and then led her onto a rocky path that led upwards and round a shoulder, to where she could see a dark opening to a cave. Above her the hill rose in a steep cliff, and to her left the hill fell away in a sharp fall down to the valley far below.

"It was the mountains of Gwynned that saw my birth," came a soft lilting voice. "These are a poor substitute but they suffice to remind me of whence I came," and there, seated at the very edge of the sheer drop, was the dark shape of a woman. "Come, the sooner this is over the sooner we can both get to our beds," and she led the way into the cave.

It was not large, but roomy enough, and flickering light from a peat fire lit the rocky walls with dancing shapes. At the rear of the cave were wooden shelves and cupboards, and Enid could see earthen mugs and pots, and wooden platters, and jars and bottles, just like any other kitchen, and to the left was a rocky shelf on which clean fresh straw was heaped; and on them a pile of animal pelts, wolf and bear if she was any judge.

The women grabbed an armful of sticks from the wood pile and fed the fire, and flames leapt high and Enid could see her for the first time, and she gasped at what she saw. Beautiful she was, with glossy black hair to her shoulders and eyes that the firelight suggested could be green. Her form was slim and rounded as any man could wish, but there was about her an air of authority. "But you are as lovely as any maid at court," said Enid.

"Ah, you expected an old hag, did you, with wild and staring eyes and a great hooked nose." The woman laughed. "A poor wise woman I would be to sell unguents for beauty and remain a hag myself."

"But you are so young for a wise woman; I had not expected that."

"Well, I am perhaps not as young as you think, but enough of that." She motioned to three stools set by the fire. "Come, seat yourselves. I am called Benen-y-Caf. It is not my real name, of course, it simply means 'woman of the cave' but it will suffice."

Tygry came forward and sat himself on one of the stools and motioned Enid to sit beside him. The woman bent and retrieved a small cauldron that Enid had not seen and placed it on the fire. "Tygry here has told me of your trouble, but before I am willing to help you I need to know from you the truth."

"That I swear," said Enid.

"Yes," said the woman drily, "everyone swears thus but often even that is a lie." The woman sat on her stool, her knees apart, the flames leaping in her green eyes, and leant forward to stare at Enid intently. "Adultery is rife," she said softly. "There is scarcely a man the length and breadth of the land who has not worn the cuckold's horns at one time or another. Wives and maids bed whom they like, as often as they like, even Arthur's court, or so I hear, is rife with lechery. So tell me, wife to Gereint of Kernow, does your husband wear the horns unknowingly?"

"No, he does not," said Enid emphatically. "I have known no man but him, and no man but him has known me."

The woman stared at her thoughtfully. "No other man, not ever? Not even a kiss?"

Enid snorted. "I have been kissed against my will before now by drunken oafs who claimed to be friends to my father, and I have had unwelcome hands paw me before I could escape – what woman has not endured such torments – but nought else."

The woman grunted and stirred the fire to fresh flame. "You are a rarity, Enid of Kernow."

"If you are a wise woman you must know whether I speak the truth," she said boldly.

"I am not a god that I should know your soul," the woman said harshly.

"She speaks the truth," Tygry suddenly. "I vouch with my life that she speaks truly."

"Nobly said, but your life is not at stake here – only hers."

"My life?" said Enid.

"Oh yes. If I help you and you have lied to me you will pay in blood!"

"I have not lied."

The woman stirred the contents of the cauldron and with a cloth she hefted it from the fire. "Tygry, turn your back," and when the bard had complied she reached with a wooden spoon within the cauldron and spooned out a brown, soft unguent and blew upon it to cool it. "There," she said, proferring the spoon, "loosen your tunic and smear a little upon your bosom."

Enid frowned but did as she was bade. "And this will bring my husband back to me?"

"Not of itself. It is but a link, something that will trigger a response. The real work will be done when you are gone from here, a ritual working that perhaps will rescue him from the darkness that envelops him."

"Perhaps?"

Again the woman shrugged. "No sorceress worth the name will guarantee anything; she does but set forces in motion, tides upon the inner, and directs them." She watched as Enid smeared a little more ointment on her chest. "There, that will suffice. It may be that he is too far gone, too enmeshed, if so then nothing will bring him back." She rose. "Tygry?" The bard handed over a small bag that chinked as the woman hefted it in her hand. "Go now, I have the real work to do."

"But . . ." said Enid, but Tygry took her arm and led her away.

"Look to the dawn," said the woman cryptically as they mounted and rode back down the trail.

When they had gone the woman stripped herself and donned a robe embroidered with strange sygils. She then stirred the fire and sat before it. Then she rose and pointed to the east and began to utter words of power in a strong voice as she moved deosil around the fire, and when the circle was complete she sat herself again and slipped from her body with an ease of long practice.

The mist swirled around him. "Enid, Enid," he called, but there was no sign of her. His horse snorted fearfully and stamped its hooves. He urged the animal forward, but carefully, for he could see little through the murky haze. Then briefly the mist rolled away and he found himself at a crossroads, and there seated on a rock was a dwarf. "Have you seen a maid on a horse pass this way alone."

"No," said the dwarf, shaking his head, "and what maid would travel alone in these dark times unless abandoned by some dishonourable knight."

Gereint bit his lip but kept his temper. "Then which way to the court of Earl Owein?"

The dwarf pursed his lips thoughtfully. "Well, there is the lower way, and the upper way. The lower way," he said conversationally, "is highly dangerous, only the intrepid traveller should go by the lower way. The Earl would not want you to go that way. No, you be advised by me and take the safer upper road."

"And what danger lurks on the lower road, then?"

The dwarf shrugged. "It depends on the traveller. For some it is one thing, and for others quite another."

"You speak in riddles," said Gereint irritably. "I shall go upon the lower way."

"As you wish, but you will not return alive."

Gereint turned the horse's head to the lower way and soon the mist came down more thickly than ever. Cautiously he edged the horse forward almost step by step. The mist clung damply and the horse snorted in fear. Then once more the mist rolled aside, and there was the dwarf. "So, there you are again," said Gereint.

"Or another. We look so much alike, we dwarves."

"How much further?"

"To where, your reckoning? Ah, you have come to that already," and the dwarf waved his hand and the mist roiled around them and rose up and up, and Gereint gasped and edged his horse back, for there before him was a great hedge of mist rising so high that the top of it was beyond the sight of mortal man to see, and standing within the mist, side by side, were hundreds of sharpened stakes, and other stakes pierced the hedge through.

"What black art is this?" cried Gereint, for he felt fear for the first time, a great fear that pierced his heart and froze his bones.

"It is death," said the dwarf. "As I told you, for some it is one thing, and for others quite another." The dwarf stood before him. "Gaze now upon the stakes and tell me what you see."

Gereint looked and his heart was cold. "I see skulls," he whispered, "skulls of dead men upon every stake save two."

"And those two await your coming, you and your lady. Mayhap soon thy skulls will adorn their vacancy."

"Enid? What has she to do with this?" cried Gereint. "If I am to die in this foul place she will be well cared for."

"Fool!" cried the dwarf. "Do you think that she will choose to live if you die? You knowest not the depth of her love for you. If you plunge thyself into your death then she will follow gladly."

Gereint was silent for some time and his horse snorted fretfully. "Is this then to be my death?" he said sadly.

"Who can say? Only you can choose to ride boldly in and face what ere befalls you. Gather thy courage, brave knight, and ride to meet the testing of thy mettle."

And Gereint gathered his horse and held firm his lance, and with a great cry of challenge he rode forward into the mist of death. Dank and foul it roiled about him and he could see nothing and he felt a great fear. But he plunged ahead and then emerged beyond into a fair land. He found himself upon a green meadow and beyond it a pleasant wood from which he could hear the song of birds. The sky was as the blue of summer, and a fresh wind blew sweetly upon his face. He looked back and saw the hedge of mist, and then saw that it encircled this whole land, and again the fear lanced him, for this was magic beyond his poor ken.

Then upon a rise he saw a gaily bannered pavilion and he urged his horse up the slope towards it, and there he saw a maiden so fair that she took his breath away, and when he dismounted and drew near he saw that it was Enid. "No!" he cried in great dread. "Go thou back through the hedge, this foul place is not for thee!"

"Whereso thou art," she said softly, "there shall I be beside you, for your life is my life, and your death my death."

"No!" he cried, his heart pierced with anguish. He stepped forward and bent over her hand, and the perfumed unguent upon her bosom filled him with its sweet fragrance and he knew that he loved her beyond life, beyond death.

Opposite her was a golden chair and he flung himself into it. "Sit not there," she cried, "for that is the chair that another has claimed as his own and will permit no other to sit therein."

"Who is this other? Let him stand forth that I may do him battle!"

She looked upon him and her eyes were sad. "It is thyself, Gereint."

Then a figure hove upon the slope and rode quickly towards them, and Gereint saw an auburn-haired knight in the full flower of his manhood, clad in green armour with a green shield with a fiery dragon emblazoned in yellow upon it. "Who gave you permission to sit upon that chair?" the stranger knight cried.

Gereint rose and drew his sword. "I need no permission, for this is the seat of this lady's love, and none may sit upon it save myself."

"Or another who is better than you. Lady, rise, come you to me, leave this varlet to his surly humours."

Enid rose and gazed upon him. "I shall not come with you. Here is where I choose to be even unto my death if that shall be the price."

Then the knight in green sprang from his horse and charged down upon them, but Gereint met him sword to sword, but Gereint's own sword went over the top of the other's guard and pierced his chest, and the knight in green gave a great cry and the life sped from him and he fell dead at Gereint's feet. But the green knight's sword had found its mark as well and pierced Gereint's chest and he fell back on the sward, his eyes glazing.

Enid came to him and knelt beside him. "Do not give in to thy wound," she said softly, "fight against it. Rise, rise, Sir Gereint, and blow the Horn of Life!" and there upon the pavilion he saw a horn hanging in readiness. He reached for it but fell back. "You must, you must, or else die thy knight's death here and now!" and again he strove, and she helped him rise, her arm around him, supporting him, and he reached up and with a great effort seized the horn.

And Gereint son of Erbin blew the Horn of Life, and the mist rolled away and the pavilion vanished, and he found himself sitting bolt upright on a straw bed in a strange hostelry, and there was Enid, his beloved, and he opened his arms to her and she gave a great shout of joy and rushed to him and there they renewed their love.

Then they went below and there was Tygry, waiting, and he saw their joy and was glad for them. And straight way they gathered the horses and rode that day to Arthur's court, to great rejoicing at his return, and there was feasting and jousting to any knight's heart's content, and the people saw the love that Gereint had for the fair Enid, and she for him, and they were glad.

Then when the celebrations were over Tygry gathered his horse to set out once more upon his travels, and King Arthur said to him: "Well, Tygry, is thy tale done now?"

The bard smiled. "Oh yes, my liege, now the tale is done and I shall sing it throughout the land, and the telling of it shall pass from generation to generation and shall never be lost."

Sir Sagremor in
THE PERFECT STRANGER

R. H. Stewart

Sagremor is introduced in the story of Erec and Enide *by Chrétien de Troyes as Sagremor the Impetuous though, by the time of Malory he had become Sagremor the Desirous. He was apparently the son of the King of Hungary, descended from the Emperors of Byzantium. In the following story, Rosalind Stewart considers what might have been Sagremor's real background, from out of Africa. Rosalind Stewart (b. 1938) was born in Surrey, but grew up in County Durham, and later moved to Cumbria where she and her husband ran a farm just north of the Roman wall. She has long had an interest in Roman Britain and in the following story gives us a glimpse of what the real Arthurian world might have been like.*

In truth, I neither liked nor trusted Guinevere. That is a sad fact, but unavoidable. She was fair to look upon of course, and full of charms – but too manipulative, too tricksy by half for my taste. There was always that tinge of malice beneath her laughter. Yet, I suppose, set against Arthur's Pendragon relatives: his combative half-sisters, Morgause and Morgan; that baleful cousin, the druidic Prince Merlin and his lover, the priestess Nimue (there was always talk that she, too, was related in some unspecified degree) Guinevere, it must be allowed, had her work cut out. She came very young to Arthur's life, which, by necessity of the times, forever swirled and shifted. She had no choice but to carve her own position and hold it against allcomers. We needed every ounce of energetic magic we could muster, keeping the Angles and the Saxons and the Jutes at bay.

It should be said equally that Guinevere never liked or trusted me. She desired me for a while, but that is different. She was not averse to adventure and what Arthur did not see, he never grieved over. He hadn't the time to waste.

But I was Arthur's man from first to last: one of the little handful of his original chosen officers and friends. I was among them and of them, yet even in this I was different.

I? Who, then, was I?

I was the dark one, out of Africa Nova.

The Angles and the Saxons feared my face.

I owed my soul and my skills in battle only to Mithras; my life, honour and possessions in Britain to the Dux Bellorum – so long as they all might last – and whatever small treasure of love that I once held, to my dear, brave, dead wife Alianyr.

In Britain Arthur set me on the warrior's road I craved. Being generous, he gave me trust and no small renown of deeds. He renamed me, and truly, I was integral to his strength. Yet my stature and my skin rendered me singular: the outsider, the nighthawk, the perfect stranger – always.

I did not set out to come to Britain. Arthur, so to speak, acquired me in what was, on the face of things, a chance encounter. Yet nothing that had to do with Arthur was quite so straightforward as it might seem. Not that the man was ever other than himself – but in his circumstance. It is my belief there was no accident in the bringing of us together: Mithras made the pattern, in His awareness of the aspirations of the heart.

I was nineteen when my father died. My inheritance was a pick of twenty horses from among our current crop, and a purse of silver. Well and good. It was what to do with them, to turn to my advantage which exercised me.

Father was not a great man but he had served with distinction in a fine cohort of cavalry, rising to command a whole squadron. He had retired to a comfortable, sprawling family villa with farms in hand. He bred horses successfully – sufficient to supply the army on contract and to fill the occasional racing team in the great hippodrome at Thamagadi, near where we lived. His name was L. Palomides Morbenius.

Father was all African, but with a high-bridged nose and fine cheekbones. There was that in him, I always thought, which must have come down to him from the lost times of Pharaohs and their chariot divisions. My mother, on the other hand, was Celtic with fair skin and red-gold hair. She was out of further Gaul – a find or trophy to Father out of some expeditionary action of his regiment in the diminishing Imperial effort to stem Frankish and Visigothic incursions. (Alaric had long since sacked and broken Rome. We were governed from Constantinople in the east, and influences were as much Greek and Roman.)

Thus it can be seen that I was slave born and half-brother only to Nargiles, father's heir. Of all his children, only Nargiles and I grew up.

Thankful that I was healthy, Father made no difference between us boys, feeding, clothing, exercising and educating us alike. Yet difference remained, slumbering, as I was to find when we reached the edge of manhood.

After the funeral and the settlement of the estate, Father's lawyer still came puffing round to dine – a porcine but shrewd individual.

"You're not bereft, Sagramides," he said, eyeing me beadily over the roasted, herbed goose, "indeed, you are very lucky. A man of business, already! Take what you want and go – and quick about it."

"Where to?" I demanded dourly.

"Go north. I know that sounds cockeyed, but it isn't. For your best sales, head up what they call the Celtic corridor as far as you can reach. Word is: the Britons are beset by enemies and desperate for breeding stock to help maintain their mobility in the field. But rich. They'll pay whatever you ask for anything decent on four legs. Believe me – I have your interests at heart!"

I doubted that, but went to Carthage and asked around. Many Iberian dealers confirmed the trend.

There was a strange atmosphere at home.

Nargiles – two years my elder – was already an optio in the cohort. We grew up in friendship, he and I, yet – though he was competent – he had always been at best lukewarm about military life whereas I had never dreamed of anything else. In truth, from when we both came into our man's strengths, at exercise I was by flair and instinct far the better warrior. I badgered Father to get me into the cohort also. Seeing my embryonic talent, when I turned eighteen he did not wait for illness and death to secure my manumission, but formally freed me and then (to the scandal of his nearest cousins) legally adopted me, in his effort to do so.

Nargiles made no complaint, but perhaps that was because he had made sure that the best the cohort would offer me was a quasi-private posting as his groom and servant. This annoyed me but I accepted for want of betterment, and on the thin promise that in a year they might "review" me for proper training. But I suspected quickly that they'd only fob me off, while Nargiles' Decurion made himself pure hell – "requisitioning" and ruining the good gelding father had sent me in with and addressing me at every turn as: "Oi. You: 'Half-and-half'!"

Nargiles' inheritance now had him buying himself out of the military, a factor which reduced my chances in the cohort from very slender to absolutely nil. They were a choosy lot, carried away by their three hundred years of valour and corporate history. Nor did I in the least fancy my best expectations at home: a stewardship, perhaps, among the farms – that subtle form of belonging and yet not-belonging. To be fair, Nargiles never pushed me but he wasn't about to waste breath in persuading me to hang around.

I passed days out in the grazings and the dusty corrals, finding and halter-breaking my pick of the hardiest, fastest yearlings and two-year-olds we possessed. (I was a better judge of horses than Nargiles, too.) Almost on a whim, it seemed, I included one pure white colt because he was so forward and promised great nobility of spirit. It was exacting work for which I got no help except that of a silent youth called Bargres, also slave-born to the property and now also free, by virtue of my father's death.

Trailing back to the villa one night, tired and hungry, looking for bathwater and food where there was neither in my brother's temporary absence back at Cohort HQ, I blasted through the suites of rooms and caught my mother and the house steward naked in my father's bed. That hadn't taken long.

Perhaps I was oversensitive, but I passed an angry night feeling as though one betrayal had heaped itself upon another. In the morning I packed saddlebags, ignoring all my mother's pleas for understanding. Whatever that might be.

When I went out to fetch in my strings and choose a mount, Bargres was waiting in the stable yard, silent as ever. Neither of us looked back.

In Carthage I acquired us trading and travel warrants. Going west along the coast, we found stowage spaces aboard a proper transport and crossed the narrow Straits of Hercules, whence, landed in Iberia, we turned west again, then at last north and always hugging the seas until we reached Galicia and traversed Biscay round. From there we passed up into free Brittany and the great horse markets of the north. Where Arthur had come: buying.

"By all that's Good – this one I shall have!" said a voice at my horse's near shoulder. "And the man with him if needs be . . ." The tone was one of enormous, undefeatable confidence, and humour.

I had been trying the white colt.

In Galicia Bargres and I had lingered. I was tempted to sell there until I realized the buyers were nothing but middle men who would run the last of the corridor and skim a profit. Instead, we had taken time in secret to mouth and back the best of what we had, and the white colt in particular. Now he might be ridden, approximately, though he needed schooling to finish him.

In Morbihan, now, his paces and his courage were beginning to show. I had run him up and down, and halted him to back three steps. "I am Arthur out of greater Britain," this voice continued, "Dux Britanniae. I need horses for war and horses to breed, but whatever they have told you, I don't pay silly prices! And who are you, with your Roman cavalryman's seat?"

I glanced sideways to find a big, well-knit young man with an open, weathered face, sea-blue eyes and a thick tangle of rich brown hair. One broad, calloused hand was gentling the colt's neck. It was as though a brief play of summer sheet lightning flickered and died between us – then, like the colt, I trusted.

"Come down," he said, "and I shall look at all you've brought. Surely we can come to some agreement?"

He tried the colt himself.

"I'll take him. Absolutely."

And that was the first and only serious customer I got.

He picked out all he wanted, leaving me four. We went to my camp fire and dickered prices. We were alone, except for Bargres, hunkered down, watching my saddlepacks. This Arthur brought out a bag of coin from deep inside the bunchings of his tunic. Together we tallied gold and decent silver. The money he was paying with was good, but very old-fashioned. As I picked it over, he told me shruggingly, "It gets hoarded. We don't have means to strike coins in Britain any longer."

I fetched out a skin of wine and also a stylus and two-leaved wax tablet, listing him out receipt.

"Sagramides of Tha . . . Them . . . Timgad," he made out, reading, accepting a drink. "Thank you. My Council will be impressed!"

It was the first reminder since he'd introduced himself that he was more than just anyone.

"And what will you do now?" he wanted to know.

"I've four to sell yet."

"Mhhm. They only need rest and a bit of feed. Then what? I learn your name but you don't explain yourself to me. Your bloodstock is from Africa Nova. You sit a horse like a cavalryman born – and a Roman one at that. You are educated. You have passable Celtic, bar the accent. If I owned a straw hat to garden in, I'd eat it whole if you were no more than some itinerant dealer. Do you fight? I need fighters. My country is ringed by raiders and foreign landgrabbers. Or are you perhaps a clever runner-away?" he challenged me with a look. "Whatever you are, you're a mystery, Sagramides – lean, dark and falcon-eyed!"

We sat on sharing the wine while the afternoon advanced round about us and I told him something of myself. He listened patiently. "If fighting's what you're after, I can give it you in cartloads! Come into Britain with me and we'll try you out. That, and endless riding. I hardly lay my head twice in the same spot. Come to my camp at least and meet my close companions. Bring your man . . . bring everything. It would be safer so."

What was it about the man? Turning tamely back for Africa had never seemed less inviting. By evening's end, he'd won me. I set my hands between his, Celtic fashion, and swore allegiance.

There were with Arthur at that time Cei, his older foster-brother and High Steward; dark, Welsh Bedwyr and Breton Galahad. To learn me, they tested my temper.

"Your name is what, you say?"

"Sagramides. P. Sagramides Morbenianus."

"Wonderful! What does P. stand for?"

"Palomides. My father's name."

"Palomides Sagramides Morbenianus?" they chorused on a burst of mock pomposity. "Mithras protect us!" and all hooted with laughter. "At full gallop, we'd have gone five miles while shouting that! It's too much! Arthur – what shall we call him?"

Arthur, on his feet, was looming bearlike between the glow of firelight and the sinking rose-violets of encroaching dusk. He took the question seriously.

"Sagramor?" he asked me quietly – already remaking me to his purpose. "That gives you half the middle and one quarter of the last. What do you think?"

He waited courteously as I turned it in my mind and shrugged acceptance.

"And you lot," he added forcefully, "hear me! This is my falcon. Never again provoke him!"

And so I adventured into Britain.

Arthur was a year younger than I. Yet when I joined him he was already the seasoned victor of battles and two sustained campaigns which had mended prompt alliances among the British kings and sent the Saxons reeling. This had given him a kingly authority which he wore easily, like a cloak, and which combined to great effect with the strengths and gusto of his nature. And I learned quickly (it was well known) that there was question regarding his birth. Arthur was styled Pendragon in Britain – a king's son and descended of their line of High Kingship – but King Uther had got him by desire on the Lady Ygraine of Cornwall, whose husband he first tricked and then had killed. Although Uther had married Ygraine immediately, nonetheless Arthur's conception had been presumptuous.

I suppose all these things won me to him. He attracted the displaced and dispossessed, using the alchemy of his character to work them into something sword-bright and new.

White was Arthur's chosen colour: white his horses and white-brindled his huge hounds. He wore white with gold trim into battle, so that no man might fail to see him – especially his enemies.

He was not married when I joined him.

"Well – nothing so's you'd notice, is it?" Bedwyr would say, grinning.) But I learned he had been – briefly – to a girl who'd died within a year, of their stillborn child. Only once did Arthur speak of her to me.

"I loved her, Falcon. Loved her and killed her of it! My poor, dear Mouse. Perhaps the Risen One required her of me in atonement. I cannot – dare not – love like that again . . ." and he looked away, biting off his words. I had no idea, then, what it was he meant, though I came to it eventually.

And I? Stranger that I was? Britain herself was what I had to learn to love: her legionaries' roads; her rounded hills and furzy woods; her crags and meres and unexpected hollows. There are those who find Britain unfathomable – haunted, chill and uncanny. But she drew me. I learned her mists and moods; her snows and bitter winds; her piled skies and cold rains; her sharp green springs, her mild, relenting summers, her bronze and tawny autumns – her shape, her feel, her scents. No woman filled my life like the land I rode through.

We travelled constantly. Knowing where kingdoms lie, memorizing terrain, judging distances and getting there first, were all part of the secret of Arthur's success. In those days we were never still: we the Companions, the Comites.

What Arthur retained, as his personal guard in peace and as the nucleus of a much bigger army in war, was a band about the size of a quingenary cohort. That may not sound much – and for reasons, I suppose, of their own labyrinthine politics, the Council of Britain would never vote him more. But we were a compact officer corps, readily expansive in a crisis. We were trained to lead and deploy tribal levies raised to face invaders. Standing armies cost money, and Britain had very little. It was true, as Arthur had told me, that they had long ceased to mine their precious metals, or to strike coinage. What there was dribbled in from abroad by way of a dwindling class of merchants and sea-captains who had to chance hostile fleets – or it was old and hoarded.

Arthur placed me under Galahad's tutelage, until I had learned my trade.

I remember Galahad remarking to me cheerfully in camp one night:

"Of course you realize Arthur secured your horses virtually for nothing?"

I watched him squinting down the lifted length of a new sword-blade that he'd just had hilted and ground sharp. Firelight danced gold across the metal as he oiled and polished it.

"No . . ." I puzzled. "He paid me. And mine weren't the only ones he bought."

"Yes, yes – he paid you! The famous receipt and all that. But where's the money now?"

"Safe," I told him darkly, "and mind your own damned business!"

Galahad laughed.

"You miss my point. Where? Not in Africa surely? Nor Brittany?"

"No. Where I can get at it when I have to."

"I'm sure. In Britain, see? It doesn't matter a bean whether it is stuffed down your tunic or Arthur's. Either way, the moment he turned you round, that money came home. Plus, he had a warrior – or one in the making. All the Council admired him for managing that!"

I thought it over. It meant that much – everything, perhaps, in the end that was savable about the Roman-British way of life – hung on Arthur's thought and Arthur's sword-strength. We were as secure only as our last victory, and every next battle could be our end. But famously, whatever happened. Such stark choices make living infinitely beautiful.

"Then he's a very cunning Bear," I answered equably – and smiled.

We lived everywhere and nowhere between Cornwall in the south-west and Elmet in the north-east: lending weight here, stamping on encroachments there. The big trouble was the permanent, slanting wedge of old Saxon treaty lands clipped off Britain's south-east corner, and its extension nowadays north of Thames where Anglians held all the rounded eastern bulge. Such landward perimeters we had to hold, but there were mounting pressures from inward migration across the German sea.

Arthur had no centre then, no fixed headquarters beyond a series of decaying, wind-ridden Roman forts which we could use as winter refuges, and as supply stores. In this way we passed several hardbitten, restless years and I made my progress from trooper to optio and then decurion. And all the time they gathered and made common cause, these Teutons, until they brimmed and spilled over from behind their pales and dykes – and we had to meet their host at Badon Hill.

But Arthur had watched their coming and knew their rashness. He lured them on, to the killing ground of his choice, where we were ready, steel-bright – knowing precisely all we had to do.

No one who entered that battle for Arthur was less than heroic. Even Prince Merlin came, clad in rich colour and fighting like ten under Arthur's vast Pendragon standard, screaming Druidic imprecations. Maybe he'd put himself on mandrake root. I knew the man from a distance, when he came to join the Council, and had been accustomed to a middle-aged, veiled personality dressed usually in hodden grey, given to hooded stares and deep, intimidating silences. When I'd stopped being surprised, I found I had to dress my lines of levies, pivot them around, and take them smartly down a slope into the flank of some greasy Saxon rabble.

Arthur greeted me at the feasting afterward. "Sagramor . . . Falcon . . . my dear man – what can I say?"

He pinned his red and gold dragon badge on my cloak's shoulder, making me commander. And since he named me Falcon, it was a falcon I set on my shield as my device.

I took instruction, and followed Arthur into full Mithraic brotherhood.

That day at Badon Hill we thought we'd won the world. What we had afforded Britain was a precious interlude. But all things change.

After the success of Badon Hill, Arthur assumed the full style of kingship. The Council, moreover, voted him usage of craftsmen and materials in plenty, urging him to make for himself some permanency of place. He chose Caerleon-of-the-Legion, westward in Gwent. This afforded him many benefits, not least that here he did not impinge on other rulers and yet he was accessible through a web of roads and other forts. Also, much of its structure was still sound, or renewable. Above all, since Caerleon had been built to accommodate thousands, it gave us space and military facilities such as we had not previously enjoyed – an increasing necessity once news of Arthur's victory had spread wide enough to send men crowding the roads to serve with him.

The King and Prince Merlin oversaw Caerleon's renovations between them.

Merlin enjoyed engineering and structural problems – as I found once he decided to mend the bath-houses and set them functioning. Because this was a much larger version of all I had known at home in Africa, I rashly let slip I understood the hydraulic principles, so he roped me in to assist him.

"What were you in Africa?" Merlin asked me austerely one autumnal afternoon, as he and I traced a first flow of water down patched-up drainage channels and saw it spill satisfactorily out into a newly clean, if long disused, plunge pool.

"Prince?"

Merlin repeated his query, turning on me such sudden intensity of mind that it felt like a physical blow.

I sighed.

"I was a soldier's son – but my brother's half-brother only. Albeit Father adopted me in full."

"I see. And what caused you, I wonder, to walk here among the guttering lamps of Celtic Britain?"

"The Bear – King Arthur – caused me. None other. From youth I sensed my destiny – yet Father's cohort would not take me, or at least as a menial only. But Arthur, the King, looked into me for what I am, and offered me self-worth."

"And if we lose? As we must eventually when Arthur wanes, or is struck down? He has – will have – no child that he can truly recognize – and that one which lives in secret may well prove his undoing. I know this."

I bowed my head.

"Whatever I am sworn to, I do not desert. And still I have had honour, and high friendship unsought but freely given – and the clear, cold ecstasies of war well waged. How else can a Falcon be?"

For a long moment we held each other's eyes.

"You do not lie, it seems," Merlin granted. "And Arthur could have great need of you some time. I possess skills, Falcon, which the ignorant miscall magic. Arthur's wellbeing is my life's charge. If and when you have necessity, send to me, mind to mind. Do you understand me? In Mithras, they teach you – surely – techniques of visualization and concentration, to aid endurance? I would not fail to answer."

I nodded acceptance.

His probing awareness left me as quickly as it had come.

Prince Merlin walked away, his expression lightened, as though we had ended the merest pleasantry. Out into the filling, tiled basin sailed a stray leaf from the holding cisterns – crisp and curled like some brown, elfin boat, bound for it knew-not-where.

Merlin commended the anxiously waiting foreman of our work-gang. When I caught him up, he resumed: "Now, Sagramor – were we to have the furnaces and flues examined, perhaps we might begin to try the heating. *Hot* water has to be civilized – don't you think?"

Bargres took care to establish me within Caerleon's fortress walls, in what had once been centurions' rooms. Together we broomed out, whitewashed and repaired – and went bargaining in the town below, for modest furnishings.

When the armourers' forges and metal shops reopened, I secured us both new mail in good chain mesh, and had our swords rebladed.

The King issued all commanders with a distinctive pattern of helmet crested with streamers, and the entire Comites received long cavalry spears which required practice in handling.

The fort provisioned for winter.

King Arthur occupied the Legate's courtyard residence, central to the whole castra. This was not only still heatable (as Prince Merlin and I were to prove) but handsome – and it provided guest rooms for such visitors as Arthur might choose to honour. Indeed, visitors soon arrived in the forms of Queen Ygraine, Arthur's mother, and his younger sister, the Princess Morgan.

The Bear himself presented me to Queen Ygraine. Although advanced into middle age and no longer in the best of health, one could see how beautiful she must have been in youth. Within her elegance, her graceful carriage and her schooled containment, lay all the implications of what had drawn the late King Uther. Yet she and Arthur were stiff and awkward in each other's presence – a kind of glazed formality never dissolving to give them warmth of each other. It is true that at Uther's behest the Queen had sent her son into obscurity, mere days after the boy's birth, and he was virtually a man grown before ever they met again. Such severances may not be rejoined. Nor did they dare, at this late stage, to venture affection – for fear of pain.

Some say that this sending away of Arthur was done out of security for the boy; some that it was guilt at the manner of his begetting. No doubt Uther sought more sons of the Lady Ygraine. But the gods, undeceived, had sent them only daughters living: the princesses Morgause and Morgan. Morgause, I had learned, was already Queen to the ruler of Lothian and Orkney – and breeding her husband sons, they said, with annual monotony.

The Lady Morgan, on the other hand, was considerably younger than both Arthur and her sister – a dark, feline beauty, most vividly alive. With her, Arthur appeared on surer ground: the self-assured, brilliant elder brother to whom, in any case, she must look for bestowal of her future. Uther had been dark, they said.

Between Arthur and Morgan there was much teasing and springing of practical jokes. She lightened him at that time, undoubtedly.

If Queen Ygraine kept to herself, her daughter did not. The Lady Morgan came exploring in Caerleon with frank curiosity.

I saw that Bargres had been seized red and dumbfounded, in answering her call at my door one day. There was some maid or other in attendance, and Prince Merlin was visible loitering aloofly in the background.

"Who lives in here?" the Lady Morgan was inquiring busily, "Sir Sagramor? Really? Do you think he might object if I were just to look in? No? Thank you so much . . ." and in she stepped.

I doubt Leviathan could have prevented her, let alone tongue-tied Bargres.

I stood too hastily from where I was burnishing mail (the job is endless) and stumbled heavily across the stool I'd been sat on.

"There you are! Sagramor. I remember you from dinner the other night. You're the exotic one – all the way from Africa Nova . . . and enormously brave, my brother tells me. Even the Queen our mother finds you interesting! You don't mind me coming in, do you?"

I did not – of course – still furiously untangling my legs. She shimmered with suppressed mirth, then softened and laid a hand soothingly on my arm.

"I am sorry. I didn't mean to discompose you. Please forgive me . . ."

There is always wine to be had in Britain, once you know where to trade for it. I set out a flask for her, and my own small silver cup. Bargres astonished us by appearing smartly bearing a dish filled with fresh bread, cheese and sliced apples.

"Oh, truly, this is kind. I had no intention . . ."

She sipped and nibbled, kept up lively conversation, and all the time flicked constant, interested glances about her: at me, at Bargres, at the rooms and their sparse contents. She even vanished momentarily behind my partition screens, to view my sleeping arrangements.

"You keep it awfully neat, don't you?" she commented, re-emerging, "Quite inspiring, really! I'm hopeless, you know – the girl is always picking up after me."

Merlin shifted impatiently in the doorway and the movement wasn't lost on her.

"I've taken enough of your time. You are so tall and solemn and mysterious! But cousin Merlin warns me starkly that you are on no account a person to be trifled with. So I won't. Trifle. But *I* think, Sagramor, there is some unusual air of aloneness about you. Sadness, almost. So I wondered if stirring you up just a little, might not help. Do you think? You have been kind . . ."

When she'd gone I experienced a kind of ringing stillness.

The fragrance of her lingered.

A most notable setter of frogs in other people's beds, the Princess Morgan. How she had done it, I could not imagine, for she carried neither bag nor basket and was nowhere close to the maid.

When her gift croaked and leapt out from under my brychan blanket, it took Bargres a very long time indeed to corner the thing and dispose of it – being large, green and vigorous.

I think my laughter rather aggrieved the lad.

Arthur was quick to exploit the new Anglo-Saxon weaknesses, and not least by reinvesting the ancient fort in battered and abandoned Londinium. For Britons, this place was talismanic – having once been their most flourishing provincial capital. Just to possess it was to hold much. Arthur considered the shored-up, regarrisoned fort as a pricking spear-head lodged to divide Angle from Saxon, either side of Thames.

Towards the end of winter he sent me to command there.

The outgoing officer due to take his troop back to Caerleon was not known to me, and seemed dour to a fault, though he proved to be an efficient, if somewhat unforgiving, leader of men. His name was Meraugis and he clothed himself for preference in grey and russet-brown. One could appreciate why Arthur had nicknamed him "Wolf".

Meraugis showed me round and gave me tips about the few folk already creeping back behind our swords to try a little trade. But when we gazed out from our wallwalks across the city's utter decay and emptiness, it did not seem likely the place would ever be anything in future. Pointing me out landmarks among the dereliction, Meraugis shivered once – and realized I'd noticed.

"My only similarity to the Saxons," he explained tersely. "My dislike of cities. They actively fear them as well, of course. Oh, they'll strip bare and wantonly demolish wherever they go, but they don't stay. They're off back to their rustic hovels and clearings the moment they're done! Leaving everything to wind and rain, and moaning desolation. Me: close-packed streets and stone buildings stifle."

"Why so?" I asked.

"Brought up in forest. There are densities and densities, Sagramor. Forests are at least a living density."

I had brought in some good wine, and broached some. At supper that night it turned out that Meraugis was a king's son, "but," he added bitterly, in a deliberate echo of Bedwyr, "Nothing so's you'd notice, is it?" When, finally, I broke through his terrible reserve, it was to have him tell me that he'd found out eventually his father was his mother's uncle, and though she had fled him with her infant son, this king had her hunted down and killed for silence of his infamy – and the child dumped deep into forest. Meraugis had survived by pure chance and the passing of some childless forester.

"So there you have it. Much good my connections ever did me, Falcon!"

He passed one narrow, nervous hand across his troubled face.

"We all carry scarring in us somewhere," I commented. "And Arthur discerned the worth in you, did he not – as he did in me?"

We parted the next morning almost friends.

"You listened, Sagramor, and that is much to me," he said, gripping my arm just before riding out. "Best of luck here."

I had quiet duty. The dragon standard flew unchallenged over Londinium fort. My men repaired a wharf – more in hope than any belief in its usage – yet one morning's tide brought a cautious, nudging hull.

It was summer before I returned to Caerleon.

Queen Ygraine, they said, had become Christian and retired into a convent, southward in Avalon.

The Lady Morgan, for whom even before I left, formal negotiations of betrothal were in hand, was now married: Queen to Urien of Rheged, in Caerluel city.

I believe I missed her more than most.

Marriage, it seemed, was this year's diplomatic pastime. Arthur vanished into the blue distances of further Wales, taking with him only Cei, Bedwyr and a small peacetime escort. When he came back he brought with him the daughter of one King Leodegrans: the new Guinevere.

Guinevere. The White Lady. It was less a name and more an assertion of her status in the land. Guinevere: fair-haired, pale of skin, clad in white, inquisitive, cold. It was difficult to look at her and not wonder . . . and not want her. And yet also she filled me with unease.

She and Arthur were already wed, though by what rite was a mystery. In any case, it was all to be done again at Caerleon with

Christian ceremony and public celebration. Guinevere favoured Christians, despite rumours that she had been initiate in some cult of the Moon. Arthur, ever Mithraic, did not find Christians impressive – but sought to please Guinevere. In turn, she perhaps thought to make a gesture toward Queen Ygraine, who would, of course, attend.

Queen Morgause of Orkney and Lothian declined, pleading sea-storms and childbirth.

But Queen Morgan accepted to come, riding down from Rheged escorted by Urien's handsome heir, Prince Owain.

Queen Ygraine's bishop officiated – a fat, unbelievably fussy man, not overclean in his person. For lack of a church he elected to "sanctify" the old Legionary shrine within the fort's headquarters building. Christians were in there; the rest of us must needs cram together outside the low stone half-screens, in the cross-hall.

I worked my way among the throng until I stood a little behind Queen Morgan, at her left shoulder. She looked ripened, beautiful – and was richly dressed.

"Sir Sagramor," she said, without turning and on a hint of amusement.

"Queen Morgan," I replied, testing my emotions deliberately and after a pause I asked her, "How are the frogs in Rheged?"

Her mouth curved while she watched the bishop have incense smokes wafted over her white-robed brother and sister-in-law.

"Toads."

"Lady?"

"Toads, Sagramor. In Rheged: toads. Large, warty and deliciously ugly! You've no idea . . . Once one knows where to find them. Luckily, in that respect I have a young ally in the Prince Coel who loves mischief and laughter above all things."

"How is it in Caerluel?"

"Remarkably civilized. Come and see. You might like it."

"And King Urien?"

"An honourable, generous and vigorous man – for all his years and his grown sons from his late wife. I enjoy my state."

I sighed and said I feared as much.

She favoured me with a quizzical, sidelong glance.

"And you?" she countered. "What do you make of ladies?"

"Enough to take comfort of them from time to time, whenever such is permitted."

"Truly? I am relieved . . . You troubled me last autumn –

so severe and self-contained. You and that dark, inarticulate man-servant!"

I barked mirth – causing heads to come round.

"Fret nothing there, Lady! I got back from Londinium only to find that your platter-carrying Bargres has now also found a wife. All the world marries this summer!"

"But not you. Do you love?"

I was silent for so long that at last she touched me with one, long-fingered hand.

"Sit by me at the banquet tonight," she said, "that we may pursue our talk."

The feast also was in the cross-hall that evening – it being the only place wide enough to accommodate the great circular table which was part of Guinevere's dowry. This was a piece of Roman furniture of some antiquity which could be fitted together in ingenious marble-topped segments. It was said to have been made for the last true British emperor, Magnus Maximus – whom the Welsh call Macsen. King Leodegrans – a willowy, self-regarding man – claimed descent from Macsen.

Not knowing how the seating was to be, I awkwardly approached a harassed Cei, who had oversight of such matters.

"Yes, yes – I know," he waved me away, "Queen Morgan has already made herself plain. You are on her immediate left. Consider yourself much honoured!"

Arthur and Guinevere were together in state with Arthur's trophy of arms and his magnificent sword behind them. His white hound lay at his knee. The rest of us made a brave show: kings, queens and princes, and then the Companions ranged in order all around.

I remarked on it to Queen Morgan, who uttered impatience. "Huh – this won't satisfy Guinevere for long!"

"Lady? Why not?"

"But the food is half cold. All must be fetched a distance from the cookhouses and residency kitchens! See how she eyes her dish? Be thankful, Sagramor, that it doesn't rain. Think how our ale and wine would be reaching us diluted! To say nothing of the sauces . . ."

I smiled.

"Already," Queen Morgan went on, "she talks of Arthur making for her a summer palace, as she puts it. Caerleon is too masculine, too military, it seems."

"Would that be so bad?"

Morgan stared at me sceptically.

"She isn't getting to you as well, is she? So soon? Bad? No, not bad – unless you count ruinously expensive as bad. But there you are . . . Arthur ought to have the state of a king. God knows he's fought for it. She'll bring him that, if nothing else."

I gazed along the curve of faces to where Arthur dispensed kingly affability and Guinevere was demurely accepting the toasts of princes.

"Merlin isn't here."

"No."

The honouring of Guinevere in wine was proceeding from man to man in due order, right round the table. In my turn I stood and bowed to her over my cup, encountering the blue conjectural stare.

"You've been noticed! Have a care, Falcon," Queen Morgan was saying drily as I resumed my seat.

"Lady – you are too shrewd," I protested.

"I don't think so," she replied, flatly.

I turned the subject to Queen Morgause's absence. Morgan crumbled bread.

"You have not understood us yet, Sagramor. Our passions run deep. It was not that my sister could not come: she would not come. But one day she will – and Guinevere won't relish that!"

"How so?"

"Because – my dear, earnest, honest knight – nothing is ended between Arthur and Morgause. Nothing. It was before your time, but you must have heard the story?"

I shrugged and shook my head. Gossip, only. Morgan studied me carefully.

"Arthur was fostered in obscurity, unknowing of what he was. Cousin Merlin only brought him to court when Father was dying. Arthur was barely sixteen. You have that much surely?"

I agreed.

"If I tell you more, it is in trust. Arthur's first act was to win a battle Father was too sick to fight; everyone celebrated rather well. Morgause picked her moment when Merlin wasn't looking and took Arthur to bed. She was, after all, virtually the first beautiful thing in skirts he had ever set eyes on. Pharaonic love. They know of such in Africa, yes? At the time, Arthur had no idea of his sister's identity, but on him she practised a terrible deceit. King Uther's rage when he found them out is legendary. Morgause he had betrothed, and her traps packed, in a trice. Lot was paid handsomely to take her away and keep her in far-off

Orkney. But the first son she bore was never his. We have skryed it. And the boy lives – though Merlin has raked the kingdoms to make an end of him."

"To kill him? An infant?" I was aghast.

"A viper, Sagramor. A small, sleeping viper. Infants grow to men. If this one does, he will prove my brother's downfall. Of that, also, Merlin and I are certain."

"Now I comprehend . . ." I answered slowly. "Arthur spoke to me once about his first Guinevere's death perhaps having been required of him in atonement."

"Poor, dear Mouse. If only she had lived! She gave Arthur such peace. Whatever he has married this one for – it cannot be love! Sagramor," she touched my sleeve, "you will watch out for my brother, won't you?"

I assured her I was sworn to it.

"There are times even yet," Morgan told me starkly, "when I have envied my sister with him. But then, Arthur would never make the same mistake again," and, seeing my dismay, she added, sighing, "We are all three of us as much the product of Merlin's tutelage as of our parents' act. Come. I have made you sombre, such a schooled observer as you are. Perhaps you should write us down one day? It would please me to lighten you once more. How if I were to skry your future, Falcon?"

I am not a seeker after augury – but she drew me so.

I could not forbear to look at Arthur anew. In doing so, I caught his eye and he, seeing me in company with his sister, raised his gold goblet in salute. He was not troubling to hide the depth of his drinking, this night.

Following Queen Morgan's instruction, once she had retired from the banquet with the other ladies I allowed some time, then went discreetly to the Residence, where she was lodged. Prince Owain himself opened the outer doors, barred them swiftly behind me and led me along the colonnaded walk to reach Queen Morgan's rooms.

She met me cloaked in some rich stuff dyed midnight-blue – sewn on its shoulders with sun, moon and a galaxy of stars in bullion threads. Her dayroom smelled of sandalwood and frankincense, such as I had not encountered since Thamagadi. In answer to my open amazement, she smiled.

"We trade well out of Rheged – our coasts being harboured and our fleets defended. How else would Arthur have disposed me there? And I have said: Urien is generous. Come. Sit by me."

She had been a girl last year. Now she was a woman of authority, and in authority. What faint hopes of her I might still have had, died in the few steps I took joining her at a small table, on which a bowl faceted from rock crystal held water, with a lamp behind it.

Owain guarded the screens.

There was a maid in one corner, bent over fine sewing against another lamp.

"I looked over water for you," Queen Morgan touched the crystal, which rayed out the colours of light, "You show to me as a man of honour and of true courage who, however tried, will not be broken. You are also a man of journeys, lifelong. Sagramor," she paused. "At the moment you think yourself in love with me," her mouth quirked amusement, "but that will pass."

"Yes, Lady?" I queried dully.

"You will find love – where you least expect or look for it. Its great reward will prove a foil to Guinevere's baser purpose. Beware of Guinevere. Do you heed me, Sagramor? I tell you this advisedly, and not from petty jealousy. Here is a woman of deep appetite and you underestimate your attraction. Moreover, your refusal will constitute her challenge. She would seek your harm."

"Yes, Lady."

"When you reach your love – bring her to me. I shall help you."

Was it the wine she offered? Or the sympathetic visions of her mind? We talked long. When at last I rose to leave, Queen Morgan took off a silver ring, gemmed and cut with her badge.

"Keep this, Falcon, and wear it for me. I would be your friend, now and hereafter."

Again, Prince Owain went ahead of me to the outer doors. From across the street in headquarters issued the muffled roar of late revelry. And even as I paced in Owain's slim shadow, I grew aware of a pale glimmer from the far side of the enclosed courtyard – behind the tubbed herbs and little, sprinkling fountain. Guinevere – in solitude – watched my going.

For a while she tuned herself obediently to Arthur's hands.

Eastwards in summer country, Merlin found them an empty hill fort and fashioned it for them into a palace – all lofty rooms and towered walls, topped by the bravery of banners. Camludd, Guinevere called it.

* * *

I have remembered how I came to look.

Guinevere, playfully insistent when she cozened me for her pleasure, would face me with myself in the great polished silver disc which was her mirror.

I was of Gallic height but, like my father, fine-boned, hawk-nosed and walnut-brown. All my life I have stayed lean but muscled also, for warfare. I possess unsettling, light grey eyes, flecked with gold. There was then a reddish glint within my dark, close-cut and crinkling hair which all the henna in Egypt might not reproduce. I had narrow, down-curving, dark moustaches,

"Well, Sagramor – are you not just formidable?" the White Lady would inquire, on a little, gasping laugh – stroking my forearm with one cold, inquisitive finger. Curiosity gripped her and desire stole out from her like scent. I was as a lion, it seemed: a foreign rarity made attractive by very virtue of its strangeness and potential danger.

For Arthur's sake, at such moments, I would keep countenance with a waiting stare, until she shivered involuntarily – and gave me leave to go.

I was by then Captain of the Guard for the summer palace. She had toyed with Galahad but put him by as being too transparent. And there had been a strange incident in which, out hunting, she had apparently been abducted and held against her will. Arthur had had to be sent for. When he recovered her, the precise details of her captivity were kept a mystery.

With me, Guinevere knew better than to cross old ground twice. With me, she set out to flatter and charm – admitting me to private suppers. I found I was expected to attend her for orders not only in her dayrooms but into her bedchamber if she were resting or rising. I sent urgently to Arthur, requesting to relinquish this command. He gave no answer.

It was not easy for Arthur to control the Comites in peacetime. Within its ranks men jostled for place and distinction. Officers and companies had to be rotated, or sent out on detached duties, if jealousies were to be kept at bay. And because Arthur was himself so frequently absent, making or mending alliances, patrolling borders, Guinevere had soon come to wield much influence in the making of appointments. Her capacity to please and tease me being slow, she began subtly to harry me in my business of setting guards.

Late one evening, after her excuse of altering yet again my proper choice of night-watch, I looked up, at the end of patience from my scored-out postings, to find she had barred her door and was slipping off her robes.

It must be said: she was most beautiful. As she came toward me I was goaded into recklessness, lifting her to the bed. Almost, she had me. Only, Mithras intervened, filling my head not with visions of this false romance, but of the grossness upon which I stumbled with my mother, all those years before. A bitter disgust swept through me. I remember covering Guinevere roughly with something and saying, "Lady – I will not be your plaything! Find another . . ."

She could not fail to see the scalding hatred in me – my fear of dishonour and my own weakness.

"What is it, I wonder," she countered – hissing, "that Queen Morgan offers you, and I cannot?"

Rearing up off the bed like some striking serpent, she spat full in my face.

I expected Guinevere to have me dismissed momently, but in fact my term of duty had almost run its course before she presented me, her voice icy, with Arthur's new commission. Beside her, in the great council room to which she'd summoned me, lounged a handsome refugee – a Breton prince whose lands were said to be freshly overrun by Franks. As she held out to me Arthur's written command to meet him in Uriconium in twelve days' time, the Breton smirked at me, leaned and said something low in Guinevere's ear. With an arch expression she replied clearly, "Yes, there is," and continued mockingly, "Well – he hasn't seen her yet, has he? I have!" at which they both laughed.

I bowed stiffly, and left.

Calling in at Caerleon to collect my men, I found Meraugis padding fretfully round the walls, so took him with me. We sped north on uneventful roads, reaching Uriconium with days to spare, but Arthur was already encamped, waiting.

I presented myself to him as soon as possible. For the first time in years Arthur sent everyone away, even Bedwyr, and sat with me alone.

"I got your request," he informed me levelly.

"Then why in the Name of all that's Good, Sire, did you not act?"

He humped his shoulders.

"Because I trust you."

"She weaves cat's cradles! Mithras be thanked – there is no

dishonour between you and me, though I came a whisker from it. My rejection of her earns me spite."

"I understand. You're not the first, Sagramor, nor will you be the last. When the air clears, she'll seek another."

"She has, I think. His name is Lancelot."

"I cannot afford to care! Nor, in truth, do I have that right," Arthur spoke bitterly.

We stared at each other, disconsolate, men toeing the threshold of middle age.

"You must not think, Falcon, if I send you into north-west Wales on a placement of my Lady's suggesting, that this is in any way a punishment. Prince Peredyr is a good man, suffering grievously from Irish raiders. I send you because you are cool-headed and I can rely on your success. Nor will you be greedy and overbearing in a situation offering small reward. Peredyr has nothing much, and now he even loses heart."

I waited.

"How does the Wolf suit you?"

"Well enough, Sire. We talk when he feels like it! Neither of us minds the other's silence."

"Good. One thing: Peredyr has a daughter – unwed. Despite Guinevere's further suggestion, and this new convention of marriage where possible setting a seal on my Companions' secondments – I do not ask you to tread that path." Arthur shuffled letters embarrassedly on his campaign table.

"No, sire. If there is war – you will send for me?"

"My dear Falcon – whatever else?"

Next morning we took the roads west, to the sea.

Peredyr's little, shore-fringed principality was tucked between two rivers in the lee of Wales's northern promontory. His stronghold was a draught-ridden rickle of stones up on a crag, and he himself went cleaner but hardly better clad than his youngest henchman. Even my junior optio could outdo him for well-dressed leather and a bit of ornament. But it is wrong to judge purely by appearances, and within all he could manage, Peredyr was studiously hospitable. He had, for instance, only one carved and silver-rimmed horn beaker, but for the duration of our stay, he insisted I must use it, making do himself with a plain, turned-wood cup. I suppose that at Arthur's court, of late, we had grown insidiously accustomed to easy living.

In physique, Peredyr was black-haired and thin – dried-out looking – and plunged, as Arthur had said, into a kind of resigned melancholy. Suppers, between him, Meraugis and me, were essays in withdrawn silence.

There was no single, relieving woman's touch anywhere, and only once did Peredyr mention somewhat of "my late wife."

We began by hunting Irish all along his shores – a pursuit just about as fruitful as catching mist, for they drew off at every first hint of our arrival. Then we had a real stroke of luck. A tub-bellied merchantman, lost off a convoy and partially disabled due to storms, came crabbing in to shelter in Peredyr's northern estuary. As she struck sand she was rushed by an Eirreann galley intent on nothing but loot. Both captains were surprised, to put it lightly, at the sudden eruption of our hidden force, to assist the one and annihilate the other. We took no prisoners. Why feed pirates?

The merchantman was Rhegedian, and her cargo valuable. I showed her master Queen Morgan's ring, and he was content to have his vessel in plain ballast for a while and cruise, apparently cripple-winged, till we rused in other ships and destroyed them also. After which, mended and reloaded, he left on a brisk following wind, towing a skin coracle wherein sat the last Hibernian leader, alone. Our captain had undertaken to cut him loose off the far side of Man so that, if he drifted on to Irish rocks, he could at least relay the fact that Peredyr's land was now strongly defended.

In time, a south-bound convoy from Rheged called in on Peredyr, depositing King Urien's thanks and a chest for the Prince containing fine cloth, brooches and clasps gold-wrought, and a packet of foreign spices.

Separately, there was a letter for me from the Queen which read: "Dear friend, You have saved more in that hull than you can know and I am grateful. Look upward, Sagramor, to find your love and do not flinch at its first sighting. Remember to bring her to me . . ."

We had by then been with Peredyr for most of that fighting season and in all that time not once had he shown or spoken of, a daughter. Inasmuch as I had thought of her at all, I had assumed that, like her mother, she must be dead.

It was Meraugis who found the place.

He had been hunting inland to replenish Peredyr's larders. At supper he told me curtly, "I have discovered a curiosity. Come with me tomorrow and tell me what you think," then, casting a glance at our host, would not elaborate.

We went at dawn, though for the look of things we borrowed a couple of Peredyr's deerhounds. By midday, having run down two useful stags, Meraugis led me round a steep shoulder of hill into a narrow corrie. "There," he pointed, "what's that for?"

Against a backing of sheer rock and among a scrub of wind-bent trees stood a slender stone tower, conically capped. We approached it cautiously, keeping always in cover, until eventually we sat in a fernbrake near its foot. There was no discernible entrance, yet towards the top but well apart there were two small, roundheaded windows, each heavily shuttered.

"Concealment?" I answered.

"Well, of course!" the Wolf was scornful. "But of what? Of whom?"

"Look upward, Sagramor . . ." Queen Morgan's voice echoed in my mind.

"His daughter! Peredyr's girl," I replied with sudden amused certainty and half-rose.

Meraugis caught my arm.

"Hold. Think. Why does he hide her so? Ought we to intervene?"

But I shook free, seized with a raging curiosity. "I know so – yes. This is for me, at any rate."

It was a matter of patience in the end – of making camp in the adjoining valley and returning by stealth, to watch and wait. Some middle-aged woman gowned in russet, full bodied and red-cheeked, pushed out from a fissure in the rock nearby. The split she came from seemed nothing, and was half covered by bramble and a loose slide of stones. But, after careful hesitation, she puffed and scrambled down a thread of path to fill water pots and skins at the valley stream. Once she was occupied, back turned, Meraugis and I flitted like shadows into the opening she had come from.

It was hardly a cave, but at the back behind hanging canvas grey as the rock, was a stout wooden door, unlocked. There was a short, angled tunnel cut through slate, then a further door which we entered softly and closed – and we stood within the base of the tower itself. A tiny rushlight flickered on a metal pricket. The only other gleam came from above, where a removable ladder led up through an open square in a floor that was riven slate laid on beams.

Meraugis shrugged.

I led quietly up the steps, getting out into an empty room lit only from more rush lamps and the slits in the plank shutters of one window. There was a table with bowls and such; one freestanding brazier; stools and two well made, backed chairs – and boxes with book-rolls all packed into them. A further wooden stair led up again.

We stood like errant boys raiding an orchard, breathing into a prickling, listening silence. And then Meraugis sneezed.

There was movement overhead – a light footfall – a sussuration of the dark stuff of a gown, and she had half descended. I saw a young form, a draped scarf covering much of the face.

"Are you the man to change my books?" she asked, with a small, persistent sibilance of speech – and then, quickly perceiving her mistake, added defensively, "No – I see not."

I loved her on that instant – all unknowing. It hung in the very air between us. I bowed.

"Lady," I began. "My name is Sagramor . . ."

Meraugis could no longer bear being so shut in, and left. Below, distantly, we heard his encounter with the woman bringing water: shouts, protest and a long, drenching pour. The servant erupted up the stair in Meraugis' place – all fear and fury. The girl calmed her – sending her commandingly away. Then she herself came fully down her steps.

"You're the Companion Arthur sent us. My father told me of you. I see the dragon badge. I am Alianyr – and all the child Prince Peredyr possesses."

She came to me, muffled.

"May I not look upon you?"

She sighed.

"If you must," and went by me to the shutter, setting it open. Day shafted in, bathing her figure in a fresh, milky light. I reached and turned her gently under its access.

"I would not hurt you," I said.

Truly, she was beautiful: black haired with vivid blue eyes and pale skin. Only her mouth was marred – caught at its upper right into a hare's lip, leaving two teeth exposed.

"Is this all, that you dwell in darkness so?" I was amazed.

"No, it is not. And you would loathe the rest!"

She stood defiant beneath the touch of longing in my fingers.

"Perhaps before I judge you, Lady, you should first judge me. For I am out of Africa – and I am different too."

A long time she studied me – frankly and close. And I understood in full the unkindness of Guinevere's stratagem –

that here singularity might be joined to singularity, for half the world's prying mirth.

"How is it Guinevere knows of you?" I asked.

Alianyr shrugged.

"We are cousins of a kind," she answered, comprehending me all too well. "In my mother's time, she stayed with us. I never was sad for my condition until Guinevere came."

"I would wed you, Lady."

But she flared up, hostile.

"Fool! Do you think yourself the first along this road? Had you not better view your fate?" she rasped at me.

In a swift and strange inversion of what Guinevere had shown me, she unlaced gown and shift, dropping them from her shoulders to her hips.

"Look well! I have learned not to care. Ask yourself how to endure a body so reptilian as mine!" she spoke low and fiercely, "I grow tired of this game first of pity and then horrified rejection."

She moved in front of me and I saw that while her left was whole and lovely, all her right was patched and blained with dry, discoloured, scaly, warted skin. But I reached out and kissed her, on her soft, split mouth; on her proud neck; on her sweet and pointed breast.

"Put back your gown. I would wed you, Lady!"

"The last one fainted at my feet," she said – indignantly.

"More idiot he!"

I held her gaze and from smiling we fell to mirth.

Peredyr could hardly credit my intent.

"There's no dowry, man! She swallows texts as the lioness her meat! All I can spare goes to the book-copying down in the monastery – to keep her fed."

"Then let her books come with her. I read – but have none."

"You'll take her from me."

"Not so. We'll dwell here. Only in war, when Arthur sends, would I leave. Consider a grandson-heir to strengthen your principality."

"You wouldn't cause her pain? She knows too much already. If I see hurt in her, Falcon, I'd kill you – Arthur's friend or not!"

"If you see hurt in her from me, Prince, I'd deserve that death."

"You mean it then?" he marvelled – and watched us married in a haze of half-belief.

* * *

I took Alianyr to Rheged before winter closed the roads.

Did Morgan see our coming? Prince Coel was sent to find us at his father's southern borders and led us to Caerluel, royally escorted. Urien himself welcomed us in.

After a day or two Queen Morgan spirited my wife away. So, having time and chance, I went to the wharves and warehouses on Ituna river, about business of my own.

With south-west gales and storm clouds at his back, Arthur arrived, flourished in at Caerluel's gates by trumpeters. Prince Owain captained his bright new Guard of younger men. Eventually, Arthur sent for me.

"Falcon. Good to see you. You married Peredyr's girl, they tell me. How is she?"

"Scaly, like the Worm," I answered harshly. "As no doubt Guinevere acquainted you."

I had presumed and knew it. Following a sharp silence, I could see his hurt.

"Your pardon, sire. I fear I'm touchy. The truth is: I love her deeply, warts and all – and they've taken her from me for this while."

"Man: you're luckier far than me! You were quite right regarding Lancelot. The affair grows celebrated, it seems. I keep away and on the move."

I stared out from Urien's tower windows at rain, and driven leaves.

"Where will you live?"

"With Peredyr. My lady needs her home, and I have plans for it."

"I miss you, Falcon. I miss your fierce honour and your plain truth."

"In battle I will join you, always. Perhaps in the years ahead, I'll ride with you again. For now – King – grant me a little peace."

Alianyr was restored to me only on the morning of our going home – richly dressed, furnished with a sumpter pony bearing laden packs and swathed in veils, above which her blue eyes danced at me in delight. Who could begrudge her this?

We made all haste south in the first thin promises of sleet, parting from Arthur's gallantry at Deva, where we took the road to Caer Gai, and thence to Peredyr's crag. Because of our need to outrun snow there had been little rest and no privacies for Alianyr and me.

Peredyr, anxious, met us looking uncommon princelike: he and Meraugis had captured a storm-struck raider – Danish, this one – who ransomed himself with ornament and hacksilver.

After supper, presents and a great exchange of news, Alianyr and I were at last alone. Still she had kept to her drapes.

"Your gift is last of all, Sagramor," she said. "But yours is best. Set back my scarf."

I did – and her lip was whole. Only the merest tuck and a fine silvery line remained.

"Mithras! How can this be?"

"Queen Morgan's work. I don't know how: I was in waking sleep. That, and a spring with mystic properties in which we bathed. But this is not all: unparcel me and see!"

Carefully – for her bad side was used to fissure and bleed – I slid away her garments. It was true. All her skin was made clean and smooth. In a fierce dream of love, I kissed all I might reach. She occupied herself unlacing me.

"You and I have a great duty, sweet," I told her sternly, holding off.

"And what is that?"

"Your father needs a grandson – urgently!"

Alianyr laughed aloud – taking me to her in the bed.

"My stranger," she said. "My dear, different and most perfect stranger . . ."

Even as she received me, I knew that for this while I had found haven.

Sir Tor in KNIGHT OF THE GOLDEN COLLAR

Peter Tremayne

Tor appears in the Arthurian legend as a defender of Guinevere. He was apparently the illegitimate son of King Pellinore, fathered upon the wife of Aries, who, unaware of the child's origins, raised him as his own. This would make Tor the half-brother of Perceval, Lamorak and Elaine, the wife of Lancelot. In the following story, Peter Tremayne gives us a different origin to Tor, as Torcán, the son of the Irish king of Cashel. It was Tor's battle with the knight Abelleus that made Tor a knight of the Round Table.

Peter Tremayne is the alias of Celtic scholar and author Peter Berresford Ellis (b. 1943). Under his real name he has written several books of interest to the Arthurian reader, including A Dictionary of Celtic Mythology *(1992),* Celt and Saxon *(1993) and* The Druids *(1994). Under the Tremayne alias he has written over thirty books, including two collections of Irish horror and fantasy stories,* My Lady of Hy-Brasil *(1987) and* Aisling *(1992). Most recently he has found fame with the character of Sister Fidelma, a seventh-century advocate and investigator of the Irish Brehon Court, whose adventures have appeared in a series of novels starting with* Absolution by Murder *(1994).*

The tall, muscular man stood at the doorway of the wayside inn and watched the approach of the mounted stranger with narrowed eyes.

The advancing man was obviously a warrior. That much had been clear since the details of the figure's clothes and bearing had become discernible to the eye. He sat upright on his horse, a burnished shield and javelin carried loosely on his left side. The scabbard of a long sword could also be seen slapping below the cover of the shield.

The tall man shifted his weight and folded his arms in a firm stance, and remained framed like a giant in the doorway.

The approaching stranger was obviously a foreigner, perhaps an accursed *welisc*? He wore a saffron-coloured woollen cloak, which barely concealed a polished breast-plate. The tall man could see the symbols, the curious whirls and circular patterns, studded with semi-precious stones, occurring both on the shield and the breast-plate of the stranger. The same patterns could also be seen on the accoutrements of his horse. The stranger did not wear a war helmet, but the quick eyes of the tall man saw it hanging from a strap from the pommel of the saddle. The rider wore his jet-black hair long and loose but he was clean shaven. The eyes, now that the stranger grew close, were bright, glinting against the sunlight, but the tall man could not tell whether they were blue or green. Around the warrior's neck he noticed a golden collar, a torque of the heavy, twisted precious metal, and a hint of envy and greed appeared in his own dark eyes.

The stranger drew up about five yards away from the front of the inn and leant forward in his saddle, regarding the tall man with an expression of amusement on his handsome, youthful features.

"God's blessing on you this day, innkeeper," he greeted in the language of the *welisc*.

The tall man drew himself up and sniffed.

"I will not reply to you in that outlander language," he answered in Saxon. "You are in the land of Abbo, thane to Eadric, king of all the Saxons dwelling in the west."

"A territory much disputed, so I hear," rejoined the other, slipping easily into the man's language. So fluent was he that the innkeeper started in surprise. "So once again, God's blessing on you."

There was a sneer now on the tall man's thin lips.

"God's blessing? Which god? We Saxons do not believe in your gods, *welisc*. Woden is my shield among the gods!"

The stranger still had not dismounted. He sat back in his saddle and chuckled.

"I have been told that you Saxons believe in a god of battles called Woden. That's a strange god for an innkeeper to have as a shield."

The innkeeper stirred uncomfortably as he glanced over the stranger's well-muscled form and his well-kept weapons. The man looked a like a professional warrior.

"Who are you, *welisc*, that ride unafraid into the territory of Abbo? Are you the one they call the dragon's chief? Chief over the accursed race who fight under a dragon banner?"

The stranger, smilingly, shook his head.

"I am not from any part of this land, nor am I acquainted with this dragon's chief of whom you speak."

"Are you not?" grunted the man, eyes still narrowed suspiciously. "But you must know of this man whom they call Pendragon? They nicknamed him 'The Bear'."

"Arthur Pendragon? Surely, of him I have heard. Why would you think that I was that man?"

The tall man shifted his weight again.

"You are a stranger and you dress more in the manner of a *welisc* than a Saxon. And what man would dare ride through the country of Abbo alone?"

"I believe that you call all Britons *welisc*, or foreigners, in your Saxon tongue. Well, I am no Briton, though I speak their language as I do your own. I have only recently come to this land."

"Then speak your name and your own country."

The stranger gazed at the innkeeper in mild surprise.

"You have an arrogance for one of your calling, my friend. Or are all Saxons as opinionated as you?"

The tall man unfolded his arms and let them hang loosely at his side.

"You do not answer," he pointed out sullenly.

The stranger suddenly swung from his horse, dismounting in a light easy motion, his shield and javelin still undisturbed at his left side. When he stood on the ground, he was a lofty man, almost as tall as the Saxon, whose body had tensed when the stranger came to stand a few yards from him. But the stranger was smiling softly and made no threatening motion.

"I will answer you, courtesy for discourtesy, innkeeper. I am Torcán son of Crimthan, King of Cashel, and a knight of the Golden Collar."

"And where is this Cashel?" demanded the innkeeper, undaunted by the stranger's announcement.

The young warrior raised an eyebrow in surprise but amusement still tempered his expression.

"It is the capital of the kingdom of Mumhan, the biggest of the five kingdoms of the land of the Éireannach."

"Ah," the innkeeper breathed out. "So you are Irish? I have met some of your race before. Pious priests of your religion who come to the lands of the Saxons, prattling about your gods. Gods of love and forgiveness! Well they need to be, for I have seen many of these hymn-singing priests perish on the sacrificial fires to honour Woden, Thunor and Tyr!"

The young warrior looked serious for a moment.

"I have heard that you Saxons were barbarians and not above the slaughter of the servants of God."

The tall man thrust out his chin.

"You speak of servants of your god, but to us they are unbelievers and we sacrifice unbelievers to our gods."

"You are very bellicose for an innkeeper. And this conversation wearies me. I am thirsty and have ridden hard this day. I have crossed from Kernow through the kingdom of Gereint of Dumnonia. A long journey. Prepare food and drink for me."

The warrior made to move into the inn.

He was surprised when the tall man held up a hand to stay him.

"I would leave this place, Tor . . . Torc . . . I cannot pronounce your outlander name. You are not welcome here in the land of Abbo, thane of Eadric."

"Doubtless you speak truly. But you are an innkeeper and bound by the sacred laws of hospitality to supply me my needs."

Torcán's hand slipped lightly to his sword hilt and he smiled once again.

The Saxon hesitated and then grimaced angrily and stood aside to allow the young warrior to entered into the inn.

At the gesture, Torcán laughed, a deep roar of amusement.

"After you, innkeeper, for I think it best for me not to present my back to you since you have told me that there is no welcome at this place for me. Only my thirst and hunger make me prevail upon the hospitality that you have to offer. So, get you in, innkeeper, and I will follow."

The Saxon hesitated a moment and then shrugged. He turned and pushed in to the tavern. The young warrior of Cashel followed close behind, his hand in readiness on his sword hilt.

There was nothing remarkable about the inn. Tables and benches were placed for customers, while to one side a great fire roared in an open hearth, above which a black iron cauldron simmered away. Barrels and bottles stood in another corner. The young warrior stood for a moment or two, waiting until his eyes adjusted to the gloomy interior. Nothing then escaped his swift glance of inspection. The windows, the doors, the points of exit in case of attack; the weak spots from where hidden dangers might lurk. He covered them all in one quick examination.

There was one other occupant of the inn. On a bench, crunched up in a sleeping posture, was a figure wrapped in a rough homespun travelling cloak. There was a smell of alcohol permeating his body which could be discerned even from a distance. The man's features were dishevelled, blotched with dirt and the hair was grey and matted.

"Who is that?" The young man nodded.

"That?" The Saxon grimaced in disgust. "That is one of the *welisc*. A drunken mendicant."

"Yet you give him the hospitality which you would have denied me?"

Was there a shifty look of guilt in the Saxon's eyes?

"He arrived drunk and fell asleep. I was not here when . . ." The innkeeper hesitated and shrugged.

The warrior examined the slumbering figure with some distaste. Dirt and alcohol combined in a putrid odour. Loud snores reverberated from the recumbent figure. The warrior turned away, assured that there was nothing to fear from the only other occupant of the tavern. He found a table, put his shield and javelin aside, leaning them against the wall, and seated himself, back to the wall, to observe the rest of the inn. Torcán had not achieved distinction in the King of Cashel's bodyguard, as one of the elite warriors of the Golden Collar, without being a cautious as well as a brave man.

"Prepare food and bring me a jug of wine, good rich red wine."

The Saxon sniffed.

"Where do you think an inn like this gets wine? There is mead to offer and not much else. Mead, cheese and bread. If that is what you want then you may have it."

"By the Holy Cross, this is a poor country. Our hostels in

Mumhan would have an abundance of hot food and wine." The stranger paused. "Very well, get me what you have."

The Saxon moved across to the corner of the inn in search of the food and drink. After a while, he brought a platter with some badly cut bread and cheese on it and an earthenware pot of mead. It was a bitter mead, unlike the honey-tasting brew that Torcán was used to.

"Anything else, *welisc*?" sneered the tall man.

Torcán smiled brightly.

"An improvement in your manners, innkeeper," he replied easily.

Anger creased the Saxon's brow and his hands clenched as if to contain his fury.

He was about to speak further when there came the sound of hoofbeats moving rapidly towards the inn.

The Saxon moved surprisingly quickly, turning to the door.

Torcán had no time to register surprise. He drew his sword and was hard on the heels of the innkeeper. They reached the door together, just moments apart.

The innkeeper gave a deep sigh and his shoulders dropped, the tension that had been there was gone in a moment. The warrior from Cashel stood stock still, rubbing his chin in surprise at the newcomer.

A young woman had ridden up to the inn. She was attractive, clothed in such finery as indicated that she was a woman of rank and means. She wore a red silk dress, trimmed with golden threads, a cloak of green and red woollen plaid fastened at the shoulder with a circular brooch of silver inlaid with precious jewels and there was a small circlet of silver which offset her hair, which was as black as a raven's wing. Her horse was also richly adorned.

She slipped lightly from the saddle. Her features were attractive, the skin fair, the cheeks tinged with red, the eyes dark. Though there was some quality of hardness about those alluring eyes which seemed to belie the innocent attractiveness of the face.

Torcán returned his sword to its scabbard and went back to his table to resume his refreshment.

For a moment, Torcán could hear the swift whispering between the newcomer and the innkeeper as the young woman entered the inn. Then the innkeeper turned back to his host's duties. The dark eyes of the woman glanced on the figure of the dirty tramp and her nose wrinkled with disgust as she caught the putrid odour of his body and heard his drunken snoring. Then they alighted on Torcán and she moved forward with quick deliberation.

"God's blessing on you, knight of Éireann," she greeted in the language of the Britons.

Torcán stared up in surprise for a moment, and then, remembering his manners, came to his feet, swallowed a piece of bread before inclining his head in acknowledgment.

"God's blessing and those of His Son and the Mother of His Son be upon you, lady."

The dark-haired young woman sat down before Torcán and she smiled swiftly.

"I am Morgan of Ynys Afal."

"And I am Torcán, son of Crimthan, King of Cashel."

"I see you wear a hero's collar."

She indicated the golden torque around his neck.

"I am a Knight of the Golden Collar in the service of my king."

"What are you doing in the land of the Saxons?"

The young man's eyes narrowed slightly.

"I did not realize this was the land of the Saxons," he replied. "But I should ask first, what are you doing in this land? By your speech, you are a blood enemy to the Saxons."

The young woman shrugged.

"Simple enough. This is the borderland. Those hills mark the boundary with my people. When I was a child we Britons controlled these lands as far east as the great sea. Then the Saxons came and gradually we were driven west beyond those hills. I am using this trail as a short cut to get back to my people."

"A dangerous short cut."

"There is only a defenceless innkeeper here."

"Defenceless? He is a tall and surly man, built more like a warrior than an innkeeper, and he has an unhealthy dislike of all strangers, particularly those he calls the *welisc*."

"He will not harm me. But the thane of this country is a man that is much to be feared. He is a merciless man and a warrior of repute."

"Ah, you mean Abbo, thane of Eadric?"

The girl raised her eyebrows.

"You know of him?"

"Only what the innkeeper has told me."

"You have not heard of him before you came here?"

"I am a stranger in this land."

"Why have you come here?"

Torcán compressed his lips at the urgent curiosity in her voice.

"Come, you may trust me, stranger," she pressed.

The young warrior nodded slowly.

"You are a Briton, and therefore, perhaps, I should trust you, for you may be able to help me in return. I seek the war chieftain of your people who is called Arthur Pendragon."

The girl chuckled softly.

"Him I know well. I am half-sister to the man."

Torcán pursed his lips in a soundless whistle.

"Can this be so? Then truly the blessings of God are with me this day."

"I swear the truth of it, by the Holy Cross. But why do you seek Arthur? Are you in his service?" Her eyes glinted in excitement. "Has he sent you to this land to kill Abbo?"

Torcán shook his head.

"I told you that I had not heard of Abbo until I reached this inn. Nor, as I have said, do I know this Arthur."

Morgan frowned.

"Then why do you seek him?"

Torc glanced across the gloomy inn to where the tall Saxon was bent over some pots and, assured the man was out of earshot, the warrior from Cashel leant towards the girl in conspiratorial fashion.

"In Cashel, we heard how the Saxons invaded your lands; how your people are being driven westward from the territories they once inhabited. There are many Britons who have sought refuge in the five kingdoms of Éireann; sought to escape from the marauding hordes of strangers who dispossess them. We, in our kingdom of Mumhan, have been at one with our cousins of Britain. The daughters of our Kings of Cashel have often married with the kings of the Britons. I, myself, was one of the bodyguard sent to escort our lady Iseult safely to the land of Kernow where a week ago she married King Marc'h Cunomor of Dun Dór."

The young woman nodded impatiently.

"Speak on, warrior, and get to the point of this story."

"While I resided in the kingdom of Marc'h I heard many tales of the battles being fought against the Saxons. I heard of the stories of Arthur, 'The Bear', whom all kings acknowledge now as supreme among the war chieftains – the Pendragon, the dragon chief because he fights under the ancient dragon banner. I have heard of the many victories he has won over the Saxons. And so I left Dun Dór, where Marc'h is king, and have journeyed these last few days in search of Arthur Pendragon to offer my sword and service."

Morgan sat back, regarding him with a frown.

"I still cannot understand why you would do so? The conflict between Briton and Saxon is not your concern."

Torcán shrugged.

"It is the concern for all who pursue truth and justice to take up weapons in defence of a country invaded by foreigners, where the people are massacred or driven westward and even to lands beyond the wave. We warriors, who take the oath of the Niadh Nask, knights of the Golden Collar, are sworn to the pursuit of truth and the defence of the oppressed. This also, so I have heard, is the pursuit of Arthur Pendragon."

Morgan sniffed deprecatingly, as if not quite believing his answer.

"Is this the truth you tell me?"

"I swear it, by the Mother of Christ."

She gazed for a long while into his eyes and then nodded slowly.

"You are not cunning enough to invent such a tale, Torcán of Cashel."

Torcán frowned at her choice of words.

"Then can you tell me where I would find your brother, Arthur Pendragon?"

The dark-haired girl gave a sudden abrasive laugh. At the sound, the tall Saxon turned and came towards their table.

Morgan rose swiftly and turned towards him.

"He is not the one you fear, my friend," she called sharply in Saxon, perhaps not realizing that Torcán spoke the language. "Deal with him as you please. I have done my part." Then, with a toss of her dark hair, she strode quickly from the inn. Bewildered, not understanding, Torcán stared after her, hearing the creak of leather as mounted her horse and the clipping of its hooves as she galloped off. Then he realized his danger. The innkeeper was coming at him with a sword in one hand and dagger in the other. There was no time to draw his own sword.

Torcán swung his chair round and raised it just in time as the innkeeper's sword fell with a slashing stroke. The blade edge bit into the wood of the chair but not through it, causing splinters to fly. Then, the innkeeper, who appeared no slouch at weaponry, thrust with the long dagger, and it would have found its mark had not Torcán jerked his body aside at that moment, having anticipated such an underhand jab.

His muscles straining, Torcán pushed with all his strength with the chair, sending the tall innkeeper staggering backwards and tripping over a bench behind him. The Saxon recovered his balance but not before Torcán had time to unsheath his sword and grab his shield.

The innkeeper rushed forward on him again, his slashing sword smashing down with thick and fast strokes while the jabbing dagger hand was forever seeking an opening.

For a moment, Torcán allowed the Saxon to have his way, driving him backwards. To this there was a purpose, for Torcán allowed the Saxon to momentarily exhaust himself by the fierceness of his attack. The moment the man paused, then Torcán went on the defensive, pushing forward with his shield before him and swinging with his own long sword against his enemy, who did his best to parry the stream of strokes, sometimes having to use both sword and dagger as barriers to prevent the landing of the Cashel knight's blows. Finally, as he drove the innkeeper back towards the door, Torcán gave a sudden push with his shield, catching the man full in the chest and sending him staggering backwards through the doorway to measure his length on the ground beyond.

Torcán paused and shook his head in disbelief.

"And here am I, elite of the Golden Collar, having to struggle to defend myself from a mere innkeeper – Saxon or not," he rebuked himself bitterly.

The tall Saxon was on his feet again. Sword swung against sword with resounding, reverberant clangs which sent the birds screeching from their perches in the surrounding trees. By the Living Christ, thought Torcán, but there was power in the innkeeper's sword arm. No matter how swiftly he fought to find a way through the other's guard, the Saxon was always there, dagger and sword defending and parrying. The sweat was on the young warrior of Cashel now, round and round the two combatants moved, circling, thrusting, parrying, until their breaths came as short nervous gasping barks.

Torcán had no idea how long the combat had gone on but he knew that he could not last much longer. His sword arm felt heavy, so heavy that he could barely raise his arm above shoulder length. And his left shield shoulder was already bruised by the smashing of his opponent's sword on his target, which was battered and dented almost out of recognition.

Then, as he moved back to gain better foothold to meet the next barrage of blows from the Saxon, his foot slipped. He measured his length on the ground and lay stunned for a moment. With a cry of victory, the Saxon came forward, tossing aside his dagger and raising the hilt of his sword in both hands above the young warrior's undefended breast.

For a split moment Torcán saw death approaching and then, as if by some instinct, he pushed up his sword, as heavy as it was, even though he felt like screaming in anguish at the pain in his muscles. He thrust the point of the blade up into the torso of his opponent, up under the rib-cage and into the heart.

The tall Saxon stood swaying a moment, he coughed some blood and then, dropping the sword, he fell backward without another sound.

Torcán, in reaction, rolled swiftly to the side and sprang up, sword still ready and regarded the prostrate body of the innkeeper suspiciously.

Finally the young man straightened from his fighting crouch and he gazed down in disgust. There was no need to question whether the innkeeper was dead or not. Thus much was obvious to the experienced eye.

"You've killed him."

The voice was gentle, the words spoken in the language of the Britons.

Torcán swung round, raising his sword and shield in preparation for some new danger.

At the door of the inn stood the bedraggled figure of the drunken mendicant. Yet there was something different about the old man now. He was still dirty and bedraggled but he stood tall and firm and his voice held a tone of authority, as if he were a man used to being obeyed. His eyes were wide, their colour that of steel. They seemed to pierce through the outer coverings of men's flash to uncover their hidden souls.

Torcán did not move; his eyes were still suspicious.

"I have killed him," he said slowly. "I killed him in defence of my life for he would have killed me."

The elderly man nodded slowly, as if in agreement.

"Then you have nothing to reproach yourself over, my son."

Torcán shivered slightly. How did this old one know he was bitterly reproaching himself? The soft tones and manner of address were those he associated with some of the religious of his own country.

He sheathed his sword.

"Oh, indeed?" His voice was nevertheless harsh. "Have I no reason to be judgmental over this act?"

"None whatsoever."

"I am a warrior, pledged to a warrior's code. I am one of the elite of Cashel, a knight of the Golden Collar. That is why I have cause to judge myself harshly."

"You do not make yourself plain."

"I have killed a Saxon innkeeper." Torcán's voice was almost a wail. "I, a warrior, fought and slew a lowly innkeeper. Do you not find this a cause for distress? Is that not cause for every poet within the five kingdoms to compose satires that will bring blemishes to my face?"

The old man gestured at the corpse of the Saxon.

"Do you claim that he was not a worthy opponent? Was it not a hard task to overcome his sword arm? Did it not take you some time to lay him so low?"

Torcán's eyes narrowed in anger.

"In truth, it was so. But it will not be the fight that the bards will sing of but the fact that a warrior of the Golden Collar was hard pressed to overcome the sword of an innkeeper."

"Why did you fight?"

"Because he thrust the fight on me."

"And what made him attack you?"

Torcán shrugged.

"I have no idea. Perhaps all Saxons are mad – he hated strangers, of that I am sure. Indeed, he warned me to leave here as soon as I arrived. He thought at first I was one of those he called a *welisc*, a Briton like yourself."

The old man smiled and nodded.

"Indeed, he did. What else?"

Torcán groaned. He had almost forgotten in the excitement.

"The woman! The woman who called herself Morgan of Ynys Afal! She told the innkeeper to attack me! But why?"

"What did you tell her?"

"I told her who I was. I told her that I was coming in search of Arthur Pendragon to offer him my sword. She encouraged me – she claimed she was the sister of Arthur Pendragon. She lied and tricked me and tried to have me murdered."

The old man shook his head, smiling sadly.

"She did not lie but, indeed, she told the Saxon to kill you."

"She did not lie? How so?"

"She is, indeed, Morgan of the Island of Apples, half-sister to Arthur, war chieftain of the united kingdoms of the Britons. She is his bane, for she hates her half-brother with all her heart. To destroy him she would destroy all Britain and hand it over on a platter to the Saxons."

Torcán ran his hand through his hair.

"I pity a woman with such hate. But I had not wronged her. Why did she seek my destruction? Anyway, how do you know all this?"

"In good time, my young warrior friend. Come, there is someone we must release from imprisonment."

The old man turned and walked back into the tavern with a firm gait and no trace of the alcohol of which he still reeked. Torcán, sword still held carefully in hand, followed him across the room.

Behind the barrels was a small door leading into another chamber of the inn, a small chamber which was doubtless meant for the living quarters of the innkeeper. Inside was a small cot. A rotund figure lay on the cot. He was gagged and bound.

"Use your sword to cut the poor churl's bonds," instructed the old man.

Torcán found himself unquestioningly cutting at the ropes that bound the man.

"Are you hurt, Ine?" asked the old man in Saxon.

"No, my lord. My pride is hurt and my blood stopped flowing freely during this last hour. But that is all."

Torcán was shaking his head totally bemused.

"Who is this man?"

The old drunk, who was not a drunk, smiled gently.

"This is Ine, the innkeeper."

The warrior ran his free hand through his hair in distraction.

"Then who . . .?"

"The man you killed? That was Abbo of Abello, thane to Eadric, King of the West Saxons. He is the most renown warrior in the Saxon kingdoms. So know now that you have no cause for shame in slaying him."

Torcán swallowed hard.

"I have no understanding of this matter."

The old man took the young warrior by the arm and led him back into the main room. He called, over his shoulder, "When you have recovered sufficiently, Ine, break out some of your red wine for I fear our young friend has need of it." He laughed as he saw Torcán's features. "Poor Abbo had no idea, during his brief role as innkeeper, that Ine has a special stock of red wine for certain guests."

"Explain this matter before my thoughts drive me berserk," pleaded Torcán.

"Easy enough. Abbo of Abello is – was – one of the best warriors of the West Saxons. A man to be feared. A merciless man. He had already slaughtered nine of Arthur's greatest warriors."

"So why did he skulk here in the guise of an innkeeper?"

"Arthur decided that he could risk no more good men in single combat with him. Abbo had to be challenged and the only person capable of meeting that challenge, or so Arthur assumed, was the Pendragon himself. Arthur arranged to meet Abbo and put the matter to the test of combat. It was agreed that both men would meet at this inn and that neither Abbo nor Arthur would bring any companions with them.

"Now Arthur and Abbo had never met before, so neither knew what each other looked like. Not being a man of honour, Abbo decided to come here and disguise himself as the innkeeper. He would pretend to Arthur that Abbo had not yet arrived, persuade Arthur to relax and, when his guard was down, he would slaughter him."

He paused as Ine, the rotund innkeeper, brought them wine. Then he continued.

"Abbo came here, tied Ine up and took his place. Thankfully, Arthur is not a foolish man and he knew Abbo was treacherous. So he sent me here to pretend to be a drunken beggar in order to see if the Saxon thane were plotting some trap. I arrived here before Abbo and when he came I pretended to be in a drunken sleep. I saw him tie up Ine and assume the role of the innkeeper. I waited ready to warn Arthur when he arrived. But you came instead."

Torcán nodded slowly. He began to see the logic of the explanation.

"But then, when Morgan came, she could have recognized you as Arthur's man and put you in danger as well."

"A lady would not deign to stoop over a smelly, drunken beggar. No, she was not concerned in identifying me. She came to find out if Abbo had killed her half-brother. But Abbo asked her to discover if you had been sent in Arthur's stead or, indeed, were Arthur himself."

"She came to betray her own brother?"

"Such is the nature of her hatred," sighed the old man.

Torcán shook his head sadly.

"Well, I am grateful for your explanation, old man. If I had gone from here thinking that I had slain an innkeeper and that innkeeper had nearly bested me in a fight, I would have had to return to Cashel and hand back my golden torque to my king. As it is, I shall continue my search for this Arthur of yours." He paused. "But I do not know your name, old one."

The old man smiled.

"My name is Myrddin. I am confidant and adviser to Arthur. And if you seek him, I hear the sound of a horse approaching. That will be Arthur. He will be amazed to find his adversary already defeated."

The young man stood up eagerly.

"I must show him that I am worthy to offer him my sword."

Myrddin chuckled.

"I think you have already done that, Torc . . . Tor . . . I have difficulty with your name. I will call you Tor. And the story of your combat with Abbo of Abello shall proceed you. By that act you have become a warrior fit to join Arthur's circle of chosen warriors."

Sir Lionel in TOURNAMENT OF ROGUES

Keith Taylor

Sir Lionel was the younger brother of Sir Bors, always ready for a scrap, but somewhat frustrated by always appearing in the shadow of his brother, or that of his cousin (or uncle in some traditions), Sir Lancelot. Arthur eventually gave him the kingdom of Gaul to keep him quiet, though as the following story shows Lionel was no easy knight to keep quiet.

Keith Taylor (b. 1946) is an Australian writer who has an avid interest in early British history. He has written a series of historical fantasy novels set at the time of the downfall of the Roman Empire in Britain: Bard *(1981),* The First Longship *(1989),* The Wild Sea *(1986),* Ravens' Gathering *(1987) and* Felimid's Homecoming *(1991).*

1

> *". . . as I hear say that the tournament shall be here within this three mile . . ."*
>
> – Malory, *La Morte d'Arthur*, VI:6

I hadn't the look of a knight of my lord Arthur's Round Table that day. Riding in errantry is seldom a matter of holy visions and magic castles. Having been lost in mountain wilderness for some time, I was travel-stained and weary. My shield was half defaced from a battle with a band of scurvy gallows-bait robbers. Two of them stumbled along behind me now, carrying my injured squire in exchange for my sparing their lives.

I rode light. My helmet was an open-faced casque with cheek-pieces. I wore nothing to protect my body but a hard leather gambeson. No, seeing me, my friends, you would not have taken me for a man of consequence, much less a member of King Bors's mighty house. Yet I will soon make clear that I bore myself like one.

Facing me across a ford I saw three knights mounted on destriers nearly as superb as mine. Well, perhaps I praise the beasts too highly, but they were good. The men wore full mail and heavy, massive tilting helms. The devices on their shields were new and clear. Their bearing was haughty.

"Come no further!" the foremost called out. "This tourney has enough worthy knights entered. We therefore hold this ford, and command all comers to turn around and withdraw."

"I know nothing of any tourney, fair sir. My squire was injured in the mountains. He requires a leech."

"Let him be treated by those curs who bear him along," the second knight suggested. "What think you, Sir Vallulf; birds of a feather?"

"It's all too likely, Sir Grum," Vallulf said.

"These are not knightly manners," I said.

A gentle and seemly response, I think you'll agree; but wrath was rising thickly in my throat.

"I'm Sir Vallulf of Lombardy," the spokesman thundered. "Impugn my manners, child, and it's the last name you may hear, by the Pope's shoulder-bone!"

I quit speaking mildly. "So? He men call Vallulf the Burner because he makes such a custom of arson, even to torching barns filled with wounded soldiery? I'm happy to meet you. Indeed, I believe I'll come across in hopes of knowing you better."

"Any knight who crosses here must run a course against us," Sir Grum shouted. "When spears be splintered, we continue with weapons of our own choosing."

The third knight spoke for the first time. By the shape of his helmet and shield, he was Thuringian. "If you *can* continue!"

"My squire cannot wait while we seek to win honour!" I protested.

Grasaut lifted himself on one elbow and said clearly, in his soft Welsh accents, "Head of Bran! I'm not dying, Lionel! I can well wait while you correct his errors of thought and talk."

I smiled at him. "My thanks, comrade. Well! Then I'll even see how these knights' deeds match their big words."

Looking across the ford again in the morning sun, I saw a party of men riding along the road, coming up behind Sir Vallulf and his friends. Leading them rode a knight banneret on a huge brown horse, and his arms were a leopard's face jessant-de-lis on a purple field. Pardieu, but he was Bricus de Souvene! Ten lances followed him, and beside him on an ambling cob rode a short man wearing a herald's hat and tabard.

Whether they would be for or against me, I did not know, nor was it knightly to care. I straightened in the saddle. "My squire assures me he can well bear to wait while I clear our path," I cried through cupped hands. "I'll happily fight you for the right to cross this poor ford!"

"With unbated lances?" the Thuringian demanded.

"Just as you like. Wait while I arm myself, for I must do it unholpen."

"No, fair sir," Bricus called to me, so that heads turned and Vallulf, seeing the newcomers, spoke an oath. Sir Bricus ignored him. "By these golden spurs, it would honour me if I might assist you."

"Then cross the ford, sir knight, with a good will."

Commanding his men to bide, he rode through the water, still paying no heed to Vallulf. It appeared they were not friends. Sir Bricus looked keenly at my shield, and then at me, a knight some dozen years his junior. I'm a large man. Bricus was tall himself, with a forked beard and an able, unsparing look about him. He seemed to assess me at a glance.

"Welcome, sir knight," he said. "If I mistake not your device, and it be the red gryphon sergeant, then I might guess your name in two or three attempts. But if you have vowed not to give your name, then I'll take it that I err."

"No, fair sir," I began. "I'm under no such vow, and – "

The egregious Vallulf interrupted us.

"Wait!" he thundered. "Who are you, stranger? I encounter no man without knowing his name and lineage! It would disgrace me, for all I know, to ride against you!"

"No disgrace!" I thundered back. "I'm a true knight, and of king's blood! I'm Lionel de Gannes, the younger son of King Bors, and a knight of King Arthur's Table Round in Britain! Wait a short while and I'll prove it!"

"Indeed," Sir Bricus remarked suavely. "Since he's so impatient, you may as well give him the recognition he merits. Permit me to arm you, Sir Lionel. I'm Bricus de Souvene."

"I'd already surmised so, fair sir. You do me honour."

My Flemish mail was packed in a bundle on Grasaut's dun courser. Sir Bricus helped me into chausses, hauberk and coif, and last of all, proudly, I donned the surcoat. It carried the gryphon of Gannes, red, between three red estoiles – my difference as the younger son. I buckled on the sword that had been my father's gift when I was knighted. For a reserve weapon I opened another bundle. This contained an axe, flange-headed mace, and morningstar. I chose the spiked ball on its short length of chain. Sir Bricus lifted an eyebrow.

"You seem in a ferocious humour, fair sir."

"It's a fiend's toy," I admitted. "I've seen some hard men flinch from it. Perhaps I am curious to know how hard those windbags yonder really are."

"Be assured, though they have been boasting, brawling, jealous trouble-makers since they arrived here, they are no mere windbags. Treat them lightly and it could be your last mistake." Seeing me frown, he added calmly, "It's intended as wholly friendly advice."

"From you, Sir Bricus, I will accept it."

I hadn't one of the massive tilting-helms, and so perforce I covered my head with an ordinary barrel-shaped helmet. Sir Bricus fastened it for me, and I mounted my grey horse, Pertinax. He was the fresher, and Probus, my sorrel destrier, was limping slightly.

The Thuringian faced me first. We took deadly, sharp-headed spears from a rack the trio had set up nearby. Dressing our shields, we spurred forward, all the world reduced to what we could see through the slits of our helmets, and the ground vibrated beneath our charging horses.

Impact boomed like thunder. The Thuringian broke his spear but did no harm. I aimed for his helmet, and scored a mere glancing hit. A fastening burst. The big helm turned half around on its owner's head, so that the eye-slits were in the wrong position. The knight reeled, yanking blindly at his reins. He fumbled with his sword.

This was not courteous jousting in the lists. I gave the Thuringian no grace to adjust or remove his headgear. Drawing my own sword, I struck him on the shoulder in a rough accolade, snapping the collar-bone through mail and padding. He yielded and withdrew.

Sir Grum confronted me next. Althought I didn't know him, I soon learned he was a superb jouster. Leaning far out of his saddle, and in full mail, he avoided my lance completely, then hit me clean on the helm with ease, nearly breaking my neck. The world turned red. I reeled sideways, and swooned for a moment, I believe. Pertinax carried my half-conscious weight back to the starting point, as his training and loyal nature bade him, while I regained my senses.

My neck felt as though it had been dipped in hellfire. With a curse, I took a new spear and charged Sir Grum. I holed his blue shield, snapped my lance and then rode straight at him. Pertinax's chest hit the other horse's shoulder and brought it down on its haunches.

Sir Grum's shield dropped low. I swung my blade strongly, to hack through mail and cut slantwise down to the bone, so that a wedge of muscle hung away from Grum's upper arm, bleeding greatly. He lurched in defeat from the meadow.

I was nearly blind with pain, and my helmet felt red hot. Sucking great raw breaths through the air-holes, I cantered up to face Sir Vallulf. Unlike Sir Grum, he was no very skilful jouster, and preferred the melee or tourney any day. When we ran together, he broke his spear at once. So did I.

"Some real work now!" he boomed.

We engaged with swords. His edge rang my helmet like a flawed bell. Agony ate me alive. I thought he'd snapped my neck. I faltered; he drove down the lower edge of his shield to fracture my shin, but I pulled my leg swiftly aside, bringing it out of the deep stirrup. Bracing my other foot, I struck so fiercely that I hacked a cantel from Sir Vallulf's shield, and toppled him sideways out of the saddle.

For a moment the lust was on me to ride him down and trample him. But I remembered the vows of the Round Table and Arthur's lordly standards of honour. I dismounted slowly. Sir Vallulf gripped his reserve weapon, a beaked German war-hammer that could punch through mail as a woodpecker pierces bark. In response, I seized the morningstar.

Crashing impacts rolled across the meadow. My gryphon shield, much defaced to begin with, soon bent over my arm from a score of forceful blows, like pastry doubled around meat. The smashing morningstar put dints and depressions in Vallulf's shield everywhere. It began bending double like mine. Oh, there were few fine points to appreciate in that fight! We battled like titans in the days when the world had newly emerged from chaos!

I made that lethal spiked ball whirl and fly. Suddenly it spun around the handle of Sir Vallulf's hammer. We both yanked strongly, each trying to deprive the other of his weapon. Neither gained an advantage. I brought my other arm around, dealing a tremendous buffet with the deformed, doubled shield. It struck his side and cracked ribs, I think. Aye, through mail, gambeson, padded vest and all. Vallulf stumbled to his knees. Hauling with both hands, I took possession of morningstar and hammer together, then kicked Sir Vallulf on his back before untangling the weapons.

"Yield!" I croaked, throwing the hammer aside.

Vallulf did nothing of the kind. Holding his shield before him, he rolled forward, gaining his feet and starting to rise. That's a feat in full mail. He wasn't nimble enough, alas. I swung the morningstar to the side of his helmet. It cratered a massive dent over the temple, stunning him. He was fortunate indeed to be wearing a great thick tilting-helm! That blow on an ordinary casque might well have knocked the brains out of his skull.

I'd cast down three damned strong men in half an hour. Let them doubt now that I was a son of King Bors!

I wondered why they had been holding the ford against all comers. They had said something about a tournament, and that they wished no more contenders to arrive. It was the first I had even heard of one! *Fete dieu*, I might take part!

Always supposing my head did not come off with my helmet.

2

"The whole place was decked with silks and banners, crowns and draperies, lights and torches, and with some amazing devices and contrivances."

– Matthew Paris, *Chronica Majora*

"Yes, indeed, Sir Lionel," the little herald chattered, "this joust and tourney will be a great event! My lady the Countess Chimene has sanction and charter to occupy Castle Brulant and hold a hastilude, all knights of noble descent to be welcome! Sir Bricus is appellant in her name."

"She must be a triumphant lady," I said. Bricus de Souvene

was not known for lending his name or his prowess to ladies for the mere sake of chivalry.

"*Tonnerre*, Sir Lionel, she's indeed something rare," he agreed. His dark, bearded face lit with a genuine smile. "I haven't known her long. She ransomed me from a dungeon where I seemed to have no future worth mentioning. I took oath to serve her for a year and a day. Master Rufo here has been her herald for a decade."

"Since the old days in Spain," Master Rufo declared. Short, dark and almost globular in shape, he did not look well in the herald's tabard. It bore arms I did not recognize, but then I have never been to Spain. "Each night I drink a toast that we may soon return there."

He chattered all the way to the castle, about his gracious, renowned and noble countess and her chequered fortunes. We arrived ere long. Having travelled in those parts once, I had vaguely remembered the castle as square, strong and plain, of indifferent size. When King Claudas ravaged the land in his wars against my father and uncle, it was gutted and blackened by fire, and became known as Castle Brulant for that reason.

That isn't how it looked now. I wondered if I had come to the same place. It appeared taller and more graceful, the stones honey-coloured, a warm rich hue in the noonday sun. The Countess Chimene's banner flew from every tower.

Riding into the courtyard, I drew rein, amazed. Instead of the usual well I saw a marble and malachite fountain with clear bright water asplash. Flowerbeds and rose bushes filled the place with colour, while near the kitchen there flourished beds of purple herbs. The Countess's people, even the scullions, for the most part were handsome. I saw milkmaid skins, straight limbs and good carriage everywhere I looked.

Pardieu, my friends, it all seemed so perfect that I had a quick sharp suspicion of faerie glamour! Dismounting, I rubbed a rose-petal between my fingers. It felt real. Even the scent of roses filled the courtyard, and Lancelot du Lac had told me that the greatest enchanter cannot deceive such deep and intimate senses as taste and smell. And Lancelot ought to know.

"I release you, *vous deux coquins*," I said to the robbers. "Set down that litter and go."

"Go where, fair sir?" asked one.

"Where? To your hoof-footed master the devil if you like. What is it to me? Depart! Disappear!"

Within the castle, I received a bath and massage that was no illusion. Nor was the embrocation a physician applied to my neck with the barest touches of skilled fingertips. Then he probed muscles and felt bones while I gritted my teeth.

"It's sorely ricked, sir knight, but not dislocated," he said at last. "Will it please you to rest until tomorrow, and then greet our lady in the hall?"

"It pleases me if it pleases the Countess," I agreed. "However, I'm anxious to behold so remarkable a lady. And she'll grant me the favour, I would have great joy to meet and thank her now."

She gave me my will. Treading into the castle hall, I saw a place of velvet, coloured glass and silken banners. A gallery ran around the upper level on three sides, and a sculpted stone fireplace dominated one end below.

Midway along one wall stood a clepsydra ten feet high. Lifelike figures of a knight and his lady moved as the water dripped, the knight kneeling, the lady offering her sleeve as a token. The living lady, mistress of all this, the Countess Chimene, waited by the high seat at the hall's far end. Two women attended her, with her seneschal and Rufo the herald.

God's light!

It was worth being lost in the mountains, attacked by bandits, and then challenged by a trio of haughty knights, just to look at her!

Splendid, sensuous and noble are good words for my first impression. I'm two yards high. She might have been a palm shorter, with a deep-breasted, wide-hipped shape and proudly poised head. Blood of some ancient line of Visigoths there, I would guess, and her rich gold hair confirmed it, but her face made me think of a Roman empress. Her eyes were a smoky, slumbrous brown, and deep within them I thought I saw shadows of grief, just as I thought I saw something tender soften the cast and expression of her full mouth. She redefined woman.

All right, I rave. Grant me indulgence; I was twenty.

"I address Sir Lionel, whose father is the noble and puissant King Bors, one of the greatest knights alive?" the Countess asked.

Believe it or not, she didn't dash my illusions by speaking. Her voice was a mellow contralto that made me think of mandolins and bronze windchimes, and if her accent was Spanish, all women should acquire one. God's light! I ought to have known then that it was too grand to be true!

"Gracious lady," I said through a daze, "for your welcome, I thank you greatly. You have right. I am Lionel de Gannes, younger son of King Bors and the splendid Queen Evaine."

"Splendid indeed. All Christendom knows how that great lady defended a castle against siege by King Claudas." She smiled at me. "I am Countess Chimene of Naubet and Corracha, which lands be part of the Spanish kingdom of Sovrar."

"Your distance from home is Gaul's great good fortune, lady, but I am ignorant of Spanish matters. Where lieth Sovrar?"

"Between Lusitane, Galicia and Layaun. 'Tis somewhat new on the maps. To create it, Ferdrugo the Cruel wrested half a kingdom from his brother, and then married a fair portion of a second. Bloody disputes followed, so that a bandit baron slew my husband and now lords it in our demesnes with none to hinder."

Her voice throbbed with grief. I was outraged.

"*Fete dieu*, countess! If you told this tale in Camelot there would be no lack of knights to take your part! This brigand should soon lose his head!"

"I've heard as much. Perhaps I should have sailed to Britain! These seven years I have sought a champion who may journey to Spain with me and destroy this tyrant. 'Tis for the purpose of finding one, Sir Lionel, that I have declared this great tournament here. In each land I enter, I make a practice of doing so."

"Why, gentle lady, may I know how many you have entered thus far?"

"Carthage, the Sicilies, Greece, Illyria, and Lombardy."

"And found no champion of the right quality in all those places?" I was greatly tempted to burst out laughing. Nay, most certainly, she should have begun her search in France or Britain! "By this hilt! But I am amazed! Surely you need look no further than Sir Bricus, lady? He has equal renown in the lists and as a captain of war."

"Gramercy, fair sir," Bricus said. "I think so too. God knows I am eager to set out for Spain. I'm greatly in this fair lady's debt, for that she ransomed me from an imprisonment in which foul death seemed certain."

"And I'd be loth to deliver you to such a fate again!" the Countess exclaimed. "I protest I'm sure of your might and good will, Sir Bricus. But this tyrant is a man of such strength that I must in justice and wisdom throw open the field to others."

I bent my knee to her at once.

"Then I would take part! Lady Chimene, I'd be pleased to serve you against this monster! Be assured, also, that if any knight surpasses me and wins that right instead, he must be glorious and worthy!"

"I'm assured of it, and I thank you," she said gravely. "But what of the injury to your neck? Might you not be fatally hurt if you were struck again upon the same place?"

"How long until the hastilude begins?" I asked.

"Seven days, Sir Lionel."

"Gracious Countess, I'll be ready. And may mine be the hand that rids you of this pest!"

Chimene smiled sweetly. I stood fast without staggering, God knows how. "Enter Sir Lionel's noble name and ancestry upon the rolls, Rufo my herald. I believe it will be in fair company there." She hesitated a moment. "I'm honoured and much heartened, Sir Lionel. But tell me. Is your cousin, Sir Lancelot du Lac, haply in France at this season?"

I suppose I'd been half expecting her to ask that, sooner or later, and still I bridled. Always Lancelot. Yes, he's the best of knights, and yes, he's saved my life, but –

"No, lady," I answered, curt as I had been voluble and impassioned the moment before. "He bides in Britain."

"Ah," she said, and to my surprise she did not appear disappointed at all. Surely she'd hope for the greatest of all knights to be her champion? But already I was learning that in ways this countess was as enigmatic as charming.

About Lancelot, my friends . . . he was indeed in Britain, and nowise fit to travel. He'd been gravely wounded in his great fight with Sir Turquine the Black. You will all know about Turquine . . . no? Splendour of God, how quickly men forget! He was our lord Arthur's greatest enemy in the early days. Huge, strong and great, he never met a knight of Camelot without fighting him, and those he did not kill outright he tossed into his dungeons, to suffer foul abuse until they died.

He captured *me*, in fact, had the better of me with shameful, galling ease, so you will conceive how mighty he must have been. But my captivity was not long. Lancelot challenged Sir Turquine, fought him most of the day in a combat I wish I had witnessed, and cut the head from his shoulders at last. He nearly died in the doing, though. His wounds were frightful. He said himself it was the hardest battle of his life.

Still, I wanted to prove myself again with great deeds, and also be clear of Britain for a while, the scene of my humiliation. Begging King Arthur's leave to visit France for a time, I crossed the Channel and wandered in errantry with my squire (and blood-brother) Grasaut.

I didn't, you may be sure, divulge any of this at Castle Brulant. That nobody there had heard of Turquine the Black was the best of reasons for liking them.

3

> *". . . and well may ye wit there were all manner of meat plenteously, all manner revels and games, with all manner of minstrelsy that was used in those days."*
>
> – Malory, *Le Morte d'Arthur*, VII: 35

Dinner in the Countess Chimene's hall was as lavish as most banquets, but then, the local seigneur, Count Hurguse, had come to visit with his lady, Danielle, and their children. They were important guests, not only because of their rank. Hurguse was the lord who had granted Chimene licence and charter to hold her tournament at Castle Brulant, which was one of his possessions.

"Matters go well, Lady Chimene," he said happily. "I've seldom seen preparations for a tournament proceed more featly. Truly, your people know what they're about."

"Thank you, my lord count. 'Tis most true. The noble Sir Bricus and Master Rufo, there, my good herald and secretary, in especial I could not do without."

Rufo beamed all across his chubby face. Bricus smiled, but I was beginning to think there was something hidden in those smiles of his, something sardonic or rueful. Didn't he like serving the countess? Of course, he was a mercenary captain, landless, and maybe he saw his vow of service to the lady as a necessary evil he must endure until he discharged it. Then he could go back to earning his living.

Count Hurguse, a bald man with a pepper-and-salt beard, cut into a spiced pastry, handing a portion to his wife. "More knights arrive each day. We've had good response from all parts of France. Twenty-three knights of Brittany have sent their acceptances, and ought to arrive within three days, the King's son, Kehydius, leading 'em."

"Others from Flanders and Payarne, also, my lord," Chimene said, "with over forty from certain German princedoms, by the letters I've received. There should be almost 200 knights in all."

The count's happiness increased until he nearly glowed. I well saw why. Tournaments bring gain and increase a lord's repute.

Splendid and varied dishes never stopped coming to the tables: boar's heads with gilded tusks and flames in their mouths, swans and peacocks dressed again in their feathers after cooking, the centrepiece of a huge pastry ship, sweetened and laden with sweetmeats, the spices and sauces, pork, venison, truffles, apples and nuts, figs simmered in honey and wine, and more things past counting. Trumpeters in satin announced each new course from the gallery with flourishes. Musicians in velvet who played while we ate came from Italy; the dancers and acrobats who entertained us between courses were, I think, Illyrian, and two young Greek wrestlers in leather kilts fought best of five falls at the end, lithe, quick and skilful. It was clear the Countess had travelled in all the lands she said.

And still things troubled me. Little things, odd things, like a slightly sensitive tooth your tongue cannot leave alone. The torches burned too clearly; there should have been more smoke. A tall servant who passed me cast a short shadow. The varlets' liveries fitted impossibly well. I started looking closely. Never a stain or a loose thread among them all!

Now I am not bothered by finicking details as a rule. Surely there was much else I did not notice or remember, but which added to the unreal air just the same. I applied myself to the wine, which was unmistakably real, like the viands, and soon was cheerful again.

Count Hurguse's two daughters and a local baron's lady, all pretty women, let me know by hinting that they would not be displeased if I carried their tokens in the jousting. I'd rather have had Chimene's, but Sir Bricus was her consort and champion, so that would be his honour. I answered their hints with courtesy, but did not commit myself. I could decide at the banquet and ball that would precede the tournament. *Fete dieu*, but it's magnificent to be young and to have noble beauties wishing you to ride and fight in their names! I forgot those bothersome little fancies I'd had, which no doubt amounted to nothing. Belike my damnably stiff and painful neck had engendered them.

It was Chimene who had truly taken my fancy, though, and the next day I rode to the tilting-field with her. Not alone, alas. A party of her guests went with us. As Count Hurguse said, preparations were going briskly. The plain was already enclosed with the standard double barriers, four paces apart, and lists were complete. Men were painting them in the Countess's colours, alternating with those of her patron, Count Hurguse. Beside the field, carpenters were hard at work on stands for the judges and the ladies, hammers banging, saws rasping. Elsewhere, lines were being marked out for the knights' pavilions, for the country was going to see a small army of us in residence, by all accounts. Several blacksmiths' forges, an armourer's workshop, extensive temporary stables and a fairground were going up too, the stables three-quarters done. Master Rufo the herald, as King of Arms, and the four Judges of the Combat, were supervising all this; they looked harassed, and I didn't wonder. To organize a large joust and tourney is a task fit to chastise the devil, as old Philippus my father's herald used to declare . . . loudly.

Seeing all this busy reality rid me of any last traces of that odd disquiet I'd felt the night before. I felt excited and eager. Each step my horse took hurt my neck wickedly, even though I went no faster than a walk, but I knew I'd be fit to joust within a week. And carry the field before me. I'm Lionel de Gannes, not a feeble old woman!

"You will have to fight hard," Sir Bricus said. "I intend to carry the field before *me*, Sir Lionel. With respect, you are young. As you were gracious enough to say, I'm experienced in the lists and in warfare. The Lady Chimene will need me when she returns to Spain."

"She said, I believe, that she has need of the best knight she can find."

"And she has found him. I believe her concern for your injury was as sensible as it was kind. Let me advise you. Find that your neck worsens daily and withdraw from the hastilude."

"*Fete dieu*, Sir Bricus, you are no less kind," I retorted, staring at him, "but it seems that my neck has been improving with each word you've uttered. It's wonderful! I believe you must have healing power."

"I hope you still hold the same opinion after riding against me."

Ha! I might be young, but I had grown up in a royal court. My knowledge of the world was enough for me to see what this landless man wanted; Countess Chimene's hand in marriage, her castles and demesnes. Yes, and her wealth. To refurbish a castle as she had done, and hold a tournament at her own expense, she must be rich as Croesus! That, too, I could see.

Well, my friends, after that exchange, I did not care for Sir

Bricus's company over-much. But with Chimene's I was still enchanted. To my delight she seemed pleased with mine. Although busy with a constant round of guests and new arrivals, she always included me in the party when riding, hawking or hunting, and twice invited me to her bower for refreshment and a game of chess – with her maids present, of course. The first time, her seneschal was also there, and the second, Rufo the herald acted as chaperon. *Once I prevail in the tournament*, I thought, *there'll be no such nonsense*.

"Lady Chimene," I said, lifting my eyes from the chessboard, a wonderful thing of white marble and scarlet porphyry, "you know it is my great desire to win the right to accompany you to Spain and overthrow this tyrant."

"Yes." She met my gaze. "Your desire honours me."

Pardieu! Was she teasing, promising, mocking, or all three? Desire can be an ambiguous word.

"Never believe I think this a game," I said earnestly. "I know war. Besides, there is a gallant, seasoned commander at my father's court, and a life-long friend of mine, who would come with us, lending me his experience and judgment. A hundred knights would also follow me if I request it. These are men who would march across purgatory and lay siege to the barbican of hell! When I win the degree in this tournament, I should not wish you to feel regret because I am not Sir Bricus. On my knightly honour, I can bring more to your cause than green eagerness."

I couldn't read that glorious face. From the way her eyes widened and a pulse throbbed in her throat, I thought I had moved her, and then it seemed for a second that her expression mingled amusement and regret, and that she lowered her gaze to hide it – and then she spoke, and her voice was husky with feeling.

"I'm grateful, gallant sir. I know you can, believe me. And – I should like to see you win the day, though I ought not to say so. Let's leave the subject there. Ah! A good move."

It wasn't good enough. She checkmated me six moves later.

4

". . . that is a great pity that ever so noble a man as ye are of your deeds and prowess, that any man or woman might find in their hearts to work any treason against you."

– Malory, *Le Morte d'Arthur*, IV:12

The days passed, and they were good. Knights continued to arrive, singly and in parties. Kehydius, son of King Howel of Brittany, came with a score and two chevaliers, and I was glad to welcome him. Knights of King Claudas and his greatest vassal, the Count of Estrangot, also appeared, and I was glad to see them, our ancient enemies, though in a different way. Men of rank and prowess from several German princedoms came last of all, having the greatest distance to ride.

All these men submitted their arms and crests to the scrutiny of the *juges diseurs*. They were then free to enjoy the banquet and ball that would precede the tournament. On the morrow, the judges would examine their characters and records more closely, and anyone guilty of dire offences against knighthood would be barred. Then the ladies and other highborn spectators would be admitted, all in accord with the usual practice and custom. The utter familiarity of it put my mind quite at rest.

Alack, it couldn't remain so. I've wondered many times since what might have happened if I had ignored Grasaut's well-being and left him to the physicians. But no, I had to visit him, to see how he was coming along. Pardieu, I had not asked the young fool to fall into that ravine, injure his leg, and strike his head besides!

Grasaut looked at me so wild-eyed as I entered that I thought, for a moment, the concussion had sent him crazy. Sitting up straight in his bed, he blurted, "Lionel, by the gods my people swear by! I hoped you'd come! I was ready to fashion a crutch and go hopping off to find you, except that would have too desperate and urgent a look – and desperate and urgent are the true words for what confronts us here!"

I overlooked his heathen oath. I've never been over-devout. "What, comrade? I've heard excesses of Welsh excitement from you before. Lie back and take your ease. It's a command. You have suffered a broken head. This is the last time I'll say it. I am not going to fuss o'er you like a mother with cold towels."

"Welsh be damned," he said with heat. "It's a derogatory foreign term I hold in scorn. I'm Cymric, if you please, and will you listen?"

"Why, if you insist. What's wrong?"

"That fat little herald came to visit me twice, sitting for some time, and he so busy. I talked a lot. He kept bringing the talk around to you and Lancelot."

"Oh, Splendour of God! Don't tell me you gossiped about my

time in Sir Turquine's dungeons! I came over here to escape the shame of that and win new glory!"

"That's neither here nor there." He *had* divulged it. "The herald looked in again today. I didn't feel right, so I feigned sleep and heard him giving tongue to the physician. What they said . . ."

"Well, speak it! Do not shake your head like an old woman who has just learned her granddaughter's with child unwed!"

"That rogue of a fat herald said, 'He's safe. His master is but riding a knight-errant for a while, and Lancelot will not arrive here. We have nothing to worry about.'

"'Nothing but the banquet tonight,' answers the physician. 'I've done my part there. The rest depends on the lady and the steward.'

"The herald chuckles then, and rubs his hands. 'They won't fail,' he promised. 'All's done as for a genuine tournament. God knows our lady presided over enough of those. Her accursed husband was mad for them.'

"'I'll answer for the food and drink,' said the physician then, showing himself a bigger rogue than the herald. 'All those who eat and drink heartily will sink into drugged and opiate slumber – and few, I'd think, will be abstenious. If any prove so, why, that's the purpose of the special wine.'

"'I'd admire to see their faces when they awake to find us vanished and the castle transformed,' said the herald, and they smirked together, the black deceivers! Lionel," Grasaut continued, gripping my arm, "we're surrounded by glamour! Can you not sense it? There's trickery toward, of a kind that Gwydion himself would be proud to commit, as when he swindled Pryderi out of the pigs of Hades in exchange for horses with gold bridles and saddles that didn't even exist, and I declare it!"

"I can't believe it," I muttered. "Grasaut, you must ha' misheard! Your broken head caused you to fancy that wicked colloquy. Nay, but think! Who would announce and prepare a tournament at such great cost if it were not genuine?"

"Maybe they hope to gain more," he said darkly. His eyes glittered with the fancies of his dark western mountains. "Suppose the tournament is just a pretext to gather enemies on Count Hurguse's soil, the German knights and those of Estrangot, that they may pick their time and sack his castle?"

I burst out laughing. "Oh, comrade, that's rich! Pardon me, but such a nefarious scheme could only come from the brain of a Welsh, eh, *Cymric* chieftain's son! You barbarians, you fierce, tricky, changeable raiders! Long-time enemies these may be, but still, they're noble, high-hearted knights, and gallant in emprise. When they come to a tournament, they have nothing in their minds but the glory and honour they may gain therein. They never would use it as cover for villainy. Pardieu, it would be beneath even Vallulf the Burner! Take my word."

"I heard what I heard," Grasaut answered stubbornly. (I doubted it.) "Lionel, have a care at this banquet tonight. Do not let them drug you senseless and fire the hall around you."

"No, no," I said soothingly. "I swear I'll not."

Leaving him, I went out through the courtyard. How pleasant it would have been to dismiss all he said, but the discrepancies were mounting. Were they not? I leaned on the fountain's rim and felt the smooth warm stone under my palms. Maybe some masters of glamour could deceive even the sense of touch, as well as sight and hearing . . . maybe. But Lancelot had been so certain about the other senses. These, he assured me, were at once so intimate and subtle that no enchanter could baffle them. And Merlin himself had agreed.

Well, that meant the food and drink here were honest past all doubt! The roses in the courtyard, too. Breathing their scent to assure myself, I suddenly realized it had become fainter. Much. The air had been drunk with their perfume the day I arrived. Was I just accustomed to it now?

Thoughtful, I walked over to the kitchen garden and picked a sprig of basil. The leaves felt fresh and light between my fingers, quite as they should, but when I crushed them, they did not yield the fragrance I expected. They stank, in fact, like common weeds.

So. Grasaut was right in one thing, anyhow; we were surrounded by glamour. The lovely, incomparable Chimene was an enchantress. It didn't follow that she was wicked. She might well have learned some sorcery during her misfortunes and travels, and if she used it to add splendour to a tournament on which so much depended for her, well, then, I had no fault to find. *But was that really all*?

Grasaut's notion that the knights might be planning treachery was pure folly. I dismissed it. If this event covered some evil design, then the knights were being duped. Thinking of Chimene's wondrous face, I hoped with all my heart it was straightforward. Or reasonably so. But I might no longer count on that.

It appeared I must follow Grasaut's advice after all, and be wary at the ball, keeping my eyes wide open for mischief.

5

". . . in our situation we need not hold long councils . . ."
– Froissart, *Chronicles*

The Lady Chimene appeared in a hawk-mask of topaz and gold and a matching gown. I wore a gryphon costume. Four or five times we danced together, surrounded by dryads, tribunes, a black-furred wolf, the Amazon queen Penthesilea, a Lapith with waist-long hair, a Persian fairy, Thoth in a baboon-mask, and a spirited gypsy girl. The evening was merry, even by the standards of my father's court.

But Grasaut had been right. After a trifling two hours, most of our revellers were *hors de combat*, sliding under tables, slumping over their gilded platters, or just sitting in owlish stupor. I'd been careful to eat little and drink less, and still my wits were drifting.

Indeed, something was amiss. Chimene's guests fell drowsy around me in growing numbers. When I walked with slow careful steps from the hall and subsided in an alcove, snoring, the varlet who followed me looked at my huddled shape once, chuckled, and went away.

A quarter-hour later I was on top of one of Castle Brulant's towers, clearing my head in the night wind. There was activity down by the tilting-field, much of it, torches blowing and the stamp and neigh of many war-horses. Getting hold of my sword, dagger, shield and casque, I climbed down a buttress and was soon prowling through the purple night.

Sang dieu!

The best war-horses in France were being taken out of their stables and herded together in the lists! Where would they have gone by the flamingo-hued dawn? Who'd find them again with the countess's enchantement to hide their trail, and the wild mountains so near to receive them? More angry each minute, I saw knightly mail and weapons packed deftly into bundles, then loaded onto the backs of the horses. The rascals were lifting a king's ransom; no, an emperor's!

Pardieu, but they had their larcenous daring! I thought of hangings and the rack. Strangely, at the very same time, I had a perverse urge to shout with laughter. Never had I heard of such audacity as this. One almost had to admire it. And each passing, outrageous second, I became more convinced that Chimene had conceived the scheme.

Almost as I thought of the Countess, I beheld her. Tall, stately, wrapped in a silk mantle over her gown, she still wore the gilded hawk-mask. Sir Bricus stood beside her, also in his costume from the masque. I was appalled. He was a *knight* – one of the best famed in France! As a page and squire I had longed to be like him! How could he be part of this?

"It goes well," he said. I heard amused satisfaction in his voice. "The beasts should be out of here by cock-crow. Nay, my lady, your thieves are so efficient we may have time to take all the horses with us."

"Alas," she said regretfully, "it isn't a matter of time. We lack the men to drive so many war-horses in the dark. Two hundred are all we can control. And remember, I must make them appear a herd of cows before they leave!"

"*Dommage*. Ah, well, my sweet, you are right. Many a man has finished his course holding nothing because he was too greedy. The armour and weapons – "

"– shall remain here," I told him, and showed myself.

"*Lionel*," the countess said, shaken.

"Yes, my sweet," I said viciously, mocking Sir Bricus's words. "It's different with a witness, is it not? I'm curious; indulge me. Have you ever set foot in Spain at all?"

"She has not," Bricus answered, after the briefest pause. His panache would have suited a better situation. "However, she's a most genuine countess by marriage, my youngling, and descends from six generations of barons in her own right, so address her with respect no matter how ruffled your red gryphon's feathers may be."

"With respect, my lady Countess, where is your husband now?"

"Lionel, listen, if you will," she pleaded. "My husband is a beast. God grant he never finds me!"

"This will probably be as true as that other tale you told me, of his death in Spain as lord of Naubet and Corracha."

"No reason for you to hear it," Bricus said. "We're still in haste. You are correct, Sir Lionel, it is different with a witness, but if you are the only one, I can quickly remove you."

Coolly as you like, he took a shield and helmet from a nearby pile of gear. Seeing his intent, I drew my sword simultaneously with Bricus.

"No!" the countess said sharply. "Don't be foolish, sir. You cannot kill this young man. By the Cross of God! You know the greatness of his kindred; he is a son of *King Bors*!"

"And difficult to kill," I taunted.

"Sir Vallulf, Sir Grum and the Thuringian found you so. I doubt that I shall. My lady, you must leave this to me. There is no other way now."

"Oh, stand back, sir," she ordered, fearlessly stepping between us. "We are neither of us murderers. Lionel, will you listen? My husband – "

"Your husband, lady, is not of interest," I said harshly.

"If I'm to be condemned, I wish to be heard first," she said bitterly. "Or dare you not?"

I lowered my sword and folded my hands over the hilt.

"My husband is Count Trephison of the Eastern Empire. So powerful and haughty is he that no imperial tax assessors dare go near him for dread of being skinned alive. He's mad for jousting and pageantry and knightly glory – and he has his own concepts of the latter."

"Lady, this gains us nothing," Sir Bricus said grimly. "I pray you, stand aside and let me deal."

"Oh, wait! Sir Lionel, my husband affects these notions of courtly love. When a famous jouster wished to carry my token in the lists and declare himself my champion, my husband was willing, indeed flattered, and all but thrust me into this other man's bed so that the charade might continue. It's fashionable in the east."

"In parts of France, too," I said grudgingly, "but not in the north."

"Then hurrah for the north," Chimene replied with spirit. "This . . . jackass . . . did not love me, but found a mistress more convenient than a wife, and I soon detested both him and my husband. I turned for comfort to a handsome young falconer. We became lovers. My husband and his knightly friend found out, and, if you can believe it, they were appalled. They joined as one to take revenge upon me and my lover."

I curled my lip. "Pardieu! Lady, you make it sound as though they'd have done best to marry each other."

Despite my scorn and anger, her story had gained my attention. I reminded myself that she was clever, and fully revealed, now, as a rascal and leader of rascals. Eh, well, let her finish the tale. It wouldn't move me.

"They tied us in shrouds of sacking and buried us both alive in the same deep grave. My champion, the lover my husband approved, this courtly knight and jouster, had me thrown in last, on top of the falconer, 'Because,' he said, 'she's nobly born.'"

"*Christus*." I couldn't refrain.

"And so said I," Bricus said sardonically.

Chimene continued, "It was Rufo the herald who came and dug us from that pit at the risk of his life, but too late for my lover. Only I still breathed. Having no wealth, rejected by all who had known me, I've made my living ever since in such ways as this, Lionel – and yes, I have gained great riches. That's neither here nor there. Forgive me if you can, but in any case, forget you saw this tonight and return to Castle Brulant. Consider it a favour for a favour. You said I was kind to your squire."

"What? Letting you escape with your plunder?" My choler increased again, the hotter for having been briefly beguiled. "My horses among them?"

"I gave instructions that your horses and gear were not to be touched; a gesture of liking."

"A gesture?" I said incredulously. "I see well that you think me stupid, but what causes you to think I am deaf? I heard you talking. You cannot take all the horses, having too few rogues to handle them. And by the saints, I'm here to tell you that you may take none! I command you, end the thieving and let you be the ones who return to Castle Brulant!"

"You hear, my sweet?" Sir Bricus asked. "It's sad, but you did try. I warned you not to waste your time. Now let me deal with this conceited pup."

Not brutally, but firmly, he thrust her aside. His sword flashed in the night. Ducking and slashing by the wavery torchlight, we fought without mail, on ground littered with thieves' loot and baggage. It was more like an impromptu brawl in a captured war-camp than anything else.

This mercenary captain meant to kill. His quick hand sent the blade shuttling, leaping, seeking a way to my flesh. I stepped back from a whistling stroke that would have opened the whole front of my head, then brought my shield low to the ground to save myself from being hamstrung. Hacking in my turn, I carried away a wedge of Bricus's shield. Then I tried to break his hip. He twisted aside like a cat.

I was twelve years younger, broad in the shoulders and chest, my limbs greatly muscled. Bricus, although about my height, was leaner. He hadn't, I believe, my strength, but he had something else;

a natural grace, co-ordination and quickness that even reminded me of my cousin Lancelot. Not that he was Lancelot's equal! How many ever were? Turquine, that great and evil knight, and Sir Tristram, maybe. Not Bricus de Souvene – but still he had some of it, that leopard ease of motion that so few men possess. And he'd slay me with it, or cripple and then slay, in a few more moments if I played his game.

The devil with nice swordsmanship, thought I, and the devil with knightly manners. I smote three crashing, thundering blows on his shield, one after the other, swiftly. Then I dealt him the best stroke I could on his casque. That was none too good. I had to launch the cut too fast, could get neither my back nor my full force behind it. But he felt it.

The second's distraction let me spring in close, throw my sword-arm around his waist and toss him over my hip in a wrestling throw. He hadn't expected that. His quick agility saved him, but he used it all to avoid falling on his sword, or breaking bones on his own shield's edge as it went down with him, clattering. Thus he still fell. Before he could move, I had my foot on his arm, my sword menacing his neck.

"Unless you swear an oath to me, I'll slay you where you lie, Sir Bricus. And Count Hurguse's justice will deal with the Countess."

Winded, it took him a while to answer.

"You are surrounded by men . . . who would kill you to save her. I don't think . . . you conceive . . . how she's loved by her folk . . . rogues as they are. You know what she did for me. Half of them she saved from fates as bad."

"Maybe. We'll waste no time discussing that! It's my sword at your throat, not yours at mine."

Bricus acknowledged it. "What's the oath you require?"

"You'll swear on the relics of saints and your souls' salvation, both of you, to abandon this thieving scheme. Restore everything by dawn, and let the tournament take place as everyone expects."

"*Tonnerre*!" Sir Bricus gasped. "Are you serious?"

"Serious enough to swear an oath as binding as yours to say nothing of what you intended."

"Why, Lionel?" the Countess asked. "I mean, why so merciful?"

I shrugged. "I desire to win glory in your tournament. I cannot unless it takes place! And – doubtless I'm a soft and gullible fool – I credit that dreadful tale you told, lady."

I removed my foot from Sir Bricus, knowing he'd agree to nothing while forced to lie abjectly prone.

"You have the strength of a bull," he said feelingly. "Are those the only conditions on which we're to get off so lightly?"

"No. Once the tournament is done, you must both leave France and never return in your life's days – and particularly not to my father's kingdom, or my uncle's!"

I boomed the command forth like the judgment trump, and my sword was ready to enforce it. Common sense told me that I was being weakly lenient. I wondered if these two, older, more worldly-wise, were laughing within. I felt dangerous, ready to change my mind in an instant, at the first excuse.

It may be she sensed it. "Agreed," she said quickly.

"Agreed," Sir Bricus echoed, after a pause.

"Then set your rascals to work. The night won't last forever. Nor will the effects of your drugged food," I added with some rancour. "Come with me, lady, if you please. I'll have more confidence if you are under my eyes until morning."

"I'm grateful for your mercy, Sir Lionel," she said, in that damnable, charming voice of warm bronze. "But it were best that we return to the castle now. Unless I renew the enchantment, it will fade like mist when dawn comes. I did not believe I'd have any more use for the illusion. *Tu comprends*?"

"Yes," I said grimly. "Indeed, you had better make good that lack without delay, hadn't you? That is why you asked if Lancelot was in France. You know he was fostered by the Lady of the Lake. He's accustomed to such things. He'd have discerned the truth in a matter of hours."

"He would. However, you did not do badly."

I wasn't in a mood for her flattery. Passing through the courtyard, I smelled again the faint scent of the roses, and wondered. Although small, it was one of the things that had induced me to credit Grasaut's warning, and I was moved to ask the Countess about it.

"Lady, I've heard that enchanted glamour can't deceive what one smells, or tastes i' the mouth; is that verity?"

"It is. The eye and ear are not difficult to hoodwink, because they work at a distance, through the void air. The sense of touch is more intimate, and so much harder, but I can even mislead that. Taste and scent, though, no." She smiled. "In justice to my cooks I must say they are as skilled as they seem."

"Your false roses had scent."

"Oh, that! We cast rose perfume around the courtyard with a lavish hand, that is all . . . and I'm grateful for the reminder. We mustn't forget to renew it by morning."

Epilogue

"Sirs, now may we go where we will."
– Malory, *Le Morte d'Arthur*, IV:14

Well, my friends, to quote the woman I knew by the name of Chimene, so long ago, that's all. Or all of it that matters. The tournament did proceed; I even took part in it as one of Sir Bricus' companions, and we both won considerable glory. Bricus, in fact, won several men's war-horses and armour as well, though hardly as many as he'd planned to get.

Afterwards, he did leave France with his mistress. Not so swiftly as to arouse suspicion, though. I gave them some latitude there. Pardieu, I was happy to do so, for although I never became Chimene's lover, both her lady's-maids and I were the sweetest friends for a time. Esther was a dark, sparkling Greco-Persian demoiselle whom her mistress had saved from a brothel in Illyria, and Veronique had been accused of witchcraft until Chimene's magic provided an unmistakable sign from heaven that the girl was innocent. I daresay she was, at least of witchcraft. Esther and Veronique, yes . . .

I cannot regret letting them go. The longer I've lived, the more convinced I became that only a prig would have given them over to justice, and even if I did wrong, by my hilt! I've worse things than that to answer for. There was a monstrous day when I would have killed my own brother Bors in the belief that he had betrayed me. I did kill Sir Colgrevance and a holy hermit who made the mistake of interfering between us. The price of that was a pilgrimage all the way to the Holy Land. And when I returned, I found the Round Table cracking, the bravest fellowship of knights ever known, under the greatest king.

No, this foolish little story from my youth ends more pleasantly, doesn't it?

I would I might tell you what became of Chimene and Sir Bricus at last. I don't know. In my last exchange with her, I asked her where she would go, and she said, of course, that she was not yet sure, but that the German princedoms and Hungary beyond looked tempting. Having said Hungary, she doubtless went to Ethiopia.

But I answered fervently, “Jesu help Hungary!”

Sir Bedivere
A TRIBUTE OF FERNS

Peter T. Garratt

Sir Bedivere is best remembered as the last knight to attend Arthur after the battle of Camlann, who returned Excalibur to the Lady of the Lake. It is perhaps the most unforgettable scene in all Arthurian legend. Bedivere's connections with Arthur go back a long way in legend. As Bedwyr he was one of Arthur's earliest companions and his adventures are told in several of the stories that make up The Mabinogion, *including the following. Peter Garratt (b. 1949) is a writer and lecturer, who reviews Arthurian literature and has given talks on the subject.*

They always come at certain times. Pentecost is a favourite. Suppliants never choose any old day to plod up the hill on foot, or sway up it on a donkey . . . and of course they hardly ever come in a carriage, or riding a fine horse. No, whoever they are, and whatever their real situation and the secret reasons that underlie the most banal of their requests, they always plod in on a Holy Day, like pilgrims, slumping exhausted in front of the diners when you can still smell the cooking.

This Vortiporix, "Protector of the West", was no exception. He knew how to approach a Christian High King, that the King would be more Christian and sympathetic if he had enjoyed his meal and the bishop had made a special effort over the sermon and the rituals. Perhaps Vortiporix had prayed with the Bishop beforehand, and made a grant of land to the church. The sermon that morning was about a warrior called Uriah the Hittite, whose death was a great shame on his king. I could see Arthur was moved by the sermon. He was wondering if it was a shame on him, to often let his best men go alone on quests which should require the effort and expense of a small army.

I, Bedivere, care little for sermons. I've been at the court since it was more like a camp. I knew Arthur when the idea that his rule should be juster and more Christian than any other was no more than a glimmer in the back of his mind. It hadn't reached his eyes, which sometimes glimmered in other ways.

I'm not a religious man. Oh, I go to the chapel, but often my mind drifts off. The readings don't change; things I had to learn by heart at school, or even copy out. That was my childhood: a brief period of peace when priests took charge and tried to tell boys the pen was more important than the sword. My real learning I did later. I gave up wondering why some of the Good Books are sermons about turning the other cheek, while others are full of war stories a lot like the tales you hear from bards. Some are even set to music . . . we had a harpist and a drummer in chapel that very Pentecost morning. No, if you study priests, especially bishops, you realize there's a story in the Books to suit every point they want to make, every point of view they want to make it for. Monks are a different matter. No one knows what books they spend their lonely lives poring over, in languages only they can read. I've heard strange things about the powers of monks, seen some of them myself.

Vortiporix didn't enter the Hall till after the Feast. From the titles he gave himself, Protector of the West and Consul of Caerleon, City of the Legion, he should have been entitled to an invitation to dine, but he pointedly arrived looking hungry and tired. This probably wasn't hard, as from his shape he was more used to food than exercise. He wore a Roman breast-plate, muscle armour with some of the muscles bashed in by swordcuts, and a tattered white toga with a purple border, worn the wrong way as a cloak. He looked like the last heroic, impoverished defender of the ancient way, though I noticed his tunic and hose were of fine linen, his boots of expensive red leather.

Arthur himself was simply dressed, no toga or coronet, but Vortiporix hailed him grandly, "*Riothamus*", "High King", and

"*Amhrawdyr*", "Emperor". "I seek not vengeance but justice!" he went on. "And not for myself alone, but for you!"

Arthur looked surprised, as did many round the table, but I smiled to myself. Vortiporix went on: "Your justice is famous for turning the other cheek, but will you turn the first again if the second is abused? Have you forgotten the three of your men, and thirty of my own, all loyal to your Imperial Majesty, who were murdered by the heretic bandit Ligessac?"

I started at that name, as an uneasy hush fell. Up till then there had still been whispers around the table. The Consul and Protector hadn't merited silence. Arthur used a cool voice, one I knew masked strong emotion: "It's true I sent a few men to help you, and it seems it was a bad decision, for even fewer came back. But that was ten years ago. Didn't you report that Ligessac had been vanquished, and driven from your lands?"

Vortiporix shifted uneasily. "We attacked the brigands and killed three times more than we lost. Ligessac fled: I hoped he was dead, but then I heard he had taken refuge with Gwynnlym of Glevissig, almost my neighbour! I demanded he be given up, but to my amazement the old king showed me a letter from your majesty giving him powers to grant sanctuary to fugitives."

Arthur tried to not look interested, but dissembling wasn't his strongest point. I could see he was as upset as I was. He said: "He wasn't that old! You can't mean Gwynnlym is . . ."

"Dead? Yes . . . he did an outrageous thing, left his kingdom, not just Glevissig but all the lands between Brychan's Beacons and the Severn Sea, to a monk! How can a monk be a king?"

Bittersweet memories flooded back, of my only visit to that region. I saw what Vortiporix was after, and felt afraid. Glevissig lay across the roads between his little empire of Caerleon and lands further west which he also claimed to protect. Arthur looked very troubled. He was saying: "You mean his . . . *his* son, the boy Cadoc? He's young to be an abbot, but he's said to be a very great scholar, a credit to the church."

"Church!" Vortiporix shouted to the whole company round the table: "This so-called churchman, this puffed-up boy-abbot, this spayed dog, this so scholarly monk has refused a direct order from the Bishop of Caerleon to hand over the traitor! Hasn't he learned his first monkish duty is to obey? He keeps his father's retinue of a hundred armed men! What holy man of God needs an army? What treason, what heresy or worse are they plotting in that monastery? While loyal men lie unavenged!"

It was a clever move. Some of the monks in Britain may have obeyed austere rules, but every soldier round the table knew that the majority led rather easy lives. Men said they had secret rites and rituals whose purpose and power were unknown outside those abbey walls. If they obeyed neither bishop nor king, and were even starting to build up armies of their own, it would not be difficult for Vortiporix to put himself at the head of a mass expedition against Cadoc. That was the last thing I wanted, so I started to argue that monks were learned men, who had preserved far more of the ancient wisdom than priests had, but I made no impact. Someone, I think it was Cei, shouted: "Why not ask him for a tribute of ferns!"

That settled it. That spring, the Emperor of the East had sent word from distant Byzantium, all round the world by sea. He was planning to reconquer the lost lands, and looking for still-loyal Romans to send help and tribute. Arthur considered the distance and the number of barbarians between the two empires, and sent as tribute a beautiful maze work made from dried ferns. It would mean little to the Romans, whose art depicts only what they see outwardly. We Britons prefer our subtly knotted mazes, which express the inner essence of a situation. Thus the tribute of ferns indicated that Arthur valued the friendship of the Byzantine monarch, but did not fear him enough to send a tribute he himself would value.

Arthur said hastily: "The loyal dead will not be unavenged! How many men do you need?"

"Threescore and three would do it. Or perhaps a few more."

Threescore and three would be about half as many well-armed horsemen as Vortiporix already had . . . they would give him almost twice the muster of Cadoc and Ligessac but not overwhelm his own retinue. Arthur must have known that, for he said: "To ensure that justice is done with the minimum of violence, I will come myself with 300 and threescore and three!"

That night as I packed and oiled my weapons and armour . . . I dress well, but not showily, and prefer new mail to battered Roman plate . . . I thought about the land west of Caerleon, its wild, scarcely Roman peoples, and the last time I had visited its mist-soaked valleys, so many years before.

They're a strange lot, Westerners, poets, not always loyal. Far from the Saxons, their ancestors made their names fighting the Irish, who've been no problem since someone taught them Christianity.

I sat on my bed and I remembered, and whispered the lines: "If my heart is full of Bliss/ I must have thought of Guladis!" and after a while I drifted into a dream so vivid it was as if I lived those long-gone days again, riding the hillside paths, smelling the rain in the air, hearing sheep and the distant calls of shepherds, staying at night in forts of thatch and stone or farms with damp turf roofs.

I dreamed of the old imperilled times when Cheldric's Saxon host had only been made cautious by Arthur's early victories. Much of the East had been occupied, and old men shook their heads, saying it was a bad omen to lose the sunrise part of the Island, and those lands would never be regained. The middle of Britain was exhausted, with food in short supply, many of the fortified towns abandoned. We knew Cheldric would come again, and Arthur needed men, guaranteed supplies, and treasures he could trade in a hurry for one or the other. He didn't expect money, for by that time there was very little of it left in the land, but he needed treasures that could be used as money.

A tyrant like Vortigern would have sent squads of armed men, but Arthur wanted to spare the small army he had, and reasoned that if he could not arrive with enough men to overawe, it would be best to go alone like a pilgrim, or with a few trusted companions. He chose Cei and myself, not counting the servants who handled the pack animals. (They are never counted.)

In my dream we went again to Deva on the Wirral, a similar place to Caerleon but more run down, only able to offer a few men. Then west to the land from which Cunnedag's sons drove the Irish in the old days. The local ruler promised us many men, and though those steep hills breed strong warriors and lean sheep, he took us across the narrowest sea to the known island of Mona, which is very fertile, and promised us the best of the harvest if the ghosts of the Druids which haunt the place would permit it. He told us of the secret island of Mona, which lies lost in the sea, half-way to Ireland. He would give us that harvest also, for a favour. "I've kept the bloodsucking monks from the very heart of my territory, for they seek grants of land and rich gifts and don't do a thing in the world to deserve them. But I keep finding they've got footholds around the edges. Bloody fools give them wealth which should go, as you put it so well, on our nation's defence. Take Paternus. He says his life is one of poverty, but it's well known that his embroidered coat is one of the thirteen great treasures of the Island of the Mighty. Make this upstart respect us, and you can have both island harvests and keep the coat for yourself."

We rode the shore of the the great bay, which looked from the mountains as if the giant Bran had taken a huge bite from the land. We knew our cause was just, our opponents no fiercer men than monks: but we had sombre thoughts. Is it not written that the battle goes not always to the strong, nor riches to men of understanding? God's ways are mysterious, and one is to favour men who neither work nor fight. Are their prayers worth more than those of we who lead more useful lives? Yet we knew the One God had driven his rivals into the shadows which are the edge of the Otherworld, and could do worse to men.

So we rode into the monastery of Llanbadarn. It had a lot of land, good soil for the region. The monks used peasants called half-brothers to work the fields, but tended the herb garden themselves. Their cells were simple round stone huts: the only sizeable buildings were the chapel, the library, a dining-hall and a kitchen whence I could smell the fermentation of mead.

Paternus met us in front of the chapel. It was upwind of the kitchen, and I could only smell incense. He had the nerve to imply that Arthur had come with donations for his monks . . . we were all angry, especially Cei, who shouted: "Coward! Leech! Do you expect to be given every last drop of the nation's blood? Well, don't wait for it! Cheldric will get that if you have your way, before he drinks yours!"

Paternus paled slightly, and crossed himself, but several of his monks were listening, and he said: "If the Lord wills it."

I was alarmed by the way increasing numbers of monks were pressing towards us, though there should have been nothing to fear. We three could have killed all of them, though Arthur wouldn't have done so. Even Vortigern wouldn't have done more than threaten. We dismounted and, young though he was, Arthur said as calmly as he could: "Brother Paternus, we have much to discuss. I suggest we go inside, away from the crowd."

Even Cei and I were left outside. There was a wind off the bay, but I fancied I could smell something that wasn't mead or incense. I didn't know what it was. The chapel had thick walls, but there were windows with no glass, just open shutters. After a while, we started to hear voices raised inside, Arthur's, then the abbot's voice. I heard him shout: "Thief! Tyrant! Help your servant Lord! May the Earth swallow the tyrant!"

Cei put his hand to his sword and headed toward the door. I

made to restrain him, then I heard Arthur cry out, an anguished cry. I never thought to hear him cry so, even in battle with the heathen, let alone among Britons, men of God. We charged into the chapel, swords half out, then stopped in our tracks.

The place was lit by more candles than a minor king uses at a feast. The abbot was kneeling by the altar, and beside it was his embroidered coat. It wasn't British work . . . it was set with gems and thick gold threads, but they didn't forms knots or mazes. There were pictures woven into it: God above, priests and abbots passing his message, tiny laymen at the bottom where it swept the ground. It was a thing a rich bishop who fancied himself as a Roman would have given half his lands for. The stones glittered in the candlelight: it was moving, for Arthur had hold of it. To my horror, I realized he had indeed fallen into a pit in the chapel's earth floor. It must have been a trap prepared against thieves, though how it worked, I could not see. It looked like a quicksand: Arthur was struggling, but made no progress in getting out. Paternus was saying: "My son, this tunic was given to me by the Patriarch of Jerusalem. It shows us the way to reach the next world, not succeed in this. Yet God *may* grant you success, if you humbly repent your sins."

"Yes," Arthur said. "Yes. I am guilty of . . . Pride. I must continue as a true pilgrim, without even my two companions."

At that moment the ground stopped oozing like a quicksand, and Arthur was able to scramble out, but he remained on his knees at a lower level than Paternus, who said: "You must be a Christian pilgrim warrior, and protect the defenceless."

"Yes. Yes, Father, your blessing is worth more to me than the tunics of all the Patriarchs!"

Cei and I were bewildered by this, but Arthur sincerely believed that God had thrown him into the pit for his sins, and released him for his repentance. I hoped a worse pit awaited the Saxons for their greater sins. Arthur resolved to go alone South West to Caer Myrrddin: Cei was sent to Glevissig, I to visit Brychan, Lord of the Beacons. Later we pilgrims would meet at Caerleon, where we had once fought sea-raiders.

I rode alone through the empty hills, pausing only to speak to shepherds, memorizing directions well ahead. A thing was said of Brychan that I didn't like: that he regarded himself as a kind of monk, but at the same time had fathered threescore and three children. Pilgrims were said to travel for many miles to hear his wisdom, though these visitors seldom included priests or recognized churchmen. And in those hills no one had removed the small shrines and wayside statues to the Other Gods, the kind one still bows to but does not quite worship.

Brychan's fortress was on high ground, dominating one of the better valleys. It had once been Roman, unusual for that part of the world. The walls were well kept and forbidding. There were a few men in armour on the gates, so it at least looked like the home of a warrior, but it was crowded with people whose plain robes resembled those of monks, though with more variety of colour and cut. Many of these pilgrims were women, and these too wore odd clothes, usually single-coloured and decorated only with maze-patterns; but their dresses were low-necked and short for religious women.

I arrived in mid-afternoon and was taken to see Brychan at once. He was in a room called the atrium, which still had its Roman wall-paintings, most notably a striking depiction of Mary Magdalen washing the feet of Christ. He was a fit man of fifty, dressed in a plain, but not monkish robe, a fine leather swordbelt and a gold torque. He asked me to sit, listened to my explanations carefully, and questioned me: "So, you are an officer and close companion of this young man who calls himself 'High King'. I hear good things of him. But how does a High King's right-hand man come to ride alone through my gates?"

I stirred uneasily, wondering if he thought I'd stolen the seal ring Arthur had given me to identify myself. I also had a letter, but it wouldn't do to ask a ruler if he could read it. I had no idea if anyone could read in those wild hills: but it seemed best to hand it over without comment. He scanned it and then sent a servant to fetch one of his daughters.

It was thus that I first saw Guladis. She ran lightly into the hall, as if called from a game: but though she had the bare feet and skipping pace of a child, she had the body of a woman, and the face of an experienced one. Her black hair was piled on her head in elaborate curls, a strangely similar style to the Magdalen in the picture; her dress was of fine linen, a shade of pastel pink which seemed in parts to deepen into red. It was tighter than those of the pilgrim women, but not constricting: as she moved it flowed over the curves of her body like a gentle wave over rocks. Brychan said: "Come, my dear, and check your letters against this missive, which is from the Great King himself. It says this fine young man is his ambassador."

Guladis looked at me, very nervously at first, but then her

expression changed, and I started to feel I might be a fine young man, which perhaps was true in those days. She sat beside her father and began to read. After a minute she looked up in excitement: "It says the Great *King* has become a pilgrim, and his best friends too. Isn't that wonderful news, Father?"

"Hopefully. Show our new friend to the best guestroom, then to the baths."

It seemed a strange task for a lord's daughter, though Guladis explained that she had more sisters than there were maidservants, so they all had to help. She was vague as to exactly how many, but mentioned so many names in a short time that I wondered if the rumours about Brychan could be true. One shepherd had told me that far from leading a monkish life he seduced nearly all of the girl pilgrims who came to his hall.

Nor had he trained Guladis in modesty. Most of the bathhouse had been converted to a kitchen, but there remained one plunge bath and a small steam room. Guladis told me to undress by the plunge, which was filled by a pipe from a spring, while she prepared the steam. The door between the two sections didn't close properly, and she made no real effort to hide while pulling off her dress and shift and wrapping herself in a towel. Admittedly it was hot work, starting a fire and carrying large kettles of water through to bubble over it, but the towel reached only from her knees to just above her breasts, where she secured it with a clasp in the shape of a fish. When the steam was going she invited me through and offered to scrape me down with a strigil. By that time I was excited by the thought, but felt enough pilgrimish self-restraint to protest that the job was menial and might compromise her.

"What do you mean, compromise? Was the Blessed Mary Magdalen too proud to tend to the needs of Our Saviour?"

I don't know what went onto the fire, but it had a richer scent than any wood I knew. Such fuel can be more potent than wine: this must have been. I did deny the comparison to Our Lord, but willingly allowed her the role of Magdalen. The bathhouse still had mosaics: delightful pictures of the kind no one now makes. They showed soldiers being rubbed down by voluptuous camp-followers. I wondered if letting Brychan's daughter act as my camp-follower in the heart of his fortress might be dangerous: but I wasn't afraid. Perhaps it was the scented smoke. She scraped me with delicate strokes, almost like a massage. I could smell her body, sweeter than the odd fuel.

Halfway through she became distracted. She told me abruptly

to go through, and hastily lugged the kettles over to warm up the plunge bath, nearly spilling boiling water onto both our feet in the process. She then went properly out of sight to get back into her clothes, and hurried through, wiping the sweat off her face with her towel. "Hurry up, hurry up!" she scolded. "You mustn't be late for dinner and evensong on your first night! I've brought your clean tunic."

I hadn't realized it was near evening: the sky was still bright and not very red at the small windows, and I had been relaxing in the bath listening to a lute player nearby who was singing in a very fine voice:

Fair and unfair are the daughters of Our Lady,
Fishers of men and their souls
Planting sweet feet in the steps of Saint Joseph,
Entangling men and their souls.

We walked out into the late afternoon air slightly apart. The sun was setting across the Black Hills. The harpist was a tall young man, fair-haired, good-looking, but on the thin side. He wore a fine tunic, one side white, the other red. Guladis introduced us nervously, as if hoping without belief that we would be friends: "Lord Bedwyr," she said my name with the music of the hills in her voice. "This is Gwynnlym, from Glevissig. He is prince and poet both. And this is Bedwyr, one of the famous pilgrim warriors of the Great King of the East!"

It was a tense encounter. We were close to Gwynnlym's land, there on the edge of the Black Hills, and I sensed this girl who for some unfathomable reason had been trying to seduce me was at heart much more interested in him. But Gwynnlym was no warrior. He gave Guladis a hurt look like that of a spurned dog, plucked a sad air from his lute, and sang:

If my heart is full of Bliss
I must have thought of Guladis!

though blissful was not how he sounded.

Evensong was celebrated exactly at sunset, outside in the clean air. A great crowd attended, too many, I realized, for the chapel. Brychan led the service himself, though he was not dressed as a priest. He welcomed me by name as a pilgrim sent by Arthur, went on to say that the Lord had a special place for pilgrims. "For did not the very first pilgrim, Joseph of Arimathea, make his way here to bring the light to this chosen island when the rest of the gentile world still suffered under the Roman darkness?" I had heard this story before, and felt it wise to not indicate that I didn't know if it was true. Priests trained by bishops denounced it as a falsehood, made up to encourage heretical ideas. Brychan went on: "And are we not all pilgrims and fishers of men, whether we serve as anglers or as bait? Must not many of you go soon into the world to do your duty as I have taught you, and spread the word of St Joseph? To be bait, as Jonah was, for the greatest fish?"

He looked then at Guladis, as if she had the most difficult pilgrimage, and she stepped forward from the group of his daughters. I noticed that there were indeed far more daughters of about the same age than one married mother could have borne. All were good-looking, but Guladis was the most beautiful. She began to sing, Gwynnlym accompanying her on a harp:

Pure the feet that trod these pleasant hills,
Dark the clouds that folded back,
Joy filled hearts that turned those gritstone mills,
Golden light filled spirit's lack.

We had supper in the atrium. It was then I met Ligessac. He looked familiar, and was Brychan's Master of Horsemen. Guladis poured the wine, but I noticed Gwynnlym had not been invited to join us. Guladis had made herself up to look exactly like the painted face of the Magdalen: her dress was tighter than that afternoon's, a deeper red, and much lower cut. When pouring my wine, she bowed especially deeply. She wore a silver pendant in the shape of a fish: when she bowed it would swing forward, and as she straightened fall back into the gap between her breasts, as if playing hide-and-seek. She was more intoxicating than the wine, though that was hot and spiced with something that reminded me of the afternoon's perfumed logs.

Remembering whose table I was at, I tore my eyes from her and began to explain my mission and Arthur's need for help.

Brychan nodded sagely. "I have heard he is a great warrior."

He glanced at Ligessac, who said: "We rode to join him when the pagans attacked Caerleon from the sea, little though we like the Protector or the Bishop. If bards are to be believed, Arthur has already defeated the barbarians eleven times. But not driven them back into the sea, as was once promised."

It was the comment of a man who had only faced the enemy once. I said: "That is true. But Saxons cross the sea the other way. Sometimes it seems that for every one we kill, a shipload arrives. It's clear they mean to steal more land, perhaps abandon their original homes altogether. Driving them out of Britain would be harder than driving the Franks out of Gaul!"

Brychan nodded. "I hear your leader has already fought and won in Gaul."

"Yes. The people of Little Britain asked Arthur for help, and now they send the Franks no tribute but knotworks of fern."

Ligessac said slyly: "What if he were to raise a great army, perhaps let the Saxons join him, as they did Vortigern, and drive out the Franks instead?"

I felt furious that anyone could think Arthur would march beside Saxons, but I said as calmly as I could: "If that were possible, and it couldn't be for many years, why would it be his priority? His life is the defence of Britain!"

Now Ligessac got angry, and he did show it. "He's already crossed the sea once! He could attack the Franks, and if he succeeded it would tempt an ambitious man to march on Rome. Then the Bishop of Rome would declare him Emperor, at a price!"

It wasn't a bad plan, and if anyone could have carried it off, it was Arthur. Brychan said with passion: "The price would be that any wisdom found by holy monks here in Britain, that Romans were not enlightened by, would be suppressed as heresy! Already their priests tell us what to read and how to pray!"

I felt shaken. What warrior enjoys being ruled by priests? But I only said: "Arthur doesn't need any bishop to declare him Emperor. If he wants the title he'll take it, here in Britain!"

I left the meal as soon as diplomacy permitted. Brychan hinted at things no bishop would allow, while Ligessac was drinking and showing no respect for Arthur and we who sat round his table. I did not wish to quarrel with them: indeed, though it does me no honour to say so, I was afraid to. I was alone among warriors who were loyal to these men and their strange version of the Faith, and though I have no time for the petty arguments of priests, I fear division and hate disloyalty.

My room was in another building, and I walked to it under the stars. The night was cold and clear: they were very bright. Simple folk say stars are the lamps of angels, but they felt older and colder than that, as if they had looked on at the Creation and the Fall of Man, and would still be there after Judgment Day. No one moved, though I could see lights in the windows of many of the dilapidated buildings, and strange music was playing in more than one place. All around, I was aware of the walls, high and dark as the mountains beyond, and I sensed eyes seeking me out from the watchtowers.

My guestroom was decorated with faded religious murals. Above the bed was one of Joseph of Arimathea at the burial of our Lord, holding the fatal, dripping spear: behind him the Magdalen raised a jewelled cup, I supposed as a communion.

I started at a knock at the door. Had they decided I had heard too much, and come to murder me in my sleep? I was trapped, surrounded, and could only hope that for that they would not have knocked. I threw open the door. Guladis stood there, carrying a candle and a pitcher. She said: "I brought you water, for tonight. Or would you prefer some more wine?"

I thought she was the most beautiful thing I had ever seen, the light of the candle making a halo of her curls and the silver fish glittering in her cleavage like the morning star. I said as firmly as I could: "I've had enough wine."

She took a deep breath. Her breasts swelled like stormclouds and she brushed past me into the room. She put the pitcher and the candle on the table. I saw there was an old, faint painting on that wall too. I thought it was the Magdalen performing her old profession. Guladis turned to face me. "Your sheets are clean, but the bed is cold, poor hospitality for a pilgrim."

She pulled at the maze-work pattern on the front of her dress, and it came apart. The dress fell to the floor, leaving her wearing only her fish pendant. I was a young man then, and had never had such a temptation, not from such a woman. I followed her to the bed and undressed, but before I actually touched her, I controlled myself enough to say: "Is this wise? It could damage your reputation, infuriate your relatives!"

She stared at me in what seemed to be genuine amazement. "My reputation? How could taking the holy sacrament of Mary Magdalen damage that?" She knelt on the bed and, seizing my wrists, made me kneel before her and pushed my hands into a position of prayer between her own. "Lord," she said, "as you offered your body, and Mary in her way offered hers, so we offer ours, his to the barbarian sword and mine to the Roman fire, but first in this sacrament. Amen!"

She glared at me till I too said "Amen", then gave me her fish to kiss, then her breasts, and then it proceeded as you might suppose. I should say that none of the few respectable women nor the many less respectable with whom I have done that was at all like Guladis. She had an openness and ecstasy in her love-making as though she were indeed performing a sacrament.

Afterwards she knelt across me and dried me carefully with her hair. Then she gave me a little smile as if we were not really lovers, but shared a special friendship which was in some ways a better thing. She said: "That is but one of the many wonders the bishops would deny us."

"There are others?"

"All the knowledge found by my father and the holy monks, in books which Joseph brought to this land, not then part of Rome, which the Romans later suppressed. Do they not deny that good works can help one to Christ's mercy, which is surely obvious?"

This was the Pelagian heresy, which I knew only from sermons warning against division. It never occurred to me, as it might have to some priest or Rome-inclined monk, that she might be a bad woman, or even a demon sent to snare me. What I did think was that this was too complex for me, and that for Britons to fall out was a mistake when there were Saxons in the land.

I remained there for three more days and three more nights, A pattern developed: I would demand help for Arthur. Brychan would equivocate, and Ligessac would rail that Arthur meant to restore the Roman way and give power to the bishops. Guladis spent her days with Gwynnlym: playing music and singing. Gwynnlym's songs became sadder and more plaintive. By night Guladis came to me, and she made love and spoke of the church of the other Joseph and Mary with equal passion. On the last night I said to her: "I have never met anyone like you."

"You should come more often. Some of my sisters have never had the chance to do their dut . . . to take this sacrament."

"And you have . . . perhaps too often?"

"No!" she said anxiously. "But perhaps enough!" She went on: "Our law allows a girl who has done her duty to choose her husband. Father's interpretation is that as I have been called on most, I shall be allowed the most . . . the greatest . . ."

She stopped, confused. I said: "You are fisher, but also bait. You were promised marriage to the biggest fish you could haul in. You allowed yourself to think you had caught the biggest who was likely to swim in these remote waters. Then . . ."

"Yes!" She grasped my arm firmly. "You understand me so well . . . I love . . . but duty . . ." She took a deep breath to compose herself, looked me in the eye: "If you will swear to prevent the

Great King of the East imposing the Roman way of the bishops on my father and my people, then I will swear to make you a good wife, if that is what you should want."

"At this moment, it's what I want more than anything in the world. But I can't swear as you wish. I'm already sworn to Arthur, and like him I think Saxon warriors are a bigger peril than Roman priests."

She rose then and left without a word, going for the first time before dawn. Later that day I confronted Brychan:

"I go today to Caerleon to meet Arthur. I must be able to tell him what help you can send."

He shrugged. "Perhaps I will follow you there and meet this High King. But I will send my own pilgrim ambassador. Perhaps you would care to escort my daughter Guladis?"

I said Arthur needed men not women, and took my leave. I didn't know if I would return: as it happened, I never did.

I rode south, and at sundown came to a ford in the river on the boundary of Brychan's lands. Beyond it the road crossed one which led from the West to Caerleon. Nearby was a rough inn, a farm where they brewed beer and kept a clean round house for guests. There I met Cei, who had heard that Gwynnlym was at Brychan's Caer, and was waiting for him to return so they could discuss a contribution to the war. I cursed myself for not doing this myself, though I was scarcely the best person to persuade the forlorn lover. I realized that I had taken it for granted that he was a younger son, allowed to work on his music because he wasn't needed for anything more important.

We had scarcely sat down to our meal and ale when Arthur himself arrived. His luck had been better than ours. The ruler of Caer Myrdinn had promised threescore horsemen with arms and supplies, and other western lords had also rallied round. Cei had achieved nothing, while my conquests were personal. Beer flowed, and I found myself speaking indiscreetly of Guladis, almost boasting. Cei was envious: so, more surprisingly, was Arthur: "Y'know, being a saintly pilgrim is the right life when you have to, but what warrior could carry it off all the time?"

Next morning we slept late. It was cool, but the dew had almost vanished by the time we went out to our horses. Birds were singing, but there was a noise in the distance we couldn't ignore: the drumbeat of many horses, being ridden hard.

We armed and saddled up. We found a vantage point, and almost at once saw a small group riding out of the North as if fleeing from Gwyn ap Nudd and the Wild Hunt. They were almost at the ford, but even at a distance I felt that some of the horses were about to fail, and we could hear the sound of a far larger number not far off, just around a bend in the road.

We trotted toward the ford, and before we got there saw the fleeing group reach it. A man rode across, then allowed his horse to rest. It was Gwynnlym: he wore no armour and had his lute on his back where his shield should have been. He was followed by a few servants, some leading pack animals. Then I sat up abruptly in my saddle. In the middle of the group, a slighter figure had crossed the ford and at once jumped off an exhausted pony and started trying to soothe it. It was Guladis, but before I could react to seeing her thus, the following hoofbeats got louder and a cavalcade of some forty or fifty men came round the bend. They made for the ford, though not as fast as the fleeing group had done. They wore mail but no helmets, as if prepared for action but nothing serious. I recognized several: Brychan was in the lead, with Ligessac beside him.

I continued down to the ford with my weapons sheathed but my shield with its dragon emblem forward. I didn't know what to feel: this woman I more than half loved evidently eloping with a man she loved more: behind a father who preferred me as a suitor. Unless of course he cast for bigger fish. Behind, I could hear Arthur making a remark to Cei about the opportunity the situation presented, which I found shocking coming from him: Cei replying without much sincerity that we warrior pilgrims had been committed by him to help the defenceless.

The fugitives looked up expectantly as they heard us, then their faces fell. Gwynnlym turned back toward the ford and, Brychan and his men being already within earshot, shouted at them to stay out of his territory of Glevissig. They did not slow their advance, and Guladis drooped against the exhausted pony. Something was dripping down her face; I could not tell if it was tears or sweat. It saddened me to see her so desperate, and I spurred forward to the ford as if I was part of the relief she had hoped for. Arthur and Cei followed. I shouted: "Lord Brychan, you must respect Gwynnlym's request!"

"What!" he yelled back. "Respect a guest who has stolen his host's daughter?"

Unfortunately, Cei and even Arthur laughed at that, which infuriated Brychan. Clearly, his Magdalens were not to be known as such anywhere where they might bring shame. He had his own strange plans, but Guladis had failed him, had removed the strongest piece from his board. I said: "Yes. If you have come as I asked with your men to support Arthur, then of course, cross and then ride with us to Caerleon. But if you are distracted by a personal quarrel, then when the greater battle with the Saxons is won, loyal Britons will remember!"

It was a desperate situation. Brychan was furious: I doubted he would be used to contradiction. Even if he felt no guilt at using his daughter as bait, her elopement had led him to be laughed at, and who likes that? His face went a sickly red and veins stood out like fat worms; he looked as if he might die of a seizure if he did not order some terrible act, so what had he to lose? Arthur and Cei rode up, and we three stood guard over the ford, as we had four times guarded the ford over the Dubglass against the Saxons. I felt it would be a great irony if we should die so obscurely after all that, but passions were high and numbers against us.

People were looking at Arthur with no more curiosity than at Cei or I. I realized they did not know him. A Roman ruler would have been known from his portraits on coins: but we Britons do not make graven images on gold. Arthur took his helmet from his saddle bag, and raised it as if to put it on. It was a famous piece that had once belonged to Macsen, the last Roman Emperor of Britain: it was of bronze and gold, and had a laurel wreath of emeralds set round its brows. Everyone gasped: even Ligessac bowed. Guladis came forward and bowed very deeply, one of her special bows. She said: "High King, a poor grand-daughter of Mary Magdalen begs your protection!"

Gwynnlym looked hurt, but also relieved, while Ligessac looked at Arthur with begrudging admiration. He said: "Lord Brychan, this is the victor of Caerleon. Perhaps we should collect supplies for this new campaign, while your most trusted daughter can explain our special problems to his Excellence!"

Gwynnlym and Guladis spent the rest of the day negotiating with Arthur on behalf of the monks and Brychan's strange community. That night Cei and I plied Gwynnlym with ale till he collapsed, oblivious to what was happening in the guesthouse, which had been reserved for Arthur and Guladis. Next morning Guladis rose early, and by the time the rest of us were up, she had made an elaborate wreath of ferns. She presented it to Arthur, saying: "In the name of Mary Magdalen and Joseph of Arimathea, I declare you Emperor, in Britain only!"

Later, Arthur was given a more elaborate wreath for the same title by the Bishop of Caerleon: but I know which one he valued and had carefully dried. And not long after Arthur conquered the Saxons and forced them to beg terms, as all know.

I dreamed all this three times on the way back to Caerleon, many years later, when I went with Vortiporix, Arthur and Cei, and 300 and threescore men. Caerleon wasn't much of a place by then: only the Protector and his men, and the bishop and his retinue, lived within the walls, and there was a market once a month. But times were settled, letters, traders and priests found their way from Rome, and the bishop had persuaded Vortiporix to destroy Ligessac. Even Brychan's heirs were silent. Only within monasteries were the old ways of the other Mary and Joseph whispered, and perhaps in the monastic kingdom of Cadoc, Gwynnlym's heir. But it wasn't the thought of Gwynnlym that made Arthur and I ride in silence. We both had secret thoughts as to whose son Guladis might have borne.

We came to another ford, on another river, which was also a boundary of Glevissig. As well as his horsemen, Vortiporix had twice 300 foot soldiers, so we were over 1,000 men in all. Cadoc did not bring his 100 warriors to the ford: instead he came with his monks. Their habits looked a little more comfortable than those of Rome-inclined monks, and each was red on one side and white on the other. Behind was a separate group of nuns, their habits red and white on the opposite sides, faces covered by their hoods. Even after all those years, I thought I recognized the stance of the abbess; but she did not unhood or step forward. Cadoc threw back his hood and said: "Lord Emperor! Have you forgotten your solemn word, that you would protect the monks who study the wisdom of Britain in preference to the orders of Rome?"

It was a shock to see he was not that young, well past twenty. From his thinness, fair hair, and gentle, melodious voice, it was clear who his father was: Arthur said roughly: "Wisdom, yes, but your guest Ligessac has killed three of my men, and that is no wisdom to me!"

"Ligessac is old enough to have fought beside you, unlike his enemies." The Abbot-King glared at Vortiporix, who despite his sagging belly was not much older than he was. "Your old companion is sick now, a limping scholar not a soldier. Have you no respect for our monastic duty to provide a hospital? Why not send Bedivere, whom all trust, to see my words are true?"

Arthur hesitated. I could see he wanted to compromise, and

I said: "No one doubts the word of an abbot, or the right of sanctuary. But you monks have never contributed to the upkeep of the armies which defend Christendom. How about a gift of supplies, to show respect?"

"You want monks, men of God, to pay tribute?"

"Yes." Arthur replied. "Some tribute my men won't have to sweat to move, cattle perhaps."

Vortiporix opened his mouth to protest, but saw Arthur was determined, and instead said: "At least 100!"

"A hundred will do," Arthur said. Indeed it would, in that territory where most farmers raised only sheep.

Vortiporix shouted: "He is said to have a special breed which are red in front and white behind. A hundred of those!"

Arthur nodded: Cadoc looked upset, but said: "We will search our herds, and pray for three days. If God wills it, we will find the 100 and bring then to you."

The tribute arrived on the evening of the third day. I saw the cattle and heard them bellow in protest at the unexpected trek, and I smelled what they left on the path. They were not wondrous cattle as poets saw can be found in the Otherworld: but three and thirty of them were of good age with full udders; three and thirty were a little old, with udders starting to fail; and three and thirty were a little young to be milked. There was one bull. All were red in front and white behind.

The bull was walked on a chain by a nun. As Cei and I finished counting, she pushed back her hood, and I recognized Guladis. She had aged, though perhaps less than I. She said: "This is all the tribute God will allow a Roman king to demand from a British monk!" and returned across the river.

We herded the cattle into a field with drystone walls, and made camp. The men had found a farmer who brewed beer, and we drank him dry in celebration of the triumph of soldiers over monks. But it was a cold night, the coldest I can recall for that time of year. Drunk or not, I woke several times, but I heard nothing. At other times I dreamed of things I had not seen, strange ships landing in our country, with men from distant climes: monks singing a service I did not know, a procession with a cup and a spear.

I woke in the morning to find the camp in silence. I realized it was almost summer and the night had been short. The sun was rising, but there was a cold, hard white frost all round our camp. The sentries were huddled round their fire . . . nothing seemed amiss with the troops or the horses, but something told me to check the tribute. I was the first to do so: the sentries had not been over-zealous, but what I found could not have been done by men without them hearing.

The cattle were there, but they were changed. They had gathered on the side of the field furthest from us, looking over the river towards their old home. At least, I assumed they had gathered, for they were changed, and could no longer move. Every last beast had been silently replaced by an elaborate fern maze work in the shape of an animal. I studied several carefully, and each seemed to be made from a single incredibly long fern, with neither tip nor base. They stood there in utter silence, facing towards Glevissig and Cadoc's House of God. It came to me that we were all part of the great maze, and that we would never know its beginning or end, why some men flaunt God's wrath, but others cannot escape his justice.

For it was, in its way, a just tribute. Every one of the 100 beasts was there as a fernwork: I noticed there was only one bull. And all of them were dry, so the fronts at least were red: but in every case the rear end was thickly coated with white frost, so the terms of the agreement were kept, and we had cattle part red and part white, like the habits of Cadoc's monks and nuns.

Sir Blamor in DIEU ET MON DROIT!

Eliot Fintushel

Blamor and his brother Bleoberis were the nephews of Lancelot and rather hot-headed at court. One day Blamor accused King Anguish, or Agwisance, of murder with the result that Blamor faced Sir Tristam in trial by combat. It is that story that is retold here.

Eliot Fintushel (b. 1948) is a teacher and performer of mask and mime and has twice won the US National Endowment for the Arts Solo Performer Award. His short stories and essays have been appearing in American science-fiction and literary magazines since 1993, including the spoof Arthurian story "Hamisch in Avalon". Eliot discovered a book of Arthurian tales when he was nine. "I gobbled them up," he writes, "right up to the last chapter, called 'The End of Knighthood', which I didn't have the heart to read!"

Blamor woke early. He tiptoed past Bleoberis, dead to the world. He let his squire Edmond sleep where he lay, on a cot behind the stairs, and rode out of Camelot into open country, to think.

It was wrong, *but human*, to hate. Christ himself was both God and human, so the fathers taught. Christ overturned the moneylenders' table – he had not played the gentle lamb for *them*. And this world was filled with such tables, tended not just by moneylenders but by every sort of malefactor, thieves with fine lineages, buggers in sackcloth, lying, gossiping chamberlains, Sir Rape-Your-Wife, Lord Stab-You-In-The-Back – and murderer kings. Blamor hated them all. They thought they ran the world, "*mundus Caesare*", swiping helpless lads like his cousin Anselm, but he would overturn their tables for them.

Blamor tethered his horse – and his anger – to an oak tree by a stream and went walking beside the water. God dwelled in such places more than in the towns. No king here but He. How often in their childhood Blamor had fled the dominion of firstborn Bleoberis – it chafed, even from him, who surely loved Blamor and had only Blamor's good at heart – to the woods! The priests might get it wrong, seduced by power or papish gold, but not the wind and water!

In the rushing of the stream and the soughing of the leaves above was God's voice and his comfort. Blamor followed the stream into a woods, leaping down among wet, dark rocks, a wattle of fallen branches, and scurrying things. He picked and threaded his way, keeping the sound of the water close at his right when grasses and limbs obscured it.

Sometimes even the water sound dwindled to the loudness of his own thoughts, and then, willy-nilly, his brother's doggerel hung in his mind. He shook his head, but it lingered. He'd heard it coming from up in the garde-robe, accompanied by the sound of Bleoberis's piss as it sprinkled into the cellar, two stories down, through the hole in the garde-robe floor:

Poor Anselm, on the bier you lie,
Whom Agwisance with palsied eye
Fewtered his cruel lance upon . . .

Delicate lad, it had been suicide for Anselm to have gone to Ireland. How should he train for knighthood who was hardly fit to squire? He never should have stepped foot in a tilt-yard, King Agwisance's or anyone else's!

Wherefore my father's lesser son,
Stricken to his saintly marrow,
Appeached the king and gargled, "Haro . . .!"

"Haro!" *I accuse*! What else was there to do once his brother Bleoberis had told Blamor of Anselm's murder? Bleoberis, the elder one, had wanted to wait, to weigh things, he'd said, to politic a bit before breaking lances, but Blamor would never dilute righteousness with circumspection. "Dieu et mon droit!" *God and my right:* – justice for Anselm's killer!

God would secure the proper outcome without any politicking. Wasn't Agwisance King Arthur's vassal? He would have to face the charges or forfeit his lands.

A huge, fallen branch blocked his path, and Blamor picked his way around it. At last Bleoberis had seen the truth of Blamor's plea, relented, and allowed Blamor, the passionate one, to go to Camelot to settle the matter by a contest at arms.

Now must Ag to Camelot,
Where he may brother Blamor gut,
Or brother Blamor him *may gut . . .*

Blamor recalled the words of Bleoberis's drinking friends, the "Black Monks" who helped him home from the *Messe Des Fous* on the brown hillside in Cluny: "Young devil, you embarrass even us!" they'd laughed, as Bleoberis improvised mock liturgies in Latin and French, "Don't stop, blood of King Ban, or we'll tell your Uncle Lancelot on you!"

. . . Or brother Blamor him *may gut*
And we Ag's benefice obtain
For Ansy's broached and shattered brain
Upon the noyous bloody lance
Attributed *to Agwisance.*

"*Attributed*!" Strange choice of words, but maybe Blamor had misheard it, charging up the steps of the burgher's house where they were staying in Camelot, afire with the news that Agwisance had arrived with his champion, a young knight named Tristram. Or it could have been Bleoberis's Cluny wildness. He was entitled to that – God needed all sorts of souls to work the salvation of his creatures. Bleoberis was a bear of a man, thickly bearded, burly, with nostrils like oubliettes in his squat face. But Bleoberis loved Blamor, blue-eyed and blond. He even took joy in the younger brother's superior skill at arms: he told him so time and again!

"Here's the standings," Bleoberis had said, pulling up his leggings. Behind him, on the garde-robe wall, a samite gown hung from a hook, and a vest and a fancy doublet under it, the stench of human waste proof against vermin. Blamor stood panting and listening in the dark hallway. "Agwisance is a little rat, and Tristram is Agwisance's lump of cheese."

"But, Bleoberis, I heard that Tristram once gave Sir Marhaus, Agwisance's man, a mortal wound; he left a sliver of his sword edge in Sir Marhaus's brain pan, so I heard, and sent him packing back to Ireland to die – and he kept Marhaus's shield and sword for souvenirs!

"They found a rune cut fresh in Marhaus's belly. It's said he had it tattooed there for a spell against Tristram, *but no one feared Tristram then*! I think Tristram did it, Bleoberis – black work, to disfigure a man and slay him! Now he champions the Irish king!"

"Death was Marhaus's due, little brother. The *truth* is, Marhaus was overrated, a milksop. Ask anyone! For us blood of King Ban's line, your *cavalier triste* is a squire's toady, and if you ever yield to him, by God, you shame us all, and I'll kill you myself."

Of course, Blamor would never yield!

The way cleared, the stream widened, and Blamor found himself under a mackerel sky, in a brisk dry wind, with the whole world now squinting, now widening its eye, as the sun beamed through the clouds or was lidded again. As still in his soul as a monk or a dead man, Blamor stared down at the patchy green ahead of each next step. More than seeing, he *felt* the changing light against his skin. God's voice was in it as in the water and wind.

Memento mori! the light whispered to him. *Be mindful of dying*!

A horse whinnied, and Blamor looked up. A hundred yards away, violet brocaded silk swelled and rippled. The fabric was stretched between tentpoles surmounted by huge gold pommels; even at this remove, Blamor could make out their figure – a hawk in flight bearing in its beak a small animal.

Agwisance!

Abruptly, the light and air stopped speaking to Blamor. He felt himself blush. He had been as if invisible, with God, and now he was skulking about the enemy's encampment, spying on the murderer-king or, God forbid, seeking to strike a bargain with him – that's how it looked. Blamor glanced in all directions to see if he might have been observed. It flustered him: willy-nilly he found himself trying to convince an imaginary judge of his intentions. He had been out walking, purifying himself before God, preparing himself to be an instrument of His justice. He had had no idea that the encampment of King Agwisance was nearby.

The judge was unconvinced.

Thoughts scattered, pulse jumping, he wanted to flee his body. He began to reach back to untether his horse, but of course, he had left it half a mile behind.

Then he saw Sir Tristram. He was taller by a head than Blamor; he walked as if supported from above, so lofty was his carriage and so graceful, even though he was wearing a cumbersome hauberk, all of woven silver links that flashed when the sun shone. His helmet flashed as well, dangling from his hand by a chin strap.

Behind Tristram a huge black horse ambled. It *felt* closer than Blamor *knew* it was – his eyes and heart had somehow separated and perceived the world at odds. An awesome beast with fiery eyes, Tristram's mount snorted thunderously and shook its massive head. Its mane flew up: sparks from a flint. When it shuddered, the sweat sprayed and sparkled like St Anthony's fire. Tristram led his mount with clicks of the tongue. Once or twice he petted the creature's neck, and it seemed to Blamor a supernatural act, like placing one's head in a lion's mouth.

Blamor felt paralyzed, a sheep at the slaughtering block. He stood stock still, exposed and vulnerable in the middle of the field, like a post one tries arrows on – even rabbits and fowl knew to stay along the edge of a field for safety. A 100 yards away, Tristram turned and rubbed his forehead against the black horse's lowered forelock – and at that moment Blamor realized that his brother had lied.

This knight was his death.

Inside Blamor the panic burst. He felt all blood and lightning. He thought nothing, decided nothing, but found himself running back through the woods, splashing in and out of the stream, pawing branches out of his way, charging into dark confusion, heedless of thorns and sudden ditches, falling, rising, scrambling, face and palms scratched bloody.

At last his foot caught on a rotting, fallen limb, and Blamor fell to hands and knees, the breath rasping like sobs in the back of his throat. He stayed there, a hunted animal, panting and dripping mud. As his breath grew less ragged, he began to hear a strange sound above the wind and water sounds – not the whinney of Tristram's mount and not the voice of God, but a sort of singing.

The singing became clearer as the hoofbeats of his heart grew dimmer. At first, he could not understand the words; the singer's voice was thin and crackly, punctuated by little coughs, but gradually he made them out:

Endurez, endurez les doux maux de mors!
Plus genté de vous les endurent!

It seemed to Blamor that he had heard that chant from one of Bleoberis's Cluny *fous*, but that the words had been "*doux maux d'amer*," sweet pangs of love, and not "*de mors*", of death.

Endure, endure the sweet pangs of death!
More gentlemen than you have endured them!

Blamor slaked the grime from his cheeks and stood. Limping at first, he groped in whatever direction made the singing louder. With the singing, the sound of water swelled – she was at the stream, then. He followed the sound. *Perhaps Bleoberis had just been trying to guard his little brother from anxiety* – les maux de mors, *and nowise sweet*! Blamor squeezed through tangling, twisted vines and overgrown trees, ripping and chopping whatever got in his way. *It was Bleoberis, Bleoberis, Bleoberis choking him . . .*!

Endurez . . .!"

He stopped at the edge of a glade and leaned against two saplings, bowing them slightly as he gazed between them at the woman by the stream. She sat on a flat rock, sewing, her work half-hidden by the fall of her long hair, pale and dry as old flax. Her own clothes were tatters, a gown once white, perhaps, stained ochre and patched helter-skelter with beetle spit and leaves that were veins and powder now. She rocked back and forth from her skeletal waist as she guided the needle through her cloth, and sang.

In the seeing of her Blamor forgot himself. He drew nearer. It was a *gambois* the woman was sewing on, a knight's undergarment of quilted cotton; he'd never seen one so fine. He came within a few yards of her. She didn't notice, but sang on with a child's rapture – "*Endurez, endurez les doux maux de mors*!" – and rocked and stitched, and the stream burbled and sparkled below. He came within a foot of her, and still she didn't stir. "*Plus genté de vous . . .*" She was not *mending* the garment, he saw, but *embroidering* letters and images in a circle with gold thread. He was inches behind her. He saw the shapes of shoulder bones beneath her pale skin, wrinkly as the skin on boiled milk. From above, through rents in the gown, he saw her shrivelled breasts. He could smell her – pennyroyal and sulphur. He drew closer still, leaning to see what she was writing.

His cheek touched her hair, nearly – and she stopped singing. She clasped her knees together, folding the *gambois* in-between and out of sight. The needle dangled over one thigh at the end of a golden thread.

The sound of the stream. The sough of the old woman's breath. Clouds shuttering the sun: light and dark like a sweetness melting and vanishing in everything.

She turned her head. "I was waiting for you, Blamor."

He trembled and shrank back, his heart pounding again. "How do you know my name?"

"Sit you down before me, Blamor. Don't you be afraid, now. I only brought you *here* because my legs have gone too weak to take me *there*, and I've a gift for you. A gift and a great gift! Sit you down!"

He sat where she pointed. He was not aware of going there, but found himself before her, on a slightly lower rock, facing her, his back to the stream – its sound could have been the rush of his thoughts or his blood or the wings of angels. Now he saw the moonstones and sapphires mounted in little pendants of bone and of boiled, hardened leather. She must have a dozen necklaces inside the ochre tatters. *Maybe*, he thought madly, *they are her children*.

He fancied that she had heard his thought. She reached toward him her chicken bone arm and, with an indulgent smile, caressed his head as if he were a child. "Have they none of my ilk, then, in Brittany whence you come, Blamor de Ganis? Have they no one to teach you the end you lean toward? None to remedy your fatal pieties, Blamor?"

"No," he confessed. She laughed – her laughter wounded him. It threw Blamor inward, grasping for a principle. He imagined he was reaching for a sacred scroll, but when he touched it, he felt the powder of moths' wings. They pulsed, then separated and swirled inside his mind like snow. "Well, of course, there is my brother . . ."

"Bleoberis? Ah, poor thing, you know better now! You've seen your death in a hauberk! But never mind, I can save you. It's why I've brought you to me. Come closer and pull up your smock. I want to see your belly, Blamor. I want to write something there with a knife."

"You want to kill me?"

"No, that's a gift I cannot give you. I want to save you, child, with a rune."

"I know you now!" Blamor leapt to his feet. "Witch, you sew spells into blouses or tattoo them on a knight's body, don't you? Do you think I'd stoop to that? It's my God and my right that give me strength, not *your* sort . . .!

"Your 'right' – *if only you knew*?"

". . . And do you dream that a trick like that would get past King Arthur, madam? Was it you who secreted a spell inside the cloak of the bishop's champion when the Earl of Salisbury brought suit against him? Much good it did him! He was found out before the contest, and the bishop forfeited his case – I wonder if he *slew* his witch after."

"King Arthur is not judge today, mannikin, though his is the right of ban. King Arthur sojourns at Joyous Gard with Lancelot, your uncle. King Carados and the King of Scots, at Arthur's request, will probe you for unlawful spells and talismans, will see you shriven, and will judge you recreant, victorious, or dead. They will find no *grimoire* of mine before or after, though they flail you and stretch your hide in the midday sun, sir knight! I know everything.

"Come to me. See here the pretty ink I'll lay into the pretty cuts. Don't you fear my gimlets now! *Plus genté de vous les endurent*!" A pouch of worn leather hung from a thong between her legs like a stiff furry scrotum. Cooing to it, she worked the drawstring open and withdrew two small knives, narrow as boning knives, cruelly sharp, and a phial of purple dye. "Come! For naught, then, did I show you Sir Tristram and your death? Aren't you afraid of *that*, you foolish pizzle-mound? *That* you should fear, surely, *les doux maux de mors*!"

"No! I only fear injustice!" The words had a dull ring to Blamor's own ear, as if spoken in an earthen cellar and by someone other than himself. The old woman smiled so slightly that he could not be sure that he wasn't imagining it, and yet it cowed him. Her eyes made him feel small, shut in, sealed in a hollowed rock, his insides draining and collapsing, no principles left, no thoughts even, but only the desiccating skin, *as hot lead dripped in at the rims of the joined halves of stone, dulling, hardening . . .*

"Oh, come!" Her rebuke woke him from the daydream.

"Did you cut the rune on Sir Marhaus's belly?"

"It saved him!"

"But he died!"

"Not of Tristram. Whoever says so lies! Marhaus died his own death, days later, in Ireland. My rune saved him!"

He was sweating. He felt like a small child before her, like the child Bleoberis used to order about – Bleoberis, who had been king and pope to little Blamor. What was it about her voice, dry leaves crackling in a fire, that turned his own thoughts to smoke? He came to her.

"This is to humor an old crone. This has nothing to do with my case. Death is nothing to me." He advanced toward her on his knees. He couldn't stop trembling.

"Just as you say, Blamor dear, but death is *everything*." She tucked the mystic *gambois* out of sight behind her, she lifted his smock, and she began to cut.

He winced. "This will save me?"

"This will save you."

Light and shadow as the sun slipped higher through galloping clouds – Blamor was that slow winking, outside himself and time. At some point, she said, "Oh, this is more better and more worthier than a lodestone on a sleeping lady's head or the pebble from a rooster's craw, be sure!" Another time it was, "*Endurez, endurez* . . ." And again, "*Votre droit* – if only you knew!"

The old woman nodded, sighed, and was tracing the completed circle of her rune with the point of a gimlet, when Blamor woke to a voice – Tristram's, he was certain – calling, "Elizabeth? Elizabeth?" He heard branches snapping, water splashing. Blamor shot to his feet. The old woman shrieked; her knife streaked blood, then fell from her hand.

Blamor ran.

In Camelot, a cripple with an arm and both legs bandaged together dragged herself along the street. She was pulling a dead dog behind her at the end of an old rope she'd wrapped around her forearm. Now and then she looked back at the carcass and grinned.

The brothers Blamor and Bleoberis were riding abreast to Arthur's castle, to the lists, to Agwisance's *dies irae*. Behind Blamor and Bleoberis, squire Edmond walked, leading his horse, piled high with Sir Blamor's armaments. Blamor subdued his soul with *Holy Marys*, like a surgeon's lackey sitting on the patient's chest. Never mind the itch and tingle between navel and groin, where a rune and words may have been cut – *don't think of that*! He no longer smelled, thank God, the ashes of burnt glasswort leaves soaked in vinegar and olive oil with which the hag had blotted her grimoire.

Blamor halted at the sight of the cripple. "While some men eat themselves sick on dainties!" he muttered. Bleoberis, oblivious, had skirted the impediment and ridden on a few paces. He looked back and grimaced impatiently. "Edmond, give the woman a few coins for a proper meal."

Edmond, with practised equanimity, produced the coins and, wrinkling his nose, held them out to the crippled woman.

"What? Should I let go my supper to receive your pittance? Let an honest woman be!" She dragged herself and her dog down the street. People stepped over her. Neither she nor they seemed to mind much.

Edmond shrugged, tossed the coins straight up, like a juggler, snatched them back, pocketed them again, and looked a question at his master. Blamor winced, then looked away. He clucked his tongue, pulled lightly at the reins, and caught up with Bleoberis.

Nearer the castle, the townspeople were bustling. Piping and shouts, like wind across water, confused Blamor's prayers. A few jongleurs luted and sang, each with his own little gathering, mostly of women. In their rude, improvised songs, the jongleurs were already memorializing what had not yet occurred: in one song, Blamor could not help but hear, he was made king of Ireland, Agwisance fallen on his own sword and Tristram cleaved in two, coif to crotch, by a single sword stroke.

In others, Blamor was dead.

At tables along the street men played chess passionately, japing and arguing. There were dice games in the square where merchants hawked vegetables, herbs, spices, wax, and caged fowl. Men with monkeys and trained bears throated balleys. In the streets, in and out of houses, clogging alleys, upsetting every ordered thing, children dashed and tussled. Blamor held the reins tightly, *hail Mary, full of grace*. Some cheered him. Some pulled at his stirrups, and Edmond had to pry them off with kicks and slaps. They wouldn't bother Bleoberis; his scowl cowed them.

Before he turned away, Blamor saw one raucous group of dice-players, a few of them half-naked, beside a pile of their clothes. He heard one shout: "Hey, *there's* a better game! That's your accuser, your Sir Blamor de Ganis there! I'll give good odds he's recreant by nightfall – no, *dead*! I say, *dead*! Who'll take me on here? Where's your money?" In spite of himself, Blamor strained to hear what response that would bring, but there was none, *pray for us sinners now and at the hour, amen.*

They threaded the streets and cantered across the field before the castle, Edmond following at forced march with the armaments. They crossed the bridge, passing under drab brick arches, inhumanly high, that seemed to radiate cold. In that dark, Blamor shivered.

The chill didn't leave him until the moat and curtain wall were behind him, when his own anger warmed him up again. King Carados and the King of Scots and their bailiffs stood and chatted in the guardhouse archway, and not at all grimly. Bleoberis waved. A bit behind those kings stood King Agwisance, looking ruffled and impatient, though at one point he said something that made the others laugh.

A wit then, thought Blamor (*. . . the fruit of thy womb, Jesus . . .*) and so much more a scoundrel, then, japing on Anselm's murder!

Sir Tristram emerged with his squire and joined the kings just as Blamor was dismounting. Blamor's foot caught in a stirrup, making him hop to find his balance. Edmond rushed to assist him, but Blamor held up his hand. "Get away from me! I know where my feet are!"

Bleoberis was already ahead of them, among the kings. Their men tethered his horse for him, laughing with Bleoberis as he handed them the reins. Perhaps they were all just nervous.

Blamor strode toward the assembly. "Shall we wassail instead of jousting? Your worships seem jolly enough! Or shall we go whoring together, while the worms eat my cousin?"

Behind their beards Carados and the King of Scots paled. The entire company stared at Blamor, stony-faced. Only Agwisance stepped forward. He was dressed as if to general, in breast-plate and cape – an affectation, since Tristram was his surrogate. His eyes were full of fire, and the unruly curls of his red beard gave him a fierce look. He was Tristram's height and not the least bit afraid to march close enough to bite Blamor's nose if he wanted to. "You wish I were a kitchen knave, don't you, so you could cry *haro* and have me flogged, or get my ear lopped off, or see me strangled in a noose, burned or pulled apart by four horses – *gehenné*!"

Four men approached Agwisance to calm him; of them, Bleoberis was first, laying a gentle hand on the King's shoulder. Agwisance smiled contemptuously and shook his shoulder from under it. "You are so self-righteous! The whole affair is built on a falsehood. I never touched the boy, and so my champion will swear in due course. It was my knight constable, the boy Anselm's tutor at arms, who touched him with the butt of his lance, as was his right – *touched* him, merely, the puny child – to speed him along his duties, and the boy died."

"Lies!" What a wondrous antidote to fear was anger! Blamor jettisoned his *hailmarys* on the spot and even forgot the burning at his loins.

"Knight," said Agwisance, "you are unworthy of your famous uncle. Your Anselm was a maladroit who counted clouds when he should have been dressing his shield."

Bleoberis whispered to Blamor, "Save your fury for the lists, brother."

"Save my fury, Bleoberis?" Blamor said aloud, and his brother flinched. "Where is *yours?*"

Bleoberis smiled obsequiously at Agwisance, then took Blamor's arm. "Brother, you know I love you!"

A cool breeze seemed to accompany Tristram. Suddenly he was standing at Agwisance's side – Blamor felt the drop in temperature before he saw the man.

"My lords and fellow worthies, perhaps we should swear our oaths in the chapel, and then to the lists where *God* will judge. Gouvernail . . .!" Tristram gestured toward the chapel, a long hall across a courtyard, beyond the looming keep; his squire bowed and started toward it with an armful of silver mail.

"Wait!" King Carados spoke at last. He was a squat, blubbery-faced man with a bulldog's voice. "It's not time for the chapel and oaths yet. Arthur has enjoined us, me and Scots here – by God's grace and all that, of course – to preside at a trial by combat, and by Christ's bloody ankles, I'm going to see to it, jot and tittle." He stared them down, one by one. When Carados came to his fellow judge, the King of Scots, a big man, but pigeon chested, short of breath, and bald, Scots nodded like a man afraid of reproval. Carados slapped him on the back, then turned to address Tristram and Blamor. "Sir knights, before any oath-taking, we're to check your undergarments and secret places." He motioned for the bailiffs to come near

Blamor felt faint. The skin on his belly burned so hotly he thought the others must see flames or smell the burning flesh. He couldn't look at Tristram! *Damn the hag*!

"I will forego the examination of Sir Blamor," said Tristram, "if he will excuse me that same discomfiture." The man was slick as a paynim's dagger. Blamor strove to keep his mouth from dropping open. "I trust him, sirs. Are we not two honorable knights?" Agwisance grumbled, but concurred. Scots shrugged, and King Carados called his bailiffs off.

Tristram bowed, stepping backwards a few paces toward the chapel, then turned and continued walking after Gouvernail. Carados blustered, "To the chapel, then!" but it was all anticlimax. They marched across the bailey, past the keep, to the chapel.

Blamor lingered behind, staring after the tall knight. Then, his blood rising, he galloped past the crowd to Tristram, who had overtaken Gouvernail now and led the pack with an easy powerful stride.

With ragged breath, Blamor slowed to match the pace of the taller man. He caught Tristram's elbow, stopping him, making him look Blamor in the eye. The witch's rune danced on Blamor's gut, sending shivers through him – could the thing that made him quake make him prevail? "It moves me deeply how Christian ready you are to trust a knight whose skull you'd shatter for a traitor's patronage!"

Bleoberis, huffing, caught up to Blamor and Tristram. "What the hell's going on?"

Tristram's face darkened. "I'm no whore for patronage. My father once wanted my stepmother killed, and I defended her."

With a dragon's rasp, Tristram exhaled slowly and became once again the alabaster column of a knight. There was a slight catch in his voice, no more, when he said, "She was the only mother I knew, the only *live* one . . ."

Bleoberis japed, "'Only *live* one?' You know the *dead* one?"

"My father couldn't stand the sight of me after that. I went to live with Mark . . ."

"Only *live* mother he knew!" Bleoberis guffawed, nudging Blamor with his elbow. "Aside from the dead one!"

Tristram fixed his grey eyes on Blamor. "*I* know justice! My *live* mother" – inclining his head ever-so-slightly, cuttingly toward Bleoberis – "my stepmother, tried to murder me, Blamor. She wanted my inheritance for her son. I saved her, and my father sent me away. Don't talk to me about whoring for patronage!"

Bleoberis laughed. "His father was out whoring when his live mother bore him and became a dead one!"

Tristram abruptly turned away. He called to Gouvernail. The squire trotted to his side and Tristram began to speak to him in a low voice. Gouvernail nodded, nodded. "Yes, sir!"

Bleoberis trumpeted, "He'll *kill* you, Tristram! My brother will *kill* you! This is the seed of King Ban you're trying to hoodwink with your sad tales. Blamor'll give you something to be *triste* about – won't you, Blamor?"

Blamor clapped a hand over Bleoberis's mouth.

"Here, now! Here, now!" King Carados, red in the face and sweating like a pig, shouted after them, striding nearer. "This isn't proper! Damn me if this is proper! You shut up now! Say it with your lances, where God can decide, or Arthur'll scribe his judgement on our hides, me and Scots here – with a knife, *in capitals*. Dieu et son droit, sirs!"

Bleoberis pried his brother's hand away. "What's the matter with you?"

"This knight may well be my death. Look at him! He's an oak, he's an iron pike, and his steed is hellfire. Why did you lie to me?"

Blamor watched his brother flap his lips, shrug, cock his head, and finally decide to be angry. "This is the thanks I get! You think that petrified foreskin of a man can stand against Lancelot's nephew, a knight of the Round Table? You shame us, little brother!" Bleoberis's high dudgeon gave place to an ingratiating smile. He shook his beard at Blamor. "No, Agwisance will lose everything, don't you see, and if we play our cards right, we'll have his fiefdom, you and I, and all its wine and wenches!"

"*We?*" Blamor charged ahead of him to the chapel.

Bleoberis shouted after him, but Blamor kept right on walking. There was a rage in his voice that Blamor hadn't heard since their boyhood. "That's right – insult your big brother! You know, Blamor, they say that Cain was a bad boy, and God tattooed him and sent him east of Eden and all, but who knows? Maybe 'twas a fine, healthy tattoo – and I hear east of Eden isn't a bad place at all. Lots of wenches and wine there, I hear – and no goddam Abel to pull your chain, ey?"

The chapel doors were just now edging open; the priest emerged. He stood on a stone landing, rubbing his hands together and blinking as if sunlight were new to him.

Bleoberis caught up to Blamor, laid his hand on his shoulder and cooed, "Just see you don't shame us, Blamor!"

A madman with a cross shaved on his head was chained to a railing near the cross. Someone had dressed him in a choirboy's gown, but it would not stay on him long. He clawed at it, drooling and blathering, sometimes making a sentence. When the doors swung wide and daylight bathed him, he stood spread-eagle against the lattice, blinking, as the priest had done. His head jerked like a monkey's from nobleman to squire, inspecting each as he paraded in.

"Gawd . . .!" Carados threw up his arms.

"Gold!" aped the madman.

". . . I mean, by the five wounds of Christ, is this *necessary*, father?"

"What – *Leo*, your majesties? Does he offend, sirs? The man's absent his wits since his wife and children died of a fever, God have mercy! I shackle him near the rood: let him see every mass, says I, and Christ will wipe his mind clean as ever a mother swiping her baby's buns. I pray your lordships indulge poor Leo this favor – by your leave and by God's good mercy!"

"Goggle murky?" said Leo. He started to weep, then stopped, all for no reason.

The King of Scots had been whispering something in Carados's ear. Carados nodded. "Puh! I suppose I don't care, if nobody else does. Just see he keeps out of the way and holds his piss."

The priest stroked Leo on his crisscross, then retrieved the reliquary from the altar, an ornate pewter box with sapphires set like fruits in branching, Italic swirls. "Saint Sebastian's thumb bone," he said.

"Bastard's thimble!" said Leo.

Throughout the mass, Leo moved his head as a man would whose eyes were fixed in their sockets, darting to follow the wafer, the hand in benediction, the bowing head, or whatever moved most. And Leo aped the words – his private Cluniac *Messe des Fous*.

Tristram swore his mendacious oath – *Agwisance's mendacious oath* – over the reliquary; then Blamor swore his contrary oath – *or was it Bleoberis's mendacity he aped*? Then they kissed the Bible, each pronouncing his "*Pax vobiscum*," but Leo hissed, "*Pox upon you*!" and in a burst of lucidity, added, "Death, all! All are Death's!"

Then to the lists. Blamor sat on a carpet for Edmond to dress him in his mail and breast-plate, pauldrons at the shoulders, poulaines at the toes, the iron skirt about his waist . . .

"Is something the matter, sir? Does it chafe?"

"Never mind. Get on with it!"

As Edmond cinched, strapped and clapped him into his carapace, Blamor watched, as if from the grave, his judges, King Carados and the King of Scots. They were settling onto their camp chairs in the loge, with the moat behind them and the midpoint of the field before them. Agwisance sat nearby, and Blamor wondered if that could be quite right, for a party to the dispute to be so intimate with its judges. It was too late for such a consideration, of course.

"The helmet, Edmond. Try the vision slot." For a moment, while Edmond adjusted his visor, Blamor thought he spied through the ventails another person in the judges' loge, an old, white-haired woman standing behind them with a hand on each of their shoulders. Then Edmond lifted the helmet off his head to make an adjustment, and she was gone – a flash from the metal, sunlight glancing off the moat.

Farther off, between the bridge and the northern rampart, a man and woman with their two raucous children struggled to stretch the fabric over a second loge. It was the burgher whose house Arthur had expropriated for the brothers de Ganis. He had brought a caged bird along, jugs of ale, and spice roots for the boy and girl to chew. Just now, despite his ostentatious dress – brocade and ruffles – he was not looking so elegant. When he reached up on tiptoe to pull the canopy snug, he hiked up his blouse, baring his navel in front and part of his backside behind. His wife knocked the children's heads together and jabbered at the bird, trying to make it sing. It would not.

Bleoberis stood midway between the two loges, at a polite remove, gazing coolly at the judges, the horses, and the men. Bleoberis's last words to Blamor – to his *back*, actually, as Blamor strode to the lists, still trying to riddle out the precise extent of his brother's deceit – had been these: "Yield to the orphan knight, by God, and you shame us all, remember!"

Tristram had already mounted. Gouvernail was handing up his lance with an adroitness that made Blamor anxious at his own squire's fumblings with thongs and hinges. Tristram trotted his ebon charger crosswise at the far end of the marked field. Good, gentle Tristram pulled suddenly at the reins to make it rear up and spit fire, it seemed like – an adolescent thing to do, but effectively terrifying. *What was it that happened to men when they mounted horses caparisoned for war? Was it Death Himself,* Mors, *preparing* les doux maux, *taking possession of the man, as Blamor and Bleoberis had taken possession of the burgher's house?* The burgher's family cheered at Tristram's display; their little girl saluted with half a capon.

Edmond gazed at Sir Tristram. Blamor had to lift his hand: "The other gauntlet, boy!" The gauntlet placed, Blamor hugged Edmond and maneuvered himself to his feet and into the saddle, Edmond supporting him. He thought of Jesus being hoisted on the rood. That first precarious moment, finding his balance in the solitude of his iron casket, he felt nauseated, weak, no instrument of Death, but Death's breakfast. His horse would not stand still; it kept dancing under him, making him twist and torque to stay in the saddle. When he tried to think of Anselm, to squeeze out some revivifying anger, all that came was despair: the image of the sweet boy lying broken in the tilt-yard, just as Blamor soon would be – but for the witch's spell.

Someone was thrusting something at him; Blamor took hold of it, and he saw that it was his lance, and he heard Edmond say, "God be with you, sir."

"Dieu et mon droit, Edmond!" was the unthinking response.

Now the warriors faced each other from opposite sides of the field. Blamor located Tristram not by sight but by intuition. He fixed the butt of his lance against the fewter, lowered it, and charged headlong, like a man leaping from a castle window. His battle cry rang in his helmet like a falling man's scream. Tears streamed from his eyes, blurring his vision.

Skeletal fingers curled around Tristram's pauldrons – Blamor could see them now. He could see the straw-like hair whipping like a pennant behind Tristram's head. It was the forest witch, cheating Blamor! Between the drummings of the horses' hooves, he heard her cackle, "*Endurez, endurez . . .!*"

Now he understood who she was. "Elizabeth! Elizabeth!" Tristram had called to her in the forest. She was Tristram's dead mother, and Blamor's death.

The moment he saw that death, his own, real and palpable before him, the rune on Blamor's loins began to spin and swell. He fell through the rune into another world, into the world of a single heartbeat, a single breath, an infinite expanse of time hidden between the hoofbeats and between the numbered grains of the hourglass. The jousting field became a vast, dark plain in which drab, hooded hunchbacks bore corpses on biers draped in black. The dead were being carried to hollowed stones, where more hunchbacks sealed them in with lead and circled each stone, each corpse, with candles. When one of the hunchbacks fell, others bore him to his stone and sealed him in and circled him with fire. Sealed stones lay everywhere, everywhere there were biers on backs the shape of crosiers, and the earth sparkled everywhere with cold fire. The horizon was a ring of candleflame, the witch's rune.

Another pulse.

The woman with bandaged limbs was sealing what remained of her dog into one of the stones. She dripped molten lead into the seams of the split hollowed stone. She became aware of Blamor's gaze, and she looked up at him as if he were the sky. With her one good arm she pointed to another stone, and Blamor followed her gesture to a rock not yet quite sealed. Its corpse's death seeped out the unsealed edge like light through the keyhole of a shut door: fever. From a stone nearby, another's death shone, an ecstasy of pain: impalement on a spear, a warrior's death. There were many more.

Another breath.

Heat lightning illumined the field, and Blamor saw that on every stone the same single word was chiselled, the word the thunder said, one of the four words the witch had cut below the rune on Blamor's skin:

DROIT

Another hoof beat.

The knights met. The last thing Blamor saw before the impact was Sir Marhaus's shield, the one Tristram had taken from the Irish knight when he'd split the man's skull. There was an explosion so intense that Blamor could not tell if it were sight or sound or pain he sensed. Sparks flew up where the metal covering of Sir Tristram's lance point struck Blamor's breastplate. He felt his chest collapse and breath and spit shoot out of him as he was propelled backwards over his horse's croup. He crashed to the ground.

He landed on his heels, and then the momentum of his fall tumbled Blamor backward over his head, so that he ended with elbows and knees on the dirt, still holding his shield in one hand and, in the other, a few slivers of his shattered lance.

He saw stars, he felt his skin turn to stars: it wasn't pain so much as a sort of physical amazement. By sheer will, he righted himself and drew his sword. The witch had lied. Bleoberis had lied. Everyone had lied. The rune did not shield Blamor; it *damned* him. He felt the hag's arms like ropes around him, holding him still for Tristram's thrust. His hand, its own animal, found the pommel of his sword – the feel of it surprised Blamor – and he pulled it from his scabbard. He lifted his shield like a battle standard and brandished the sword high over his head. "Fight me, you murderer's whore!"

His impulse was to thrust his blade twixt his own gut and groin to skin the tattoo off him. Instead, he boiled, he screamed, and he made for Tristram, sword aloft, bellowing, threatening to cripple Tristram's horse with a mad swipe.

Tristram dismounted. He swung the dead man's shield before him. His sword was already in his hand, held at the angle of an executioner's axe. Around Tristram's shoulder the forest witch glowered.

Inertia and blind rage carried Blamor forward. In all those pounds of plate and mail, it would have taken more of a superhuman effort to stop than to keep on charging. The heaving mass he nearly tripped over, he realized, was his own fallen horse. *Never mind!*

Without quite knowing how he had got there, Blamor found himself squarely in the path of Tristram's blade. He heard it clang against chain mail in the pit of his own raised arm, he heard it bite into the metal links, he heard a softer sound, like a butcher's stroke – he *felt* nothing yet – and he saw his death again, as sure and present as earth and rain.

Again, at the sight of it, he was in the witch's tattoo. The dog woman was upset with Blamor: why had he peeked into the wrong stone? It was the *next* one she'd meant to point to . . . and there was Anselm, dead, in a hollowed stone – *DROIT* – half-sealed with lead and circled by candles. His death spoke to Blamor from the stone:

> *The constable struck me to hurry me. I fell. My head hit a stone, and my life flowed away from me. My soul endured the sweet pangs of death. I saw the man shriek and call my name, but I was no more . . .*

A hunchback finished sealing the stone.

Blamor felt sharp metal at his ribcage. "Dieu!" He retreated a step and held his shield before him like a cottage roof against an avalanche. It was as thin as the lie that had brought him to Camelot. Tristram hacked at it. Blamor watched ridges form and light shine through small holes where the metal had wrinkled and split under Tristram's blade. Now and then he was able to push Tristram's sword aside with a thrust of the shield, and so manage a swipe of his own. *Was it Tristram's blood or his own that spattered the tall knight's breastplate?* Hot, sticky blood flowed inside Blamor's armor too. He smelled it. He smelled his own death – and changed worlds.

Not fair! Not fair! was all that Blamor could think, just as when he was a boy, playing soldier with Bleoberis and Anselm. There were the three of them now, in the field of stones and candles, children again, fighting as they used to, with plantain spikes for swords: strike the tiny green flower from the enemy's spike, and you have killed him . . .!

> *. . . Anselm, skinnymalinks, all in a heap, with eyes blank and round as communion wafers, is staring up at his fractured spike. Blamor sits on Bleoberis's chest, about to take the prize, when suddenly, with perfect aplomb, his brother says, "You can't win, you know," and Blamor, for the briefest moment, is so astonished and confused that Bleoberis throws him off, whacks the flower from little Blamor's spike, and declares himself champion.*
>
> *"Not fair! Not fair!" But it is fair – Bleoberis convinces him of it, Bleoberis who always knows more and knows it first and has done it first, and Blamor always comes after, when Bleoberis has told him the way . . .*

. . . When Blamor came to himself again, he found his shield in tatters. He dropped it, freeing his left hand to grasp his sword arm above the elbow to steady it; Tristram's first blow had sapped half his right arm's strength. Now Blamor's game must be to attack so ferociously that he'd have no need to defend.

Tristram's blade flashed out at him again and again, his death again and again singing to him – but on the field of stones and candles he saw Tristram, cold and white, in *his* hollowed stone – *DROIT:*

> *I harped for my love, la Belle Isoud, Aqwisance's daughter. My uncle, her husband, crept behind me and slew me where I sat singing. The sweet pangs of death I felt. The last thing I heard was Isoud weeping . . .*

Blamor was the thunder over the field of stones. He blasted the hunchbacks and set them scurrying. Corpses tumbled from dropped biers, their dead limbs flailing at ghastly angles. He didn't want to know these things. The past was hard enough; now future things afflicted him as well. Damn the witch! Damn Tristram's undead Elizabeth! Kill him!

"Kill him!" Bleoberis was shouting, and Blamor de Ganis realized that it was all over. He lay broken in the tilt-yard dirt with Tristram's sword at his throat. All that was left was to say, "I yield," but he woke to Tristram and the lists and Camelot already shaking his head *no,* already refusing to yield; just that much power remained to him, his second-son's defiance, as the sawblade of Elizabeth's rune spun and cut at his power of will.

He heard Tristram speak to the kings, their judges: "I beg you, my lords, let me spare him for his uncle Sir Lancelot's sake."

King Carados and the King of Scots had left the shelter of their loge and ventured closer to the marked field. Agwisance was with them. "If Sir Tristram can forgive him, I suppose I will," the Irish king said. "He fought like the devil, didn't he?"

"Yes" – this was Carados's gravelly voice – "there's no need to kill the man. God has judged by sword and blood, and de Ganis must see his error, as we all do, by Christ!"

"Kill him!" Now Blamor realized it was *he* his brother wanted killed, and not Sir Tristram! "Kill him," said Bleoberis, "rather than let Blamor declare himself recreant and shame us all. Honor my brother by killing him!" After a pause, he added, in a milder voice, "It's for love of him I say it," and Blamor closed his eyes. Nothing mattered now.

"No!" barked Carados. He murmured something nasty that Blamor could not quite hear, then trumpeted, "We three concur with Tristram. Let the knight live."

But Sir Blamor de Ganis had already set upon a different, darker path. While Tristram, battle weary, regarded the kings, still holding his sword at Blamor's throat, Blamor began to raise his head – it took straining at the belly to do it, invoking the long chain of muscles from groin to chin, and the effort made his skin burn again where the witch had written, "DIEU ET MON DROIT!" He felt the cold metal touch his neck and press deeper.

Then, in the space between breaths, an odd glimmer caught his eye. It was the gap in the edge of Tristram's blade, a foot or so from the point, where a sliver of iron had broken off in Sir Marhaus's skull. In a second, his own blood would spurt up and fill it . . .

. . . But Sir Marhaus stopped him. From his hollowed stone in a circle of candles, the dead knight spoke:

> *It was Tristram's blade, but* my own *death! It came to me sweetly at last!* Mon droit! Mon droit!

The witch's stone was empty, but her voice echoed in it, like the shimmer in a horn's bell when the breath has ceased:

> *I died before I could suckle my Tristram; such was my right. Now I nurse him with the milk of death, him and all who break lances with him. I put on my withered old body, shake the grave's muck from my wrinkles, and I make men wise. Thus my soul endures the pain of bearing and losing my Tristram!*

Other stones flew open, their dead men pushing them apart like dragons hatching. Agwisance was there, and Carados, and Scots. "*Mon droit!* My right!" they wailed. "My death is my only right, at last!" And the burgher and his wife and their children, all dead at last, cried from their stones, "See! *Mon droit!*"

Lancelot was there, and all the other knights, their bones poking through their skin like pens through wet parchment. They pointed spectral fingers toward Bleoberis, and he, from his stone, said:

> *I found Sir Lancelot a monk at a hermitage between two hills where the Bishop of Canterbury sang mass, and he enjoined me to go to the Holy Land. Many Turks I slew there with Sir Bors, Sir Ector and other Christian knights, but on a Good Friday, as I rode across Solomon's porch, my horse knee-deep in Saracen blood, a paynim soldier slew me. The sweet pangs of death came upon me, and I inherited my right,* mon droit, *this hollow rock, my death.*

"Bleoberis! Brother!" Blamor cried; his voice was the thunder. "Are you done lying? Is *death* the right you always boasted of?" Bleoberis said nothing more, but pointed to a rock where Blamor himself peeked out – a corpse – and the dead Blamor said:

> *I was with my brother in the hermitage between the hills, at last, and I died with him on Solomon's porch, for the glory of God – this was my right!*

Blamor de Ganis lay broken in the tilt-yard dirt with Tristram's sword at his throat – but his death was not yet due him. He let his head fall back, and Tristram threw down his sword. King Carados, the King of Scots, and Agwisance stood over him now, and the judges' bailiffs knelt to help him to his feet. Edmond hurried to remove the heaviest pieces of armor, careful where blood might spring when a wound was freed of the pressure. Tristram took his hand, and Agwisance came nearer. Behind Agwisance, Bleoberis hovered, all darkness.

On his feet at last, Blamor fell into Tristram's arms, into the arms of the man who would die harping for his beloved. Bleoberis, his fellow corpse at Solomon's porch, came nearer tentatively, and Blamor opened his arms to him. Bleoberis, with a dark, confused look, suffered himself to be drawn in.

As they all embraced, Blamor spied through a rent in Tristram's hauberk, the embroidery on his *gambois*, "DIEU ET MON DROIT!" and his dead mother's rune.

"Forgive me!" Blamor said.

Sir Brandiles in THE GEST OF SIR BRANDILES

Kurt Roth

One of the great French romances tells of the battle between Sir Brandiles and Gawain over the honour of Brandiles's sister which Gawain had despoiled. Sir Brandiles is sometimes believed to be the same as Sir Brian of the Isles, who falls in league with Sir Kay against Arthur. Some scholars believe that Sir Brian was based on a contemporary historical character, an illegitimate son of Alain de L'Isle. Alain was the Bishop of Auxerre in the 1150s and wrote a commentary on Geoffrey of Monmouth's Prophecies of Merlin. *It is more than likely that his son, Brian, would have been fascinated with the Arthurian legends and may even have contributed to them himself.*

Kurt Roth (b. 1969) is an illustrator, musician and martial artist whose short stories and reviews have appeared in small press and literary magazines since 1989, but this marks his first professional appearance. He was attracted to the Arthurian legend when he saw John Boorman's film, Excalibur *(1981). He writes: "I'm drawn to the thematic scope of Arthurian romance. From one angle, these tales can be seen as unadorned adventures. Viewed from another, they explore our greatest joys and sorrors. Maybe it's the simple template of knights and ladies and shining swords that makes for this amazing facility. All I know is, I keep coming back. We all do."*

He found her on the forest floor, in the place she had called her Secret Place, on a bed of bright colored leaves. He found her by following a scent he knew too well. A stench that belonged on battlefields.

It was the reek of the slowly dying.

He didn't recognize it at first. It didn't belong here. This was home. A world of sweet bread and clean linen, thick blankets and warm fires. This was a place one could leave, as Sir Brandiles had left it, and expect it go on unchanged. But it *had* changed while he was away. Someone, somewhere near, lay dying.

He reined in and turned to Erec, his brother and squire. "Do you smell that?"

"Smell what?"

"Never mind," he said, dismounting. "My sword. Now."

The moment it was in hand he charged into the wilderness. He had no trouble picking his way. As a child, he had played in these woods; as a man, he had hunted them. He knew every twig, every stone. And the further he ran, the harder he pushed himself, for with each step he became more aware of his immediate surrounds, more conscious – terribly conscious – of his destination. That boulder there. The ravine. The way the two birches formed a low canopy. And the wall of tangled conifers.

This was the Secret Place. His sister's private glade, where she came to be alone.

The reek of death was overwhelming.

"Ragnelle?" he cried. But there was no answer.

He screamed for her again as he chopped at the wall of brush, heedless of how angry she might be at him for wrecking it. *Be angry!* he thought. *Please, dear God, let her fury scorch me to ash*. He had stood outside so many times – but had never learned the way in. No one but her knew it. So he hacked wildly at the brambles, damning his sword with every stroke for not being a hatchet. After what seemed an eternity he managed to push his way through.

What he saw . . .

"*In nomine Patris*," he said – or tried to say. The words caught in his chest as he crossed himself.

There she lay on a bed of leaves. His sister. Bathed in blood, her dress torn away. Her limbs shot out at odd angles, snapped like so much kindling.

But she wasn't dead. Not yet. Her eyes were open, her mouth moving wordlessly.

Brandiles fell at her side. "Oh, my sweet Ragnelle," he said, words coming now as he tried in vain to patch her dress together. "This can't be happening. Not to you." The dress was shredded and sopping with blood. He stripped off his tunic and draped it across her naked breasts. "Can you speak? How did this – who – ?"

Her lips trembled, but only a thick, gurgling sound emerged as she spat blood.

"Who?" he said. "Who did this?"

She closed her eyes.

"No! Don't go!"

Her jaw clenched.

"Please, God, don't take her – "

Her left arm moved. Against his knees, Brandiles felt it buck. It must have been excruciating for her to move it at all. It was visibly broken in at least two places. Brandiles scrambled out of the way, in case she was trying to point at something. Then he saw it. Her hand was curled into a claw and a chain – gold or silver or steel he couldn't tell for all the blood – began to pour from her palm.

"The chain?" he muttered, as if she could answer. He snatched at it, careful not to jar her. He pulled it slowly until it caught. There was a pendant of some kind on the end. He pulled a little harder and it came free.

He recognized it immediately. The chain, beneath the crusted blood, would be silver. The pendant was a crystal – a six-sided gem of deep red, as long and as thick as Ragnelle's little finger. It belonged to his best friend.

Gawain.

Brandiles dangled it in front of her face and said, "Gawain? Is this his doing?"

Her eyes grew round with terror and her lips began to tremble as she tried once more to speak.

"Please, you have to tell me," he said, though he hated to draw her through any memory of it. "If I'm to avenge you, I must know."

She closed her eyes. Tears cut channels through the blood on her temples.

"Did Gawain do this?" he said.

She opened her eyes, met his gaze. And blinked once, slowly.

"He did?"

Another slow blink. Then she closed her eyes completely.

"Ragnelle?" She didn't answer. "Ragnelle? Don't go yet! Your confession! You must have the Last Rites!" Scrambling for a cross, he plunged his sword into the ground beside them.

She started at the force of it and her eyes opened, again filled with terror. Or was it sorrow?

"What is it?" he said. "Mouth the words, my love. You don't have to speak."

Her lips began working.

Bay . . .

"It's all right," he said. "God will hear you."

Bee . . .

"Bay bee," he repeated.

Like his sword in the earth, the word sank home.

"Baby?" he said.

Her face screwed into a knot and she mouthed it again. *Baby*.

"Gawain's baby?" he said, reaching for her belly, careful not to touch. "It can't be."

Baby, she said.

Then finally, mercifully, her tears ceased and her trembling stilled.

Brandiles pulled her head up into his lap and cradled it while he stroked her hair and washed her face with his tears. In his mind, he stumbled through what little he knew of the Last Rites, praying that Christ would take her into His care no matter what her useless brother got wrong.

He was still weeping some time later when he felt Erec's hand upon his shoulder.

"Is she . . . gone?" the boy whispered.

"Yes."

"But – what happened?"

Brandiles held up the pendant. "Gawain."

Then he clutched it tightly to his breast and he felt the fury fill him.

The first time Brandiles had seen the pendant was the day he met Gawain, on a fine afternoon in May, only a few months before. Gawain had come to the courtyard at Balallan from the south, on foot, having just landed at the docks. He was dark-eyed and haggard – as if he'd been to sea for weeks instead of days – but still managed to carry himself proudly, shoulders broad and square, stubbled chin held high. He was dressed in a tunic that was plain but for the devices it bore: a two-headed eagle beneath the royal wyvern-and-crown. Together, these marked him as none other Sir Gawain – a prince of Orkney and knight of Arthur's Table.

Brandiles felt an instant dislike for the man.

"Who's *that*?" said Ragnelle, who stood gawking at Brandiles' side. He told her. "Are you sure?" she said. "We really should find out for certain, don't you think?"

"Why would we want to do that?"

"Well, if we're to be good hosts – "

"*We* are not," said Brandiles. "That is up to Father."

"And what would Father say if he knew we had passed up the chance to demonstrate his hospitality for such an esteemed visitor?"

"Who says he has to know?"

"Brandiles! I think you're jealous."

"Jealous?" He waved the notion away. "Of Gawain the debaucher?"

She laughed. "Perhaps his sword is bigger than yours?"

He no sooner began to protest than Ragnelle took him by the arm and dragged him toward the newcomer. "Sir Gawain? Sir Gawain!" she cried.

Gawain's head swivelled their way and his face lit with a wide grin. He strode briskly to them and sketched a bow.

"My lady," he said. "And good sir. You mark me well. I am Gawain of Orkney, at your service."

Brandiles rolled his eyes – an action observed only by Ragnelle, who elbowed him in the ribs. He shot her a scowl, cleared his throat, and said, "Welcome, Sir Gawain. I am Brandiles. This is my sister Ragnelle."

Ragnelle extended her hand. Gawain took it in his own, studied it for the briefest moment, then kissed it gently and stood. To Brandiles's surprise, Gawain's attention then shifted not from Ragnelle's delicate hand to her shining emerald eyes, but instead to Brandiles himself.

"You are Sir Brian," said Gawain.

Brandiles suppressed an urge to grit his teeth. "If it pleases you, yes. I am sometimes called Sir Brian of the Isles. But in truth only my father calls me Brian. Please, call me Brandiles."

"Sir Brandiles, then. It's very good to meet you. After all, it is you I'm here to see."

"Really?" said Brandiles.

"Really?" said Ragnelle.

"Really," said Gawain. "I've come to invite you to court."

"Arthur's court? Have I done something wrong?"

Gawain chuckled. "On the contrary, sir, you've done everything right. You see, I was not long ago on the mainland, in Melvaig, where I heard a man speak endlessly of your deeds. Since it's my duty to send my liege any man who might bolster our ranks, I addressed this gentleman. He was called Meliot. Sir Meliot of Logurs, who professed to be your sworn brother. He's the one told me where I could find you. And here I am."

Brandiles could scarcely believe it, and said as much. "Meliot has served well yet again. Imagine the company we'd keep if I employed *two* liars."

They had a good laugh, after which Ragnelle insisted they join their father, Sir Lac, in the great hall where they might embarrass Brandiles further and enjoy some excellent food while they were at it.

As the afternoon wore on, Brandiles found himself actually liking this Gawain. They had many things in common – not the least of which were the hard-willed women in their lives. By evening they were sitting at a table together in a dim corner of the hall, just the two of them, sipping rich, woody wine and enjoying long silences.

"She reminds me of my aunt Morgana," said Gawain, breaking the latest lull.

"Who? Ragnelle?" Brandiles watched as she taunted Erec and their father at the high table. "In what way?"

After some consideration, Gawain said, "Her fire, mostly. They both have a mischievous air about them. As if they live to cause trouble. Do you know what I mean?"

"I should say that I do."

"Look here," said Gawain, fumbling at his collar. He pulled forth a silver chain, on the end of which was an odd pendant. A six-sided crystal, pointed on both ends, and wrapped with silver wire for the mount. It looked black in the candlelight. Gawain pulled it over his head and dangled it in front of Brandiles. "Have a look at that." As it twirled it seemed alternately opaque and translucent, with a spark of red flaring at its core.

"What is it?"

"A charm, given me by my aunt. She claims it imbues its wearer with great strength in battle. 'It stokes the inner fires and makes them burn more brightly,' says she."

"And does it work?"

"Well, I don't know about that. But it keeps her in my thoughts, which is always inspiring."

"It certainly is beautiful. Is she?"

"Oh, yes. She and Ragnelle both." He watched the crystal twirl. "Says everything that needs be said, doesn't it? It embodies their grace and their spirit. It stirs the hearts of men."

"Careful there," said Brandiles, making a point of glaring at his new friend. "One might think you're falling in love with my sister."

"One might."

"Or that you're smitten with your auntie."

Gawain raised an eyebrow, then burst out laughing. "I'm so glad I made this journey. Boats like me little, but it will all have been worth it if I can bring Arthur a new jester."

Brandiles grinned.

"Of course," said Gawain, "I'll need a few days to rest before I dare board another ship."

"Of course you will. And you can while away the hours with failed attempts at wooing my sister."

"Oh ho. I'm to fail then."

"No man has succeeded yet."

"Methinks I perceive a challenge."

"You most certainly do not," said Brandiles. "Your reputation precedes you, sir. You are a famed reprobate. What makes you think I'd let you anywhere near that sweet young lady?"

"Well, I should think I'm sufficiently handsome."

"True. You would have beautiful children together. But it'll take more than that."

"I'm healthy as a horse."

"Except on ships."

"I'm a son of nobility. She would have a good life."

"She already has one."

"I'm also famous," said Gawain.

"So is her brother Brandiles, from what I hear. You'll have to do better."

"What if I were to tell you I think I could love her?"

"*Think* you could?"

"Oh, the devil with it. I'm sure I could."

"You could."

"I think I may already."

"There you are thinking again."

"Right! You have caught me, sir!" cried Gawain at the top of his lungs. He stood and banged his cup against the table. As the others' attention turned his way, he strode across the room to stand before Ragnelle. There he dropped to his knees, took her hand, and kissed it with dramatic flourish. She seemed bemused – until he opened his mouth and shouted, "I cannot deny it! Though I've known you only a few hours, dear Ragnelle, I must declare: I love you with all my heart!"

Ragnelle frowned at Gawain, then spied Brandiles in his corner and gave him a hot stare.

Gawain stood next to her and turned toward Brandiles. "Will that do?"

"Yes," he muttered, thankful for the gloom that veiled not his abashment, but his joy. "That will do very well, thank you."

And that was the way of things. They decided to wait a few days for Gawain to recover from the first leg of his travels. In that time, Arthur's knight became more and more deeply bewitched by Ragnelle, and she by him. When it came time to depart and Brandiles stood ready on the dock with Erec, his horses, and gear, Gawain arrived late with nothing in tow.

"You pack so little for such a long journey," said Brandiles.

Gawain winced. "I'm afraid I won't be accompanying you."

"That much I had gathered."

"I can't leave her, Brandiles. Not right now."

"Shall we wait then?"

"No," said Gawain, a shade too quickly. "You go on. Arthur isn't expecting you, but I've written a letter that should serve you admirably." He reached into his tunic and pulled forth a folded leaf of parchment. It snagged on his pendant and pulled it free as well.

"Ah, your Aunt Morgana's charm," said Brandiles. "You'll need the strength if you keep on with Ragnelle, you know."

"I know."

So Brandiles and Erec went on. They never did venture as far as Camelot. They caught up with Sir Meliot in Melvaig and joined him for a hunt. Then for another. As it happened, they stayed through Midsummer's Night and on into autumn. The truth was Brandiles didn't have the gall to beg Arthur's leave, with or without Gawain's endorsement. He was just a boy from the isles. A boy with a title and holdings, true; a boy with a sword and the skill to put it to good use – but he was no knight of the Table Round.

In the end, with winter not far off, he returned to his isles.

And as he staggered out of the woods onto the road south of

Balallan – as his arms grew leaden under the weight of Ragnelle's corpse and his mind buckled under the mass of his grief – he wondered if Morgana's pendant would give him the strength to strike her nephew down.

He delivered Ragnelle's body to the great hall. He didn't expect to find Gawain there and he wasn't disappointed. Did anyone know where the butcher might be? He was last seen that afternoon, when he and Ragnelle asked the steward to get them some food from the livery cupboard.

"Are you sure it was Gawain?" said Sir Lac, his craggy face moist with tears.

"Yes," said Brandiles. "We found his sword discarded some ways further on."

"And his tunic," said Erec, presenting both the weapon and the garment. "Left by a muddied spot in the stream."

The lines in Sir Lac's face deepened.

"Father," said Brandiles, "I must go. Now. I'm sorry I can't stay to comfort you. I pray that if I bring you the devil's head, it will be comfort enough."

"A cold comfort, indeed," said Sir Lac. "And if he kills my oldest son, too? What then?"

Brandiles began to speak, but Erec cut him off. "If there's any man who can best Sir Gawain, it's Brandiles, father. He's more skilled than any knight at Arthur's Table." He met Brandiles's gaze dead on, daring him to say otherwise.

"The squire is now a judge of knightly prowess," said the old man, bowing his head until it touched his chest. "Go then. And Erec – you go with him."

Brandiles said, "He can't help me, Father."

"I don't pretend that he could. But he can tend to your wounds when it's over."

Brandiles nodded. *Or bring my body home.*

The ship was still moored as it should have been but Gawain was nowhere to be seen, so they went to the inn in Balallan – and there he was. Sitting in a corner, bleary-eyed, sodden, and alone.

Brandiles thundered through everything in his path and seized Gawain by his still-damp hair.

"On your feet!" he screamed, slamming him against the wall. "On your feet and outside, if you're not a coward!"

Gawain sputtered, his breath heavy with bitter spirits. "You're . . . home? But – "

"OUT!" It was enough to rattle the walls.

Gawain lurched to his feet and went for the door, looking over his shoulder every step of the way. Outside, he said, "What's this all about? Did . . . did Arthur refuse to see you?" The inn's patrons had followed and other townsfolk were gathering in the street.

"Don't play games with me, you bastard. I should kill you where you stand." He turned to Erec. "His sword. Give it to him."

Erec, his face more twisted with grief that Brandiles had imagined possible, said, "Why should I? Let him die like the beast that he is. You've led him to slaughter. Now finish the job."

"Erec," said Brandiles. "His sword. Don't make this harder than it already is."

The boy hesitated, but drew Gawain's blade – the length of it still crusted with blood – and handed it over silently.

Gawain stared at it like something foreign. "What's this? I don't understand."

"It's quite simple," said Brandiles. "You are going to die for your crimes against my sister and my family."

"This is about Ragnelle?"

Brandiles felt the pendant grow warm against his chest and his heart filled with rage. "Enough!" he said, and he struck. Hard overhand at Gawain's head. Gawain barely countered in time, and he stumbled back from the force of it.

"By our Lady – you really mean to kill me!"

"That I do," said Brandiles. He feinted at Gawain's head, but the knight countered smoothly this time, looking not at all surprised as Brandiles reversed the feint and went for his arm. Gawain deflected the blow with the flat of his blade.

"Very well," said Gawain. "I will fight if I must, but if I'm to slay you in my own defence, I would like to know why."

Brandiles felt the world going red around the edges. "Don't play the fool with me. You know very well why."

Gawain was aghast. "If this is about what's happened between Ragnelle and me – if this is how you treat a brother – then I should be happy to kill you."

"Do your best."

"Erec," said Gawain, turning to the boy, "look at him. Look at his eyes! He's gone mad."

Brandiles turned, too. "Have I now?"

He expected the boy to goad him further into the action he

so desperately desired, but upon meeting Brandiles's gaze, Erec's expression mouldered from rage to terror.

"Brandiles?" he whispered.

"What's wrong with you, boy? Don't turn on me now!"

"But he's right. Your *eyes* – "

"Damn my eyes!" he screamed. "Damn them for ever seeing this devil as kin!" And he attacked again, on a wave of fury that boiled up from his guts and flowed through him like molten pitch. He stepped in toward Gawain and slashed at his left arm. The knight tried to counter, but was too slow or too weak to turn it away. Brandiles's blade chopped through his sleeve, into the meat of his forearm. Gawain wailed and tried to deflect the blow that followed, but Brandiles beat him again, this time slicing through his left shoulder nearly to the joint.

Somehow, Gawain managed to spin away and open a distance between them. "Sweet Jesu!" he cried. "Your eyes are afire!" To the spectators, he said, "He's bewitched, I tell you!"

They gaped at Brandiles then and began to slink away. Like weasels. Drifting back, back into the shadows.

Don't do this, Sir Brandiles, they said, their voices fading with every word. *There is an evil upon you.*

He swung his blade wildly and they disappeared.

"Brandiles," said Gawain. "Look at me."

"Look at you?" he heard himself rasp. "I'd as soon drink your blood. You raped my sister. You beat her and left her to die unshriven!"

"No!"

"Her and the baby both," he went on. "Is that why you did it? The great Sir Gawain won't be caught siring a bastard?"

Gawain's handsome face was etched with confusion and terror. "A baby? But it's not true! I didn't – I wasn't – "

Brandiles tore the pendant from his chest and threw it at Gawain. It bounced and landed in the dust. "As if your sword weren't enough," he said. "She gripped that in her dying hand."

Gawain scrabbled at his collar, bewildered.

"That's right," said Brandiles. "And that's the last anyone is going to say about it. It's time – "

But a spasm tore through him and the world began to flicker from red to black to red. The faces before him swam and melted together.

"It's . . . time . . ."

Red. Black.

The faces became one: that of a beautiful woman, whose blazing –

Red.

– eyes seared him to the core. He didn't know her, but he *knew* her. The lady. The lady. As he reached for her, she, like the weasels before her, slid back into the –

Black.

– and as she faded, she changed. The years peeled away and she became Ragnelle – Ragnelle, or something like her – pure and beautiful, falling back into the shadows, helpless, terrified, calling for him.

Brandiles . . .

"Brandiles?"

The cold night air was thick with sea salt and wood smoke. Erec hovered over him, pushing something in his face.

"Drink this."

"What?"

"It's water. Please, drink it. You're pale as bones."

"Gawain?"

"He's gone."

Brandiles knocked the water away and rolled onto his side. A few onlookers had returned, but the streets were mostly empty. Beyond the buildings, the gate to the south road gaped black and forbidding.

"Did he . . . the boat?"

"Yes, and it will have sailed by now."

"The pendant?"

"Gone."

Gone. Like Ragnelle. Like Gawain. Like everything.

Gone.

They laid her to rest in her secret glade, on the very spot where she had died. Brandiles visited her once a day, every day. He fashioned a gate where he had chopped through the hedge to gain entry. He used it each afternoon, still wondering how she ever got in without it. He quizzed her silently about that, and many other things.

Why had she trusted Gawain?

Why had he?

Why did she have to go?

Or perhaps he wasn't quizzing her at all. Perhaps it was his way of holding back from questioning God. When Brandiles was a little boy, his mother was felled by a fever. His father told him then, as they sealed her in a stone box, never to doubt His love for them; never to questions His ways.

"Father is a great man," said Brandiles to the empty glade. "Far greater than I can ever hope to be."

As the months went by Brandiles gained strength, his father withered, and Erec grew more and more distant. The boy's affection for Brandiles had somehow been quelled by whatever happened in the street that night. It had been replaced by an unreasoning fear.

Then again, that fear might be very well reasoned, for Brandiles's heart was brimming with a lust for vengeance. While he spent each afternoon by Ragnelle's grave, his mornings were devoted to prayer and to practice. Where he was skilled with a blade before, he would settle for nothing short of mastery now. He swore to himself – to his father, and Ragnelle; to his dead mother, and Erec – that if ever he laid eyes on Gawain again, it would mean a fight to death. And he fully intended to be the one left standing.

His chance came in the spring, on an afternoon like any other – excepting that when he swung the gate wide and stepped into the glade, he found himself staring at Gawain's back. The knight knelt before Ragnelle's grave, his head bowed in prayer.

"It would be so easy to kill you now," said Brandiles.

Gawain stiffened momentarily, then stood and turned around. "Hello, Brandiles."

"I can't believe you came here."

"I had no choice. I couldn't go on."

Brandiles snorted. "Couldn't you?"

Gawain peered around the glade. "No, I couldn't. It's been a strange time, these past few months. A hard winter."

As much as Brandiles wanted to hate him – as much as he wanted to slit his throat then and there – something in Gawain's expression raked at his heart. His eyes were empty and rimmed with purple, his skin pale and drawn. It was the face of a man being torn apart from the inside.

"I killed her," he said.

Brandiles nodded.

"I don't know why or how, but I did. I can see it in my dreams. Whenever I close my eyes, they're there. Ragnelle and the child. I can't escape them or myself, Brandiles. So I've come to make peace. I'll make it any way I can. Any way you choose."

Brandiles felt a sneer creep across his lips. "I see her, too," he said. "Every day. And when I do, all I can think of is the pain you brought on her. I have spent my days since in the company of a cold grave and colder steel. The only thing that will bring me peace is to bring her peace. The only way I can think to do it is to take your life as payment for hers."

It was Gawain's turn to nod. "An eye for an eye, then. That's as it must be." He dropped his arms to his sides and lifted his chin. "I am ready."

"But, your sword," said Brandiles, pointing to where it lay still sheathed beside the grave.

"I'm not going to fight you. I said I'd make peace any way you chose. You asked my life in return for hers. I offer it peaceably."

"What?"

"You heard me. I am prepared to die."

Brandiles looked down at his own blade. "I can't just kill you," he said. "I am charged to respect all weaknesses and constitute myself their defender. To do otherwise would be expressly against the code. I cannot kill an unarmed man."

"What would you have me do then?"

"'That shalt not recoil before thine enemy,'" quoth Brandiles. "It's your code as well as mine. Pick up your sword, man."

"You're not my enemy."

"Then fight because I ask it. You said you'd make peace however I chose. This is my choice. I swore that if ever I saw you again, I would fight you to the death."

Gawain bowed his head. "It's not really for her then, is it?"

"You're in no position to judge. Defend yourself."

"Very well." He leaned over, picked up his belt, unsheathed the blade, and assumed a guard position. "You know, I thought we would be brothers."

"I did too," said Brandiles, raising his own guard.

"Ready then?"

"Ready."

Brandiles made his first move swiftly, lunging to Gawain's left, which he hoped would still be weak from their first encounter. His hope was ill-placed. Gawain pivoted smoothly to his right and countered with a slash to Brandiles's sword hand. The blade bit into his wrist, drawing blood, and he cried out.

"Are you sure you wish to fight?" said Gawain.

"Dead certain," said Brandiles, and he struck again. This time he made a high cut for Gawain's right forearm. Gawain's response was exactly what it should have been – a simple parry, high, catching the top quarter of Brandiles's blade. But then Brandiles stepped in. Gawain fell back, clearly expecting to draw Brandiles with him. Instead, Brandiles jerked his blade back in a short, quick motion. Its own weight pulled it down. Then Brandiles shifted forward, coming in under Gawain's guard, and planted the tip of his sword squarely in the knight's upper arm.

Gawain screamed and tumbled backward. His sword fell across Ragnelle's grave.

"You bleed on my sister's deathbed," said Brandiles. "That falls out rather well, don't you think?"

Gawain clutched at his arm, trying desperately to staunch the flow of blood. It wouldn't work. The cut was too deep. Nothing short of tying it off would do, and perhaps even then it wouldn't be enough.

"I think you've killed me."

"Good," said Brandiles. He lowered his sword. "Then justice is done."

Gawain struggled to his feet. "Justice?" he said. Somewhere in the middle of the word, his voice changed tenor – from the high rasp of agony to the low rumble of distant thunder. "There is no justice."

When he looked up at Brandiles his eyes flickered with red fire. Below his burning face, the pendant glowed. It had tumbled free of his tunic when he fell. Now, out in the open, it flared like a tiny sun, too bright to gaze upon.

Morgana's charm! That was the key. It was the pendant that had done this evil. Not Gawain. Not Brandiles.

Morgana.

"Gawain," said Brandiles, "the crystal! Throw it away!"

But Gawain was beyond hearing. His face was as stolid as any statue. He grabbed his sword and got to his feet. He charged Brandiles, blade held high, ready to bring it down and crush his skull.

Brandiles did the only thing he could do. He charged Gawain and came in under the blow. He snatched at the pendant, taking it in his fist, and pulled with all his might. As he did, the thing burned him. Not just his hand, but the entirety of his body and mind. The fire was his fury and Gawain's mixed. He barely noticed as Gawain's sword came down and sank deep into the back of his leg. All he could feel was the fire that ripped at his brain. All he could see was his poor lost Ragnelle, writhing in agony as he beat her, as Gawain broke her – as their hands tore at her dress, pinned her down, and stripped everything from her that might be stripped.

Then the chain snapped.

The pendant flew.

The two men fell away from one another.

And the blazing red nightmare faded; faded to cool, cool green as the brothers who weren't brothers bled their lives into her grave.

He found her again in the Secret Place, as he lay on the spot where she died. He found her by following the sweet voice he knew so well, and missed so sore. A voice from beyond the grave.

He didn't recognize it at first. After all, it didn't belong here. This was the world of the living. A world of hatred and pain, of sorrow and loss. When one left this realm, as his dear Ragnelle had done, it was for ever more.

But she had come back. The voice told him so. The voice that drew him out of dying.

"Brian," she said. "Brian, you must wake up."

Brandiles forced his eyelids open.

She stood over him, pure and clean in white gowns that flowed like water. In her arms she held a thick bundle of linen. "Tend to your wound," she said. "Then see to Gawain. He'll die if you don't."

There was no room for questions. He tore his shirt into strips. He wrapped his thigh in the middle and knotted it as tight as he could manage. Then he crawled over and went to work on Gawain. He wondered though, as he did, if there was much point. The earth was so sodden with blood.

When he was finished, he said, "He loves you, you know."

She smiled and knelt beside Gawain then. She leaned over and kissed him on the mouth. And as her tears bathed him, his pale face seemed to color.

"I know," she said.

"Will he live?"

"He will now."

"And what of you?" said Brandiles, reaching out to dry her tears. "Are you alive? Have you come back to stay?"

"No, dear brother. I've come only to bear this gift. Then I must go on."

"Go on?"

She nodded.

He pointed at the bundle. "Is that it? The gift?"

"Yes."

"What . . . is it?"

She didn't respond with words at first. Instead, she held the bundle out to him. She placed it in his arms and uttered a single word; a word filled with pride; a word that was itself a gift from Heaven. A gift of forgiveness. It was a word that might never have been spoken, but for the grace of God.

She said, "Guinglain."

Then the swaddling fell away and Brandiles could see it was an infant. A baby boy. Guinglain. He had Ragnelle's eyes – Brandiles's eyes – and Gawain's nose. His mouth was scrunched up like old Sir Lac's. He seemed terribly concerned about something well beyond their comprehension.

"My nephew," said Brandiles. "But how?"

"Here," she said, gesturing at her grave, soaked through as it was with his blood and Gawain's. "Your love and your life is what did it. And here," she said, caressing her son's breast.

A pendant hung about the boy's neck. It was so transparent, so pristine, Brandiles hadn't noticed it. Like Morgana's charm, it dangled from a silver chain. But this charm was clear as rainwater.

"Now it will protect," said Ragnelle, and she brushed his cheek with a warm, soft hand. "Peace to you, my beloved. Watch over Guinglain. Watch over Gawain. I must be on my way."

Brandiles nodded, understanding. "I'm sorry you couldn't go before. I'm sorry I failed you."

"You did not fail," she said. "Look on this child now and speak no more of such things."

Brandiles did as instructed. And when finally he looked up from the child's wondrous face, a cool breeze brushed past, and Ragnelle was gone.

He had no real notion of how she'd managed to return, or how she might have brought this child into the living world – but she *had* done it. The proof was cradled in his arms, smiling up at Life. A gift from God, whose love could not be doubted or denied, and whose ways would never more be questioned.

Sir Yder in
MY LADY OF THE ASHES

Paul Finch

Yder appears in the Arthurian legends as an occasional companion of Gawain. He was renowned as a fighter of giants. In fact in some Celtic legends he appears as a giant. In the following story, in his quest to help a young maiden, he comes up against one of the fiercest giants of all.

Paul Finch (b. 1964) is a journalist and former police officer who used his early experiences to contribute scripts and storylines to the television series The Bill. *He has since contributed stories and essays to many magazines and has had many of his stories issued on a series of audiotapes such as* From the Graveyard *(1996),* Spilled Blood *(1996) and* Creatures of the Night *(1997). He was born and raised in Wigan in Lancashire which is where his interest in matters Arthurian began. He used to play on the banks of the River Douglas, enthused by a local belief that Arthur had once fought a battle there. Arthur did indeed fight a battle on the banks of the River Douglas, though scholars dispute over where that was. The general agreement is that it was in Lindsey, in Lincolnshire, but who's to say it wasn't in Wigan!*

1

The leper was late for her own funeral. So late that those who had gathered to watch were there before her. Many of them.

Yder and Polidamus tethered their horses, and had to push through ranks of villagers before they could see. The forest chapel was small and squat, built of rocks, with a roof of turf, the open space before it a glorious swathe of bluebells. Insects danced in the light shafting through the new canopy of leaves. The atmosphere was grim, however.

Yder glanced at his fellow spectators. Angles, to a man. A tough, untrusting breed in his experience. They were tall and strong, but surly, bred more as hunters than farmers, and hateful of their subservience to the British. Though many carried hoes, they wore the sheepskin of the dalesman rather than the coarse Hessian of the rood-hand. The faces beneath their hoods were broad and strong-boned.

Even so, when the leper appeared, they stepped back in a fearful wave. Yder and Polidamus watched. At first they saw only a priest, barefoot and clad in the black cowl of Benedict, approaching along the wooded path. He was praying, and with one hand giving blessings. With the other he swung a brazen censer, tailing purification fumes. The leper came next, walking slowly and stiffly.

The crowd fell silent. It was a girl – this was clear from the shape of her, but only from that. She was clad in a shroud, which had been tied at the waist with rope, and was swathed in linen bandages. Every inch of her was covered, her arms and legs bound separately. Even her head was wrapped, though straggles of fair hair hung down.

The priest stopped in the chapel door and turned to face her. He swung the censer to the north, south and west, then moved on into the darkness. As he did, he began to sing:

Dies irae, dies illa,
Solvet saeclum in favilla:
Teste David cum Sibylla . . .

Doggedly, the girl followed him. Nobody else seemed to want to, though several peasants ventured to the door and peered inside.

Yder felt mute horror. "To attend your own funeral," he finally said. "I've never heard of such a thing."

His uncle shrugged. "It's a symbolic gesture. But the villagers don't want their stock tainted. To dispense with her, like this, is the lesser of two evils."

After a moment, they walked back to their horses. Neither knight was clad for court. They wore heavy cloaks over their leather travelling clothes, and wolf-skin boots. Only the longswords slung at their hips revealed their rank. Polidamus was now aging, but still as broad as an ox. His hair was long and white, his face nut-brown and seamed with ancient cuts. Yder was taller but leaner. He shared his uncle's strength, however, and the dark sullen looks so typical of the Armorican Britons.

As he climbed into the saddle, he heard a muffled requiem from inside the chapel. He imagined the shadows in there, the smoke, the diseased wretch standing alone by the altar as the priest said the Last Rites over her. And he was glad he couldn't see it. The roads of pilgrimage could be hard on the eyes of even the coldest man; an endless tale of begging bowls, clawed hands and grizzled things in rags and tatters. The shrines were no better; filled with the limbless, the demented, the twitching, all clamouring to kiss whatever relics they'd crawled so far to see. The crypt at Caistor would be no exception. Yder and Polidamus were on their way there to honour the Pope's new season, Lent, but the young knight had never expected anything so grotesque as what he'd just seen.

They rode slowly past the church. On one side, grassy mounds stretched back into green and golden glades. In the middle, a man was digging. From his black habit and tonsure, Yder realized that he was another brother of the order. He was preparing a grave.

The knight reined up. "They mean to bury her too!"

Polidamus rode ahead. "What if they do? Leave them to it, boy. It's God's choice."

Yder held his ground. Fireflax, his horse – a handsome red, with a huge chest and flowing golden mane – pawed the earth nervously, always sensitive to the moods of its master.

At that moment, the leper appeared around the side of the chapel, again in the wake of the priest. She now wore a cow-bell at her throat, a square, ugly thing, which tolled as she walked.

The knight watched as they approached the grave, another thrill of horror passing through him. He'd seen condemned men walk bravely to the gallows. He'd even seen a Saxon chieftain throw himself into the adder-pit, rather than submit to the shame of being pushed. But this . . . somehow this was more horrible; this woman, *this girl* was meekly accepting banishment from human society. They were casting her into the darkness to die alone, and she was resigned to it!

As she lay down in the grave, he urged Fireflax closer. Further up the trail, Polidamus looked over his shoulder, then turned around and trotted irritably back. "There's an inn at Looth," he said. "If we hurry along, we'll probably get a bed and a roof for the night, instead of having to camp in the woods again."

"I like camping in the woods," said Yder.

"You are young, I am not," his uncle retorted. "And the longer we dally in this place, the older I feel."

Yder was too distracted to answer. "Can you *believe* this?" he muttered.

The leper's grave was little more than a trench. It barely covered her. Even so, as the final verse of the litany approached, she folded her arms on her breast, and the monk with the shovel sprinkled soil over her. A second shovelful followed, and a third.

Both clerics then knelt for a brief moment of prayer, rose back to their feet and walked away through the trees, one behind the other. The girl lay still.

"God," said Polidamus with a shudder. "Let's away from here."

Yder made no move. "She might need help."

The older knight stared at him aghast. "Nephew . . . she is dead!"

"She is not dead, Uncle. As you know perfectly well. We can't just abandon her."

They both looked back to the grave, but after a minute, Polidamus, recognizing the compassion of Urzi, Yder's mother and his own beloved sister, put a hand on the young knight's shoulder. "Yder . . . this girl is diseased. She's not a captive you can free; there's no one you can fight. We must go now."

Yder pulled away. "I'll meet you in Looth, Uncle. Find a stall for me, if you can."

Polidamus snorted and wheeled his beast around. "It won't be with me, I'll tell you that. Not if you're consorting with lepers now."

His angry hoof-beats receded into the distance, as Yder walked his horse forwards. He'd almost reached the grave, when the girl finally moved again, sitting slowly up, climbing to her feet and brushing off soil.

"Can I help you?" he asked uncertainly.

She started violently, then scrambled from the pit and backed away. Through the folds of her wrappings, he saw piercing blue eyes.

"I mean you no harm," he said.

She gazed at him for another moment, then turned and stumbled towards the forest. The knight made no effort to follow. The moment she reached the trees, she slowed down to a walk, but never once looked back.

She'd been so maltreated already that any approach was deemed a threat, he supposed. She likely thought him mad, as well. Who would offer help to a leper?

Who indeed?, he wondered as he trotted back to the road. There were thousands of wretches like her, lost and wasting, no one to help them. This occasion would be different, though. *This* wretch had chanced on Yder. To aid her somehow was now his obligation, no matter how vile, degrading or dangerous.

Was that not the essence of the Quest?

2

Looth was on the baronial demesnes of Lindsey, but possessed its own charter. It was essentially a gaggle of thatched buildings meandering along a tributary of the Humber. Its streets were narrow and muddy, and filled with pigs and geese. Animal dung lay in reeking heaps, while the air was thick with wood-smoke. Hammers clinked in the smiths' shops and tannery sheds along the river, traders called out their wares, laundry-women cackled, madmen gibbered on corners.

When Yder arrived, night was drawing down and rain falling. He hurried to the inn, left Fireflax with a stable-lad, and ambled inside.

It was dark, crowded, and smelled of onions and beer. He found Polidamus at a table by the hearth, a jug of ale in front of him. The older knight raised an eyebrow as Yder sat. "Still ten fingers and a nose. You've done well . . . so far."

Yder ignored the jest. "I may as well tell you . . . in the morning, I'm going after her."

Polidamus took a swill of ale, then wiped his mouth. "What are you talking about?"

"The leper. She can't have got far."

The two knights gazed at each other. Eventually, Polidamus laid down his mug. "Have you lost your senses?"

Yder shook his head. "At first I didn't know how I could help her, but then I thought of the holy man Gawain told us about. The one he met while campaigning in the north. Oslac . . . Oslac the White, I think. You remember? Gawain said he had the power of healing."

"Another of Gawain's stories, Yder."

"It's a chance, isn't it?"

Polidamus swore. "For Christ's sake boy, he's a hermit! He's supposed to live on the coast of Galloway. *If* he lives at all."

Yder was resolute. "If he's there, I'll find him."

His uncle sat back scornfully. "And you intend to take this leper . . . this girl, who you don't even know?"

"If she'll permit me."

Polidamus roared with laughter. "*If she'll permit you!* This is madness. Sheer madness. If the leprosy doesn't claim you, wolves or brigands will."

Yder shrugged. "What choice do I have? I'm a knight of the Round Table. As are you."

"Don't talk to *me* that way, sirrah!" A warning note crept into his uncle's voice. "Some of us have had a bellyful of war in the King's service."

"A bellyful, that's for certain," said Yder.

"And what does *that* mean?"

Yder leaned closer. "You were a great knight, Uncle, and for years the champion tourneyor of Armorica. No one is disputing that. Yet, like so many, you made it pay. I watched you grow fat on ransom and booty."

Polidamus now glared at his nephew, a fist on the table. "Ransom and booty with which I financed your squiredom!"

"For which I'm eternally grateful." Yder adopted a more respectful tone. "Don't get me wrong, please. But there has to be more than this. We aren't just soldiers of fortune . . . like Balin or Agravain. Don't you see, serving the Round Table must *mean* something. Look at Arthur. In a land riven by strife and war, he started next to the bottom but emerged a triumphant king. I not only want to emulate that, Uncle, I want to take it further.

"Remember when you first brought me to Camelot? We only came to help Arthur fight the Saxons, because we dreaded a Germanic state founding in Britain. But we stayed because in *his* household we found something different, something special."

Polidamus grunted and took another draught of ale. "We stayed, Yder, because after the sodden fields and stone towers of Armorica, Camelot was like Heaven."

"Exactly, Uncle! And Arthur was like God. I idolized him. I longed for nothing more than to ride side-by-side with him –

to be if not his equal, his lieutenant. Now, after so many years in the company of elite knights from so many lands, I know how groundless that hope was – at the end of the day, I'm a country lout from Gaul. But I still serve the Round Table, and no greater honour could any man have. Its name is seared into the fabric of Christendom. Yet it's a name we can carry to even greater glory.

"Uncle, the Round Table has never just stood for might, but for purity, justice, charity . . . all the things Rome lacked, the things even Byzantium yearns for. And when it makes that call, I'll answer. I'm still errant – I've no fief to manage, no place on the bench at the shire court. I have the time *not* to turn a blind eye, *not* to be hard and say 'It's God's decision, let them die!' Oh, I'll still ride in the tourneys, still fight the King's enemies, but to help one crawling, broken creature, in the name of the Round Table, would be a greater service still. Is that not the true crux of knighthood? The real test?"

There was a moment of silence, then Polidamus sat back, a sour look on his face. "Well, your mind's clearly made up. I'll not try to convince you otherwise. If only we knew where Merlin was. You could take the wretched creature to him. That, at least, would be safer."

Yder shook his head. "You know I couldn't. Merlin's lore was the forest lore. The King has forbidden its use. It upsets our Roman priests too much. But this Oslac the White – his powers come from God. Not even the Pope could object to that."

"Nephew," said Polidamus solemnly. "Your ardour will be the death of you. Maybe not *this* time, but soon. I respect your vows, but this is the real world we live in. The *Chansons* . . . they're works of fiction. Just poems and stories."

"And now we'll create stuff for another one," said Yder, smiling and rising to his feet. "I'll need an early start, so I'll try for an early night. I'll speak to you in the morning?"

Polidamus nodded and watched as his nephew moved away. He emptied his cup, then ordered another. He didn't doubt the young knight's prowess. Through his affection for Yder's mother, Polidamus had overseen the boy's training personally, entrusting him as squire to only the finest knights. The name 'Yder', itself was significant: in their native tongue, it meant 'bowman', indicating a sturdy yeoman devoted to his lord before all else. The boy had shown such devotion in battle many times. Unfortunately, he'd also shown devotion to the naive beliefs of his zealously

Christian mother. Little wonder the realm of Arthur, with all its courtly ideals, suited him.

Polidamus remembered the battle at Chester, when they'd stormed the famous 'City of the Legion' to eject a Pictish horde in the pay of the Saxons. He saw again those mighty outer walls, their parapets bristling with spears; heard the repeated 'crash', as the great iron-headed ram swung at the barbican gate under a deluge of rocks and burning pitch. Above all though, he remembered the King's army launching itself from between the battle-engines, laden with ladders and grapples, arrows blowing down on it like a wind of death. Many companies disintegrated, falling in heaps, but not Yder's. With suicidal courage, they'd scaled the rampart and hewed their way over the battlements into the barbican, securing the gates and eventual victory.

Afterwards, proud to have served his king so well, and streaming blood from several wounds, Yder had handed over six Pictish chieftains, whose lives he'd spared. Only for Arthur, who of course had no choice, to hang them all. Lancelot and Bedivere had quietly congratulated the young captain for his honour, but Balin, another to win renown that day – through the sheer numbers he'd slain – had laughed. At the victory feast that night, he'd drunkenly proclaimed Yder "an ignorant fool, but more a scoundrel, to make a promise to heathen murderers and then expect his king to have to keep it."

Polidamus was not sure whose cheeks had burned with greater shame, Yder's or his own.

3

Yder rose at cock-crow, but when he turned to the bale of straw beside him, where his uncle had lain, he found it empty. Curious, he walked down the guest-hall. Most of its denizens were still asleep, snoring under their cloaks, but of Polidamus there was no trace. Across the yard, in the stable, the older knight's horse was absent. When asked, the yawning stable-lad said the white-haired gent had long gone.

Yder gathered his belongings with a heavy heart. In the cold light of day, the task he'd undertaken was beginning to hang over him. A kind word from his only living relative would have lightened the load considerably.

It was a dull morning in March, the spring-like conditions of the previous day having fled for leaden skies and chill rain. When Yder approached the leper's meagre camp, a few hundred yards from the forest chapel, his sense of gloom increased. The ragged figure was seated on a log by a pile of sodden ashes, staring into nothing.

The knight reined up. "Good morrow," he said.

She made no response.

He dismounted. "I wonder if I might speak with you?"

After a moment, she looked round at him. Yder wondered what raddled face lay below those bandages – at some stage he would have to find out, vile as the thought was. As if sensing his revulsion, the leper rose to her feet. She was now very stiff, clearly racked with pain.

Feeling suddenly guilty, the knight fell to one knee. "My lady, I am true, I swear it. Look you . . . I serve the royal house." He pulled off a gauntlet and showed her his equestrian seal.

"Go away, sir knight," she said. Her voice was muffled, but very soft. "Please. It is not safe for you."

Yder stood up quickly. "A certain wise man would argue. He once told me the affliction is not so contagious as people believe."

"Easy for him to say," she replied, slowly turning.

Yder jumped in front of her. "I wish he was here now, so that he could tell you himself. Alas, no one I know has seen him for years."

The leper stared at him for a moment, her blue eyes inscrutable among the rags. "Why are you toying with me? Leave me alone, please. Didn't you see? They buried me. I no longer exist."

She moved away, but still the knight barred her path. "My friend was a druid of the old gods," he said. "Perhaps his powers are on the wane. There are others though. Jesus Christ, for instance."

"You know him personally?" she wondered.

"I've heard of one who does. A very holy man."

"Those monks were holy men. And they buried me."

Yder shook his head. "Then you haven't heard of Oslac the White? A hermit. They say he has the power of healing. A woman was bitten by a mad dog. She fell on all fours, frothing and barking. A knight of our company saw Oslac lay hands upon her and drive the sickness out."

At last the leper seemed to be listening. "And where does he live, this miracle-worker?"

"A remote place, I'm afraid. Galloway."

She sucked in her breath. "This is cruel teasing. Galloway, you say? Sir knight . . . I am alone, I am on foot, I can only feed on the scraps they throw to keep me from their doors."

She turned again, but Yder stopped her, this time with a hand on her arm. She gazed at it in astonishment.

"That is nonsense," he said quietly. "Firstly, you are not alone – I am with you. Secondly, you may ride my horse. Thirdly, my bolsters are full of food and drink – more than enough for two."

"You would share your food with a leper?" Her voice shook audibly.

"I trust the wisdom of my old friend," he said.

"You are possibly mad."

He smiled. "Possibly." Then he frowned. "There are two conditions however. Firstly, I must know your name."

"I told you, I am dead and buried."

"Your name, my lady?"

She hung her head before answering. "I'd hoped to forget it. Madeleine . . . I was called Madeleine."

"Madeleine," he said. When spoken aloud, it sounded Roman or Gallic. It reminded him of home. "My second condition . . . uncover your face."

She backed away sharply. "I cannot!"

The knight folded his arms. "Do it now, or I'll abandon you."

For a moment they gazed in silence at each other, rain pattering in the glades around them. Then, very slowly, the leper reached to the back of her head to loosen her bounds. One by one they unravelled and fell. At length, every fold hung loose at her neck.

She shook out her hair and faced him, a vision of loveliness. Her features were flawless, her eyes deepest blue. The flaxen tresses hung to her waist. Aside from a faint paleness of cheek, there was no indication of ill health. At first, the knight could hardly speak.

"They call you leper?" he finally stammered.

"You must believe them. I am a leper. It is a slow-burning fire. Already my limbs are stiff. Within a year, they'll be withered to nothing."

She betrayed no emotion. The courage and dignity with which she spoke moved him deeply. He had to choke back tears. "A year is all the time we need to find Oslac." He turned to his saddle-bags. "But first . . . you must be hungry."

"I am," she said. "But now that I know you're true, I have a gift for *you*."

Yder looked round, perplexed.

She reached behind the log and picked up a heavy sack. "Another man came by this morning. He wouldn't approach me, but he said you would be coming. He said I was to have hope, because you are among the best of knights. He also said we were to have this, as a means of survival . . . and a token of his affection."

Yder took the sack and opened it. It was filled with coins, enough to run a manorial estate let alone see two wayfarers safe across the country. In addition, there was a scroll tied with cord. He unfolded it, and instantly recognized his uncle's spidery hand:

> *Nephew . . . Oslac the White can be found at a place called Whithorn, a fishing hamlet on the western coast of Galloway. Follow the Roman road north to Carlisle. Do not tarry at Carlisle. In fact, avoid it. It is Arthur's northernmost fort, and its garrison typical of the frontier scum no right-minded king desires anywhere near his heartland. From Carlisle, ride due-west. Whithorn is roughly six days from there.*
>
> *The fact that I tell you this does not mean that I approve. But to assist you, I enclose two hundred pounds in gold. I trust you are not too idealistic to make good use of it.*
>
> *Polidamus*

This time Yder was unable to stop his tears.

4

For several days, they journeyed north-west towards the great Roman highway; the knight walking, the girl mounted.

All the way, relentless rain swept over them, soaking their clothes and turning the roads to rivers of slime. At every place they came to, they met hostile receptions. Serfs fled shrieking through the fields or turned to hurl stones. Walled towns closed their gates. Village streets emptied. Yder yearned to have Madeleine take off her bell, but that would be unfair on the ordinary folk, and would break the King's law. When buying food or seeking directions, he eventually found it easier to leave the girl out of sight and venture in alone, though even then word might have got ahead, and he'd be driven off with curses. Occasions like this brought home the magnitude of the thing he'd undertaken. Several times he was close to despair, but then he would consider what it might have been like for the girl on her own, and he grew ashamed.

At least the weather improved. As they left the district of Lindsey, summer seemed to break early, the woodlands blooming and filling with twittering birds. A week later, they entered the wealthy demesnes of Barwick, and followed firmer roads through fragrant vineyards and open cornfields, finally to arrive in a broad, green meadow by the River Aire.

Here, a retinue of splendid people came cantering towards them. Madeleine watched them warily. They had dogs with them. She knew the agony of dog-bites.

"We must be careful," said Yder, as if to confirm her fears. "It's the Bishop of Barwick."

The Bishop was a portly, balding man, decked in richest purple, with a myriad of jewelled rings on his gloved hands. He was seated in a saddle of varnished leather, and rode a gorgeous roan hunter. A hooded falcon sat on his wrist, while to one side a stunted dwarf in harlequin garb held aloft a tall pole hung with game birds. The Bishop's courtiers were also clad for the hunt, the men in capes and feathered caps, the tittering ladies in embroidered gowns. Servants were now hurrying among them, handing out goblets of mulled wine. Hounds yelped and scrambled over one another.

Yder and Madeleine waited in silence, while the Bishop took refreshment. When he had finished, he regarded them carefully. "Sir Yder . . . from Camelot, no less." His voice was impossibly pompous.

Yder bowed. Madeleine tried to dismount, so to curtsey, but the knight placed a hand on her leg, to stop her. If the great magnate took offence at this, he didn't show it. "And what exciting adventure are you on?"

"I feel you already know that, your grace."

The Bishop nodded sagely. "There is little I don't know. One thing I cannot understand, however. To reach the Roman Road, you need pass through my estate of Barwick. And I do not recall you ever writing for permission."

"Do I need permission to travel the King's highways?" the knight asked.

"When you bring a leper with you, yes. That may not be the King's law, but it is mine."

Yder regarded him stonily. "And you are denying me that permission?"

The Bishop gave Madeleine a bleak look. "I should warn you, this unclean creature will not be welcome at Whithorn. Many stories are told of Oslac the White. Few are true. Most often he shuns the company of others. It's unlikely he'll entertain you."

The knight began to wonder if word had travelled about the small fortune they were carrying. He could see no other reason for this obstruction. Was some kind of toll about to be charged?

Then he noticed something odd about the Bishop's household. Far back among the horses, one of the servants had dropped to all-fours and was snuffling the ground. Close by him, a courtier was having trouble drinking from his wine-cup. The man's nose protruded in a flat, hoglike snout. Long teeth, like tusks, curled upwards past his lip, and he snorted with irritation.

A chill ran down Yder's spine. He took Fireflax firmly by the reins. "We've come this far, your grace. We'd like to proceed."

Boldly, he led the horse forward, and an avenue slowly cleared in front of them. To one side of it, a man and a woman were nuzzling each other and grunting.

"You are not listening to me, sir knight!" came the Bishop's voice, now from some awesome distance away. "I suggest you turn back! It's for your own good! You'll regret this, damn you!"

Yder glanced up at Madeleine. She was rigid with fear. "Yder, maybe we should . . ."

"Ignore them," he said quietly. "They're mindless things."

"What?"

"They've no power over us." He spoke firmly, though one hand rested on the hilt of his longsword. A dirge now sounded behind them. Gibberings, squealings, titters, squawks.

"Ignore them," he said again. "They're creatures of the forest, nothing more."

Several minutes passed before they reached the trees, where they turned to look back. The Bishop's household had vanished. Instead, animals scampered about on the meadow, chasing each other: deer, goats, wild pigs, even a fox or two. Most dragged the shreds of fine garments. An especially handsome stag, with a vast spread of antlers, stood gazing after the travellers. Tatters of episcopal purple were tangled around its hooves.

"Sorcery!" said Madeleine.

Yder nodded. "But why?" He gazed at her. "And who?"

5

Beyond the hinterland of York, the manor estates petered out and the land crumpled and folded. As Yder and Madeleine pressed on, bracken-clad hills rose in humps around them. For six weeks they passed through valleys that were narrow defiles, cut in the ancient past by flowing cataracts now long dried.

On the first day of May, however, they reached the Roman Road, and from there the going was easier. It was smoothly paved and ran northward, straight as an arrow. At many places along it, the ruins of villas or temples provided easy shelter. There were also wells, preserved by Arthur's engineers so that fresh water was readily available.

Yder talked endlessly, of Camelot, of his fellow knights in the order, of his distant childhood in Gaul. It was as much to fill in the tedious hours as to converse with Madeleine. For her part, she spoke little, saying only that she'd devoted much of her former life to prayer and contemplation. Never once did she decry God for rewarding her faith so poorly. In fact, she weakened steadily as they travelled, but hardly complained at all; a nobility of spirit the knight found stimulating and humbling. Only at the end of each day, when they were deeply fatigued and he would have to help her from Fireflax's back, would she give vent to her feelings, gasping in unbearable pain.

At times like this, Yder felt worse than inadequate, but tried to make up for it by refusing to shy from contact with her. This was something which Madeleine was at first concerned about, but which she eventually grew to accept. It didn't perturb Yder at all. Despite Merlin's wise words all those years ago, he had always feared the unclean, but on this occasion, unaccountably, he didn't. Perhaps if she'd been scabrous instead of fair, drooling and deranged instead of thoughtful and softly spoken!

Not that any of this would last for much longer, of course. The thought of the limping, degenerate thing Madeleine would eventually become spurred the knight on.

When they came within a day of Carlisle, he remembered his uncle's advice, and they pulled off the road to follow deer-paths through the wildwood. It was slower progress, but at last they reached the ruins of the great Roman Wall. Northwards from there, distant summits could be seen, wreathed in mist. Thankfully, Yder and Madeleine were now bound west, and within hours the terrain had levelled into a wilderness of heather, dotted with gorse and boulders. Galloway, the knight realized, the land of the Gaels or the alien Irish. If they encountered trouble here, they'd find few friends.

In this region there was nothing even close to a path. Awesome, empty vistas lay on all sides, and the only signs of life were peregrines and buzzards sailing far above, or fat grouse, black and red in their early plumage. The hunting was good, but Madeleine could eat little. Often now, she was feverish and fell into swoons. On these occasions, there was nothing the knight could do but mop her brow and pray beside her. Time was running out, but six days west of Carlisle, sorely tired, he heard the ocean, and, leading her down a rutted path, came out onto a shingle beach.

The Irish Sea was grey and chopping, the islands of the Firth distant outcrops, buried in ocean spume. Tar and timber sheds were built on the hillside in huge numbers. As the travellers approached, a motley band of fisher-folk emerged. Their faces were hard and red and ridged at the cheeks, their beards stringy with salt. Some carried staves, others gutting-blades and seal-spears.

"Whithorn," Yder said, hardly able to believe how primitive it was. He made a gesture to the locals. "Can you help us?"

Dumb, idiot looks greeted this. Fur-clad shoulders were shrugged. One man laughed, his teeth like brown slabs.

"We can pay," the knight added, holding up a handful of coins. "We can pay well."

Wondering looks were exchanged, but it was clear none of them understood him. For a moment he was at a loss. Whatever harsh language these people spoke, it eluded him. Finally, he mentioned the hermit's name. "Oslac!" he cried. "Is this the abode of Oslac?"

They reacted with terror, backing slowly away and glancing along the coast to a distant mass of crags, piled up in a natural fortress. Yder followed their gaze. "That's where I can find Oslac?" he asked. "That's his hermitage?"

They ignored him further, hurrying away in droves.

"I think we can assume it is," he said to Madeleine.

"Unusual way for them to react to their parish priest," she replied.

The knight had to agree. Then he recalled the spectral Bishop of Barwick's warning: "*Many stories are told of Oslac the White. Few are true.*"

The signs were ominous, but they could not turn back now, and a few minutes later were following a coastal path, which quickly became rocky and rutted, and rose steeply over limestone drops, where waves erupted in fountains of spray. They followed it for several hours, until a ghastly stench assailed them.

Yder halted in his tracks. "Name of a name!" he whispered. Madeleine, who was resting on Fireflax's neck, looked tiredly up . . . and covered her eyes with horror.

Some thirty yards ahead, human carrion had been nailed to a timber frame, and was covered in crows and black-flies. But that was only the beginning. From that point on, leading all the way to the crags, similar frames had been erected and on each one hung a corpse. They included men and women, in varying stages of decay, mouths yawning open, eyes hollow. Most bore fatal wounds – slashed throats, shattered skulls.

"Who are these people!" Madeleine gasped, a hand to her mouth as they rode past.

Yder shook his head. "Who can say? Supplicants to the hermit, maybe. Pilgrims, beggars . . ."

"But who kills them?"

Again, he shook his head.

The hellish path led on for another hour until swerving inland, the crags now looming above it. Everything here was blasted and dead; trees were naked skeletons, the marram grass grey and stubbly. Soon, huge boulders hemmed the travellers in, and directly before them a towering cliff rose into the sky.

Madeleine peered up it in dismay. "We can't go any further."

"We don't need to," Yder replied. He wasn't sure how he knew, but he did. There was a tension in the air. They were being watched.

"Why have you come here?" a harsh voice rang out.

They noticed for the first time that a great fissure had split the rock-face from top to bottom. It seemed that the voice had come down through that.

"Answer me!" it cried. "Do you not know who I am?"

"We know who you are!" Yder shouted up. "And we are appalled. We expected a man of God."

"So did those others you saw," replied the voice, full of mockery. "Now you will join them. At least *you* will, knight. The leper is as good as dead, anyway."

Yder ripped out his longsword. "Then heal her!"

"*You command me?*" The voice rose to a bass roar, and debris trickled down.

"I propose a bargain," Yder replied. "My life for this woman's.

Cure her leprosy and I'll go voluntarily to the stake." He plunged his sword into the ground and clasped his hands. "On my honour, I swear."

For a moment the voice was stilled, and from some distant place, they suddenly fancied they could hear the approach of hooves. Then the voice sounded again. "You would sacrifice yourself for this damned thing? When Mother-Church itself has abandoned her?"

"It is my vow to defend the weak," the knight replied. "Even unto my own death."

Now the hooves were much louder, echoing from the rocks as though hammering the core of the earth. Yder and Madeleine looked round, and saw the shape of a horseman pounding up the track behind them. When twenty yards short, he slid to a halt, his animal rearing and snorting like a bull. Neither had seen anything like the apparition they now beheld. It was a knight, but a knight the size of a bear. He wore mail as black as jet, and a crimson surcoat etched with a golden sun bearing human features. His helm was of darkest metal and fashioned like a boar's head, and in one hand he carried a black and crimson lance, tipped with steel. His mount was a gigantic grey, seventeen hands to the withers. Its eyes were hot coals, its flanks lathered with sweat. It tossed its head wildly, and reared up again.

Instantly, both Yder and Madeleine knew who was responsible for the carnage on the cliff-top.

"Step onto my tilting ground," the voice continued. "Defeat my champion and your wish is granted. Yield to him, and he slays you . . . and the girl too. Is that not fair? Either way, she is spared her agony."

"Aye," said Yder. "That's fair."

The newcomer then dismounted and, leading his beast by its bridle, strode past them into the fissure. The ground trembled to his footfalls.

Yder turned to Madeleine. "Well?"

"This can't be right," she said weakly. "These aren't the actions of a holy man."

The knight shook his head. "We must meet every challenge as it comes. Only then will we have an answer."

They entered the fissure and followed a passage through to a natural amphitheatre, perhaps fifty yards by sixty. It was open to the sky, but its walls were of sheer rock. Logs had been lashed together along the base of them and hung with shields, most now smashed and streaked with dry blood. Above these, wooden hoardings had been fixed, and on them were painted galleries of heads – kings, barons, bishops, abbots – a full array of nobility.

False dignitaries for a false tourney, Yder thought, as he stared around. Before him, the tilting ground was beaten earth, strewn with wood-chippings. At one end, a space had been roped off to provide lists. At the other, steps had been hewn into the rock, leading up to a granite throne on which lolled a hefty, toad-like figure. He gazed glassily at them, as if drunk. An iron crown sat on his shaggy head, and he wore a simple white habit, badly stained. Below him, his champion was mounted and waiting. As well as his lance, the giant now bore a shield, marked with the same pagan device as his surcoat.

"Is he not too strong?" the girl asked. "Look at him . . . he's colossal."

Yder smiled as he led her into the lists. "There's more to combat than strength, Madeleine. The finest knight in the world taught me that." But secretly he couldn't help wishing that Lancelot was with them now.

He helped her from the horse and began to unravel his own equipment. His spear was made of ash and honed to a needle-point, his shield of stoutest linden-wood, painted blue and white. He laid them on the ground, then undressed to his linen under-clothes and put on his leather tunic. Madeleine leaned on the horse and watched as he climbed into his chain mail leggings, drawing their straps up over his shoulders and securing them. After that he put on his hauberk, holding in his breath as he fastened the five buckles at either side. The coif followed, pulled down over his head, tightly enclosing his ears, then the gauntlets – hard leather, studded on the knuckles. He was almost ready. The final touch was a mantle of white with blue chevrons, laid over everything else and belted at the waist.

The knight fastened on his longsword, then turned to Madeleine. She looked sickly again, and as he approached her, swooned into his arms. He eased her down to the ground, his travelling clothes rolled up into a pillow for her head.

"Forgive me," she whispered.

He knelt beside her. "What's to forgive?"

"You . . . you've been strong for me. I should . . . I should be strong for you."

"You've been stronger than was humanly possible," he said. "Now rest. Leave this part of the fight to me."

He was about to rise, when Madeleine suddenly reached for the collar of her shroud, and tore a piece of sackcloth from it.

"Here . . . take this." She thrust it into his mailed fist. "It isn't much, but I've heard a knight should never enter battle without a lady's favour . . ."

The knight smiled, then kissed the rag. The girl reacted violently, almost snatching it back. "Pray, don't touch it with your lips . . ."

Again Yder smiled. "What matter? If I die, the leprosy dies too. If not, the hermit will give us cure."

Then he tied the rag around the hilt of his sword, and climbed into the stirrups. Turning to the tilting ground, he put on his helmet, a cylinder of riveted steel, with a narrow aperture for vision. The burly figure of Oslac's champion was framed in it. His own visor was down, his lance raised in mock salute.

The warriors gazed coldly at each other for a moment, then urged their chargers forward. In seconds, they were at full gallop. Yder went at it in the classical way, lance couched across his left arm, elbow high, right hand twisted below the shaft to fully support and direct his blow.

They came together in a crash of sparks and splinters. Yder was thrown savagely backwards, but he held the charge. Suddenly, the thrill of combat was coursing through him. He wheeled his horse about. Half his lance was missing, snapped off mid-way. The other knight's weapon had also broken, three feet of it standing in Yder's shield.

Yder grabbed for his longsword. He'd half-drawn it when Madeleine cried out a warning, and a thunder of hooves filled the air. His foe was bearing down on him already, armed with a second lance. Before Yder had time to evade there was a explosion of pain in his chest, and the next he knew, he had crashed face-down to the ground.

He lay there stunned, dimly aware of Madeleine calling his name, and the approaching drum-roll of hooves. Seconds seemed to pass before Yder's peril dawned on him. By instinct alone, he threw himself over, and the point of his enemy's lance missed him by inches.

The young knight climbed to his feet, now clutching his chest in agony. Oslac's champion was turning about at the other end, preparing for a fourth charge.

Yder drew his longsword to meet it. This time the giant crouched low, aiming his spear at Yder's heart. When he was only feet away, however, the knight leaped forward and swept his blade round in an arc, striking the lance hard. With a "smack" of splintering wood, the weapon broke; then, as his foe thundered past, Yder caught him a return-blow across the shoulders.

The giant stiffened in pain and lost grip on his reins. Running up behind, Yder struck him again, and again, and the giant toppled from the saddle.

The knight sank to his haunches, gasping hard. Victory at a price, he thought. A rib was broken somewhere, but at least it was victory. No man could have survived those strokes . . . he'd never hit anyone cleaner or harder.

Then he saw his opponent clamber to his feet. The knight was stunned. The giant's surcoat hung in tatters, but the chain-coat beneath was still intact. Even as Yder watched, Oslac's champion stood fully erect, hefted his shield and drew a spiked mace from his belt.

Battle was rejoined as fiercely as before, but now on foot, sword and mace sweeping back and forth. For minutes on end, they tussled, the rock walls and painted faces spinning around them. Yder thrust and parried with all his might, but never had he known anyone fight with such speed and precision. Never had he felt such force in blows. Everything he tried was countered, every hack or jab blocked.

And then, suddenly, his shield was gone, smashed from his grasp. Fleetingly, he froze . . . and the mace caught the side of his helmet, sending him staggering. He fell to his knees, dizzy. The rope barrier was before him. Madeleine stood beyond it, pale as a ghost but somehow radiant, hands joined as if in prayer.

"He . . . he'll be dead soon," the knight stammered.

The woman shook her head. "He should already *be* dead . . . you know that. Yder, he's protected. His armour, his weapons. They're enchanted. Use his own weapons against him, or he'll kill you."

Yder looked slowly round, half-blinded by blood – the mace had dented his helm, cutting his face and forehead brutally. Through a crimson mist, he saw Oslac's champion throw aside his shield, and arm himself with sword as well as mace. Tiredly, the knight rose.

For tense moments, they circled each other. Then the giant attacked, arms windmilling. Yder ducked the mace, parried the sword and thrust, jamming his own blade deep into his opponent's belly . . . and watched it bend on the coat of mail, leaving no imprint. *It was true! More sorcery!* Yder stepped back. "Damn you, Oslac the White! Have you no honour!"

A demonic laugh came down on him, then the giant threw himself forward. Yder blocked a sword-stroke and parried the mace, slashing his foe across the ribs. Again, the surcoat shredded, again the mail held.

Once more they wheeled, Yder wheezing with effort. His limbs were leaden with fatigue. Blood was still running into one eye. His foe, on the other hand, seemed to be growing in strength, puffing out his chest, head thrown back. Again, Yder had to fend off a barrage of blows. Then the mace caught his helmet a second time, and sparks glittered before his eyes. He fell hard onto his back, but had the presence of mind to roll away. The giant followed, stabbing savagely, but finding only the earth.

When Yder regained his feet, he was forced onto the defensive immediately. The mace swept down at him, and though he blocked it, his sword flew into splinters with the impact. He hobbled away, casting around for something to fight with, but was caught on the back of the shoulder. *The mace . . . again!*

Yder felt bones crack. Blinding pain lanced through him. Sickness rose in his guts.

He stumbled to his knees, but looked up just in time to see the giant throw down the mace and lift his sword above his head. Frantically, the knight scrabbled around . . . and his hand closed on his shield, broken in the dust, three feet of black-red lance embedded in it.

And Madeleine's words came back to him. "*Use his own weapons against him!*"

Yder tore at the spear, but couldn't free it. Then Oslac's knight struck, swiping down with a mighty two-handed blow. Yder blocked it, and the shuddering impact clove the shield apart, knocking the spear loose. Its point was of black steel, hard and gleaming – such metal could never be dulled. Yder grabbed it and felt a new power surge through him. He jumped to his feet.

As he did, the giant dealt him another enormous back-stroke, but this time the knight was quicker, stepping nimbly aside, then lunging forwards with the broken spear and driving its point clean through the chain aventail covering his enemy's throat.

Oslac's champion gave a shocked grunt, then a gurgle. The sword fell from his grasp. Slowly, he tottered backwards, clutching vainly at the jutting shaft, black blood billowing through his fingers. Seconds passed before he finally fell, landing with a mighty crash. He twisted in one final convulsion, then lay still.

Yder sank to his haunches, lungs heaving. He was drenched in sweat, half his body numb with pain. He fingered the strap under his chin, finally releasing it and lifting off his battered helm, then crawled over to where his victim lay. After a moment, he raised the black metal visor.

The face below was brutish, with a wide flat nose, heavy bone brows and jagged, knife-like teeth protruding over its upper lip. Warts covered it, tufted with hair. What was more, its flesh was grey, with the consistency of rock. Yder kneeled slowly up, bewildered.

"The troll, Abbadon," said a voice behind him.

The knight turned sharply and found Oslac the White standing there, but no longer the arrogant king-like figure of before. Now the hermit seemed old and frail. He had discarded the crown and was leaning on an applewood stick. His face was ashen, his hair straggling and white. Yder noticed a hump on his back.

"You were under his spell?" the knight asked.

Oslac nodded, then grimaced. He looked intolerably tired. "And now . . . now it's broken. Thank the Lord. The pilgrims drawn here and murdered for their goods are uncountable. Look at this place. He's turned my church into a butcher's shop."

Yder nodded, then stood up wearily. The hermit placed a hand on his shoulder. "You fought with exemplary courage, my friend. But I think you were helped."

A weak smile touched the knight's lips. He turned to the lists. "I was. I couldn't have won without . . ."

His words trailed off. The roped compound was empty. He turned round and round. The only living thing he saw was Fireflax. The horse trotted towards him, tossing its head proudly. He took it by the bridle, but still searched for Madeleine. Then he remembered the ghost-like radiance he'd seen during the battle. *No . . . no!*

"Madeleine!" he called, his voice echoing from the high rock walls. "Madeleine!"

"You were with someone?" the hermit asked.

"A maiden," said the knight. "As fair as you've ever seen. We came together from Looth."

"Madeleine of Looth!" The name clearly meant something to Oslac. "Then *truly* you were helped." He looked hard at the knight. "Saint Madeleine of Looth was an abbess, martyred by Saxon pirates over a century ago. They defiled her, then tore her habit of white silk into ribbons, bound her to a wheel with them, and rolled her into the sea."

Yder backed away, shaking his head. "*This* Madeleine was flesh and blood. She was stricken with leprosy, I brought her here to be cured . . ."

Oslac smiled sadly. "My young friend, am I Jesus Christ? I have salves for that gash on your brow, splints for your broken collar-bone, but I cannot cure lepers, nor make blind people see, nor cripples walk. Old tales, nothing more. Besides, there was no leper."

The knight insisted there was, but Oslac held up his hand. "Madeleine of Looth sits at the right hand of God. Through you, young man, a miracle has been wrought."

Yder shook his head again, desperately, unwilling to believe it. Then he remembered something. Something that would prove his case. A surge of hope went through him. "Wait!" he said. "I've something I can show you."

Hurriedly, he began to pick through the wreckage of the battle, the fragments of armour, the broken weaponry. At last he came back, and with a triumphant smile, presented the hermit with the cross-hilt of his longsword. Only shards of the blade remained, but the grip was unharmed, and around it was a piece of cloth.

"A favour of hers, to me," said Yder. "This piece of sacking came from her shroud."

"Sacking?" said Oslac. "Look again, my friend."

Yder did, and found that the piece of cloth was in actual fact a ribbon. A ribbon of white silk.

Sir Melleas in TWICE KNIGHTLY

Alan Kennington

Time for some light refreshment. Sir Melleas is, so far as I know, the invention of Alan Kennington, though the name sounds suitably Arthurian (perhaps because it sounds like a combination of Pelleas and Meliant). I stumbled across this story when looking through the short-story spot in the London Evening Standard *for 1936. I'm not aware that it's ever been reprinted. Kennington (b. 1906) was a typical humorous writer of the period, his work emulating the style of P.G. Wodehouse and Anthony Armstrong, both of whom have been represented in earlier volumes in this series. He produced a number of light romantic and mystery novels in the 1940s and 1950s.*

Melleas reflected again how delightful it was to be sitting opposite Melisande in the long, raftered dining-hall at Camelot. In the old days of the Fellowship of the Table Round, it had not been the custom for the sexes to mix over food: the ladies of the court ate by themselves in their bowers or in a separate hall upstairs. But modern ideas and Guinevere had changed all that, and now the whole court dined, as Lancelot had put it, cock and hen: Dame Brocas, in fact, a feminist of strongly militant views, had only been restrained by force from sitting down in the Siege Perilous.

Melleas gazed adoringly at Melisande. How well the new style of coif became her, he thought, admiring for the thousandth time the climbing grace of her thin eyebrows, her large grey eyes, the powdering of freckles on her retroussé nose and the golden hair that showed up so dazzlingly against the white samite.

With a great effort of will, he withdrew his gaze and glanced round the table. At Arthur, kindly, worried, slightly stooping now and with a touch of grey at the temples, but still to be reckoned with in the handicap tournaments. At Guinevere, beautiful in a brassy way, but tight-lipped and with something rather exhausting in the concentration of her gaze upon Lancelot. At Gawain and Geraint, with their fair hair, frank faces, enormous limbs, flashing teeth, deafening laughs and general aura of heartiness. At Mordred, the hero of a hundred love affairs, smiling suavely at a Maid of Honour and twirling his black moustache. And so on all round the top half of the table. For all who sat round that half, the half over which Arthur presided, were knights.

Melleas sighed enviously. How much longer would it be, he wondered, before he, too, won the right to wear the golden spurs? It meant everything to him, far more than it had done to any of them. For until he was knighted, he was ineligible by the rules of chivalry to ask for Melisande's hand.

And what with all these new-fangled improvements, such as the wider roads and the new system of forest patrols, quests seemed to be getting fewer and fewer these days, until now there were hardly enough to go round. Apart from his deferred hopes of knighthood, Melleas was beginning to grudge the large sums he had paid Merlin for instruction in "sundry infallible arts of encountering enchanters," with ten runes for outwitting warlocks thrown in. As for his six-foot, two-handed dragon-sword, which he had bought at the sale of Sir Peliot's effects, that was already beginning to show distinct specks of rust.

He was roused suddenly from these gloomy reflections by the sound of a disturbance at the door. A dishevelled messenger, gasping with fatigue and white with the dust of travel, was being assisted in, and Lancelot himself had risen and stepped forward with a brimming goblet of Caerleon No. Six. The messenger gulped it down and then gasped out his message, while all listened attentively.

Melleas caught the gist of it. Many leagues away, east through the Forest Perilous and over towards the Joyous Garde, the Lady Pelerine was held captive by a certain Black Knight, with none to undertake her quarrel. Who of the most noble fellowship, cried the messenger, would volunteer?

At these words, it seemed to Melleas that a certain uneasiness settled over the top half of the table. It must have been his imagination, he thought, but he could have sworn that a look of wariness, almost of apprehension, had flitted across the faces of all those fearless champions. And still further to complete the illusion, he was almost certain he had seen Mordred wink at Lancelot.

Then, however, as the messenger began to give further details, Melleas lost interest and turned to his capon again. There were at least 60 champions then in residence, and anyway, even if he were Sir Melleas, this was no quest for a lovesick bachelor like himself. For by the age-old code of Chivalry prevailing at Arthur's court, it was an inviolable rule that the unmarried rescuer of a damsel in distress always proposed to her as well.

Arthur had risen now, and Melleas, after one more lingering glance at Melisande, turned to watch him as he stood with one hand on Excalibur. Everyone seemed strange to-day, he thought. There was a certain hurriedness, almost an apologetic note, in Arthur's voice. "Which noble Knight here seated," he began, rattling off the accustomed formula, "will haste to the rescue of the Lady Pelerine?"

There was an uncomfortable pause, and the King added pleadingly. "Come, gentlemen. What offers for this superb quest?"

There was still silence, and the messenger grinned. Then Arthur was reduced to asking each knight in turn. But by an odd coincidence each one of them had some excuse or ailment that prevented him offering his services. Lancelot's armour was being overhauled. Bedivere had a stiffness in his sword-arm. Mordred had an appointment with an enchantress in Brittany.

And so it went on. The excuses varied, but the result was the same.

After the eighteenth refusal Arthur tactfully gave up asking the knights. Melisande's quick wits had guessed what was coming next, and she looked anxiously across at Melleas as the King turned towards the squires. As he caught her eye, and then saw Arthur looking in his direction, Melleas, too, had a sickening foreboding. Officially he ranked as head of the squires, and a squire could never refuse a quest – not, that is, if he ever wished to become a knight. That was not only a Royal command, but one of the first rules of the Guild of Knight Errants.

Sure enough Arthur's face brightened when he saw Melleas. "Rise, Melleas," he commanded, and Melleas rose, to find himself invested two minutes later with the quest of the Lady Pelerine.

Afterwards, while his armour was being oiled and while particulars of his record were being copied on vellum by the Court scrivener ("Just in case," as Mordred said), Melleas had a short and tender farewell with Melisande.

"Oh, dear," said Melisande, clinging to his surcoat. "What are we to do? You can't refuse or you'll never be a Knight, and then they won't let us get married. Horrible, hateful old rules. If you do go, you'll either be killed or have to marry that Pelerine, and I really don't know which I'd hate most. I'll bet she's the most awful old cat. No one else wanted to take her quarrel on till you had to, poor sweet."

"I know, it's awful," groaned Melleas, "I'd far rather the Black Knight won than give you up. If he didn't kill me, I mean. I wonder if I could get round him some way. No, that's too risky. I've got to get my spurs. For the life of me, there's no way out that I can see."

Melisande played with one of the buttons on his doublet and murmured comfortingly, "Cheer up, my sugar plum. It may all come right yet. The first thing you've got to do is to beat the Black Knight and get your spurs. Then after that, you can start making plans. After all, you never know. Something might happen to Pelerine on the way home."

Melleas considered. "That's a thought. Yes, of course, it is a long and perilous ride. Darling, there's the trumpet: I must to horse. Pray for me, will you? And remember, not all the Pelerines in the world are going to stop me loving you."

Melleas' heart was heavy as he rode through the forest, ignoring all dwarfs, white harts, ruined chapels and other distractions, and carefully skirting the estate of Morgan Le Fay. He was a modest youth and, apart from all the difficulties involved if he won, he had grave doubts as to whether he could overcome the Black Knight. Experts at the court always declared that Black Knights were far more formidable than those of the Red, Green or Blue variety, whose fighting qualities seemed on a par with their effeminate taste in armour.

And as they rode on, he began to discover that the Black Knight had a great local reputation. Whenever he pulled up at some small "King Arthur's Head" or "Lady of the Lake" for a quick horn of mead, he would be sure to hear, in reference to his opponent – "Unhorsed him in the second course," or "Only saved by the trumpet, he was."

However, the thought of Melisande kept his courage high.

Besides, he had been well trained by Ban and Bors, court coaches to the squires, and at the end of the past year had come out head of the Lists.

On the morning of the eighth day the messenger drew rein. Melleas dismounted from his jennet, donned his armour, mounted his war-horse and set his lance in rest. Through a gap in the trees he could see, about a mile away, a large castle, in front of which stood a pavilion of black silk. As they neared this he noticed hanging on the trees surrounding it twenty or thirty shields reversed, trophies, he supposed, of unfortunate Knights who had already met their fate.

About half a mile from the pavilion the messenger again halted, and pointed to a large elephant tusk that hung on a sycamore tree. Melleas glanced round warily. From a turret-window of the castle fluttered something white, which he took to be the wimple of the Lady Pelerine. The ground was fast and in good condition, with little advantage in either end. He saw that his sword was loose in its scabbard and that his vizor was securely locked down. Then he drew a deep breath, put up an orison, thought of Melisande, and took up the horn.

Scarcely had the echoes of his blast died away when the flaps of the pavilion flew open and there rushed forth a gigantic coal-black Knight on a gigantic coal-black steed. Melleas was the lighter man on the lighter horse, but he kept his head. As the Black Knight, with one glance behind him, spurred madly on, Melleas pulled his charger to one side, and got in an oblique blow with his lance on the other's shield, himself dropping at the impact, so that the spear glanced off over his shoulder. Both then dropped their lances and drew their swords, and at swordplay Melleas had the advantage as being the lighter horseman on the handier horse.

Moreover, as with sparks flying the fight went on, Melleas began gradually to get the impression that the Black Knight was fighting with a certain half-heartedness. He defended himself skilfully enough, but he made no attempt to force the fighting and Melleas had the curious feeling that he was not really doing his utmost to win.

The end came with surprising swiftness. A shrill cry came suddenly from the castle, causing the Black Knight to wince and jerk round his head. This left his front exposed. Melleas spurred his horse and crashed in a backhand cut to his gorget. Another on the forehead sent the other's sword skittering across the grass.

The Black Knight dismounted with alacrity and pushed his vizor up. He was a red-faced, heavily built man with a mild blue eye and a drooping ginger moustache. He wiped his forehead, sighed with relief, smiled amiably and held out his gauntletted hand. "Nice stroke of yours that, my boy," he said. "Yes, you certainly had me there. Ah, well, we can't always win. But to the victor the spoils, as it says in the rule-book. By that, I mean, of course, the Lady Pelerine. Take her, my boy, and be happy." He coughed and added, "By the way, I ought to tell you that the spoils include her mother as well – "

Melleas felt he ought to say something, and, accordingly, he launched into the set speech ordained for such occasions. He cleared his throat and began, "Caitiff for the insult rendered to yon beauteous damozel whom thou hast held in thrall – "

He found the Black Knight staring at him in a curious way. "'Held in thrall' is good," he said. "And 'beauteous damozel' is better still. Now if you'll come along with me, I'll just introduce you to the Lady Pelerine. And while you're changing, my dear fellow," he added, rubbing his hands together, "I'll just be telling the churls to saddle a palfrey for her mother. Well, well. Thank God for the rules of Knighthood is what I say."

"You don't seem any too anxious to hang on to your prey," said Melleas sarcastically.

"My prey! I like that. Good heavens, boy, she's camped here for six months – she and her mother – and simply would not move out. Lord love us, you don't think I kidnapped her?"

"It was given out that you did."

"Naturally. I gave it out. It was my only chance of getting rid of her. Heaven knows, it was hard enough. All the locals knew what was up, of course, and even when they were forced to come along took jolly good care not to win. By the way, you don't know anybody who might buy thirty or so spare shields? You might just mention it when you get back. Well, as I was saying, I thought of Camelot as the last resource. Pelerine jumped at it, of course. She wanted Lancelot but he's nobody's fool. I suppose you were only a squire. Yes, I thought your spurs looked a bit new. Ah, well. They say marriage is a very honourable institution."

As soon as Melleas saw the Lady Pelerine he understood completely that strange reluctance to undertake her quarrel on the part of his fellow-Knights – as he had the right to call them now. She was a tall, raw-boned woman of 35 or so, with a mouth like a rat-trap and a nose like a donjon-keep. When he had ridden below her window and sheepishly held up his lance, she had said, "I thank thee for thy fair service and gentle courtesy. Sir Knight, please help them take my mother's coffer downstairs."

And the Black Knight had whispered with a fruity chuckle, "She's got a wedding-dress in her own, my boy."

They rode back to Camelot in a little procession of three. In front rode Pelerine and her mother, discussing how the castle would be decorated after the wedding, for it had been early settled by Pelerine that her mother was to come and live with them. Melleas rode sadly behind, thinking of Melisande. Occasionally he glanced down at the glittering spurs on his heels and thought of the futility of life. Here he was saddled with this revolting pair, and Camelot was now only a bare three days' ride away.

He was roused from his reverie by a sudden interruption. A peasant, dishevelled and out of breath, had dashed from a thicket and clasped his bridle-rein.

"Succour!" he cried, "Succour!"

For a moment, Melleas thought he was being personal. Then his frown vanished as he listened to the man's tale.

It appeared that in a nearby cave a certain ferocious dragon had taken up its abode, and from it had been ravaging not only the nearby flocks but their custodians as well. The authorities had taken what precautions they could. A warning trumpet was blown on the beast's appearance, and serious loss of life had now more or less ceased. But the dragon was still alive and a menace. Would Melleas, the peasant implored, do something about it?

Melleas considered. He was weary and dispirited and for the past few nights he had had very little sleep. He felt in poor form for dragon-sticking, and besides, his heavy dragon-sword was at Camelot. Heedless of the peasant's anxious pleadings, he was just about to refuse, when suddenly he remembered Melisande's parting words. "Something," she had said, "might happen to her on the way home – "

He glanced towards the two women, who were now discussing tapestries. Pelerine's mother had just said, "And when we've had it done up, there'll be none of that lout Melleas coming into the boudoir with muddy armour on."

Melleas came to a sudden, tremendous decision. "Show me this cave," he said.

That evening they camped in a small beechwood at the foot of the downs, five hundred yards from where a large cave yawned in the hill. After supper, just as it was growing dusk, Pelerine exclaimed crossly: "There, now. There's no milk to wash my complexion in. Mother, do you hear that? There's no milk. I'd send Melleas to milk a cow, only there don't seem to be any round here. I don't know why. Really, it's too maddening. I've never passed a night yet without bathing my face in milk."

"And a fat lot of good it's done you," thought Melleas. Her mother took the last piece of venison, and said: "There must be a village somewhere about. Send Melleas to bring you half a pailful back."

"Only too delighted," said Melleas, jumping up. He seized the pail and vanished into the dusk. On the brow of the hill, just before descending into the valley below, he looked back. He saw the two wimples fluttering in the red glow of the campfire, and then he saw something else. Something long and blue and scaly was just emerging in a cloud of smoke from the face of the cliff.

"Darling, it's simply too wonderful," gasped Melisande, three days later. "I never saw such a head. Really, you must be terribly brave and strong. We'll have it mounted and hung in the hall for a helmet-stand, with your name and the date and the place below. Then everyone can see how wonderful you are. Whatever did it weigh?"

"About two tons, I believe," said Melleas modestly. "The scales are rather fine. aren't they?"

"They're blue as peacocks' tails – " She glanced round cautiously. "Tell me, was Arthur annoyed about Pelerine? I mean – losing her like that."

"Not in the least. After all, extremely sad though the whole affair was, it was hardly my fault. I didn't get back till – till it was all over. No, he was most complimentary. Suggested, in fact, that I'd earned my knighthood twice over."

"So you did. After all, you revenged her. You killed the dragon."

Melleas coughed. "Do you think a husband should have any secrets from his wife?"

"Of course not. Why?"

Melleas looked out of the window in rather an embarrassed way. "Then I'd better begin now: it's been on my conscience rather, anyway. It's about that dragon. You see, darling, I didn't kill it. I found it lying dead by the fire when I got back."

"But – but what did it die of then?"

"Indigestion, I rather fancy," said Melleas.

Sir Dinadan in THE GOOSE GIRL

Theodore Goodridge Roberts

Keeping in a slightly lighter vein, we come to one of the stories Theodore Goodridge Roberts (1877–1953) wrote for Blue Book *magazine in the 1940s featuring Sir Dinadan. Dinadan was a peace-loving knight who saw no purpose in fighting just for the sake of it. He needed a good cause, but tended to drift into trouble rather too easily, as we find in the following story.*

> *"They emptied a pot or two in sweet accord; and when the good ale got to their hearts the talk turned upon women; and when it got to their heads, they fell to gross bragging. At last one cried out villainously how the meanest goose girl of his country outshone the very pick of high dames and damosels and even dukes' daughters of less favoured regions; whereupon the other broke the braggart's head with a pewter pot."*
>
> *– The Book of Maelor.*

Sir Dinadan and his youthful squire Victor were twelve days out from Camelot on a line which the knight had never before explored beyond a league, when the squire was assailed suddenly by fever and stomach cramps. But the heroic youth kept his saddle till they came upon a rustic hermitage, though with heavy sweating inside his harness and great discomfort in his vitals. The hermit claimed to be a skilled physician, and Dinadan believed him because of his honest and kindly face. Between them they soon disarmed Victor and got him to bed, where the hermit went to work on him with brews of wild herbs, applications of cold wet moss to the head and hot wet moss to the stomach, and a lancet. He slept all night, with Dinadan and the hermit keeping watch turn and turn about, and in the morning drank a bowl of thin barley gruel, with one of them supporting him and the other holding the bowl. Then he slept again.

"I must move on today, good Brother Ambrose, or tomorrow at the latest, for our need of a profitable adventure is acute," said Dinadan.

"Then you will go without your squire, good sir," replied the hermit, kindly but firmly. "He will not be strong enough for the saddle within the sennight or maybe ten days, for in ridding him of the noxious humours which threatened his life I had, perforce, to all but drain his veins. But what blood I left in him is as pure as morning dew; and by the time Mother Nature and I have replenished the reservoir of his heart, he will be in better health than ever before."

"Gramercy," said Dinadan.

"I shall graduate his stomach from gruel to porridge with thin milk, then with cream (I have an excellent cow) – and anon to broiled troutlets from the brook, and so on, by way of the white meat of a spring chicken, to boiled bacon and peas," said Brother Ambrose. "So go your way, good knight, with an easy mind, and make your adventure with a stout heart, for both your squire and his charger shall receive the best of care and provisioning while you are gone."

So Sir Dinadan went on with his great horse Garry, leaving Victor and Victor's horse and four of his last five silver crowns with the good hermit. He had been fooled by the pretty faces of damosels oftener than he could count on the fingers of both hands, but he was a shrewd reader of character in the faces of men.

He moved in a wilderness where every track was of the cloven hoofs of wild cows and wild swine and deer. So dense were the thickets and so rough the way in places that he dismounted and led his heavy-burdened charger. Progress was slow. On the third day out from the hermitage, he decided that he had chosen a hopeless line of country for his purpose, and promised himself that if he failed to find a man-made road by sunset, he would change direction, for on this line a mad wild bull was far more likely to be encountered than any chivalrous adventure. But Fate, in the shapes of a gaggle of geese and their attendant, caused him to change direction in the first hour of the afternoon. The geese hissed and flopped about in the underbrush when he and Garry came heavy-footed and unexpected amongst them; and he knew them for domesticated birds, because they didn't take wing.

"Tame geese in the wilderness!" he exclaimed. "A sure sign of a homestead close at hand. Good! But which way did they come?"

He glanced about him and beheld the goose girl. She was a tall girl in coarse wool only, and not a great deal of that. Her face was weather-stained and hung about with tangled strands of yellow hair. She stood almost in arm's-reach of his left stirrup, and regarded him with questioning eyes and a half-smile.

"God bless us!" he exclaimed.

"Gramercy," she murmured, and fluttered her eyelashes.

"You startled me, my good girl," he said. "First your geese, then yourself. All most unexpected in this dreary wilderness. Did you come from a farm?"

After a moment's hesitation, she nodded.

"Will you lead me to it?" he asked.

Again she hesitated, then nodded again and murmured: "I can try, anyhow."

"Try? What d'ye mean by that? Don't you know the way?"

"I am thinking of you, sir. It is not only a farm, sir. There is a castle too."

"Hah! A castle. So much the better. Lead on, I pray you, my good girl: and in due course, and with reasonable luck, I shall reward you handsomely."

"Gramercy," she murmured, and moved to Garry's head.

Now in pure courtesy, Dinadan got down from his saddle and joined her there; for despite his frequent railings upon the inconstancy of the female heart, it was not in his nature nor breeding to go horsed in the company of any woman – damosel or wench, high dame or poor crone – trudging afoot. So they went side by side, and the big horse followed close.

"What of your fat geese?" he asked her.

She shot him a measuring look and said: "If you knew what awaits you, sir, you would have no concern to spare for my gaggle of geese."

"Why not?"

"All your concern would be for yourself."

"Hah! What awaits me?"

"The keeper of the castle."

"Is it an ogre's castle, then? Fie, fie, girl! I lost my faith in fairy tales years ago."

"The keeper of that castle is nothing out of a fairy tale, nor lord of the castle neither, but a great bully of a man who keeps it from this side of the moat, letting only hinds and swineherds and the like in and out; and so he has done these ten months past."

"D'ye tell me so?"

"Yes, for your own good. There is no knight-at-arms within to match him, and the lord took such a hurt at jousting years ago that he may sit nothing harder than a cushion now, and passes the days in monkish studies and the play of chess."

"Poor fellow! But has no knight from without essayed to get in the castle?"

"Two. That's to say one, in very truth."

"One or two, my good girl?"

"One made the essay and died of it. The other took but a look and ran away."

"God save us! The rogue must wear a right villainous look. But I promise you I'll not run from him, no matter how terrible his aspect."

"And his action is more terrible yet. He is the deadliest knight in the world."

"Is he, now? How does he call himself?"

"Sir Grudwyn."

"Never heard of him. But what of his arms? Are they rich?"

"The helmet and breastplate are damascened with gold, and the hilt and scabbard of the sword studded with rubies."

"Hah, gold and rubies!" exclaimed Dinadan. "Just what I need. Lead me to them, good wench."

The goose girl frowned at him and asked coldly, "Are you Sir Launcelot himself then – or a fool?"

"Nay, not Sir Launcelot," he replied cheerfully. "Lead on."

"A fool, then," she said, but in a kinder voice. "So be it, Sir Fool. But I have warned you."

A few minutes later Dinadan bethought to ask: "To what end does this Grudwyn keep the castle?"

"In wicked spite," she answered, with averted eyes. "Because he may not enter himself, no other shall enter. If the damosel be not for him, then she's for no one."

Dinadan checked so suddenly that his charger bumped into him.

"Damosel, d'ye say? But I might have known it! Is there no end to them? Must there be a damosel mixed up with every adventure I undertake, to bedevil it or me?"

She gave him an unpleasant look, disillusioned and scornful.

"Take heart, noble sir," she said. "You have nothing to fear. I will lead you around and set you upon a safe road beyond, without letting that merciless Grudwyn catch so much as a glimpse of you."

"Not so fast!" he exclaimed. "He keeps the castle from this side the moat, you say. Then I may do what I can with him, and come away afterward with his arms and horse, and all the while keep the ditch betwixt the damosel and myself. Lead on."

"You are very sure of yourself," she murmured, sighing.

"I need the money," he said cheerfully.

She sighed again and led onward, now moving three full paces before him; and after a little she gestured to him for caution, knelt and peered ahead, then beckoned to him with a finger. He advanced softly and knelt beside her; and together they peered out from the underbrush.

"There he is," she whispered. "To the left."

But Dinadan did not shift his gaze instantly, so vastly impressed was he by the view directly in front of him. He saw greensward as smooth as tapestry, and beyond it a willow-fringed moat with white swans and lilies on its still surface, and beyond the water the barbican and walls and bulging towers of a great castle, and the drawbridge cocked high in air like a gigantic arm of iron and oak raised in threat and defiance. It was big enough for a king: and yet he saw no stir of life save the deliberate movements of the swans. After gazing his fill at that marvel, he looked to his left.

The goose girl whispered at his ear: "Under the great oak there."

He saw a knight in a robe of red silk sprawled at ease in the shade.

"A sluggard, asleep and unready at this hour," he jeered.

"Ride forth, then, and you'll find him awake and ready enough, I trow," she answered tartly.

He sneered and said: "Nay, I'll walk over and slap him awake, the hulking slug-abed!"

And he rose from his knees and made a forward step – but only one step. Then she sprang and gripped him by the sword-belt and gave so shrewd a yank that he staggered back, and was all but brought to earth by her violence and the tangling of his spurs.

"Fool!" she cried in his astonished face – for now she was in front of him, and with both hands pushing instead of pulling. "If you *will* die, die fighting! He is not asleep – nor unarmed; and his horse is close at hand! Would you go to him like a silly calf to the butcher? Give him a fight at least. He might suffer a mishap."

He steadied himself against a shoulder of his equally astonished charger.

"What the devil!" he muttered. "He will suffer a mishap, I warrant you – unless you disable me before I get at him."

At that, she let her hands fall and stood still, with bowed head; whereupon Dinadan turned his back on her and readied Garry and himself for action. He loosed a sack and a hamper from the saddle and dropped them to the ground, took the greater of his two spears in hand and cast the other down, then drew his long shield around from back to shoulder and mounted.

"God defend you!" cried the girl.

"Gramercy," returned the knight, but coldly, for he did not enjoy being pushed and pulled about and called a fool.

So he rode forth from the screen of the forest, drew rein when fairly in the open, fewtered his spear and shouted: "Run, rogue, run!"

Then the sleepy scene came awake and alive in the blink of an eye, as if by magic. Another shout rang hard upon Dinadan's like an echo, and the shouter appeared, running and leading a great black horse all saddled and armed; the knight beneath the tree came quickly but heavily to his feet and cast off his robe and showed himself armored from neck to heels; and heads appeared along the battlements of the castle, and white faces at narrow windows.

"The wench was right," muttered Dinadan.

Now the shouting squire reached Grudwyn, helped him up onto the black charger and gave him his shield, and a spear like a tree.

"The good girl was right," murmured Dinadan.

And to dapple-gray Garry he said: "Action front, dear lad, and may God defend us."

So Garry tossed his head and flexed his legs and went a few paces with more posturing than progress, like a dancer who would attune his feet to the music before stepping out.

"Here they come," warned Dinadan.

Then Garry changed his gait and launched himself to the attack as straight and hard as arrow from string; and Dinadan levelled his spear and held it true. The two iron spearheads struck like one, each upon the very centre of the opposite iron-plated shield; and the hurtling onslaught checked while the two stout poles of sinewy ash-wood arched, quivering, between the stricken, stubborn shields – only to splinter and break at last, and release the arrested weights of horses and men and metal to stumble and crash together and stagger apart. Garry got his four feet under him smartly and wheeled wide and lightly. Grudwyn's charger was heavier and slower. Dinadan readjusted himself in his saddle – from which he had come within an inch and an ounce of being pushed – and cast away the butt of his shattered spear. He saw Grudwyn do the same, and Grudwyn's squire come running with a new spear.

"If it's to be spear against sword, I'll do better afoot," he muttered, speaking from experience; and he was about to dismount, but was stayed by the appearance of the goose girl at his knee, bearing his other spear.

"Gramercy," he said, and took the weapon from her, stooping sidewise. "You're a good girl – and you were right when you warned me of his trickery. But run away now, or you might get hurt in the scuffle."

She looked up at him and fluttered her eyelashes, which were darker than her tangled tresses.

"Don't do that!" he exclaimed. "That's a damosel's play, and not for an honest goose girl, no matter how pretty you are." And with that he swung away from her, straightened spear and horse and went at Grudwyn like a thunderbolt.

Grudwyn and the black charger were the heavier, but Sir Dinadan and his dapple-gray were the quicker and faster; and so it was that the murderous keeper of the castle was no more than headed aright, and his new spear was still shaking like a reed in the wind, when that thunderbolt struck him and jarred him from his saddle and heaved him back and down over his horse's tail. Thereupon Dinadan cast his spear aside, dismounted quickly and drew his long sword.

"Would you butcher him flat on the ground?" cried the squire, shrill with dismay and astonishment.

"God forbid!" said Dinadan. "Set him upon his feet and put his sword in his hand."

So the other ran to Grudwyn and strove hard but vainly to set him upright. And now the goose girl came running to Dinadan.

"Have at him now!" she begged. "He would not spare you if he had you down. Slay him for the merciless brute he is."

"Nay, I'm no butcher, but a true knight," he protested. "The wind's knocked out of him, that's all that ails him at the moment. Once he's up and sword in hand, I'll slay him, I promise you."

She cried at him: "This is no time for courtesy and the rules of chivalry! Take your advantage now. He is deadlier afoot than horsed."

"So am I," he said. "Don't worry. I'll feed him to the foxes all in good time."

By now Grudwyn was on his feet, but unsteady and still supported by his squire; and his great sword was naked in his right hand, but held limply and point on ground, more like a staff than a weapon.

"Don't trust him," the girl whispered. "He is as whole and ready as you are. Trust not his base squire, neither."

Dinadan replied, "Leave them to me, my little friend," and put her gently aside and went forward cautiously behind his shield and sword.

"He's big, but I've had a-do with and undone bigger," he told himself. "And he took such a shog he's fit to fall flat again even now, of his own weight and dizziness."

The squire moved away, leaving Grudwyn swaying alone and apparently held upright only by the support of his sword: but Dinadan, who was a fool only in his encounters with damosels, observed and took note of the fact that the point of the great sword was sunk no deeper than an inch or so into the tender sward; whereupon he uttered a hoot of scornful and hateful derision, and advanced yet more cautiously. He went a slow pace to the right, then a few jigging steps to the left, then three skips straight ahead and one backward, and more sidewise hops and deliberate paces, but ever closing in upon Grudwyn with a fixed and baleful scrutiny. Then, of a sudden, Grudwyn dressed his shield, whirled up his sword, bellowed and charged like a bull.

Dinadan avoided that onslaught lightly, and Grudwyn carved nothing but air. Grudwyn snubbed to a stop and turned heavily but with surprising quickness. Dinadan faced about to meet him, and saw that which startled his attention from the business in hand – the squire (who was in less than half-armor) rolling on the grass with his arms up and locked to shield his head, and the goose girl belaboring him furiously with her stout oaken staff. He gaped with astonishment, but was recalled to the menace of

Grudwyn by a swish of steel so close to his head that it clipped his crest and set his helmet ringing.

Now Grudwyn was upon him, pressing him back and hammering on his head, over the tops of the grinding shields with the pommel of his sword. He wrenched and staggered clear and made a back-handed stroke even while staggering. It was a lucky stroke, for though it only rattled at the bars of Grudwyn's visor, it won him a moment in which to steady himself and strike again. And this was a shrewd stroke in very sooth, forehanded and swung full from the shoulders. It set Grudwyn back on his heels with a split shield and a left arm benumbed to the neck. The wrecked shield fell to the ground, and Grudwyn cursed.

"Now's your chance!" screamed the goose girl. "Chop him down!"

Dinadan glanced aside and saw her standing a little way off, and Grudwyn's squire lying as still as death at her feet.

"Why did you do that?" he asked.

She cried: "He would have stabbed you from behind, else!"

Then he saw the foot-long dagger on the ground.

"You saved my life, good girl," he said wonderingly. "The base knave would have found the chink beneath my left arm, devil a doubt. I owe you my life. I never thought to owe it to a goose girl – nor to any other female neither for that matter, God wot! Gramercy!"

She screamed: "Fool! Look to Grudwyn!"

He leaped aside even before he looked, but even so was sent reeling and staggering with a dent in his helmet – a dent that would have been a cut through steel and skull but for her warning. He saw comets with fiery tails, and heard bells clanging in tottering minster spires, but all the while he kept his feet under his point of balance and in motion. He thrust blindly and heard a grunt; and then rushing comets and spinning darkness passed and disclosed Grudwyn swaying, stooping, on fumbling feet. His first impulse was to leap forward, but thought was quicker. He had pricked his enemy, but surely not deep enough for a mortal, or even a disabling hurt. So instead he loosed his shield from his left arm and flung it at drooping Grudwyn's feet – an act which required a mighty fling, for it was a shield of extraordinary size and weight.

"Fool!" cried the wench. "Now you've cast away your chance of life – and passed your only advantage to him – oh, pitiful fool!"

Sure enough, Grudwyn had raised the shield and dressed it

before him quicker than it can be told. But Dinadan only smiled and murmured to himself: "We'll soon know who is the fool."

Now Grudwyn charged again behind shield and whirling sword, and Dinadan avoided him lightly and banged the back of his helmet as he plunged past; and as he ploughed to a stop, and again as he came heavily about, Dinadan banged him shrewdly on neckpiece and backplate.

"Stand and fight!" roared Grudwyn.

"Nay, would you have me split my own shield?" Dinadan jeered.

So Grudwyn continued to charge and slash, check and turn, still slashing, all the while carving nothing but air; and the massy shield on his left arm sank an inch lower every minute.

"A heavy shield, in sooth, but a mere plaything on the powerful arm of the mighty Sir Grudwyn," jeered Dinadan.

"Stand still – but ten seconds – and I'll cut you in two," gasped Grudwyn.

"All in good time," said Dinadan, skipping lightly.

So Grudwyn continued to scar the greensward with his mad and weighty plunges and turns, while Dinadan circled just out of reach of the whistling sword, and the heavy shield sank lower every minute. But at last, and as suddenly as a flash of lightning, Dinadan stood firm and struck full-strength once, twice and again, forehanded, backhanded and forehanded again through steel links and bone: and Grudwyn toppled and crashed; and Dinadan made to step away lightly to avoid the gushing blood, but fouled his spurs in something behind him and went over backward.

Sir Dinadan opened his eyes, beheld a slanted sunbeam and closed them. When he opened them again he saw candlelight. He blinked, looked again and saw the face of an old man in a black hood.

"Brother Ambrose?" he queried.

His voice was so feeble a voice that he hardly knew it for his own.

"Nay, Doctor Mendax," said the old man.

"Candles," Dinadan murmured. "Where am I?"

"In bed, young sir."

"Why?"

"Why? You may well ask. But for me, you'd be in a grave."

"In a grave? Gramercy! But why?"

"You would be dead, that's why. But compose yourself. Relax, and drink this."

The doctor raised Dinadan's head a little with his left arm and held a cup to his lips. Dinadan drank, and instantly slept again. When he opened his eyes the third time, it was still upon the feeble shine of two candles, and the doctor was still there.

"It has come back to me," he said. "I was fighting afoot with a false knight – it all comes clear to me now – and cut him down with three mortal strokes. Then my heels tripped on something. What happened then?"

"You were stabbed from behind," said the doctor in a soothing yet relishing tone of voice. "A deadly stab, young man. A mortal thrust. But thanks to the knowledge and skill of poor old Doctor Mendax, you still live and will soon be sound."

"Gramercy, learned sir. But who stabbed me?"

"Grudwyn's squire."

"Nay, that tricky knave was dead. I saw him dead on the ground, where the goose girl had whacked the life out of him with her oaken staff."

"That's what she thought too; but when you stumbled backward over him and he arose and sank a poniard in you, she had to whack him again – which she did with a vengeance. And now he and Grudwyn occupy the same ignoble grave."

"A deadly wench and overprone to cry 'Fool!' at her betters. But a good girl at heart, and a good friend to me, for it seems that I owe her my life twice or maybe thrice."

Doctor Mendax chuckled and said: "Aye, you can say that, young man – a deadly wench indeed, but certainly a good friend to you, for you'd have bled white if she hadn't come and pulled me out of bed and out to you by main strength, willy-nilly. Had she been a minute slower, even my skill could not have saved you."

"So I'm within the castle, I presume," sighed Dinadan.

"Aye, and in the very best bed."

"And what of my horse Garry?"

"He is in the best stall in the best stable."

"And the big black?"

"In the next stall in the same stable."

"And Grudwyn's sword and armour? It's all mine now, you know – horse and arms – by the rules of combat."

"All safe and at your disposal."

"Gramercy, venerable sir. And will you tell me how soon I can be up and away?"

"You have faith in me, young sir?"

"Yes."

"Good. No other physician in Christendom could answer your question truly, just as no other could have stopped the outflow of your life-blood as I did, but I can and will. Follow my instructions to the letter, young sir, and you will be on your feet on the tenth day from now, and on your horse on the twenty-fifth. No other honest doctor, nor even that old warlock Merlin with all his deviltry, could do as well by you."

"I believe you," said Dinadan. "And I have, seemingly, even greater faith than yourself in your professional abilities. The diamonds and rubies which stud the scabbard and the hilt of Grudwyn's sword are worth a king's ransom: and they are all yours – less the trifling price of a croft and a cow for the goose girl – if you have me healed and horsed in half the time you mention."

"You flatter me," smirked the doctor. "Not that I couldn't do it," he went on, staring into the flame of the nearer candle. "It's a temptation, I confess. With such wealth as that, I could extend my scientific researches even to the uttermost ends of the earth and take a fling at the night life of Camelot into the bargain. Ah, me! But my inborn honest nature protests; and so I must ask, in fairness to yourself, what's your hurry to be gone from here?"

"Fear of the damosel," Dinadan mumbled, in a shamed voice. "Laugh if you will, but it's the truth. Damosels are my undoing. And there's one in this castle. The goose girl told me so. And she must be the most beautiful in the world – most of them are, God help me, and as false as beautiful – or Grudwyn would not have striven so madly and long to keep all other cavaliers out simply because he could not get in himself. But it was not to get in that I fought him and cut him down. It was for his arms and horse. But for my empty purse and pressing debts, I would have avoided the castle entirely upon learning that a damosel was involved in the adventure. But I was stabbed from behind, and here I am."

The old man scratched his cheek thoughtfully and asked: "Don't you know the reward for delivering the castle from that murderous great rogue's tyranny?"

"I've not been told it, but I can guess it," Dinadan sneered cynically. "The fair hand of the beautiful damosel – not to mention the false heart – in the holy bonds of matrimony."

"Nay, your guess is wide and high, young sir. The reward is a fair manor of six farms and a tubful of silver crowns. The damosel's hand, and the five manors and castle that go with it, are for her own giving or keeping. And you are wrong about her heart too; and as for her beauty – in my opinion, her nose is a trifle too short for classical perfection. And perhaps the same can be said also of her upper lip."

"That may well be – but, knowing my weakness, I fear she would appear perfect to me just the same. And now that I am in funds again, I care nothing for the six farms and tubful of crowns. So all my concern is to win clear of this castle with my horse and arms, and base Grudwyn's horse and body-armour, at the earliest possible moment, before worse befall me."

"Extraordinary! I'll do my best to expedite your recovery from a wound which would have proved fatal but for me. Drink this now and relax."

Dinadan slept again. When he opened his eyes, it was upon a beam of brightest sunshine which lanced through a narrow window and straight and level across the chamber to the arras on the opposite wall. He felt hungry and thought of broth, and even of hot pease-porridge flavoured with a knuckle of ham; and even of a jack of ale. He looked as far to his right and left as he could without turning or lifting his head on his stiffly bandaged neck and shoulders. But that was not far, and he did not see anyone.

"Are you there, venerable sir?" he asked.

"No, it's only me," said someone beyond his range of vision.

"Hah!" he exclaimed. "The goose girl. What brings you here?"

"Yes, sir," she murmured; and she stepped into view, but not into the bright beam of sunshine. "The Doctor sleeps, and I have been on watch since dawn."

She was dressed – if you call it that – just as he had first and last seen her, and her yellow hair still hung in tangles.

"Gramercy," he said. "But what of your geese?"

"I don't know, sir. I work in the scullery now."

"A scullery wench! But cheer up, my good girl, for with the diamonds and rubies from the scabbard and hilt of Grudwyn's sword I am now in a position to reward you for saving my life from the dastardly tricks of that knave and of his equally base squire. I shall establish you in a snug cottage with a fair meadow before it, an orchard of apples and cherries behind it, a cow in the meadow, chickens and beehives in the orchard, and geese too if you want them, and a servant to milk your cow and cut your honeycombs. All this shall be yours – and a modest fund in coin of the realm besides – forever and a day."

"Gramercy, sir."

"Nay, you have been a good friend to me. And you must have a garden, so that I may think of you sitting on a cushion, sewing a fine seam and eating strawberries and honey and cream."

"Gramercy. And what of yourself, sir? Shall you settle down in the manor which my lord will bestow upon you for freeing him of Grudwyn?"

"Nay, God forbid! I have heard of that reward, from the doctor – six fat farms and a tubful of crowns to boot. But I'll have nought to do with it. I did not fight Grudwyn to free the castle to the admittance of your damosel's cowardly suitors, but to possess myself of his arms and horse. I am a free knight-errant, and I intend to remain such, mauger my head! And the sooner I get out of here, the better I'll like it."

"Are you afraid of something? You, the strongest knight in the world?"

"Gramercy, child. But I'm afraid, nevertheless. I'd liefer have ado with Sir Launcelot himself than so much as exchange glances with any damosel. So I'm afraid of meeting the damosel of this castle, even if she isn't a raving beauty."

After a moment of hesitation, the goose girl whispered: "Why do you say that? Have you ever seen her?"

"Nay, but I've heard that both her nose and upper lip are too short."

"Too short for what?"

"For beauty."

"Who says so?"

"Doctor Mendax."

"That old fool!" she exclaimed, turning her head as if at a sound; and before he could utter a word of protest, she was gone from his restricted line of view.

"Overprone to cry 'Fool!' at her betters, but a good girl at heart," he murmured.

The physician appeared beside the bed half a minute later and inspected his tongue, counted his pulse and felt his brow for fever.

"How am I doing?" he asked.

"Marvelously well, young sir. How do you feel?"

"Hungry."

"Excellent! Just what I expected to hear from you, so I came prepared. This way with broth, Jynkyn."

A fellow appeared bearing a steaming bowl with a horn spoon in it.

"Hah!" exclaimed Dinadan, and he sat bolt upright.

"Have a care!" cried the Doctor, pressing him back on the pillow. "Would you reopen the wound and so undo all I have done? I'll feed you. But I'll risk the raising of your head and shoulders a trifle."

He stuffed a second pillow beneath his patient's head and commenced feeding him generous spoonfuls.

"Too thin for my taste," complained Dinadan.

"Perhaps it will be thicker for supper; and maybe you can have a rasher tomorrow or the next day, so marvellously have I doctored you," soothed the ancient.

When the bowl was empty, Dinadan asked for a horn of ale.

"You shall have a full jack of the best with your supper tonight, young sir. Drink this now and relax."

And Doctor Mendax pressed a cup to his patient's lips.

Dinadan was roused from his drugged sleep by hands on his shoulders, shaking him. He opened his eyes and saw the goose girl stooping over him.

"What now?" he gasped. "Have a care! The wound! Where's the Doctor?"

"Gone – and all your diamonds and rubies with him!" she cried, still shaking him. "As for your grievous wound – fiddlesticks!"

He gaped up at her, speechless with astonishment and confusion.

"Are you quite a fool – except in mortal combat?" she went on in an angry and desperate voice. "That was not a stab, but only one more bang on your silly head. When you went backward over the squire, and he – I thought I had finished him – squirmed up with a knife in his hand, I swung my staff again, but missed him and hit you instead. But I got him with the next swing, the tricky knave! And you were brought into the castle, where Mendax bandaged your neck and shoulders, and that lie was invented. And here you are."

"Why?"

"To give him time to pry all the rubies and diamonds from the scabbard and hilt of Grudwyn's sword, it seems. So up and after him!"

"Hasn't anyone gone after him?"

"Nay, 'tis your business."

"Nay, for I meant to divide them between you and him. What now of the croft and cow I promised you? Now I must reward you out of the price of Grudwyn's horse and armour, God help me! And what of them? Have I been robbed of them too?"

"They are safe enough," she said, and released his shoulders and straightened her back and made as if to turn away, but changed her mind. "As safe as yourself," she continued in a queer, shaking voice. "I'll send Jynkyn to help you arm and take you to your horse. As for Grudwyn's horse and armour, here's their price in gold and silver." She flung a heavy purse down on the bed. "As for that croft and cow – and strawberries an' cream – the devil take them!"

With that, she turned and ran to the door, but checked there for a moment and turned again and cried strangely, "Good luck to you – and thanks for nothing – you fool!" and disappeared.

"God defend me!" exclaimed Dinadan. "What ails the wench? And where did she get this purse of money?"

He sat up and tore and uncoiled ten yards of bandages from his neck and shoulders. "Fiddlesticks" was correct – there was no wound. At this discovery, he cursed Doctor Mendax for a rogue and himself for the fool of the world and leaped from the bed with such violence as to almost knock over the fellow Jynkyn, who had entered at that moment with an armful of garments of linen, leather, chain and mail.

"Is everyone in this place mad?" he asked, when Jynkyn was busy latching and buckling the iron plates.

"I be a poor knave an' knows nothing, yer honour," said Jynkyn.

Dinandan gave him a coin from the great purse and asked: "Why did Doctor Mendax rob me and run away?"

"It was only for lack of full pockets he didn't cut an' run years ago, in my humble opinion. But me lord was too smart for him, an' kep' all the cash an' jewellery under lock an' key."

"Why did your lord detain him? Of what use to him was that old fraud and thief?"

"For to play at the game of chess, yer honour, that's wot. My lord bests everyone else without hardly puttin' his mind to it, but the doctor has given him many a shrewd tussle, especially since his lordship promised him a prize of a pension and a palfrey if he ever checkmated him. That was seven year agone, come Candlemas; and the poor old gent never come nearer it than a stalemate."

"So he turned thief," sneered Dinadan. "Anything to escape from this madhouse! I feel the same way myself."

The chamber was in darkness by now, but Dinadan was fully harnessed and in such haste to be gone before worse than robbery might befall him that even his hunger and thirst were forgotten. He followed Jynkyn's stumbling guidance down twisting stairs and along crooked passages, and at last out and into the stableyard. Garry nickered at his approach. The tall charger was soon bitted and saddled, and the knight mounted; and then Jynkyn led them, by dim and circuitous ways, to the front courtyard and thence across the drawbridge. Dinadan gave him another coin.

"Good fortune, an' safe roads to yer honour!" exclaimed Jynkyn, louting low.

Dinadan returned the purse to his wallet and was about to move off, but a sudden thought struck him and checked him.

"Where did that goose girl get the money to pay me for the horse and arms I won from Grudwyn?"

"God fend yer innocence, sir," chuckled the fellow. "She be no more a goose girl nor the Queen of Sheby! She took to tanglin' her tresses an' paintin' her pretty face – an' everything else wot wasn't covered by that skimpy kirtle – with juices of yarbs an' berries, so's to win past Sir Grudwyn an' spy about for a champion."

"D'ye mean she's a damosel?"

"Aye, the Damosel Isbel herself."

At that, Dinadan shivered from his shorn crest to his spurs, then cried out in wordless and bewildered consternation; and Garry thrust forward so suddenly as to almost overturn Jynkyn.

"Who's mad now!" cried the staggered varlet disgustedly, for he had expected yet a third coin.

But he received no answer, for horse and knight were already crashing and stumbling in the dark forest.

Later, when Dinadan discovered a great wallet of meat, a leather bottle of ale, and even a bag of beans for Garry tied to his saddle, he sat on the moss a long time with his bewildered head clasped in both hands, and conflict and confusion in his heart.

"So she provisioned me for the road," he concluded bitterly. "She made sure that hunger would not drive me back. Now I can trust no female under eighty years, not even goose girls, any more!"

Sir Belleus in BELLEUS'S DEMON

Lawrence Schimel

Belleus is known primarily for one incident in the Arthurian legends but to reveal that would reveal too much about the following story. Lawrence Schimel (b. 1971) is a prolific writer with stories in over 100 anthologies and magazines, a selection of which will be found in The Drag Queen of Elfland *(1996). He has also recently edited* Tarot Fantastic *(1997) with Martin H. Greenberg, and* The Mammoth Book of Gay Erotica *(1997) for Robinson Books.*

A surprising fear haunted Belleus, and would not let go; surprising, for he was lord of many islands and a doughty fighter, of a stout heart and a strong arm, well skilled with sword and spear and shield, with arts of war that involved no weapons other than bodies. But he had slipped, in the skirmish, and nearly met his death; the image kept running through his mind: lying defenceless at his opponent's feet, de-armed by his fall, a sword upraised above his neck about to descend upon him. And all he could do was stare up at his opponent, frozen in fear.

Had it not been for one of his men, who struck the brigand from behind, Belleus's head would be severed from his lifeless body. He could not escape how his body had felt in that moment – lifeless, devoid of life, terror-struck.

This shock made Belleus want to cleave to his wife, Isobell – not to slake his passion on her, but to hold another body against his, to take comfort from her, from his love for her and hers for him, to recall the vibrant aliveness she made him feel when their bodies danced and joined together.

Belleus felt shame mixed with his fear, for he had lost his sword so quickly in the fight – he was no callow youth to make mistakes in war, nor so old that his sword had grown slow. Was he not lord, by right of arms and his just rule, of more than a score of islands?

He was, he often thought, equal to the knights the troubadours sang of in ballads, that fabled brotherhood of knights who served King Arthur and sat with him about the equally fabled Table Round.

Belleus hungered after that singular glory, to fight alongside those Knights of the Table Round, as they fought monsters and other fierce beasts, bested their foes in combat, and even managed to fend off the yoke of sorceries and other trickeries with their agile wits and pure hearts.

But that hunger paled now before the fear that gripped the pit of his stomach, as the image of a sword poised high above his head, ready to fall, would not leave him. He wanted so desperately to live, and suddenly he wanted desperately to live peacefully, never to face the sword again. He wanted only to hold Isobell, to feel her body against his, to sleep and to wake still holding her.

The pavilion was dark when he arrived, and Belleus could see the silhouette upon the bed, back toward him. He lit no light, lest he wake her, and in darkness he un-armed himself, removed his boots and outer clothes, and climbed into bed. He wrapped his arm around her sleeping form, and pressed himself against her back, holding on to her for life's sake, for holding her dear, for understanding what he fought for. His beard brushed against the soft back of her neck. He felt his manhood rising as their bodies pressed against each other, through the sheets and clothing.

But as Belleus held and caressed her and whispered in her ear that he loved her, she leapt suddenly from his arms and the bed and cried out. Her voice was monstrous strange, sounding like the bellowing of a demon it was so low in timbre. "What foul trickery is this?" Belleus cried out, wondering if a devil had lain in the shape of his wife on his bed, ready to trick him.

And what, then, had happened to Isobell?

In the dim light of the pavilion, all Belleus could see was a tall man-like shape. Belleus reached for and drew his sword, which he always kept close at hand, to save himself from this foul creature that loomed above him.

Belleus was half-grateful for the darkness, which cloaked the devil's hideous features; this same darkness, however, left him vulnerable to the creature's attack, for could not this spawn of hell see in darkness as if it were brith day while Belleus was left nearly as blind as a newborn infant?

He heard the slide of steel on scabbard, and Belleus's blood froze as he imagined the blade held high above him once again, as he lay defenceless and de-armed at his opponent's feet.

"Thought you to cuckold Nature with me, cur?" his demon attacker cried, looming above him in the shape of a giant. "Stand your guard, I shall have reparation for this base attack on mine honor and mine person."

The voice snapped Belleus from the past, to face the opponent before him. It didn't matter if this were demon or other foul creature, he must save himself – and Isobell.

"Tell me," Belleus commanded, "what hast thou done with Isobell, 'ere I strike you down."

The devil sought to battle steel against steel, hoping to unnerve him by playing against Belleus's weakness, this newfound terror of the sword. But the demon had chosen the wrong game to play, for Belleus was a swordsman born, and he would give an accounting of himself, though none were here to witness it save his own person. It would restore his confidence again, and perhaps give rest to these images in his mind.

The giant man-shape stumbled from the pavilion, and Belleus followed after, intent on learning what had been done to Isobell, and why this demon had sought to trick him, lying await for him in his bed. The night was bright compared to the darkness of the pavilion, though the moon was nearly new. The demon took the shape of a man more strongly, visible now in the moon's glow, a man unnaturally tall and with sword drawn and at the ready. They faced each other, each awaiting answers to their questions and salve for their honors.

Steel whistled their answers through the darkness.

Their swords crossed and locked. The sliver of moon, no wider than a blade, cast her light glinting along the metal. They disengaged and swung again and again parried. A fire began to sing in Belleus's blood, for his opponent's skill near matched his own in swiftness and strength. Thoughts of fear, of being terror-frozen beneath the falling blade, melted from his mind and fled before the joy of battle that was a challenge.

Belleus forgot why it was they fought, as their blades crossed and pulled apart; he was focused wholly on the combat and his opponent. But though Belleus fought with all his skill, still his opponent managed to take the upper hand, with its demonic speed. His foe lightly scored Belleus's leg with the tip of its sword, forcing Belleus to shift his weight and grit against the pain, the warm blood that welled forth. The fear, and the surprise, began to creep back into Belleus's mind, as they continued to battle one another. Belleus's breath began to come more shortly, and he wondered if the demon were not merely using its supernatural swiftness and unflagging strength to bludgeon and overwhelm him; could it have also cast a spell, even while fighting blade against blade, to steal Belleus's breath from his lungs and thereby weary him?

Before Belleus knew what had happened, as he wondered at what dire sorcery he was being attacked by in addition to the sword before him, his opponent struck a blow beneath his defence, sword slashing across Belleus's chest. He fell, crumpling with the pain, instinctively hugging his body around the wound.

He tried to uncurl and lift his sword, to block the falling blade his mind insisted must follow, to sever his unprotected head and neck. But no sword fell, and eventually Belleus was able to blink through the tears to look for his opponent. What stayed the demon's steel? Did it mean to torment him further? He prayed for the swift, clean death of battle, of a fight fairly lost.

The giant man-shape stood towering over him, sword pointed down at Belleus's body. And, staring at the tip of that blade, Belleus knew he would cling to life, even if it meant torture. He feared death more than anything, though he was certain his soul would go to heaven – unless this demon spirited it away to the infernal realms.

It seemed content to accept his defeat, however, without killing him. Belleus longed for Isobell even more fervently than he had earlier that day.

"I . . . yield," Belleus managed to whisper, though the effort caused a new flash of pain across his chest.

The being said nothing, merely nodded, then knelt to help Belleus staunch the wound.

"What," Belleus asked, as it tore his shirt to bind the gash, "have you done with my wife?"

Belleus winced as the man-shape – which acted more like a man now than a demon, though Belleus still recalled its demon-swift skill with the sword – pulled the strips of the shirt across his chest tightly. "I have done naught," his opponent replied, wrapping as he spoke. "The pavilion was empty, and I sought refuge within from the foul witchery of four queens, who beguiled me once and tried to force me from my one true love with their black arts. But I would not be moved."

Belleus wished that he not be moved, for every movement jarred his wound and caused him pain, but no pain was as great as the ache of loss he felt because he did not know what had become of Isobell. He wondered if the four witches who had chased this man – who was indeed man and not demon, if he was to be believed; though who could trust the lies of the devilkind? – had ensorcerelled her. Belleus wondered if she'd been kidnapped, or had been in an accident in the woods and needed his help. He tried to rise, to go to her, but his wound split again from the exertion, and he collapsed back onto the ground with a moan.

"Do not move," the man said, but the words were lost to a shriek, and then a woman's voice crying out, "Unhand him, villain!"

The man stood, quickly, and stepped away, and then Isobell was there with Belleus, and he felt whole again. She cried a dolorous moan when she saw his chest, and stood and beat her arms against the man who had done this to her lord, crying out against him. The knight stood his ground and withstood her blows, then grabbed her wrist to still her.

Belleus began to speak, which made Isobell forget the knight and bend her ear close to her lord's face, that she might hear him better. "He bested me fairly, love, do not fight him." He smiled at her, then looked past her, at the knight who stood above them. "Who are you?" Belleus asked. "Few there are who could best me thus in battle."

"I am Sir Lancelot du Lake," the man replied, kneeling down again on the other side of Belleus, to better hear the wounded man. Isobell gasped with surprise, before she realized what she had done and closed her mouth.

"I knew you must be one of Arthur's knights," Belleus continued to whisper, "from the way you fought with the speed and skill of a demon. Though I did not know this when I lay down in my bed and thought you wert my wife!"

"On mine honor, I meant no deceit. And by my troth, you fought me well. When you are well again, my friend, you must come before me at the Court. You would be a welcome addition to our brotherhood of knights."

Belleus could not believe the words he had just heard. Could this be more lies from this demon, tormenting him, playing on his worst fears – the sword falling toward his unprotected neck – and now offering his most fervent wish, only to withdraw it later as part of some cruel mental torture?

Belleus wanted to believe. He pushed himself up on his elbow, the pain be damned, and flung his arms about this man who had wounded him but a short while earlier.

"I thank you, sir," he whispered, each word said with feeling, though each caused a new flash of pain across his chest.

Lancelot du Lake withstood the contact as stiffly as he had Isobell's fists, but then he too embraced the man before him, welcoming Belleus as a brother.

His wound was an arc of pain across Belleus's chest, but the pain made him know how alive he was. And how much life he had yet to live for. It was a mark of the change in his life that had just taken place, which he would wear proudly. Lancelot's arms, wrapped around him, kept him anchored in this world and helped carry him to a new station in life. The image of a sword, poised above him, ran through Belleus's mind once again, and he was not afraid this time; the sword came down toward his unprotected head and neck and rested on first one shoulder and then the other, knighting him. Belleus began to weep from joy, sheltered in these arms of chivalry and the brotherhood of the sword.

Sir Balin in THE HAND OF FAIR LYSETTE

Michael Coney

Balin, known as the Knight of the Two Swords, is one of Arthur's better known knights. He was something of an irascible hothead, likely to strike the head from anything that got in his way. He incurred Arthur's displeasure by killing the Lady of the Lake, and this made him all the more keen to please Arthur with his efforts to right wrongs. In so doing he wounded King Pellam and this "dolorous stroke" blighted the land of Loegres and brought about the need for the Grail Quest. The original story of Sir Balin, as retold by John Steinbeck, was included in the very first anthology in this series, The Pendragon Chronicles. *Here Michael Coney (b. 1932) has reinvestigated Balin and given us a new portrait of this psychopathic knight.*

Michael Coney is a British writer who has been resident in Canada since 1973 and has been selling science fiction and fantasy since 1969. His first book was Mirror Image (1972). *More recently he has produced two spoof Arthurian science fantasies –* Fang the Gnorme (1988) *and* King of the Scepter'd Isle *(1989).*

Everybody knows the story of Sir Balin, who was imprisoned for slaying a cousin of King Arthur, and who alone of the King's knights was able to draw an enchanted sword from its scabbard and so became known as the Knight of the Two Swords. As the story goes, he was exiled after beheading the Lady of Avalon and, in company with his brother Sir Balan, rode to do battle with Arthur's enemy, King Royns.

After much killing, Sir Balin and a young noblewoman arrived at the court of King Pellam, and in fierce battle Sir Balin stuck King Pellam through with the same spear that had pierced the body of Jesus as he hung from the cross.

And Merlin had prophesied that as a result of this dolorous stroke three adjacent kingdoms would be laid waste for a period of twelve years. Thereupon the walls of the castle collapsed, killing everyone within except Sir Balin and King Pellam, who lay in a trance.

It is said that Merlin awakened Sir Balin and told him to leave forthwith. When Sir Balin asked Merlin what had befallen the young noblewoman, the magician replied:

"She is dead."

So runs the legend.

The truth is: Merlin lied.

He was angered by Sir Balin's murderous ways, and wanted to punish him by removing from his power the thing he desired most.

The young noblewoman Lysette, daughter of King Pendhu, had been accompanying Sir Balin and his squire Knut on their travels for the past month. This had been more than long enough for the lusty knight to conceive an almost overpowering desire for the girl. I say almost, because the presence of Knut alone had prevented the worst from occurring.

Knut, a fresh-faced and red-haired young man, had conceived his own feelings toward the fair Lysette, and they did not include flinging her to the ground and having his way with her. Neither did they include Sir Balin doing this, so Knut contrived never to leave Lysette unprotected.

At the moment when Sir Balin felled King Pellam with the dolorous stroke, Knut and Lysette sat talking in a cottage, in the village outside the castle walls.

Suddenly they heard a sound like the roar of a thousand dragons. They ran to the door and saw the walls crumble and collapse. A great geyser of dust rose into the summer sky.

"Sir Balin!" shouted the loyal Knut. He and Lysette began to pick their way across the rubble, searching for survivors. By evening they had found nobody left alive, and they returned to the cottage, distraught. Throughout the village, people wailed for the dead.

In a cloud of radiance, Merlin appeared.

"You must leave this place," he said to Lysette.

"I don't want to." She didn't say why, but she was looking at Knut.

"Otherwise you'll have to contend with Sir Balin. And I think you know what he wants."

"He's dead, surely? Nobody survived out there." The dust was settling like a grey shroud over the village.

"He's alive, in a trance. Soon I must awaken him, and then he'll come for you."

"I'll protect her," said Knut.

Merlin sighed. "How could you fight Sir Balin? He has size, strength and lust on his side. What would you have?"

Knut said nothing.

"You would have indecision," said Merlin. "You wouldn't know where your loyalties lay. You're the last person to protect Lysette. No, I'll give her three days to reach the safety of her father's castle. Then I'll awaken Balin."

And so, three days later, Sir Balin arose from the ruins and stumbled into the village, rubbing his eyes. He found Knut waiting with their horses.

"Merlin tells me the girl died in the castle."

"That is true," Knut answered.

Sir Balin eyed him narrowly. He'd long suspected Knut's feelings for the girl. "I expected to find you weeping."

"Squires do not weep, my lord. Anyway, it's been three days. One gets over personal tragedies, in time."

"Not in three days. But no matter. Have you seen Merlin, at all?"

"Merlin? The magician?"

Sir Balin's hand dropped to his sword, an instinctive and frequent gesture. "Don't fool with me, Knut!"

Frightened, Knut blurted out, "He appeared to us after the castle collapsed."

"Us? *Us?*" The sword was at Knut's throat, pricking the flesh. "Who are us, eh? You and the girl, I'll be bound. So she's alive, eh? You've been lying to me, Knut!"

"No, my lord." Faced with death, the squire decided to shift the blame onto more distant and insubstantial shoulders. "You said Merlin told you the girl had died. I said that was true. Merlin *did* tell you that. It was Merlin who lied, not me. You have my unquestioning loyalty, Sir Balin. As ever." Besides, thought Knut, if I stay close to the man, I may be able to alleviate some of his excesses. "The girl lives," he said, "by the grace of God."

"That's better, Knut. I've always found the point of a sword conducive to honesty. So where is she?"

"She went home to Castle Pendhu."

Sir Balin's improving mood underwent a swift reversal. "Went home? And you let her? You fool!"

"We thought you were dead."

"I don't die so easily. Listen to me, Knut, I must have that girl. We shall ride after her."

"If you say so, my lord," said Knut sadly, hoping that King Pendhu's castle was more soundly constructed than King Pellam's.

Merlin, who had his own method of travel, arrived at Castle Pendhu shortly after Lysette. He found the girl being harangued by her father and mother.

"Where have you been all these weeks, Lysette? Your mother and I have been mad with worry. Rumour has it you've been seen in the company of the Knight with Two Swords!"

"I travelled with Sir Balin for a few weeks, yes."

"I'd have thought a daughter of mine would have more sense," said King Pendhu angrily.

"You're not with child, are you?" asked Queen Sophia.

Now it was Lysette's turn to get angry. "No, I'm not! You must have a poor opinion of me, to think I'd allow Sir Balin so near me. The man is little better than a billygoat! I travelled with him for other reasons."

"What reasons?"

"I'd prefer not to say."

"You'd prefer not to say?" repeated King Pendhu furiously. "First of all you elope with quite the most miserable knight I've ever seen, then you leave him to spend time in the company of the most notorious knight in England, next you ride blithely home as though nothing had happened, and now you won't tell us what it was all about? You need teaching a lesson, my girl!"

"Don't thrash her, Owen," said Queen Sophia anxiously. "She is of marriageable age and comely. I don't want her marked."

"I said nothing about thrashing. I said a lesson. Yes," he said thoughtfully, "it's time she was married off, to be sure. But I'm not having this castle besieged by high-born beggars seeking a dowry. Or low-born beggars like that squire of Balin's – what's his name?"

"Knut."

"Or any damned beggars at all. What happened to that weeping Sir Harleus you ran off with in the first place, Lysette? He was a penniless fool, too."

"He was killed by Sir Garlot, the invisible knight."

"More power to Sir Garlot's elbow. Merlin!"

"Yes, sire?" For some minutes past Merlin had been regretting his materialization. King Pendhu was almost as objectionable a character as Sir Balin himself. Small wonder that Lysette had fled the castle; even the lachrymose, and now dead, Sir Harleus must have been preferable to her father.

"Since you are here, Merlin, you shall devise a means of deterring worthless knights hungry for Lysette's dowry. It's a simple enough task; Castle Pendhu, as you may have noticed, is built upon an island. I will ensure that my daughter does not leave the grounds. You will ensure that no suitor enters, unless – "

"Unless he brings wealth to the marriage greater than the value of the dowry," suggested Queen Sophia.

"I like it," approved King Pendhu. "It's neat, it's simple. And it should be well within your powers, Merlin."

"Certainly, sire," said the magician.

"That looks like the place," said Sir Balin three days later. "Peasant!" he shouted to a man tending his vegetable plot. "Is that Castle Pendhu beyond the forest?"

"Could be." The man didn't look up.

"By God!" Sir Balin rode up to him and reined in viciously, causing his mount to rear. "You need teaching some manners, fellow. Do you know who I am?"

"This is Sir Balin," said Knut quickly, before the peasant could offer some impertinence. "The Knight of the Two Swords."

Confronted with this armoury, the man became voluble. "Indeed, my lord, that is Castle Pendhu, but no man may approach it. Word has it that Merlin has constructed a deadly bridge that will throw any unwary knight into the chasm below. So you are forewarned. I tell you this because I am a Cornishman, and friendly towards strangers. And because King Pendhu is not a popular ruler in these parts. Good luck to you!"

They arrived at Castle Pendhu in the middle of the afternoon.

It is well known that Pendhu means "black head", and the castle lived up to its name. The sunshine, bright as it was that day, seemed to wither as it struck the battlements so the castle became a sinister mountain of black shadows and cold glitterings. Knut found himself shivering at the sight.

Before them lay a deep chasm with smooth sides, and the hiss and crash of waves came to them. A stone stood at the edge of the chasm with this inscription:

> WHOSOEVER CROSSES THIS BRIDGE
> SHALL EARN THE HAND OF THE FAIR LYSETTE IN MARRIAGE

"Look at Merlin's bridge!" Knut exclaimed.

It shone golden, a thing of a delicate beauty such as Knut had never seen before. Gentle arcs of braided gold hung between two marble towers each five times the height of a man; from the arcs dropped silver wires to support a deck of ivory just wide enough to allow men to cross in single file. On the far side a smooth greensward ran to the brink of the chasm. Over all this the sun shone brightly.

And on the sward a girl was tossing a red ball to a lurcher.

"Fetch, Gelert!" they heard her cry.

"It's her!" snapped Sir Balin. "By God, it's her! Bring her here, Knut!"

"I don't trust this bridge," said Knut. "Remember what the peasant said. Merlin built it, and we all know what a trickster Merlin is!"

"I said, bring her here!"

The thought of the fair Lysette in the arms of Sir Balin was too much for even Knut's loyalty. "I am not bound to you, Sir Balin. I may go my own way if I please. Many knights would welcome an experienced squire such as I."

"Then go! I'll get the girl myself!" And Sir Balin ventured onto the bridge.

But he did so cautiously, which was as well for him. He'd barely covered three paces on the ivory deck before the bridge began to tremble so violently that he was forced to cling to the supporting wires. The chasm gaped, and far below deadly waters swirled around jagged rocks. The wires sagged and his feet slid from under him. Yelling with fear, he fell to his knees. He crawled back the way he'd come and Knut helped him to his feet.

"You won't get across today, Sir Balin!" called Lysette cheerfully. "This bridge has a spell on it!"

Recovering, the knight shouted back, "Then Merlin must remove the spell!"

"He's not here." Laughing, she tossed the ball to the dog Gelert, who bounded after it, retrieving it at the foot of the marble tower on her side of the chasm.

"So damned near," snarled Sir Balin. "What manner of spell?" he shouted. "Is there anything I can do to remove it?"

"You can't remove it," she called happily. "You could cross the bridge in certain circumstances, however. But I hardly think a travelling knight like you would qualify."

"What circumstances?"

"According to Merlin, you would have to bring riches to our marriage of a greater value than my dowry!"

"I never said anything about marriage, did I?" said Sir Balin, but he said it quietly to Knut. "How great is your dowry?" he called.

Laughing, Lysette listed such a fortune in gold, jewels and other precious things that Knut gasped.

"So be it," shouted Sir Balin angrily. To Knut he said, "You are forgiven. Come with me, and we will amass a fortune. And within the year, that girl will laugh no more."

Unhappily, Knut helped Sir Balin on to his horse.

There followed months of villainy such as the fair land of England had never seen before or since. Sir Balin, made even more savage by his lust, cut a swathe of murder and robbery through the three adjacent kingdoms, thus fulfilling Merlin's prophecy. Three kings fell lifeless to his sword, their queens too, and countless subjects. Knut, appalled, tried to assist the wounded and dissuade his lord from further evil, but was pushed aside by the band of brigands Sir Balin had assembled.

"Make no mistake about this, Knut," remarked Sir Balin one evening as he washed the blood of the dead from his arms. "By the time we return to Castle Pendhu I shall be the richest man in England!"

His caravan straggled through Cornwall, a staggering line of beasts laden with gold and silver, precious stones, silks and rare artefacts from other lands, even furniture if it was encrusted with sufficient jewellery to make it worth carrying. At the head rode

Sir Balin, proud and triumphant; and behind him Knut, humble and ashamed.

Three times Knut tried to dispatch an appeal for help to King Arthur, and three times his message was intercepted by one of Sir Balin's followers.

"That's enough, Knut," said Sir Balin when the third missive was brought to him. "One more try and you'll feel my sword through you. I'm a patient man, but this is rank disloyalty."

The truth was, Sir Balin had spared Knut so far because he found him useful and hardworking, and his horror at the carnage amusing. And because he suspected Knut was himself in love with the fair Lysette. This was an unforgivable presumption, and he looked forward to the day when he would force Knut to witness his violent coupling with the girl. The sight would probably unhinge the young milquetoast completely.

"Haven't we amassed enough wealth now?" said Knut one rainy afternoon, as the caravan struggled up a hillside and one of the mules fell dead under its load.

Sir Balin reined in and looked back. By now his followers numbered several hundred and the end of his retinue was out of sight in the forest below. Matters, it occurred to Sir Balin, were getting out of control. "By God!" he shouted, "I hope they're not robbing me down there!"

"Castle Pendhu is less than a day's ride away," Knut pointed out. "We've come in a big circle."

"As I'd planned. Tonight we'll camp within sight of the castle, and tomorrow morning we shall be at the gates. Or to be precise, we shall be at Merlin's bridge. The sight of this army will wipe the smile off that girl's face, for sure!"

Knut heaved a sigh of relief. The killing, it seemed, was over.

It was a fine spring morning and the gold of Lysette's tresses rivalled the gold of Merlin's bridge. Sir Balin and his army halted noisily on one side of the chasm; the girl and her dog watched silently from the other. It was not, thought Knut, a fair contest – if contest it was. Suddenly a terrible thought struck him: perhaps Lysette would be impressed by Sir Balin's show of strength!

"What are you waiting for, Sir Balin?" she called.

"Prepare yourself, my girl. The riches I bring far exceed the worth of your dowry!" And Sir Balin stepped onto the bridge.

The bridge trembled.

Sir Balin began to walk forward, slowly, one cautious foot after another like a man picking his way through a swamp.

The bridge shuddered.

It seemed to the watchers that Sir Balin was executing a curious dance. He skipped and lurched, and made no progress forward. The golden wires of the bridge sang like a harp, but the song they sang was in a minor key, sad and sinister. And the deck of the bridge heaved like a ship in a storm.

Sir Balin fell. He scrabbled at the ivory deck with his fingers, but the bridge twisted and he slid toward the edge. His legs dropped between vertical wires and he hung above the chasm by his hands alone. "Knut!" he shouted. "Save me!"

The squire ran onto the bridge, knelt, grasped the knight under his armpits and tried to lift him. Sir Balin was heavy, bloated by the post-battle feasting of past months. "Help me!" Knut shouted to Sir Balin's men.

But they were frightened of the magic of the bridge, and held their ground.

Knut pulled again. Sir Balin lifted himself mightily, groaning with effort, and in time lay on his chest, only his legs dangling over the chasm. Knut seized him by the seat of his trousers and hauled him up the rest of the way. Together they crawled off the bridge.

Sir Balin stood, his face scarlet with rage. "You cheated me!" he shouted across the chasm.

"Oh, no, Sir Balin," replied Lysette. "Merlin made it all very clear. In order to earn my hand you must first cross the bridge – it says so on the stone beside you. And in order to cross the bridge you must bring your wealth to the marriage. I am to be married in the castle, as is the custom. Well, your wealth is still on those mules on the wrong side of the chasm!"

"Words! Mere words! Bring Merlin here!"

"That I cannot do. When Merlin revived you in the ruins of King Pellam's castle, he swore you would never see him again."

"All right. All right." Sir Balin pondered the problem. "If necessary, I will carry my riches to you piece by piece!"

So saying, he untied a chest of jewels from the back of a mule and, stumbling under its weight, stepped onto the golden bridge.

The bridge wailed and shook.

Sir Balin tottered back to safety.

"Not good enough, Sir Balin!" called Lysette. "You are bringing only one chest of jewels. My dowry is a hundred times greater!"

"But I intend to bring the rest!"

"How can the bridge rely on the promises of a murdering knight? For all the bridge knows, you might decide to have your way with me the moment you are on my side of the chasm!" And the dog Gelert, whose hackles had risen when Sir Balin had stepped on the bridge, snarled softly.

"By God!" shouted Sir Balin, "This is trickery pure and simple! Men!" He beckoned to his brigands. "Bring up the mules. We'll send them across first, and I'll follow!"

The bridge, as you have been told, was narrow. The lead mule balked, but was finally persuaded forward by the flat of Sir Balin's sword. Its flanks brushing against the supporting wires, it stepped onto the bridge.

One of the vertical wires snapped with a twang like a bowstring. The mule, frightened, plunged and bucked. Another string snapped. The dog Gelert broke free of Lysette and ran onto the bridge, snapping at the mule's forelegs. Whinnying with fright, the mule backed up until it was standing on solid ground again, trembling.

"I thought you had more sense, Sir Balin!" Lysette laughed. "Any fool could see this bridge can't take the weight of a laden mule!"

"Then what am I to do?"

"That's your problem, Sir Balin; not mine. I suggest you forget about me, return your spoils to their rightful owners, return yourself to the court of King Arthur and endeavour to make your peace! It may not be easy, that last part. King Arthur has high standards."

And Gelert, who had followed the mule onto Sir Balin's side of the chasm, began to snap at the knight's ankles as though to add emphasis to his mistress's words.

"You trollop!" shouted Sir Balin. "You've always known I wouldn't be able to cross!" Face black with rage, he drew his sword and swung it at Gelert. "This dog seems to be of some value to you. All life is short; this dog's more so than most!"

But Gelert jumped aside, then bit into the knight's meaty calf. Yelling with pain, Sir Balin raised his sword for a final and deadly blow.

"No!" screamed Lysette.

"No!" shouted Knut.

He darted forward and snatched the dog away from the descending blade. When he turned, he saw murder in his master's eyes, and the blade was now swinging toward himself. Clutching the dog he ran swiftly, without thinking, in the only direction where safety lay.

Across the bridge.

They watched, amazed.

"What manner of a dog is that, to be of such worth?" asked Sir Balin, bewildered.

"A lurcher," replied one of his men.

"I know it's a lurcher, you damned fool! But where is its value? How can it be worth more than all the wealth I have amassed? Yet it must be, otherwise Knut couldn't have carried it across the bridge. Well, that solves my problem, men. Knut!" he shouted suddenly. "Bring the dog here! I'll carry it across!"

Knut stood his ground, saying nothing, still holding the dog.

"You have it wrong, Sir Balin!" called Lysette. "Admittedly Gelert is of great value to me. But you failed because you are worthless, despite all the riches you bring. Merlin's bridge does not judge a man by his assets alone, neither do I. There are liabilities to take into account. And all the wealth in the world could not outweigh the evil you have done to our three neighbouring kingdoms. You have deprived them of their leaders, their possessions, their crops. You have killed and robbed for months on end. You have laid those kingdoms waste, just as Merlin prophesied. And you think the baubles on the back of those mules outweigh all that? Then you're a fool, Sir Balin. A murderous fool. And you're worth less than Gelert the dog!"

And, watching Lysette and hearing her words, Sir Balin's lust died at last, and all he saw was a girl, just a girl, quite pretty, accusing him. Her words caused his deeds of the past months to run before his eyes, and at last he saw clearly what kind of a man he had become. Lysette was right. Every word she'd said was true.

"In God's name," he muttered, "what have I done? What madness got into me?" Tears in his eyes, he called, "Knut! Leave the dog. We're returning to Camelot. I must ask the forgiveness of Arthur and somehow atone for my deeds!"

Knut replied, "You will return alone, Sir Balin."

So Sir Balin turned away, weeping, and said to his men, "Take all these riches and return them to their rightful owners. And do not consider keeping any part for yourselves. I am lost and sick of killing but I still have my two swords, and I shall be awaiting word from the three kingdoms."

One of the brigands, more kindly than most, said, "Do not distress yourself, my lord. It will be some atonement."

"It is nothing when compared to the killing. The girl is right. I am worth less than a dog."

So, as our story runs, Sir Balin rode away, weary of killing, and for many months he behaved as the best of knights should, as slowly he made his way towards Camelot. He ensured the return of all the wealth he had stolen from the people of the three kingdoms. He comforted the sick in those lands, and did his utmost to compensate for the damage and the death he had wrought. He behaved in every way as King Arthur would have wished, and gradually the word of his goodness spread through England.

And all the time he knew it could never be enough.

So it was with a kind of resignation that, one day as he rode, he read an inscription in gold on a stone cross:

> IT IS FOR NO KNIGHT ALONE TO RIDE TOWARDS THIS CASTLE.

Because a voice within him said that ride to the castle he must, because that was the place of his final punishment.

What followed is known to everyone.

There was dancing and merriment at the castle built on an island, but the horn that sounded on his arrival was of dismal tone. Then the lady of the castle told him, "It is the custom that you should fight the Knight of the Island, and if you defeat him you will take his place."

"I am sick of fighting," he said, but he knew he had no option, and he took the shield a knight handed him.

And so he fought the Knight of the Island, who was clad in red armour with red harness to match, but there was no device on the Red Knight's shield.

They fought for many hours because they were evenly matched, but at last the Red Knight fell to the ground, mortally wounded. Sir Balin too could stand no more. He dragged himself across the sward until he lay beside his adversary, and said, "I've never met an opponent who could fight as you have done. What's your name, Sir?"

And the other replied, "Sir Balan, brother to Sir Balin, the Knight of the Two Swords."

* * *

Sir Balin, dying, asked the lady of the island castle that he and his brother should be laid in the same tomb. Then, while he was awaiting extreme unction, he heard the voice inside his head again. And now he knew the voice was Merlin, who had sworn never to appear before him, but had not said that he would never speak to him.

"You are close to atonement," said Merlin.

"But I've slain my brother. What harm did he ever do?"

"None. He was merely a mounting block to your atonement. He would have died in his next battle, in any event. I foresaw it."

Sir Balin lay there, weakening. Finally he whispered:

"One last request."

"If it is within my powers."

"I must know what happened to Lysette."

"You did not love her," said Merlin.

"I think I do now."

"Then you will be interested to know that she is married to Knut, your squire, and they are very happy."

Sir Balin lay quietly for a moment. Then he said, "King Pendhu never intended that such as Knut should win his daughter's hand in marriage."

"A small matter of trickery. I have no liking for King Pendhu," said Merlin, "so his disappointment does not concern me. I had, however, hoped that he would emerge from this adventure a little wiser. More to the point, does the news of the marriage please you?"

"Yes," Sir Balin answered truthfully. "Knut is a far better man that I am."

"Then your atonement is complete."

The brothers were laid in the same tomb, as Sir Balin had requested. Sir Balan's name was inscribed on the tomb, but not Sir Balin's, because the lady of the castle had never learned his name.

Then Merlin appeared on the morning after the burial, and inscribed:

> HERE LIES SIR BALIN
> THE SAVAGE KNIGHT OF THE TWO SWORDS
> WHO STRUCK THE DOLOROUS BLOW

Afterwards he brought the bridge from the castle of King Pendhu, where it had served its purpose, and set it between the island castle and the mainland. He changed the spell he had placed on it too; but not greatly. The matter of wealth he set aside, so that any knight who was of exceptional purity would be able to cross it, rich or poor.

He also made a new hilt for Sir Balin's sword, so that it could only be drawn from its scabbard by Sir Lancelot or his son Sir Galahad; and he put a certain curse on it too, because it was a part of Merlin's cunning to mix the evil with the good.

Then he returned to Camelot and told King Arthur of the death of Sir Balin and Sir Balan.

Word of Sir Balin's reformation had already reached the King, so he was naturally distressed. "This is terrible news," he said. "Those brothers were the finest knights I have known."

So this final forgiveness came too late for Sir Balin to hear it.

And what of Knut and Lysette?

It is not generally known that Merlin appeared to the couple, who by that time were living in a fine house near the ruins of King Pellam's castle.

"You tricked my father, Merlin," said Lysette reprovingly. "Knut was poor and happy to be so. Wealthy knights were what my father had planned for me. Kings, even. He is furious. And that saddens me, because I love him despite his faults."

"Nevertheless you are very happy now."

"That is true, Merlin. I couldn't have wished for a better husband."

"Then I am happy, too. I will leave you." Merlin began to shimmer.

"Wait! Merlin, it seems to my father that you lied. Knut was penniless, and Gelert – valuable to me though he is – cannot be worth as much as the dowry that has bought us this beautiful house and the lands around it. Yet Knut was able to cross your bridge, carrying only Gelert in his arms. The bridge failed in its purpose and my father feels he has been cheated."

"I have lied before," the magician admitted. "All magic is a lie of one kind or another, but this time I told the truth. Knut brought you wealth far greater than the value of the dowry, far greater than all the gold, precious stones, pearls and silks in your father's entire kingdom. He brought you a true and honest love."

"That he did." Lysette sighed, regarding Knut fondly.

"Then the bridge performed its purpose well."

"So it did. I am greatly in your debt, Merlin. So greatly, that I hesitate to ask you one last boon."

Merlin himself was susceptible to blue eyes and a winning smile. This was to be his downfall in time to come, when the beautiful Nyneve imprisoned him in a cave forever. "You need only ask," he said foolishly.

"I ask you to explain it all to my father," said Lysette.

Sir Breunis in THE KNIGHT OF GOOD HEART

Liz Holliday

Sir Breunis Saunce Pyté is the Brown Knight Without Pity. Although knighted by Arthur he becomes the enemy of Arthur's knights and seems to have the remarkable ability to be everywhere at once. He's one of the more shadowy knights in the legend, but the following story brings his plight to life. Liz Holliday (b. 1958) is an author, journalist and fiction editor of the role-playing magazine Valkyrie. *She has written three novelizations of the television series* Cracker *and one for* Bugs, *whilst under pseudonyms she's also written novelizations of* Soldier Soldier, Thief Takers *and* Bramwell.

Morgan stands looking out at the moonlit forest. Her forty-two years weigh heavily on her this night. All over the tower, women are weeping. Why should they not weep? she wonders. Each one of them has lost a husband, a brother, a lover. Perhaps in the morning, they too will die. Perhaps she will.

A footfall alerts her. She turns. Shadows cast by a thousand flickering candles dance across the stone walls.

The man she confronts smiles at her. "Will you betray me, Morgan?" he asks. His eyes are hard, but there is terror in them if you know how to read it, as Morgan does.

She gestures at the window. Just beyond the tower walls her nephew, Gareth, has laid siege with twenty of his best knights. All know it is not a situation that can endure long.

"To my nephew?" she asks the man before her. "No, Breunis, I will not betray you to my nephew." She turns her head, letting moonlight and candlelight catch the red-gold of her hair, knows he must smell the citrus and musk of the perfume she has rubbed on herself for him.

He nods, and turns to leave.

Breunis's sword wove patterns in the air: down and back and lunge and back and across . . .

Sweat dripped into his eyes. His heels thudded into the beaten earth of the training area. The muscles of his shoulders began to burn.

None of this mattered. There was only the movement of the sword, now slow, now fast.

It was nothing much more than a stick with a crossguard, that sword. He had made it himself, with the help of Oliver, his father's master-at-arms. A natural athlete, Oliver had called him. A natural swordsman. Such a pity, Oliver had said, that he was bound for a monk's life.

Fury lashed through Breunis.

A monk's life, all because he was a second son, with the bad luck to be born into a family whose fortunes had been depleted by the raiding Saxons.

Without pausing, he managed to centre himself. This was his last chance. Another summer, and he would be fifteen, and bound for the monastery. But his father had brought him to visit Sir Ector and his son, Kai; and Sir Ector already had one foster-son. What was to say he might not take another?

A flash of sunlight on metal caught his eye. His father was coming, and with him Sir Ector. Kai trailed along behind him, laughing and chattering with Arthur, his foster-brother. With a tiny thrill of excitement and fear, Breunis realized that the last figure, the one trudging wearily after them, was his brother Huw. But he was supposed to be fighting the Saxons, not here.

I am better now than either of them, he thought, and strove to concentrate on his exercises. Not yet better than Huw, but one day. . . Build your strength, Oliver had said. Form will come later, and style. So Breunis had built his strength, but he had worked on his form, too; and now he was better at fourteen than Kai at seventeen or Arthur at fifteen.

And still his father and Sir Ector swept straight past him, to the far end of the training area. If they'd noticed him, they'd given no sign of it. Kai and Arthur allowed the armourer to fit them out. Perhaps now. . . Breunis thought. But his father and Sir Ector were deep in conversation with Huw, and none of them looked in his direction.

Weary, suddenly, and dispirited, Breunis let his sword fall to his side.

There was nothing for him here.

He walked away, knowing he risked a chill or strained muscles from cooling down too quickly. It didn't matter. Nothing did.

He should have called the armourer to take his sword, but that would have meant attracting the attention of his father, and perhaps facing Kai and Arthur. For a moment, he found the idea attractive. Maybe someone would invite him to join their training session . . . but probably not. He didn't think he could bear the shame of it.

So he walked the other way, in the cool shadow cast by the barrack wall. He turned the corner. And that was when he saw her.

She was crossing the yard from the Chapel to the Hall. Sunlight caught at the rosary wound between her fingers, and at the coppery gold of her hair. She was somewhat older than him, and she looked somehow familiar, but he couldn't think why. Not that it was important.

He would have liked to speak to her, but it would not have been seemly; and anyway, someone might see them. Still, he thought, it would do no harm to go to the Chapel and pray. Perhaps the Lord would take pity upon him and show him what he should do. And if his steps should take him near the maiden, well, what harm in that?

As he passed her, she looked up at him. She smiled at him. Smiled! Breunis thought his breath would stop in his chest.

"You have worked hard, good sir," she said. There was a west country burr to her voice that intrigued him.

For a moment he thought she was laughing at him. Surely she could see he was only a boy? "I have," he muttered, wondering what he looked like – all red-faced and sweaty, no doubt, and with his coarse black hair a rats' nest.

"Such a shame your father gives you no credit for your

exertions," she murmured. "I've heard you are to be given to the monks – "

Breunis felt his face flame. Did everyone know his shame – all the ladies, all the servants? And this girl – he noticed her girdle, knotted low on her hips – this woman, then, also knew. He licked his parched lips. "I hope not," he said, though he wanted to demand how she knew.

"Perhaps you should do something to change your fortunes, good young sir."

"I would," he said. "If I could. I mean, I've tried – "

"Perhaps you should try another way." She said it lightly, as if it were a joke, but Breunis could hear serious intent in her words. "I could help you," she said. "If you would let me."

Breunis stared at her. She was so beautiful, so womanly. Why would she want to help him? "I don't think you can," he said.

"Oh, I can," she said. "In fact, I'll lay you a wager: by the time this day is done, you'll have come asking for my help."

"I shall not," he said, and he started across the courtyard, suddenly craving the cool incense-scented interior of the Chapel.

She laid her hand on his arm. There in the courtyard for all to see, she touched him. "I wager you will – "

"I tell you, lady, I will not," he said, and was pleased at how very adult he sounded.

"Then you've nothing to lose by taking my wager – unless you doubt your own word."

He stared at her, and realized that she had won now, whatever he said. "Very well. But if I win, what then do you forfeit?"

"Why," she said, "the chance to give you my advice – and, I think, a kiss."

Again, Breunis felt his cheeks flame red. "And if I lose, what must I give you?"

She laughed then, and he realized she'd been teasing him all along. "Why good sir – a kiss I shall have from you, nothing less and nothing more."

And then, somehow, she was gone, and Breunis was standing alone in the courtyard.

"Let them go," Morgan says.

Breunis shakes his head. "You wanted this," he says.

"No – " She will not voice the rest of the thought: that she did not want this – the deaths of these innocents, to be closeted here in this tower with him – but that yes, she had wanted Arthur brought low. To admit that would be to admit how she had used this man. How she would use him still. And to do that would be to invite death.

A kiss, Breunis thought. She wanted a kiss from me. The thought of it confused him: that sweet, heart-shaped face, the demure-devious smile. Those eyes. The knot of her girdle resting against her hip-bone.

He stared up at the crucifix, then, realizing what he was doing, knelt clumsily to pray. He crossed himself. *In Nomine Patris . . .*

And she had said she would help him get his father's attention. *Such a shame you are to be given to the monks.*

How could any decent man want such a wanton? But he wasn't a man. Not yet, and he didn't truly know what he wanted.

Et Filii

Dear Jesus, he thought, I don't want to be bad. I don't. I want to be good, to be an obedient son, to serve my lord. But he knew even as he thought it that it wasn't entirely true. If it had been true, he would have gone uncomplaining to the monastery: but even as he thought of that, he felt the weight of a sword – a real sword, of steel – in his hand. Tasted the glory that would be his if he fought off the Saxons. Knew in his belly that he was better than Arthur, than Kai – even than Huw.

She would give him a kiss. What would she give him, then, if indeed he fought the Saxons?

Et Spiritu Sanctus . . .

It was wrong. She was wrong, a witch, a beguiling little witch, who would lead him into error.

He tried to settle into prayer, to begin the *Ave Maria*, to pray to the Virgin to banish the thought of the maiden from his mind.

"Breunis?" said Kai's voice from behind him.

He twisted round, startled. The sunlight falling through the open door made him blink, but he saw Kai and Arthur silhouetted against the light. "My father has suggested we should take some provisions up to the hermit who lives on the hill."

"I think they want us out of the way while they talk to your brother," Arthur put in.

"But I wanted – " Breunis said. Kai looked at him sharply. He swallowed his disappointment. "I'll be glad to come with you."

Huw had been on his side – had argued that a proper knight needed a proper squire; and Breunis could have talked to him in front of Sir Ector. Who knew what might have come of that? But perhaps there would be time tonight.

The steward had packed them up some food in a bit of cloth – some bread from the night before, a few vegetables from the kitchen gardens, a twist of salt and even a scrawny hen, killed specially. So this old man was held in high regard, Breunis thought as he followed the others out of the side gate. He was carrying a pitcher of milk, and it took all his concentration not to let it spill as he picked his way down the path and through the village.

"They say your brother has acquitted himself well in the wars," Arthur said.

"Good." Breunis didn't want to think about it.

"I saw you training," Arthur said. "You're really very good."

Damn you, Breunis thought. Did he have to be so nice? Didn't he know? Everybody else knew. "Thank you," he managed.

"It will work out for the best – you'll see."

Breunis looked at him sharply. The older boy seemed to be sincere. Sympathetic, even. Breunis realized that he hated Arthur for that; and even as he acknowledged it, he felt guilty for his anger. Without saying another word, he lengthened his stride. The milk slopped over his hand. He didn't care.

Some time later, they left the village and then the path, and clambered round the side of the hill. Kai and Arthur had obviously done the journey many times; Arthur in particular seemed to know every stone and tree.

It was just another thing for Breunis to hold against him as he struggled along behind them trying to keep his footing, while the milk sloshed and spilled.

It isn't his fault, Breunis told himself. Arthur had done nothing but offer him friendship. But in his heart he knew that didn't matter.

At last they came to a place where a few ragged blackthorn trees clung to the side of the hill around a narrow cleft that led inwards.

"Ho! Master Myrddin," Arthur shouted. He repeated himself twice, and then a scrawny figure wrapped in a tattered blanket appeared at the mouth of the cleft. His beard and hair were long and matted, and Breunis caught the stench of him even at a distance.

"You may come," he said. His voice was little more than a croak, as if it had rusted away through long disuse.

Arthur led the way towards the cleft. Kai followed him. Reluctantly, Breunis trailed along behind.

He slid sideways into the cleft after them, only to find that it opened out into quite a capacious cave. There was a natural slit in the roof that let in a little watery light, but the air was thick with smoke from a couple of fat lamps that burned fitfully, and from a fire burning in a ring of stones on the floor.

Breunis forced himself not to cough, but he could do nothing about the watering of his eyes.

"My father sent you food, Myrddin," Kai said. He held out the package.

Hesitantly, Breunis proffered the now half-empty pitcher of milk.

But the old man pushed it away. Close up, Breunis could see that he was wearing only a breech-clout under the ragged blanket.

"I do not eat now," he said. "It is my fasting time – a time of import is upon us, and I must see clearly."

"What do you see, Myrddin?" Arthur asked.

The old man grabbed Arthur's face. His fingers were knotted and crabbed with age, and his long nails seemed like talons. They bit into Arthur's flesh. It must have hurt, but Arthur made no sound.

"I see you," Myrddin said. The firelight struck sapphire from Arthur's eyes. He gazed steadily at Myrddin. Breunis wasn't sure he could have done the same. Then the old man shoved him away, and the moment was over.

But he turned, the old man did, and glared at Breunis, "And I see you," he said. I won't look away, Breunis thought, but Myrddin was already stumbling away.

He cried out suddenly. His limbs flailed the air. He crashed to the floor, and his arms and legs jerked and writhed. A dreadful sound came out of his throat, like the manic screaming of a bird in pain.

Breunis started forward. The old man would hurt himself, surely –

Arthur grabbed his arm. "Leave him. He does this. He'll be all right." That couldn't be right. Breunis shook Arthur's hand off impatiently. "Leave him, I said." There was a snap in Arthur's voice Breunis had never heard before.

I only wanted to help him, Breunis thought resentfully. I can't even get that much right.

There was silence. Stillness. The old man lay shivering on the floor.

After a moment he clambered to his feet. A thin line of drool oozed from the corner of his mouth.

"In all this land," he whispered, "there will be no unity, no peace." His head turned slowly, as if he were looking at each of them in turn, but his eyes were fixed on some other place. "Only war, and murder, and the raiders from over the sea. The shores of Britain will be lapped in blood, and the stones of the castles will tumble into the ocean." He reached out to support himself on the cave wall. "This I see. Unless one comes to unite the land, to enforce the peace. The greatest warrior of them all – "

And he was looking at Breunis. Surely he was. I am better than the others, Breunis thought. A better swordsman. Stronger. And because it's been denied me, I will work harder and longer . . . to serve my lord; but he could not deny how tardily that last thought came, how it trailed along behind a vision of himself riding through some grateful city receiving tribute from the citizens. And the kiss – and more – of a girl with coppery hair and a sweet smile.

But the old man stumbled past him. To Arthur. *Arthur*.

"You will . . ." he said, and his voice trailed off. He reached out his hand.

Arthur took it. Held it. "I know."

Myrddin dropped to his knees. Suddenly he was nothing more than an old man again. "Leave me now," he said.

Kai looked at Arthur, who nodded. The two of them started to leave. Breunis might as well not have existed.

As he started to follow them out, the old man reached up to him. Appalled, Breunis took his hand.

"You," Myrddin said. "What will be, will be. And what is within cannot remain forever hidden."

"I – " Breunis licked his lips. His voice seemed no more inclined to work than the old man's. "I will serve my lord."

The old man said nothing, but pulled his hand away.

Breunis went out, and stood blinking in the sunlight. I will, he thought. I will be good. I will be the best.

But there was no certainty in the thought any more.

"You should have given yourself to me when you had the chance, lady," Breunis says.

He steps in close. She can smell him now, the heavy male musk of him, that and oil and leather, all mingling. She's attracted to him: she can't deny it; she always has been. And she knows that's her danger.

Nevertheless, if there's a way out of this trap she has inadvertently forged for herself, she must step into danger, inside his guard.

So she moves towards him. "A true knight would face my nephew, rather than slaughtering innocent women."

He grabbed her arm. For a moment she thought he would hit her. "Never say that to me. You do not have the right."

"None better than I," she snapped. She can almost smell his desire now. It comes off him like sweat. "I made you what you are – "

And she's gone too far, though perhaps not further than she needs to. He slams her against the wall. She feels the breath go out of her.

"Do you know why they are here?" He jerks his head at the door, indicating the other captive women. "They're here because all my life I've sought you, and I didn't even know I was doing it. But now here you are, fallen into my lap like cherries from a shaken tree. And you will pay for what you did."

"Perhaps," she says, "I was wrong to appeal to your honour." Again, she's going too far, and knows it. But there's no help for it. "But if you don't face my nephew – if you kill these women instead – you'll know yourself for a coward. As I will."

"Only if you live, bitch," he says. She can feel his breath, hot on her face. His hand on her breast. She's so close to losing control of him.

So close. But not quite out of control. Not yet.

Sir Ector had laid on something of a feast for Huw. The high table had been decked out with the finest platters, and there was a boar's head with gilded tusks as the centrepiece of the main course.

Breunis strove to hear what was being said up at the far end of the high table as one of the stewards ladled meat and gravy over his trencher of bread. It was useless. He thought he heard someone say something about going hunting early in the morning, but with the babble of voices from the lower tables, and Arthur and Kai chattering on about how their training had gone that day, it was impossible to be certain.

Still, Breunis thought. A hunt. That would be a fine time to show what he was made of. He craned forward to try to hear. As he did so, his arm brushed against someone behind him. He twisted round. A maid was there, ready to serve him with small-beer.

His maiden! His maiden from the morning. He smiled at her, but she looked at him as if she'd never seen him before.

It was only afterwards, when she'd gone on to serve Arthur that he realized that her hair was a shade more golden, her face a little rounder and paler, her eyes hazel rather than green.

He sipped his small-beer. It was watery and bitter. Now Arthur was telling Kai of the sword he hoped to wield one day – how the guard would be, how it would balance just so in his hand – when he himself was knighted. And for his part, Kai was teasing him. Telling him to be patient, that he had years of squiredom yet to come.

Breunis took a good gulp of his beer. It tasted vile. So did the meat and gravy when he tried it. Make the most of it, he thought. It's a monk's life for you – fish on Friday and thin gruel the rest of the week if you're lucky. It was hardly a fair assessment, and he knew it.

Arthur was looking at him oddly. He stretched out his hand. Breunis stared at it.

"I'm fine," he muttered. "I will be fine." But he felt sick to his belly. He got up. "I just need a little air. Don't let them take my trencher away," he said carefully. "I'll be back soon."

Arthur nodded. As Breunis stumbled past him, he saw the other boy start to get up. Saw Kai stop him.

Good. He didn't need them anyway.

He stumbled through the clamorous hall and into into the courtyard. The cold evening air slapped at him. I only had a sip or two of beer, he thought. I shouldn't feel this way. But the world was turning and he could barely keep his feet.

He groped his way to a dark corner near the stables, where no one could see his shame, and threw up. Bile burnt his mouth. He wiped his lips on his sleeve. As he stood up, he heard a sound behind him.

He turned. She was there. His maiden of the morning. He was certain of her this time. There was no mistaking the tilt of her chin, or the way she smiled.

"Are you well, good sir?" she asked.

Coming from Kai or Arthur, the question would have enraged him. From her . . . well, he did not quite know how it made him feel, but it did not make him angry. "I think the small-beer was not to my liking," he said.

"I've heard it's sometimes so," she said. Something in her voice, a slight flicker of her eyes – as if she knew more than she would ever say. Breunis stared at her woozily.

"So," she said. "How went your day? Did you gain the ear of your father?"

She knew he hadn't. He could see it in her eyes. "Who are you?" he asked. It was better than admitting failure. Far better than asking her help. Losing his wager. Breaking his word.

"An answer for an answer," she said, and laid her hand on his arm. He felt her touch as if it were a branding iron.

"I could not speak to him earlier," Breunis said. "And when I tried again before the steward called us to dinner, he told me to be gone – that he wished only to speak to Huw."

"That was unkind of him," she said. Her shoulders seemed to sag a little. "But I know how unkind a parent can be – my mother's had little time for me or my sisters since my brother was born. We've even had to seek work as waiting women, though we are not of common birth."

"That's unreasonable," Breunis said, at once enraged on her behalf. He longed to hold her. To comfort her, he thought, in a brotherly fashion. Though if he admitted the truth there was nothing much brotherly in the desire he felt.

"Aye," she said. "Well, it will happen when a widowed lady takes a second husband."

"Who should honour his new responsibilities and be glad of the chance, if they were all so comely as you," Breunis said.

She laughed then, though from the spots of colour that appeared on her cheeks Breunis could tell that he had embarrassed her. And, he dared hope, pleased her also.

"Ah, young sir," she said, "but not all men are like you – they do not all strive for goodness and honour."

"Is that what you see in me?" Breunis could not help but think of his anger at Kai, his sudden hatred of Arthur, his envy of Huw.

"I see what there is to see," she said. "Though I do believe your great honour is doing you little good."

Breunis felt his breath catch in his throat. How could she know so much. "How so?" he asked at last.

"Your father barely acknowledges your existence. Your brother seeks your advancement only because he thinks it ill-becomes him to go without a squire of his own – oh, don't look so shocked. We hear things, those of us who wait at table."

"It is so," Breunis admitted. "But – "

"But nothing. It need not be." He stared at her. Moonlight gilded her cheekbones. "Listen to me – what has your goodness got you? Nothing but pain. What good then is goodness to you?"

He stared at her, suddenly appalled. What she was suggesting he did not dare imagine. Yet her emerald gaze held him there. He could not move. "What good am I without it?" he asked. His voice sounded piping, boyish, in his ears.

"A stronger man. A man who will do what he must to avoid a fate he cannot endure. A man of action, not a monk to be shut up in a room with books and penance and endless prayers!"

A man. She had called him a man. Yet he'd never felt more like a boy. And her hand was still on his arm. "What must I do?" he asked, and he did not know if he meant what he must do to save himself from the monks, or to please her further.

"Take action where you see the need for it, that's all," she said. "Lock up your good heart where it cannot be hurt, for I am loath to see you hurt." She laid her hand lightly on his chest.

"But I wish to be a good son – "

"You shall," she said. "In your heart. But let the world see a man who must be reckoned with." She reached up to him. "And remember this – I dub thee Sir Breunis." And she reached up and kissed him lightly first on one cheek, then on the other, as if in some strange way she was dubbing him as a knight might be made with a sword.

He was utterly bemused. "You promised me but one kiss," he said.

"Ah," she answered, "but I had a different kind of kiss in mind. Only first you must promise me you'll do it – take action where you must." Her eyes were icy now. He felt as if his soul were being reamed out. "Promise," she said. Her fingers clutched his arm.

"I do," he whispered hoarsely. He was hollow, filled with nothing at all.

She reached up and kissed him hard on the lips. He burned with the need for her. He felt her desire match his own. Yet her passion burned ice-cold. For a moment, he fought against it. But how to fight ecstasy?

He yielded to it. It ripped through him, like the blow of a blade made of ice, replacing his fire with its own freezing flame.

Anything, he thought. I'll do anything . . .

But it was over. She was moving away from him.

"Wait!" he said, too loud. She turned back. "You never did tell me your name."

"Some call me Morgan," she said. "But you may call me Anna. It's the name my father had for me."

And then she really had gone, leaving him standing alone against the wall. Moonlight poured down upon him. He was horrified to find that he was crying; and in his heart there was a new hardness. Take action where you must, she had said.

And what would come of that? Nothing good, he knew. How could it, when she'd told him that he'd be stronger without goodness, without honour?

Footsteps rang on the cobbles. Two voices giggled together. Whoever they were, they would see him. See his tears. He would be shamed.

He slid back into the shadows.

I do not want to be without honour he thought. I have only desired to be a good son. To serve my lord. He started to say an Ave Maria, but the words would not come.

And then the two people he had heard came round the corner of the building. Arthur. There was no mistaking that corn-blond hair.

He had his arm around a girl. Anguish stabbed at Breunis like a stiletto as he recognized her. His Morgan. His Anna. With Arthur. Would she give him, also, a kiss for a wager?

And Arthur – Arthur, it seemed, was intent on giving her much more than just a kiss. He drew her to him. And together they slipped into one of the empty stalls. Breunis shifted slightly. He had to see.

And then he wished he couldn't. Arthur touched her. Touched her in ways Breunis never would have dared. In ways no one but her husband should have – if anyone would have her after this.

She turned. Moonlight turned the smooth oval of her face to alabaster. Not his Anna. Relief surged through Breunis. It was the other serving-girl. The one that looked so much like her. What had she said? *We've even had to seek work as waiting women, though we are not of common birth.*

So it was not Anna that Arthur dishonoured, but her sister.

Rage boiled through him. That he would dare such a thing. That this nameless slut would let Arthur do *that*, when his Anna had given him so little.

Take action where you see the need for it, she had said. Lock up your good heart, where it cannot be hurt.

He felt something dark and hard crystallize at the core of him.

Goodness? What use was that to him?

No use at all.

* * *

"Will you take me by force?" Morgan asks Breunis.

"You wouldn't be the first." He's clawing at her skirts now.

"But so unnecessary," she murmurs. His anger excites her. She can feel her own power rising to meet it.

He isn't stupid, though. He laughs, a short hard bark of a sound. "Are you going to tell me you'll give yourself to me willingly, if only I'll spare the women? Let myself be taken by your nephew?"

She wants to say yes. Knows, even, that her power is such that she might be able to make him believe it. But the moment demands honesty. "No. I said I would not betray you to him, and I meant it."

"Then you don't want to see him put my head on a pike?" he demands. Morgan schools her face to stillness. "Or worse, drag me back in chains for Arthur to humiliate?"

Morgan summons her power. Knows it, now, for what it is – unlike when she was a girl, resenting the way Arthur and his father Uther had stolen her mother Igraine's heart, so that suddenly it was not good enough to be Gorlois's child, not good enough to be first born, certainly not good enough to be a girl. For Arthur had been given into fostership as a baby, and his mother had mourned his loss ever since. So Morgan and her sister Morgause had stolen away to find him.

And bring him low.

But not like this. Breunis has been a good weapon, forged in the heat of lust and envy. But indiscriminate.

Morgan pulls him to her, and kisses him hard on the mouth.

The day dawned fair, with blue skies and bright sun to burn off the hint of mist that lingered close to the ground.

Breunis watched the hunting party assemble in the courtyard. He longed to join them, but he was sure he would not be welcome. Besides, he felt thick-headed from the night before.

He remembered sitting at table. Drinking his small-beer. Then being ill, and something happening in the courtyard. He hoped, he truly hoped, that he'd done nothing to dishonour himself, but the next thing he knew he was staring up at the ceiling of the chamber he shared with Arthur and Kai, and sunshine was streaming in through the arrowslit. He'd dreamed though. Something about the girl he'd met the day before. Such an angry dream . . .

He shook his head to clear it.

"Little brother," Huw called. He was already mounted. "Will you not join us? Be my squire, at least for this one day?"

Breunis stared at him. So now his shame was known to all.

And Huw just sat there, smiling down at him, as if he didn't know what he had done. Challenged, he'd doubtless claim he was trying to be kind.

Well, Breunis wanted nothing of kindness. Yet if he had a chance to show his prowess off to his father, he'd be a fool to waste it.

He waited till the grooms brought out a pony for him, and when he was mounted he took Huw's sword and the spears – a great boar-hunting spear with a wicked point, and several lighter ones – which Sir Ector had loaned them.

Then the women came out, with stirrup cups – sweet wine to fortify them for the hunt. One of Kai's sisters gave hers to Arthur. Breunis was resigned to being left out. After all, he wasn't even a proper squire.

But he was wrong. The maiden he'd met in the courtyard came to him. She handed him up a goblet of wine. He sipped it. It was very good.

He leaned down to give the empty cup back. As she took it, the girl whispered, "Remember, take action where you must."

Clearly, it had some meaning for her, but Breunis could not begin to puzzle it out.

Breunis pulls away from Morgan.

She stares into his eyes. There is bewilderment there. Terror.

"What have you done?" he asks. She waits, knowing his memories are flooding through him, shifting, rearranging. "Sweet Mother of God, what have I done?"

The hunt had not gone well.

Breunis pushed through the undergrowth after Huw. In truth, the injured boar they were following had left a wide trail. The broken branches and trampled earth were black with blood.

"It will be enraged," he pointed out. "You did it just enough injury for that. We should wait for the others – "

Huw turned on him. "What, little brother? Are you such a coward? You, who craves to be a knight?"

So that's the way of it, Breunis thought. That's what he thinks of me. "No," he snapped. "But you left your boar spear in its flesh, and there's only one more light spear left – "

"Because I broke the others?" Huw's face was flushed with anger and exertion. "If you think I'm so inept, turn back. Rejoin the others – "

"I will not – "

"There's no dishonour in it."

Because I've no honour to lose, he means, Breunis thought. But he said nothing more.

A little while later, the trail bent sharply. Huw stopped. Breunis did the same. He understood immediately.

They were hard on the shoulder of the hill, and the boar had gone to bay. He handed Huw the last of the spears.

They slid forward. If Breunis's assessment was correct, there was nowhere else for the boar to run.

He was right. The beast was standing facing them, tiny eyes glinting red in the sunlight. It was coated in its own stinking blood. Huw's heavy boar spear was rammed in its shoulder almost up to the crosspieces.

Huw stepped forward. If he could get in one good blow before it charged . . . He hefted the spear in both hands.

"Have my sword ready," he said.

As he turned back, the boar charged at him. He went down. One of its tusks ripped into his shoulder. Blood spurted everywhere. He screamed.

Breunis stared at him. I have his sword, he thought. I should attack it.

Huw tried to scramble to his feet. The boar swiped at him again, and he fell. "For the love of Jesus, help me," he cried.

"Lock up your good heart . . ."

Breunis stared at Huw. His face was a gory mess where the boar had caught him with its trotter.

"My sword, damn you," Huw shouted, though he was clearly weak himself now. Somehow, he shoved himself up on to his knees.

"Take action where you must . . ."

But Breunis did not move. Inaction, he realized, was in itself a kind of action. It would have been so easy to step in. It was too late to hand Huw his sword, but the boar was weakening. Breunis could probably dispatch it. He'd be a hero. How would his father deny him then?

But it was chancy. Better to let the boar finish Huw. There'd be no question then of sending him to the monastery. Not if his father wanted a son to bear the family arms.

The boar was almost done. But not quite. It turned and trotted tiredly back at Huw. As it reached him, Huw grabbed the boar spear. He tried to hold it, but the new pain must have enraged the boar further.

If he does not die, they'll all think me a coward, Breunis thought. But that doesn't matter. What does a monk need with bravery, anyway?

The spear slid from Huw's hands. The boar bellowed. It flicked its head, and caught Huw in the belly with its tusk.

Blood and entrails spurted everywhere. Huw fell forward, clutching at himself.

But the boar, also, was finished. Its legs folded under it.

So, Breunis thought. It is done. He unsheathed Huw's sword – his sword now, he expected – and walked cautiously towards the boar. A motion of Huw's hand attracted his attention. He bent over him, cursing his luck that the man was still alive.

Huw licked his lips. "Coward," he whispered. He closed his eyes.

"Never say that," Breunis roared. He would have struck Huw a killing blow then, but even in his rage he knew he must not.

He pivoted round and brought the boar a dreadful blow that almost severed its foreleg from its body.

Let them wonder, he thought. I'll tell them how the arrogant whoreson ran on ahead of me, how I rushed in to save him. They'll believe me because they have no choice. And my father will have no son to carry the family arms but me.

The silence of the forest was broken only by the sound of Breunis, sobbing.

The light of dawn filters through the arrowslits of the room where Morgan has kept her vigil.

She stares out at the forest. The pavilions of the besiegers are plain to see now.

As she watches, the gates of the tower open. Breunis rides out alone. He is unarmed.

She sees him speak with Gareth, her nephew's shock of red hair unmistakable even at this distance. They argue. Someone hands Breunis a sword. They fight, but he puts up no defence.

When he dies, a cheer goes up from the watching multitude.

But not from Morgan. Somewhat to her surprise, she finds that she is weeping.

Sir Gawain in CLARISSANT

Phyllis Ann Karr

Gawain scarcely needs an introduction since he is one of the best known of all Arthur's knights. He was the eldest son of King Lot of Orkney, and was the brother of Agravaine, Gaheris and Gareth. King Lot is probably the same as the historical king Leudonus who ruled from the fortress of Traprain Law near Edinburgh in the early sixth century. He held his lands not only against the invading Angles, but also against the Picts and from rebellion amongst other Celtic tribes, particularly that of Morcant. This was a time of incessant warfare and it is quite likely that his sons became renowned for their prowess. Gawain, who in Celtic legend is called Gwalchmai, was originally the premier Arthurian knight, though his reputation suffered under the French writers. Phyllis Ann Karr has resurrected a near-forgotten episode of Gawain – or Gawen as she prefers – as recorded by Chrétien de Troyes in his incomplete Perceval: Conte du Graal *written around 1182. Her account is loosely based on the last episode in Chrétien's story, for which she has provided an ending.*

Phyllis Ann Karr (b. 1944) is no stranger to these anthologies, having appeared in every one. Her knowledge of the Arthurian world is profound as demonstrated in The King Arthur Companion *(1983). She has also written the delightful murder mystery* The Idylls of the Queen *(1982).*

As Sir Gawen rode alone on his great steed Gringalet – and why Sir Gawen rode alone that year, without a single squire or even one additional horse, is another tale – he came to a narrow meadow between two rivers. Across the river on the one hand, he beheld a city as fine and fair as Caerleon. Across the river on the other hand, he could see only a soft silver mist hovering. And, in the midst of that narrow meadow where he himself rode, between the rivers, one ancient oak tree stood on its rise of higher ground.

As Gawen drew nearer, he saw standing in the oak tree's shade a palfrey whose head was white on one side and black on the other. A shield too battered and bloodied to read hung from the lowest limb of the oak tree, and, beside the shield, a broken lance leaned against its trunk. The palfrey seemed a fine palfrey, but it was nevertheless a palfrey and in no way the mount for an armed knight. Sir Gawen, wondering, urged Gringalet faster forward with a whispered word, and soon came close enough to see the knight himself, lying wounded near to death beneath the tree.

Sir Gawen slung himself down from the saddle and brought his own flask of water to moisten the lips of the dying man. As he considered what cloth he could best use to dip in one of the rivers for cleaning away a little of the blood that already shrouded this hapless face, the eyes fluttered beneath their red mask and opened, shedding small crumbs of crimson. "Save my lady!" the dying man whispered. "Ah, friend, save my lady!"

"Where is your lady?" Gawen asked, gazing earnestly around. "Friend, tell me where she is, that I may save her."

"There!" With the dregs of failing strength, the wounded man pointed one bloody finger at the city fine as Caerleon. Then, his hand falling back, he clutched at Gawen's gauntlet, leaving red streaks upon the bright metal. "But, friend, you must ride her palfrey across that bridge. On your own horse, you cannot cross!"

With a shudder, the dying knight fell into a swoon and said no more. After crossing his hands over his chest to fit him as best he could to meet his maker, Sir Gawen mounted Gringalet and ran his gaze along the river bank until he located the bridge of which the man had spoken. But, when he cantered Gringalet up to it, the great horse stopped short and would not cross.

Three times Sir Gawen spurred his horse forward: the first time Gringalet stopped at the edge of the bridge, the second time he touched it with one trembling forefoot and reared back whinnying, the third time he stopped while still a good three paces distant, and would go no further.

So at last Sir Gawen turned back, left Gringalet tethered in the shade of the ancient oak, and mounted the lady's palfrey, grateful there were none of Arthur's court here to see him.

The palfrey turned its bicolored head to the bridge and ambled over as smoothly as though it had crossed this same river every day of its life.

The gate to the city stood open, the drawbridge down. But beneath an olive tree which grew near the drawbridge, as if in its pride the city scorned both siege and attack, there lounged a tall and handsome knight in shining mail. His beard and moustache were lustrous red, and one of his spurs was silver, the other gold. He did not laugh to see a knight on a palfrey, but only nodded and smiled in a companionable way.

Seeing this, Sir Gawen reined up to ask him, "Good friend, do you know anything of a lady brought here recently against her will?"

"The lord of this land brought such a lady here only today, for his lust," the tall knight answered pleasantly. "But she is a proud and haughty creature, and has so far held even him at bay. When first he crossed the river to take her, he had with him that same palfrey you ride, for he meant it as a gift to win her love. But she refused to mount it and follow him, so that at last he had to carry her across on his own saddlebow. Now she sits beneath the great elm tree in the inner garden of the keep, combing her hair and still refusing every dainty and every favor he has to offer her."

"Brave, unhappy lady!" Sir Gawen exclaimed. "I have come to rescue her and return her to her former lover, if he still lives, and if he does not, at least to deliver her out of the hands of this proud lord."

"You have work ahead of you, then," said the tall knight. "And considerable danger, for this lord claims the head of every man who crosses his will in any matter at all. Nor will the lady herself welcome you as you may expect. As for me, I will not lift a finger to prevent you from entering the city, but beware whom you may encounter on your way out."

Saluting the tall knight, Sir Gawen rode across the drawbridge. The people of the city watched him with mournful faces, shaking their heads and clicking their tongues sadly; but none laughed at him and none tried to stop him, not even when he reached the castle itself.

It was made all of grey granite, chiselled smooth and adorned like a church with statues and gargoyles, though Sir Gawen took small notice of them as he rode into the keep. Finding it deserted, save for some whispery footfalls that seemed always to be scurrying away before his approach, he allowed the palfrey to choose its own way. This the beast did quite readily, and brought him at length to the inner garden where the lady sat beneath the elm tree, admiring herself in a mirror of silver and glass.

She was altogether worth admiring, though Sir Gawen privately wondered at such an attitude in such circumstances. Her mantle and wimple lay on the ground beside her and, as Gawen watched unnoticed, she stood and held the mirror above her head so as to view the entire length of her form, slim and supple in its silken gown.

With a discreet cough, Sir Gawen said, "My lady?"

She turned and eyed him coldly, from the plumes of his helmet to the hooves of the palfrey's feet. Then she said, with a laugh of disdain, "Churl, go away!"

Sir Gawen felt his face turn crimson, but he said only, "Madame, if you come with me, I will go away from this place."

"Ah!" She lifted one fine brow. "These men! They say, 'Come!' and we are to come, 'Go!' and they expect us to go, always at their own beck and call, with never a voice of our own."

"In King Arthur's lands, my lady," Sir Gawen said, "women are paid the utmost respect, and a maiden is free to go wherever she will, and with whomever she will, always under the King's own protection."

"In that case, I am free to rest here with myself rather than go anywhere with you, churl."

"It seems, madame, that we may not now be in King Arthur's lands. But, whether that be so or not, pray allow me to protect you in King Arthur's name."

"What? Has King Arthur made a knight of you?"

"I have the honor to be both his knight and his nephew."

The damsel tossed her head. "Small wonder, then, that women should be molested in lands where such as you serve to protect them! Well, sir churl, do you intend to carry me off across the saddlebow of your fine, warlike palfrey? That once I might have had for my own mount, had I wanted it! I warn you, you are not worthy to breathe the same air as I."

For answer, after only a slight hesitation, Sir Gawen dismounted and stooped to pick her mantle up from the ground for her.

"Churl," she said angrily, making as if to spurn him with her toe, but keeping her distance, "if you mean to help me on with my mantle, I tell you that it is far too fine for your greasy fingers, and if you mean simply to do me homage, I beg to inform you that you are scarcely worthy even for that!"

Shrugging a little, he waited until she had put her mantle and wimple on herself. Then he went to hold the palfrey's stirrup for her.

She laughed. "Churl, I can mount very well without any man's help! And, again I tell you, you are not worthy to touch so much as the crumbs of dirt that fall from the soles of my shoes."

Sir Gawen trusted himself to answer not a word, but moved meekly to the palfrey's head. That, at least, the proud maiden permitted him to hold while she set her dainty foot in the stirrup and swung with ease and grace into the saddle. But then, seizing the reins, she snapped them out of the knight's hands, turned her mount, and rode away at a fast walk – almost a trot – leaving him to follow on foot.

He did so all the way back through keep and town, his spurs ringing whenever they struck stone. It seemed to him that now the townspeople shook their heads at the damsel, pointing at her in anger and muttering curses at her, while such regard as they spared for him was still of sorrow and regret. None, however, raised a hand to stop either maiden or man.

When they reached the far side of the drawbridge, the tall knight was no longer to be seen; but, near the place where he had sat, Sir Gawen noticed a green herb that awakened memories of early boyhood, of his mother exclaiming over this same herb as a rare find: a plant of such extraordinary healing power that it could restore even a diseased and dying tree to full health. He lost no time in plucking that herb.

They came at last to the river, and the palfrey put its forefoot upon the bridge. But the maiden turned in her saddle, looked back beyond Sir Gawen, and laughed. "Well, Sir Churl," she said. "unless you can scramble across this bridge on your iron-shod feet – and that you may find very difficult – you are about to win glory indeed!"

Sir Gawen turned, and beheld an ugly squire approaching on a sorry nag. The squire was barrel-chested, with red hair and brows and beard that grew together over his head like an angry hedgehog, leaving scant room for his beady eyes; his leggings were mismatched, one being green and the other grey; and he wielded a long, rusty sword. The nag was all over bones and sharp angles, with flanks scored by years of cruel spurring; its head seemed far too big for its scrawny neck; its eyes were dull and clouded; and it looked altogether too old and used-up for anyone but the knacker.

"Knight!" bawled the ugly squire. "Were you not warned that the lord of this country demands the head of anyone who crosses his will in any matter at all?"

"And an impressive champion indeed he has sent to claim the tribute of you!" crowed the damsel. "A very worthy opponent for such a knight as you, sir churl!"

Ignoring her words, Sir Gawen lifted his shield and stood his ground without even drawing his sword. The ugly squire spurred his nag into a reluctant amble and aimed his blade. The knight caught the blow on his shield and, with his other arm, seized his attacker and dragged him from the saddle.

The sorry nag stopped dead and nickered.

"Well!" the fallen squire grumbled from the ground where he lay. "You have the best of it this time, but if you'll take a piece of advice, you will mount that horse you've just won and ride away from here as far and as fast as you can."

"Yes, mount the nag!" cried the maiden. "You will make so very fine a figure on its noble back."

Partly to prove that he cared nothing for her taunts (although, in truth, they began to sting), and partly because to scorn the prize would have been in some measure to dishonor his fallen opponent, Sir Gawen leaped into the sorry nag's saddle without using the stirrups. Old and tired as they were, he feared his weight might have pulled them from the saddle.

"Oh, bravo, bravo!" exclaimed the maiden. "Now you are suitably mounted indeed!" With that, she cantered across the bridge and, on reaching solid ground, set her palfrey into a gallop.

Sir Gawen followed at the fastest pace he could urge from the sorry nag, which, seeing that he did not wish to drive his spurs deeply into the hard scars left by other knights' spurs, was no better than a slow trot.

By the time he came far enough for a clear view of the ancient oak and what lay in its shade, he saw that the damsel, so proud and haughty towards him, had dismounted to kneel at the wounded knight's side, tearing her fine white wimple into strips.

With as much speed as he could, Sir Gawen came up to her and gladly displayed the plant he had gathered there beyond the river. "My lady," he cried, "this herb, bound round the trunk of a dying tree, would soon restore it to life and health."

She frowned up at him. "Well! If you know how to bind it round the body of a dying man, then do more than sit there on your fine horse boasting about it."

He dismounted and, between the two of them, they quickly cleaned the clotted blood from the knight's wounds, rubbed them with the rare herb, and bound them up with the bandages she had torn from her wimple.

While they worked, the wounded knight gave no sign of life save that he was not entirely stiff. But, only moments after they had tied the last bandage, his eyelids fluttered open and he stared up at Sir Gawen, then at the damsel, then – with a hard blink – at Gawen again. At length he said, "I thank you! Now help me, pray, to a horse. I know of a priest who lives near here, and I would confess my sins and receive the Sacrament before I die."

"With the help of God and His gracious Mother," Gawen replied, "I think that now you may live. Nevertheless, it is always good to confess and hear Mass. Let me seat you upon my own horse, my good Gringalet."

It was as if new light came into the wounded man's eyes, but he shook his head weakly. "That sorry nag I see yonder will be good enough for me."

"It is good enough for no one," Sir Gawen answered firmly, helping the wounded man up into Gringalet's saddle.

But before Gawen could leap up behind him, the other man, who must already have recovered far more of his strength than he had allowed to show, seized the reins and pranced the great charger away to a distance of several paces.

"What's this?" Sir Gawen cried, scarcely knowing whether to laugh or rage. "Take care, good friend, or you may well reopen your wounds!"

"Do you not know me, Gawen? I am that same knight whom once you condemned to eat for a month, with both hands bound behind his back, among the dogs!"

"What?" Frowning, Sir Gawen cast his memory back through the years. "Can you be Sir Greoreas? You are changed – "

"Changed?" Sir Greoreas barked a laugh. "I was dead, and you yourself restored my life – to your own sorrow!"

"Friend, I did you no injustice! Had you not forced a maiden against her will, in wicked defiance of King Arthur's laws? It was no more than my duty to punish you – "

"As I punish you for your arrogance!" Greoreas exclaimed. "Today your horse, Gawen, tomorrow your head!"

With that, he turned Gringalet and, though the great charger whinnied in protest, spurred him back down the meadow and away from both rivers. Sir Gawen turned to see what the proud maiden might have made of all this, but she had remounted her palfrey and sped past him even as he watched, apparently caring not a whit about the other knight's past offence. Sir Gawen was left alone with nothing but the sorry nag.

No, not entirely alone; for he heard a dry cough and, turning to the other river, saw that a ferryboat had glided silently through the soft silver mist to moor at a landing site below the tree. In the boat stood a ferryman garbed all in black, with a black hood and a whitethorn staff.

"You have cost me my prize." The ferryman spoke mildly, but firmly. "Yonder knight lay defeated by the one who attacked him, and all such defeated knights belong to me by the ancient custom of this place. Or, if not they themselves, at least their mounts . . . but yonder knight's attacker took away the mount as well as the maiden. And now she is gone again, palfrey and all."

"Then it appears that you have lost as much as I," Sir Gawen answered courteously, "for the man who should have been yours has stolen away the fine mount that was mine. Well, my friend, I am sorry for your loss, and indeed I knew nothing of the custom of this place. But take – if you wish him – this sorry nag, which is all I have left to offer you."

The ferryman's eyes seemed to glow, and he pushed his hood back upon his shoulders as if for a better look. But all that he said was, "And you, friend knight? What will you do, without any mount at all?"

Sir Gawen laughed for pure loss and disappointment. "Why, as to that, I suppose I must either find hospitality at once, or go on foot until I do."

The ferryman smiled. "My friend, for your courtesy, your generosity, and your need, I will host you myself this night, and bring you back across the river tomorrow or whenever you will."

So Gawen himself led the sorry nag into the ferryboat and crossed the river with it and the ferryman, who, after mooring his craft safely on the farther side, led both nag and knight a short way up the bank. So thick was the mist that the ferryman's manor seemed to appear around them, as though it had enfolded them unawares into its courtyard.

After directing his pages to stable the sorry nag with as much honor and good, horsely fare as if it had been Gringalet himself, the ferryman took Gawen into his hall, where he had his armor removed and a robe costly enough for any count brought to clothe him for supper. They feasted that night upon plovers and pheasants, partridges and venison, washed down by red wines and white both new and old; and Sir Gawen slept all night undisturbed in bedding of sable and silk.

Following his custom, he arose next day at dawn. The mist had cleared away during the dark hours, leaving a view of a splendid castle set high on a cliff overlooking the point where the two rivers flowed together into one.

This stronghold was made all of rich black marble, with half a thousand windows blinking various colors in the light of the freshly risen sun. "Host," Sir Gawen inquired, "what hall is that?"

"The keep of a great queen," the ferryman replied, "who came here years ago and caused it to be built out of her own great wealth. With her lives her daughter, also a queen, and that daughter has a daughter, as fair a princess as any to be seen on earth or in Heaven. Five hundred ladies and damsels live there with them, all of whom came for refuge after being grievously wronged on the other side of the river, with 500 squires to protect them – 100 beardless, 100 just growing their beards, 100 with full beards of black or brown or yellow, 100 with beards beginning to silver, and 100 whose beards have turned whiter than wool as they all wait for a champion to come and dub them knight. But they have more than squires to protect them, for the great queen was served by a scholar skilled in mystic arts, red and white of hair and foot, and he wrought such marvels in that hall that no man could survive them unless he were the perfect champion for whom the people wait, free from taint of evil or cowardice, noble in heart and head and soul."

"Good host!" Sir Gawen cried. "Let us visit that castle!" So eager was he that he would unthinkingly have seized the other by the arm, but somehow, and seemingly without the ferryman's own awareness or intent, the arm eluded the knight's touch.

The ferryman was far less eager than his guest, but he had a palfrey saddled for himself and a good grey stallion for Sir Gawen, and together they rode to the castle of black marble. As they drew nearer, Sir Gawen saw that the colors in the windows were the costly gowns of ladies and damsels who stood or sat, one at every window, watching the fair countryside with its fine meadows and gardens in full bloom. When they saw Sir Gawen approaching with his host, many of the ladies saluted him with silken scarves and kerchiefs. High of heart, he returned their welcome by removing his helmet with its bright plumes and waving it in broad sweeps of his arm.

They neared the entrance to the great hall. It had two lofty doors, one of ivory and one of ebony, both carved like the panels of church doors, though Sir Gawen could not quite make out what stories the pictures showed. All the hasps and hinges were shining gold, and jewels as well as gold glistened in the carved pictures of each door. And, at the foot of the stairs leading up to the doors, a man with one leg of flesh and one of silver sat whittling an ashwood wand.

As they came up to the one-legged man, Sir Gawen paused, and might have reached into his purse for some of the few remaining coins his journeying had left him; but, judging by the silver of the artificial leg that this man was no beggar, he contented himself with a courteous greeting: "God and Our Lady give you good day, my friend."

The one-legged man glanced up and answered not a word, but grinned slightly and tapped Sir Gawen with the ashwood wand – once on the shield, twice on the sword-hilt, and three times on the breast-plate above the heart.

"Good host," Sir Gawen murmured to the ferryman as they climbed the stairs, "who is that man with the silver leg?"

"That is not for me to say," replied the ferryman. "But it may be as well that I am with you."

They reached the top step, and the great doors drew inward before them, opening as though of themselves, soundlessly and with no servant in sight. Yet servants there must be somewhere, for all was clean and shining: the high, arched ceiling painted with clouds and angels so real they seemed to move, and not a single cobweb among the gilded beams; the marble walls in which half a thousand windows of clear glass glowed with morning light; and the floor paved with slabs of every color known to stone and some that Gawen had never seen before – green and scarlet and indigo – richly gleaming in inlaid patterns unobscured by any rush, for such a floor was far too fine to cover with rushes.

And in the centre of the floor stood a bed fashioned entirely of gold, with silver cording, and a little silver bell hanging down from each intersection of the cords. The legs of the bed rested on carved dogs who sat on smooth castors and bounced their gargoyle grins back up at themselves from the mirror-like floor. In each of the four bedposts a huge carbuncle shone brighter than four candles, and a samite coverlet hung over the bed as smoothly as the soft mattress beneath it would allow.

"Good host!" cried Sir Gawen. "To sit for five minutes on such a bed as that would surely be worth three whole nights resting in any other bed in the world."

The ferryman shook his head. "To sit for even one heartbeat on that bed would be as much as your very life is worth. That is the Wondrous Bed, which no man has ever yet survived."

His words woke in Gawen's mind the memory of another forbidden bed. That other time, he had courteously obeyed the ban while Sir Lancelot, travelling with him just then, had defied it and slept in the bed, putting himself in deadly peril but ultimately winning much greater glory. Dearly as these two champions loved and admired each other, their friendship was not unmixed with rivalry, and Gawen determined to do now as Lancelot had done then. "I will sit on that bed – lie in it, if I so choose – " he declared, "until I am well and fully rested."

The ferryman threw up his hands. "Then you will rest in death! For myself, I will not linger to see it."

So saying, the ferryman quit the hall. The doors of ivory and ebony closed behind him with a resonant thud, and Sir Gawen sat down on the Wondrous Bed.

His weight instantly set every bell ajingle, and caused the bed itself to glide fully three paces on its smooth castors over the polished floor. The 500 glass windows all opened at once, and through them flew such clouds of crossbow bolts it was like a whirlwind of huge and angry wasps converging on the bed.

Sir Gawen cast his shield up over his body and head – his movements making the bed glide this way and that until it almost crashed into the walls – while its bells rang forth as if shrieking. Bolts thunked into his arms and legs, into his shield so deeply that their points scratched his face, and into the silken coverlet all around him. Nevertheless, his shield saved him from mortal injury.

At last, hearing the rain of missiles cease and the windows shut, he lowered his shield and saw it bristling more thickly with bolts than a hedgehog with quills. "Well!" thought he. "That was surely worth as much as my lord Sir Lancelot's adventure with the burning spear that all but set his perilous bed aflame!"

But even as Gawen thought this, a small door he had not noticed before flew open and someone – he thought he glimpsed one silver toe – thrust a lion into the hall.

This was like nothing that Sir Lancelot had encountered on that earlier deadly bed. Even as Gawen stood to meet the huge beast, it leapt so fiercely that its paws snapped the crossbow bolts like brittle twigs and its sharp claws buried themselves in the knight's shield like needles sinking into warm wax.

But there, fortunately, they stuck fast; and Sir Gawen, who had been knocked to his knees by the force of the charge, was able to draw the great sword Excalibur, which his uncle the King had given him for his journey. Its blade snicked neatly through the lion's neck – less neatly through its paws, for all its sharp claws were left embedded in Gawen's shield, among the remaining bolts.

Well satisfied, Sir Gawen resumed his seat on the Wondrous Bed and commenced plucking bolts from his shield. The lion's claws he permitted to remain.

"They say," he thought, "that trials come either singly or by threes, and here have been two."

As he thought this, the great doors of ivory and ebony opened again, and a maiden fairer than sunlight slanting towards evening came through them. Her skin was more translucent than the petals of a lily; her hair like the aureole round the head of a saint, so glorious as to shame the golden circlet that crowned it; her form, beneath her silken white gown, as pure and graceful as that of an angel. She was to that proud maiden with the mirror as the sun is to the flame of a smoky rushlight, and at sight of her Sir Gawen knew two things: that she could be none other than the princess of whom his ferryman host had spoken, and that he was hopelessly in love with her.

The ferryman himself escorted her on the left hand, while on the right came a youth clad almost in motley, for his mantle was of bright crimson cloth lined with sable dark as a blackberry, over a surcoat diamonded in blue and green; and one of his hose was cloth of silver, the other cloth of gold. As they drew near the Wondrous Bed, this youth threw Sir Gawen a wink, sly as Cupid.

But the maiden, never noticing her escort's wink, greeted Sir Gawen with the ingenuous offer of her name: "My good lord, welcome! I am Clarissant, granddaughter of the Queen of this castle, and you are its lord, for whom we have waited these many years, since you have proved yourself by overcoming and putting to rest forever the tests of the Wondrous Bed!"

"May God, Who made His holiest daughter to be His most holy

Mother, give you grace, good lady!" Sir Gawen replied. "But am I truly to be your lord?"

At that the youth in many colors laughed and clapped his hands, and a throng of people poured into the hall – gallant squires and fair ladies of all ages, richly apparelled and beaming with smiles.

"You are indeed their long-awaited lord," the ferryman assured the knight, slapping him heartily on the back, while two grey-bearded squires, grinning like boys, began courteously to disarm him, and two fair dames, one dimpling and one dignified, presented the Lady Clarissant with a fine ermine robe.

"Pray, my lord," she said, turning again to Sir Gawen, "accept this cloak to keep your blood from taking a chill after your noble exertions."

As she bent and draped it about his shoulders with her own hands, Sir Gawen felt giddy and faint with the nearness of her. Her breath smelt of warm spices, and her hand felt cool when by chance it brushed his jaw.

"And if you would walk about to guard against growing stiff," she invited him, laying her cool fingers over his, "the windows offer a splendid view of your new lands."

Sir Gawen rose. The blood pounded so fiercely through his veins that for a moment he feared it must be pouring out upon the silken coverlet. But a hasty glance showed him that every wound he had sustained from crossbow bolt or lion's claw was healed over as scarlessly as though it had never been.

"Yes," the ferryman agreed, supporting him on the left side. "You may look your fill, but the lord of this castle may never again go outside its walls, not even to wander through his own lands or hunt in his own woods."

"What?" Sir Gawen cried, staring about in dismay.

For the heartbeats when his gaze fell on Clarissant, it seemed a small price to pay; but she was only one, and as the ferryman, the youth in many colors, the ladies and squires, the windows and ceiling and floor besprinkled with bolts and the lion lying dead all passed in turn before his eyes . . . No, it was too much! The ferryman smiled, the colorful youth grinned, the squires and ladies watched with mouths agape, the lion yawned in death, the crossbow bolts crunched beneath his feet as he sank back upon the Wondrous Bed. And the lady Clarissant looked on perplexed and appalled.

Was he, then, a prisoner forever? And could he grieve her by complaining?

"Dear lady," he murmured, "might I beg a brief audience with your queenly grandmother?"

"It is yours to command, my dearest lord!" she answered and, after an obeisance that warmed him even through the deep chill of his despair, she hurried away.

He expected, at most, a summons to the Queen's presence. But she came in person, accompanied by a retinue of dames and damsels among whom she herself shone forth like the moon among stars. Sir Gawen knew at once, by the dignity of her walk and the venerable whiteness of the shining hair beneath her golden crown, that this could be none other than the elder queen of whom he had heard; and he saw by the bones of her face and the color of her eyes that the fair lady Clarissant had spoken the truth of her own lineage.

He rose at once to greet this great queen, and she returned his tribute with all the gracious courtesy he had seen so often in the words and actions of his kingly uncle Arthur.

"Sir," said she, "it does me honor to yield the primary rulership of my castle to you, retaining only the second place for myself. But tell me, are you not of the court of King Arthur?"

"Madame," he replied politely, "I am neither the best of that great company, nor yet, I dare flatter myself, the worst."

"Spoken with true courtesy!" she congratulated him. "Indeed, I felt sure that no knight save one of Arthur's could have passed the tests of the Wondrous Bed. But tell me now of King Lot and his four fine sons . . ."

So she drew from him, question by question, all the news of King Arthur's court. While they spoke of all the people he loved and admired, Sir Gawen felt his gloom lifting away from him. The more so as, to his relief, the Queen never asked either his own name or any other question to make him reveal that he himself was the eldest of King Lot's four fine sons. It was Gawen's custom never to reveal his name except when asked for the same in so many words.

At last he regained sufficient cheer to tell her of his dismay on learning that he might never again leave the walls of this castle.

Thoughtfully she rubbed the side of her face in a way that King Arthur also had. At last she said: "We have waited so long a while for our lord that we dare not risk his loss."

"Madame," Sir Gawen pleaded, "without the exercise of arms and the chase in open air, even the best of knights might sicken and die."

The Queen gave the ferryman a questioning look.

"Madame," the ferryman replied, "of his own free will this good knight crossed the river with me. To keep such a one too closely caged might indeed cost him his life."

The Queen smiled and nodded. "So be it, then, my good lord: ride your own lands whenever you will, on whatever horse you will. Only, I pray you never to leave this your castle for longer than a day."

Had he felt less cheered by his long conversation with her about King Arthur's court, Sir Gawen might have chafed at this condition; but, as it was, he felt that he could never again in any case wish to be further than a day's ride from the beautiful Clarissant, and so for the time he rested well content. At his request, they set up his table in the very hall of his trial, and he dined with Clarissant on one hand and his former host the ferryman on the other. More squires and damsels than he could count served them with the choicest foods and wines, and the dinner went on until well past sunset, so that the last rounds were sung and dances danced by the light of many great, smokeless torches. In all that time, had Sir Gawen noticed, no one touched or tasted sip or morsel save himself and the lady Clarissant; but he did not notice, having eyes for very little but her. As for the gracious older queen, she had retired to dine quietly elsewhere with her daughter, Clarissant's mother, whom Gawen had not yet met.

He slept soundly that night in the Wondrous Bed, and his dreams were sweet. The face of Clarissant, as she bent over to tuck a pillow beneath his head and brush his cheek with a kiss, was the last thing he saw before closing his eyes, and the first thing he saw on opening them again as earliest dawnlight stained the hall's half-thousand windows.

Also in attendance that morning were the ferryman and the youth clad in many colors, who waited on him as he rose light of heart, dressed in a robe of samite and ermine that he found laid ready for him, and washed his hands. Afterwards, when he asked to see a better view of his new lands, Clarissant took him gently by the hand and led him up into the narrowest but highest of the towers.

Gazing out through its windows, he could see all the fields, meadows, and forests that surrounded the castle for many miles; and, on the other side, the whole tongue of land beyond the river, and beyond that tongue of land the other river, and even beyond that, the city he had visited only the day before. As he stared, already beginning to regret the condition that held him inside his own domain, who should appear in the meadow between the rivers but the pair whom he had succored yesterday and who had proceeded to betray him: the maiden on her palfrey with the bicolored head, and Sir Greoreas on Gawen's own steed Gringalet!

Seeing her lord's jaw set and fists clench, Clarissant grew pale and hurried from his side, soon to return bringing her grandmother the Queen, with the ferryman and the colorfully clad youth following in her train.

"Good my lord!" the Queen began. "May that great God Who made of His daughter His Mother give you joy!"

"May God, Who sent His Son through a Maiden Mother to redeem us all, bring you every happiness, madame," Sir Gawen replied, somewhat perfunctorily, for his attention was on the scene outside the window, where the knight and damsel seemed to be searching the ground all about the oak tree, from which Greoreas had plucked his shield. "But, madame," Sir Gawen went on to the old queen, "I pray you – if I am permitted to ride through my own lands, let me also return across the river long enough to recover my steed, my own good Gringalet!"

The Queen joined him at the window, looked out, and gave a gasp. "Alas! My lord, that you are a better knight than he is beyond any doubt, and yet sometimes the smallest mischance can give the worst man victory over the best, and I have seen him kill many at this very crossing. As for the maiden who rides with him, she wears malice about her like a heavy cloak. Time and again she has led knights here for her companion to fight and, when he slays them without mercy, she laughs aloud. I beg you, after we have waited so long for you, do not leave us again so lightly!"

Greoreas and the maiden had turned to face the city beyond the other river, as if they thought Gawen had returned there yesterday. He fancied he heard them hail him by name, but none of his companions at the window showed any sign of hearing it, so perhaps it was no more than his own desire to go and recover Gringalet.

"Forgive me, madame," said Sir Gawen, "but I would be a poor coward if I allowed fear of some mischance to hold me back when, whether or not the better knight, I have at least the better cause. And that man who must never leave his own lands is not lord, but prisoner!"

"In the name of pity, madame," said the ferryman, "let him go, or he may die here of grief."

The Queen considered, and sighed. "Very well."

The lady Clarissant added, stepping forward, "But, my dear lord, if you still live, come back to us by nightfall!"

"My very dear, very gracious ladies," he replied, bowing deeply, first over the hand of the elder and then, more lingeringly, over that of the younger, "you have my solemn word: if God so allows it, I will return to you before sunset." Then, still fancying he faintly heard Greoreas and the proud damsel call "Gawen" over and over, he added, "But, if it pleases you, may I beg one more favor? That you will not ask me my name."

Sighing again, the Queen replied, "Sir, it would have been my question, but now I will hold my silence upon this matter." And Clarissant, with no further words, breathed a soft, sweet kiss upon Sir Gawen's cheekbone.

The ferryman and the youth in many colors escorted Sir Gawen to the stables, along with a crowd of squires whom they accumulated on the way. Once there, the youth said in a matter-of-fact voice, "Of course, he must ride the same steed he came here with."

"What?" cried Gawen. "That sorry nag, when I see here before me so many fine chargers?"

The ferryman likewise demurred. "That nag is mine by honest right of passage."

But the youth insisted: "The same could be said of all these animals, sir ferryman, yet here they are stabled; and the same mount he came with is the one with which he must cross the river again, as you know better than I." So at last the ferryman and even Sir Gawen – who feared that Greoreas might leave – agreed. Several squires saddled the nag, while several others armed the knight, and as soon as it could be accomplished, the ferryman brought man and mount back across the river and deposited them at the landing place below the solitary oak.

Catching sight of them, Greoreas gave a great shout and spurred Gringalet forward. Wincing inwardly at the sight of those cruel spurs digging into Gringalet's flanks, Sir Gawen leapt into the saddle and tried to urge his own mount into an answering charge: but the sorry nag planted all four hooves deep in the fine sand and would not budge.

Bearing down on his opponent at full speed, Greoreas aimed his new lance at Gawen's shield. It struck head on – but it was like striking a fixed granite boulder! The lance first bent in an arc and then snapped in two, while Gawen, the second his opponent came close enough, struck such a blow that Excalibur clove straight through shield and hauberk, tumbling Greoreas upon the river bank.

Delighted, Sir Gawen sprang down out of the nag's saddle and up again into Gringalet's, for the great steed had paused to wait for his own master.

"How false fortune can favor even the poorest of knights!" came the voice of the proud damsel. Looking up, Sir Gawen beheld her on her palfrey with the black and white head, watching from the top of the rise. "If it had not been for the wounds he received yesterday from a better hand than yours, sir churl," she went on, "you would not have enjoyed such an easy victory today."

Sir Gawen looked again at Greoreas, who rolled groaning at the river's edge. As Gawen watched, the fallen man coughed blood into the sand, shuddered, and lay still until the ferryman bent and helped him up into the boat. As if accustomed to such things, the sorry nag followed them.

"Now I have my due, good sir," the ferryman called, turning to face Sir Gawen. "And you, if you will, can come along back with me at once."

"Not yet, ferryman!" cried the damsel. "Not if he dares prove his worth by doing something for me that the man you are taking used to do every day."

With that, she cantered her palfrey back up the slope. After waving to the ferryman with the words, "Before sunset," Sir Gawen followed her on his own good steed, to find her frowning into her mirror as she waited for him beneath the ancient oak.

"Well, sir churl," she greeted him, "I see you act boldly enough so far." And, with a toss of her head, she led the way at a walk up the meadow to the place where the two rivers met and flowed into one.

From the last, triangular point of meadow one could look across on the one hand to the country of Sir Gawen's new lands and on the other hand to that of the city from which he had yesterday rescued this same proud maiden – although both castle and city now lay far upriver. Or one could look straight ahead to where these two countries faced each other across the merged waters, with no intervening land. But all these banks rose sheer and steep, naked rock and a little crumbling clay where the turf fell away into the rushing rivers far below.

"See there!" the proud damsel said, pointing. "That is the Perilous Ford. He whom you defeated just now used to cross it every day to pick flowers for me. You may fancy yourself a better man than he, but would you dare to do even once what he did so often?"

Sir Gawen was brave, but neither imprudent nor foolhardy. This time, however, the damsel had stirred his blood to anger, and the Wondrous Bed had put him in mind of that other adventure in which Sir Lancelot, by acting more rashly, had gained greater glory, not only in the forbidden bed but also at the dangerous bridges. So after only a moment to study the distance between riverbanks and judge that his horse had leaped across wider ditches than this, Sir Gawen nodded and, without trusting himself to answer the damsel in words, backed Gringalet far enough for a fair running start.

Clods of earth tumbled away as the great charger's hooves left the bank. Sir Gawen heard them plop muddily into the water . . . and then Gringalet plunged down after them, missing his distance to land in the very middle of the river.

"Oh, bravo, bravo!" came the maiden's mocking voice. "Your former mount, the sorry nag, could have made a better leap!"

But, even before Gawen leaned forward with encouraging words, Gringalet had commenced swimming. With powerful legs and chest, the great horse struck out across the sucking current and reached footing in the sands of the river bottom, then managed a second leap, still mightier than the first, for this time he had to leap almost straight up, so that for a heartbeat Sir Gawen sat in the saddle with his back parallel to the water below. And then – how, the knight could never afterwards remember or imagine – Gringalet stood panting in the grasses of the farther bank.

"You must thank your horse, and not yourself!" the maiden called across to him. "Now see if finding me flowers is equally beyond your power!"

Pretending to ignore her, Sir Gawen dismounted and saw to Gringalet. Relieving the gallant steed of saddle and saddlecloth, he arranged them to dry, then rubbed the heaving sides down with handfuls of grass. Only when Gringalet was dry, somewhat rested, and ready did Sir Gawen resaddle him and, still without a word to the maiden, ride further into the field.

He found no flowers at all, but soon saw trees that had been planted, for they stood in straight rows on every side. And planted long ago, for they were old and gnarled, even dying. And in their midst Sir Gawen met a knight as handsome as the woods about him were stark, dressed for the chase, with his hunting horse beneath him, his sparrowhawk on one wrist, and two little retrievers yapping at the horse's feet.

"Good sir!" Gawen greeted the stranger. "May God, Who made you more handsome than any other mortal, give you great joy!"

"You are the handsome one," the other returned in courtly tones. "And valiant as well, leaping the Perilous Ford and leaving that malicious maiden."

Sir Gawen looked back, and saw that, sure enough, the maiden was still in sight, gazing once again pettishly into her mirror.

"Sir," Gawen replied, "perhaps I ought not to have left her alone, after defeating her knightly companion today and entrusting him to the ferryman of that other river over there. But she herself goaded me into jumping my good horse across the gorge."

"She meant to kill you, then," the stranger told him quietly, "curse the creature. I loved her once, you must know. She might have been my own sweetheart, after I took her from the first weakling with whom she rode, but the little fool would have none of me. She ran away as soon as she could, to take up with that Greoreas whom you have happily defeated today, a victory that in itself would prove your worth, had you not doubly proved it by leaping the Perilous Ford, which no knight before you has ever survived. And now, good sir, in admiration of your great worth, let us make a pact: ask me whatever you will, and I will answer you truly; and then let you return me the same favor."

"Good sir," Gawen agreed, "I pledge you my word. And first, let me ask you what is the name of that city yonder, and to whom does it belong?" For, standing up in his stirrups, he could see beyond the wooded field the roofs and towers of that city from which he had yesterday rescued the ungrateful maiden . . . although, hearing the stranger's words, he had begun to revise his opinion of her.

"My friend," the other knight answered proudly, "that is my own fine city of Orqueneseles, which I hold from God alone and owe no part of it to any mortal man."

In that case, if Greoreas and the maiden had uttered truth in anything, this handsome knight must have captured her a second time yesterday. "And what is your name, sir?" Gawen asked, despite his usual reticence in these matters.

"Sir, I am called Le Guiromelant."

"A gallant name for a valiant knight," Sir Gawen acknowledged courteously, "and the lord of a very great land. But who is that maiden who showed such malice and lack of sense in scorning your love?"

"Sir, she is called Mirobel, but with no word ever added in her praise."

Sir Gawen turned and pointed back to his own new castle, which, being perched high on the opposite cliff, could still be seen. "And what, my friend, is the name of that fair fortress on the other side?"

But on hearing this question Le Guiromelant turned his horse's head and began to ride away.

"Sir, sir!" Gawen cried after him. "Remember your word!"

Looking back, Le Guiromelant spoke as if in angry sorrow. "Go away! I release you from your pledge – be so good as to release me from mine. I had thought to ask you news of that castle, but it appears that you know as much about it as about the moon!"

"Sir," Gawen told him, "I slept there last night in the Wondrous Bed."

"What a rare storyteller you are!" said Le Guiromelant. "And how I erred in taking you for a knight!"

"See here! The claws of the lion that formerly guarded that bed lodge still in my shield!" Sir Gawen exclaimed, holding it up.

Le Guiromelant returned, peered closely at Sir Gawen's shield, then dismounted and knelt extravagantly in the dirt, begging the other man's pardon. Upon receiving it, he remounted and went on, "And did you see its white-haired queen and think to ask her name?"

"I have both seen and spoken with that gracious lady, but I have not asked her name."

"That castle is called the Rock of Sanguin," said Le Guiromelant. "And its white-haired queen is the noble Ygerne, King Arthur's own mother."

Sir Gawen gave a violent start. Recovering himself as best he could, he objected, "As far as I am aware, sir, King Arthur has had no mother for at least forty years."

"She escaped here from the world and caused Sanguin to be built soon after Utherpendragon's death," Le Guiromelant explained in triumph. "And did you see that younger queen with silvering hair, Queen Ygerne's daughter, she who was the wife of King Lot and mother of that man whom I hate above all other men in the world – the 'good' Sir Gawen?"

"Sir," said Gawen, "I know that man well enough to say that he has had no mother on earth for a good twenty years."

"She was pregnant," Le Guiromelant continued relentlessly, "when she followed her mother Queen Ygerne to the Rock of Sanguin. Gawen's mother came to these parts already pregnant with that tall and beautiful damsel whom I love as dearly as I hate her brother Gawen."

"Upon my soul!" Sir Gawen exclaimed. "For the sake of any woman whom I loved dearly, I would love and serve her whole family!"

Le Guiromelant sneered. "Gawen's father killed my father, and he himself killed a knightly cousin of mine in combat. The world may call King Arthur's nephew a good man, meting out alms to the poor, aid to the unfortunate, and justice to evildoers – but for his very sanctimonious 'charity' and 'honor,' so much the more do I hate Gawen! But do me a service now, my friend: when you return to the Rock of Sanguin, deliver this ring to my own fair sweetheart Clarissant, whom I hope to wed, and tell her that I have such faith in her love as to trust she would rather see her brother Gawen die the bitterest of deaths than that I should stub my little toe."

With heavy heart, Sir Gawen took the ring, which was of gold set with a rich green emerald, and placed it for safekeeping on his little finger. "Sir," he said, "you have the noblest of sweethearts. And also the truest, if she accepts the situation as you have described it."

"Sir," Le Guiromelant answered with a grin, "just give her that ring from me and, if she accepts it from your hand, I may well look forward to making her my own dear wife. But now your turn has come to answer my questions. Let me begin to asking you truly, what is your name?"

"Sir, so help me God and His Virgin Mother, I will not keep it from you. I am that very man whom you hate so greatly: I am Gawen."

First Le Guiromelant whistled, and then he laughed. "You are bold enough to tell me, seeing that I am dressed only for the hunt. If I were as fully armed as you, you would soon repent your foolhardiness, seeing your head fly from your shoulders!"

"Sir," Gawen replied, "go and arm yourself. I will wait."

Le Guiromelant laughed again and slapped his thigh. "No, by my faith, such a battle as ours will be should have as many noble witnesses as possible, to give the victor his due honor. Let us meet here – " he pointed at the open land between trees and riverbank – "one week from today, and meanwhile do you send for your King and Queen and all their court. I hear that they keep this Pentecost in Orkney, which lies a mere two days from here."

"Your information is correct," Sir Gawen told him. "As God

is my savior and His Mother my true lady, I will invite my noble King and his people here to see me make such reparation as you demand for any wrong I may have done you, either battle or any other amends that I can provide with honor in the eyes of both your friends and mine. Here is my hand as pledge."

"It will be battle," Le Guiromelant replied, and gave Gawen's hand a brief shake with his own, which felt clammy as muck and hot as a coal, both at once. "And battle to the uttermost," he added, "until one or the other of us lies dead . . . and it will be you, for the love in my sweetheart Clarissant's eyes will inspire me. But now let me take you to the bridge."

"No," Sir Gawen replied, shaking his head, "or my lady Mirobel may put it down to cowardice."

So saying, he turned Gringalet and urged him into a canter at once, so that by the time they reached the bank the horse was fairly flying already. At only the lightest touch of Gawen's spur – which was, indeed, all that he ever required – Gringalet made a mighty leap and landed safe on the opposite side, as neatly as if that first time he had only taken the measure of the Perilous Ford.

Seeing Gawen back on her side of the river, Mirobel turned and rode swiftly to the ancient oak. Sir Gawen followed, and found her palfrey tethered to the tree and quietly browsing, while the maiden stood a few paces away. She held her mirror still in one hand, but no longer looked into it.

"Good sir," she began humbly, "pray hear the reason for all my arrogance. The first time that devil over there – God's curse on him! – stole me away, he slew the only man I ever loved . . . my own dearest one . . ." Tears rolled freely down her face, but she blinked them back and went on: "And, after that, to try to win my love for himself! I escaped from him as quickly as I could, and, ever since, I have gone about half crazed, looking for some knight whom I could insult and anger enough that he would hack me into tiny pieces and send me after my own dear love. Sir Greoreas laughed and answered my insults so much in kind that we became partners, after a fashion, and I was allowing him to dispose of all those others who failed to kill me, until yesterday that devil over there captured me a second time and carried me to his own city, from which you rescued me, and met such poor reward for your work!" Lifting her mirror, she said, "This was one of the gifts with which that devil tried to buy my love, but I cannot see in it whatever he sees." She looked into it and continued in wonder and disgust, "Is this a face to make men kill and be killed? A body to excite any man to vile force?" Casting the mirror against the tree with force enough to shatter its glass, she knelt in the grass and gazed up weeping at Sir Gawen. "Now, sir, do what all those others failed to do: hack me into so many pieces that no other woman, hearing of my fate, will ever again dare insult any good knight!"

Sir Gawen thought, "And yesterday, when Le Guiromelant treated Mirobel in such manner – for the second time! – he must already have been claiming the lady Clarissant as his own true sweetheart!" Even while thinking this, he dismounted and approached Mirobel on foot. Drawing off his gauntlets, he took her folded hands into his, telling her aloud, "My fair one, you have suffered too much already. God and His Mother forbid that I should give you still greater grief! Let me be to you as a brother, sheltering you in the fair castle of Sanguin. See! The ferryman is ready to carry us across."

"Best of men!" Mirobel whispered. "In all things I will obey your wishes."

He helped her back upon her palfrey with the bicolored head, then remounted Gringalet and escorted her to the landing place, where the ferryman took them all aboard – man, maid, and mounts – and ferried them to the farther side, afterwards accompanying them back once more to the Rock of Sanguin.

Its people welcomed their new lord with great rejoicing, and, for love of him, they made Mirobel welcome as well. The three ladies of the castle were awaiting his return on three small golden thrones set up before the hall. The old Queen sat in the centre, with her daughter at her right hand and her granddaughter, the beautiful Clarissant, at her left. Giving them his greetings, Sir Gawen gazed as carefully as courtesy allowed into the face of Clarissant's mother, the Queen with hair just turning silver, whom he had never seen until now . . . but no, he had indeed seen her much and often, many years ago. He had hoped against hope that Le Guiromelant, dishonorable in other matters, had lied to him in this one; but, alas! whatever the man's crimes, he had at least spoken the truth. Gawen had not yet been fully grown when his mother died – as all had believed and told him – and she did not appear to recognize her eldest son in his manhood; but her own face had changed much less, and he knew her. Feeling his heart torn in two, he made up his mind not to reveal who he was until after his mortal combat with Le Guiromelant, a battle for which now he yearned as hotly as the other.

First, however, he should sound the lady Clarissant's own wishes; for, if so be that she truly loved the man, then Gawen must both question his own assessment of Le Guiromelant and continue, perhaps, to seek some honorable settlement short of combat. At the earliest opportunity, while the people of Sanguin sang songs and danced rounds in their happiness, he drew his sister aside to sit with him on the Wondrous Bed, where all could see them but none could overhear their words.

"My lady," he began, pulling Le Guiromelant's ring from his own finger and offering it on his palm to her, "beyond those rivers I met a knight who calls you his sweetheart and sends you this ring along with his love."

Clarissant picked up the ring and looked at it with curiosity. "Is he called Le Guiromelant?"

"He is."

"So he sends more than words in token of his love." She began sliding it on each slender finger in turn, as if trying which it might best fit, but never leaving it on longer than a heartbeat. "Well, my lord, how that man knows that he loves me, it lies beyond my power to guess, since we have never met nor glimpsed each other except across the rivers . . . but he kept sending his messengers and sending them until at last I gave in, and so to that extent, I suppose he is right to call me his sweetheart."

Gawen's heart beat with relief and hope as he said, "Le Guiromelant boasted that you would rather see your brother Gawen die the bitterest of deaths than that your sweetheart should stub his little toe."

"What?" cried Clarissant. "By God, I had no idea he was that sort of fool, or I should never have agreed to be his sweetheart!"

Sir Gawen ventured to ask, "But have you ever seen your brother, my lady? Or would you even know him by sight?"

"I have never seen Le Guiromelant, except at a distance. How dare he suppose that I would value such a sweetheart's mere comfort above a brother's life?" Her fist clenched about the ring and she looked around as if to see where she could hurl it without risk of striking someone by mischance.

"My lady," Sir Gawen confided to her, breathing more easily, "that knight challenged me to a test of strength, and we have agreed to meet again on his land one week from today before our assembled people."

"Then you can give him back his ring at that time!" Clarissant almost slapped it into Gawen's hand. For the moment that their palms touched, even with the hard lump of emerald and gold in the middle, something seemed to pass between their spirits. Blinking as she gazed into his eyes, the maiden whispered, "My lord, I will pray to God and His sweet Mother for your victory!"

Very much cheered, Sir Gawen returned the ring to his own finger, and they conversed on happier topics until the table was set up for dinner. Again, Clarissant's grandmother and mother retired to their own apartments for the meal, while squires and damsels of the castle waited upon their lord. This time Clarissant ate at his right hand and Mirobel at his left.

After dinner, Sir Gawen summoned the youth clad in many colors, who seemed to him the supplest and most alert of all the squires, and directed him to choose a good, fast horse to ride to Orkney and bring King Arthur with his court back in time for the forthcoming combat. Nodding and smiling, the youth took his departure at once.

That week the squires of Sanguin bathed, kept their nightlong vigil, and received the accolade of knighthood from their new lord, so that by the day appointed, Sir Gawen had a retinue of half a hundred newly created knights of all ages, along with the gracious ladies, damsels, and other people of the castle to accompany him to the appointed place.

Some little distance beyond the point where the two rivers flowed into one, a wonderful bridge, inlaid with ivory and ebony, spanned the distance between the facing cliffs, so that here one could pass directly from the land of Sanguin to that of Orqueneseles. This bridge had no rails, but it was smooth and wide. Sir Gawen crossed first on his great horse Gringalet, followed by the queens whom he now knew to be his grandmother and mother, although, in return courtesy for their not asking him his name, he had never asked them theirs. Then came Clarissant and Mirobel, with all the other ladies and damsels after them. Next rode the knights, one by one, and after them, because there were no longer any squires in Sanguin, the serving people followed on foot. Last of all, by his own choice, came the ferryman, bringing Sir Greoreas, who ever since his defeat at Gawen's hands had stayed in the ferryman's house and (to Gawen's relief) kept very silent on all matters whatsoever. Of the man with the silver leg, whom Gawen had seen only that once, there had never been any further sign.

They came down to the meadow between the Perilous Ford and the planted woods where Gawen had first met Le Guiromelant, and found there a fighting field cleared as if for a miniature tournament, a tourney of two – which, indeed, was what it was to be – with lists, two little tiring-tents, and stands for the onlookers. Half the stands were filled already with Le Guiromelant's people, but of King Arthur and his court there was neither trace nor evidence, which greatly disappointed Sir Gawen.

"My dishonored Lord!" Le Guiromelant greeted him in a loud voice. "Where is the King you promised me would be here with his whole court?"

The lady Clarissant looked from Le Guiromelant to Sir Gawen and back again, then rode forward and addressed the challenger and instigator of the coming combat. "Sir, that they are not here present in no way dishonors my lord, for many things may happen on the way, whether to a single messenger or even to an entire party. That my lord himself is here sufficiently proves the honor of his intention."

Le Guiromelant bowed to her. "My lady, by your rare beauty, you can be none other than the fair and most noble Clarissant, my own true sweetheart."

A small, soft sound of disgust came from Mirobel. The lady Clarissant exchanged one glance with her before turning back to Le Guiromelant and telling him, "Sir, in as far as I ever consented, at a distance and knowing nothing of you save your persistence, to be called your sweetheart, here and now I withdraw my consent. I would cast your ring back into your face with my own hand, if I had ever accepted it, which, thank God! I did not." To Sir Gawen she said, "My lord, I beg you, throw it down to the ground at his feet."

"My fairest one," said Le Guiromelant, "if you only knew who this man is, you would gladly give me your favor to wear and your cheers to encourage me in this coming battle."

"Sir," she answered, "although I have known him but a week, and you but a few moments, it is enough! He and he alone shall wear my favor." To Sir Gawen she repeated, "My good lord, cast his ring back at his feet."

Sir Gawen obeyed. Le Guiromelant picked it up scowling, but then he asked, "My lady, do you know what you are throwing away? Did you at least touch and handle this ring before reaching your rash decision?"

"To my shame," she admitted, "in my innocence, before guessing anything of your true character, I did handle and admire it a little."

"Enough!" he exclaimed, slipping it onto the little finger of his own left hand. "Your touch is enough to make this all the favor I need."

Clarissant's hand went to her mouth, and the two queens looked grave; but they gave Le Guiromelant no further satisfaction than that. And so the two champions went each to his tiring-tent to arm himself for the battle.

Clarissant and Mirobel helped arm Gawen, but Mirobel left when his arming was complete save for his helmet and the favor Clarissant had promised him.

"My lord," Clarissant told him, kneeling to tie her fair scarf of pure white silk around his upper arm, "that man may have my touch upon his ring, but you and you alone have the prayers of my heart."

Often and often during the week just past Sir Gawen had looked upon Clarissant and been sorely tempted in his secret heart never to reveal his true identity to the people of Sanguin. From whence had Adam's grandchildren come, after all, if not from unions between brother and sister? Or, if all men were brothers, were not all women equally their sisters? And had not everyone in the castle gone about looking as though they fully expected a match between their new lord and their elder lady's granddaughter? Or had all those sidelong glances been only his own half-guilty, half-wishful imagination?

Now, since it was not good to go into battle with wicked thoughts, he made one last, valiant effort to put all such temptations far away from him. "My lady and my saint!" he whispered. "Your prayers are more precious to me than those of the holy Apostles themselves!" And he kissed her, chastely and brotherly, once on the forehead before lifting his helmet into place.

Minutes later, the two champions faced each other at opposite ends of the lists, Sir Gawen on Gringalet and Le Guiromelant on a coal-black charger with nostrils red as fire or blood. They leaned forward into the gallop, they lowered their lances; they charged.

But the tip of Le Guiromelant's lance dipped low, as if he were taking aim at Gringalet. Seeing this, Sir Gawen quickly dipped his own lance, to bring it up again catching his adversary's point and sweeping it harmlessly high into the air. Caught off balance, Le Guiromelant fell from his saddle, but one of his spurs caught in his stirrup, so that for a few steps his horse was dragging him.

Gawen reined Gringalet to a stop and sat watching until Le Guiromelant succeeded in disengaging his spur and standing on his feet. Then and only then, deliberately, Sir Gawen dismounted, drew his sword, and with a light slap signalled his steed to retreat well out of harm's way.

Le Guiromelant drew his own sword, but showed no such concern for his charger, which backed only a few paces off to stand snorting and tossing his head.

The combatants closed upon each other, circling for only a few seconds before commencing to exchange blows, blow for blow. Metal clashed on metal – sparks flew and clangs resounded. The onlooking throng might equally as well have roared or been silent, for all that Gawen was aware of them.

Then, of a sudden, Le Guiromelant thrust out with his shield and struck Sir Gawen a blow that tumbled the helmet from off his head!

On they fought – for such a mishap was hardly enough in itself to give the hero pause, only now he was more vulnerable, and somewhat less unaware of the gasps and cheers of the onlookers, and especially of that one among them, his most dearly beloved sister. Less unaware, also, of the sky above him, the soft winds that brushed his face and rippled his hair, even the ground beneath his iron-shod feet. The shield on his left arm grew heavier to wield warding away Le Guiromelant's blows, the very sword in his right hand seemed less perfectly balanced to strike his own. Questions swam into his brain as to the worth of knighthood itself. All this it was that helped prove his undoing, for he failed at last to observe his opponent's move when Le Guiromelant tripped him with a kick and sent him down upon one knee, at the same time embedding the edge of his shield in the dirt.

Leering, Le Guiromelant raised his sword. But in that moment, as Sir Gawen strove with his shield and Le Guiromelant's sword swung down toward his naked neck, Clarissant sprang forth from the stands to throw herself in front of the fallen man.

Le Guiromelant's face froze in horror, but it was too late to stay his hand, and he could only try to turn his stroke. His sword whickered cleanly, and the lady stood headless before them all.

A great wail went up on all sides. The two queens – her mother and grandmother – alone seemed strangely unmoved, or perhaps they simply sat deadened in their sudden grief. Nor did the ferryman's expression change, but from every other throat, of Gawen's people and Le Guiromelant's alike, even from Greoreas and especially from Mirobel, rose a terrible cry. The horses themselves screamed. As for Sir Gawen, dropping sword and twisting free of shield, he caught up her beloved head and bent over it, weeping.

Yet the lady Clarissant did not fall. Bending as gracefully as though she still lived, she touched Sir Gawen's shoulders. When he stared up at her touch, she reached out for her own head. Nervelessly, he watched as she took it in both her fair hands, lifted it up, and replaced it on her neck.

"My brother," she murmured with a radiant smile. "Gawen! My own dearest brother." Smiling still, she bent again and kissed his forehead.

And then, she vanished.

And with her vanished all the people of the Rock of Sanguin. Ladies and newly made knights, stablemen and servants, King Arthur's mother Queen Ygerne and her queenly daughter Gawen's own mother . . . all of them faded away until, of all who had crossed the bridge that morning with Sir Gawen, only the ferryman, Sir Greoreas, and the maiden Mirobel remained.

"So ends my hope," Le Guiromelant wept, dropping his sword to sink down upon the ground and bury his face in his right hand.

Sir Gawen could do nothing else except stare wordlessly at the ferryman of Sanguin.

"All of them were dead already," the ferryman replied. "All of them save Clarissant alone. Her mother died pregnant, so that the lady Clarissant was born a living child in the castle her grandmother had caused to be built in the waiting-lands of the dead. Nor could any of them go on to Heaven until Clarissant had passed in her turn through the death of the body."

Greoreas, who had not spoken for a week save to wail at Clarissant's death, asked the ferryman, "Then why do I still remain?"

The ferryman grinned at him. "Do you think they would welcome you as yet, there in Heaven?"

Sir Greoreas rubbed his beard and said, "In that case, may I make of the Rock of Sanguin a hermitage wherein to repent my sins and await my own time?"

"You may," the ferryman replied, "if you take in any others who wish to do likewise."

Mirobel asked, "And the meadow between the rivers? Does that still lie within the lands of the living?"

"It does," said the ferryman.

"Then for my part," said the maiden, "I will make a convent

there for all poor creatures like myself, who would mourn their sins away while still awaiting the body's death."

"You have more of sorrow than of sin," Le Guiromelant told her bitterly, lifting his head at last. "But I – I must return and be content with Orqueneseles alone, having lost my hope of ruling Sanguin as well."

So saying, he climbed woefully to his feet and took his departure, followed by half of his people. But the other half, with anxious murmuring and muttering, made ready to follow Greoreas and the ferryman.

As they milled about pressing their claims and desires to cross over to the Sanguin side, Sir Gawen looked beyond them and saw, in the meadow that still belonged to the lands of the living, the messenger whom he had sent a week ago to Orkney – the youth wearing a crimson mantle lined with sable, over a surcoat of blue and green, with one hose of gold and the other of silver. And the horse he rode was none other than the sorry nag!

Riding straight to the edge of the riverbank, the motley youth leaned forward in the saddle, and the sorry nag leaped the Perilous Ford as easily as a cat jumping over a string. "Swallow your surprise," the youth told Gawen, riding closer. "Without one of these two mounts – the sorry nag and the palfrey with bicolored head – no living human can pass among these lands save now and then by the ferryman's signal favor. Nor could even your own good Gringalet have leapt the Perilous Ford if you had not passed into him some of the power you collected from the back of the sorry nag."

"But who, then, is Le Guiromelant?" Sir Gawen cried. "And who are you?"

Dismounting, the youth with one silver hose handed the reins of the sorry nag to Sir Gawen and said, "Enough of questions! or there will never be an end to them. I have brought Arthur and his people as far as I could: you will find them in the meadow between the rivers. Return there now – man, maiden, and Gringalet – and do not cross these rivers again until the ferryman summons you himself. Once you are back in the meadow, unbridle nag and palfrey and let them find their own way home."

Numbly, Sir Gawen helped Mirobel upon the palfrey, then remounted the nag, took Gringalet's reins to lead him, and set off upstream. As they neared the bridge below the city of Orqueneseles, they saw, true enough, King Arthur's people milling abut their tents in puzzlement and perplexity.

"My dear friend," Sir Gawen said to Mirobel just before they crossed back to the meadow of the oak tree and the living, "when you build your convent, I pray you dedicate it to the lady Clarissant . . ." He touched her scarf, tied still around his arm, and went on, "My own dear sister, whom I have found and lost again within a week. Surely she is already a holy saint."

Mirobel replied, "She will be both our saint and our patron, and may we all come to as holy an end as she!"

Arthur's people caught sight of them when they were on the bridge, and greeted them with a great shout of joy.

Sir Uwain in JUST CAUSE

Fay Sampson

Owain, also known as Yvain and here called Uwain, was a genuine historical king. He was the son of Urien, King of Rheged, and after his father's death continued to fight the Angles who had settled in the territory around Bamburgh and York. He was killed in the battle of Catraeth (or Catterick) around the year 595. The Owain of legend appears in the Welsh tale The Lady of the Fountain *in* The Mabinogion *and in the French romance* Yvain *by Chrétien de Troyes, both of which are based on the same source. Fay Sampson (b. 1935), who is renowned not only for her many children's books, but for her* Daughter of Tintagel *sequence about Morgan le Fay, here considers the difficult relationship between Uwain, his mother – Morgan le Fay – and Arthur.*

Arthur expelled me from Camelot. Me, Uwain.

He didn't expect to lose Gawain with me. That hit him. Arthur loves that big, lusty hero with the shock of sunburst hair, always his favourite among us nephews. And Gawain *is* his nephew. Nothing more. No incest-shadow over his birth to Arthur's red-haired sister.

Not like Mordred.

My own mother is dark and different. Morgan le Fay. No

less close to her brother, though, if you could look into all their hearts.

Half-brother. Gawain to Mordred, Arthur to Morgan. The maternal half. Why, then, does he feel so threatened by the beat of his Cornish blood?

And why did he trust my mother with that which was as precious to him as life itself? The weapon which *was* his life. Why did he leave it with Morgan his sister, and not Guinevere his wife? Answer me that.

I didn't understand the half of it.

Logres was at peace that year. No Roman taxes to spurn. No giants to beard. No Grail as yet to chase. We Knights of the Round Table could do everything necessary in the way of reinstating wronged maidens, raising the siege of beleagured castles, or using valour and virtue to break a fiend's spells. An enchanted sword raised from the depths of a lake is not the weapon to wear when all that is left for the King to do is go hunting.

He entrusted Excalibur to Morgan. I was there.

"Why me?" Only I, standing close beside her, heard how her low voice shook.

His scarred hands were holding out the sword, heavy with rubies, amethysts, filigree gold. He cradled it horizontally, his palms cupped to caress the blade as much as heft the hilt. And yet, he could not let it go, even while he held it out to her. She did not lift her hands to take or touch it.

"It is not a light little thing to be left lying at Camelot while I make the round of castles to feed my court."

"Guinevere is often at Camelot when you are away." There was loss and love and bitterness in her smile.

"Is Guinevere a wise witch?"

"Am I?"

"Your mother was. *Our* mother."

Her hands moved closer. But her eyes had gone beyond the sword.

"You ask me to keep the killing weapon for you. But you have something else more precious."

He looked surprised. After all these years, and all his battles, still I think it had never truly occurred to Arthur that he could die. It was several moments before he caught her meaning.

"The scabbard?"

"Ten times the value of the sword."

He tore his eyes away from Excalibur, like a man fighting his way from a cobwebbed cave.

"The sheath that hides thes blade? So Merlin told me. As long as I wore it, no hurt could harm me that it would not heal."

"Then why do you love it so little?"

Arthur has a boyish laugh. His eyes are bluer than her green. He made them dance for her. He made the whole room dance for us. He was our May King, ever young, who could chase winter from our land.

"It's true. I've never taken a knock in a joust or a wound in war that hasn't been knitted up before the blood ran thin and cold crept up to still the courage of a king. I can't be beaten. I can't be killed."

"As long as you wear this scabbard."

"Victory is in the sword. And in my heart that wields it."

"But what would you be without them? Your magic sword, your fairy scabbard?"

"A warrior-hero who could beat the Saxons with my little finger." But I had seen alarm flash brighter than the rubies, in his eyes.

"Take it," Morgan said to me.

That shook me. I thought I was a spectator at their game.

I had not thought a king's sword would weigh this heavy. I marvelled more that he could heave it in battle. I had seen him do it, and men fall like poppies as he drove the furrow forward. I felt the thrill from it, as he must every time he holds it. This was the fairy blade, Excalibur.

Her hands were empty still, held out for what she wanted more. He gave it to her easily. No matter how many times they told him, Merlin, Morgan, he undervalued it.

She took it reverently, like a mother reaching to receive her baby from the midwife. The healing scabbard lay in Morgan's hands.

It was the mirror of the sword. No less richly wrought. No lighter to hold in her palms than Excalibur in mine. Where the sword had snakes of gold hammered over the ebony surface, this sheath showed black serpents twining over a field of gold. The same rubies, the same imperial purple amethysts. Fit for a king, or a queen.

"I would not trust my wife with these," he said.

And the two of them looked into each other's eyes a long time.

"Trust me," Morgan said. "I am a wise woman."

She watched him leave before she would touch the sword. I didn't want to let it go. Me, Uwain, holding Excalibur, as if I were the Hero-King. Which I could have been, if my mother had been the Queen. Still, I was guarding Excalibur, since I was the wise woman's son.

She took it from me. My mother was devout too in the way she held out her hands for me to lay the weapon on them. Her fingers curled about it momentarily. She slid it sweetly into the sheath, and something inside me hurt to see that blade disappear. Morgan held them together now. Her breath came loud.

"So," she said. "My mother's family were once the royal guardians of this land. It is time to put him to the test."

The weeks went by, still peaceful, until it came a perfect autumn day for hunting. Frost crackled on the fallen leaves underfoot. We were all outside the walls of Camelot early, the fellowship of the Round Table mounted, staghounds jumping, squires dodging between hooves and horses' heads.

My father, Urien, was up there with Arthur, all his vanishing youth bright in his eyes again. He would break his neck today rather than be outrun by his sons and nephews. Arthur was the same.

I turned to my own mount and threw an arm across to spring into the saddle. My mother caught my elbow.

"Not today. I have other work for you."

Loyalty twisted my head to Arthur. But I had lived long enough with my mother to know that Morgan carries an equal authority with her brother. She was the keeper of Excalibur. Arthur had given it to her.

She drew me back, past the pages with their cups of steaming wine. Past the grizzled wolfhounds whining for a hunt their legs could no longer endure, into the palace and the shadows of her room.

She had taken Excalibur out and laid it on a chest. Even without the sun, the jewels glowed. The blade had crept partly out of its sheath. It seemed to me like a holy thing set on an altar.

When she slipped the robe over my shoulders, I knew she was making me her priest. White deer-hide. The cap was harder for her to place. She is not a tall woman. I knelt before her.

It was heavy, uncertain to balance, with those five-pronged antlers. It required a very particular positioning of my head and neck. She tied the thongs against my throat. I tossed my head experimentally. I bellowed, and frightened myself. I rose on all four hooves, swaying my great branched crown. I could not speak.

Her hand stroked the soft pelt between my horns and down my furred nose. I bent my head and shivered under her touch.

"Go," she whispered in my ear. "Run."

The hay had fallen in the field, dead flowers of summer scattered and trampled by the hunt. The meadow was empty now. My hooves sent divots and grass stems whirling in the blue air. The hawthorn bushes scratched my sides. Treetrunks skimmed past. I plunged through deep forest. I heard the horn, and galloped on. The hounds bayed, higher than the blood booming in my ears. Still I fled. Leaping streams where the sudden sun was mirrored in open water. Ploughing the deep leaves and the soft silt in the valley bottoms. Up the dry sandy slopes and the higher hills. Over and on.

No sound of horns for a long while. But the pounding of horses' hooves followed me yet. I looked behind. Three riders. Arthur, Urien my father, and and a younger knight from Gaul, Accolon. Glowing darkly as the red wine he had brought for Morgan.

On. On.

A flash of a broader river. Too late to swerve. I was teetering on the bank. Must I swim? They were bearing down on me in thunder. I leaped out into sunlight.

In the seconds before the splash submerged my sweat-streaked body, a sail glided between me and my pursuers, hiding me. I had one startled glimpse. Then the cold crashed around me and the water was over my head.

I cannot surface. I am fighting against the smothering sheet that will not let me find the air. I shall never breathe again. Morgan has done this to me, for clinging to the king's sword that wasn't mine. I have fulfilled her purpose. I am finished.

The light fell soft, as though the golden evening slanted through an open window. I had won my struggle with the sheet. My face was clear. I lifted my hands, wiped the sweat from my face, rubbed my heavy eyes, ran fingers through my soaked hair.

I sat up, feeling around me. I could not steady my heart. I was back in Camelot, alone in the bed where I slept with my brothers and cousins every night. The day was not yet done. There was a distant noise from the stables. Arthur's hunt had returned, or some of them.

I shouted to a page for water and washed myself, trembling, exhausted. I dressed carefully and waited for the call to supper.

The horn was late sounding. As I made my way to the hall, the air was uneasy. There were plenty of people about now, but not the face which should have been the focus of any feast in Camelot. The high seat between Guinevere and Morgan stood empty. Fair Guinevere, dark Morgan. Nothing separated them now. Arthur had not returned, nor my father, nor young Accolon.

My mother smiled her satisfaction at me. Guinevere was breaking her bread into pellets. I made my way further down the table, between Gawain and Mordred.

Gawain yelled at me as supper was carried in, "You should have seen the white hart, Uwain! A more glorious beast you never chased in your dreams. It easily outfled our hounds. But somebody must have whispered in their horses' ears: Arthur's, Urien's, Accolon's. They flew ahead of us, far out of sight. The rest of us lost the scent."

"Urien?" asked Mordred. "I didn't think my uncle still had such a turn of speed in him. I hope he's not lying in the forest somewhere with a broken neck."

"Urien will be safe." From the high table, my mother was firm, serene.

And so he was. Waking in the bed beside her as dawn warmed the sky. When we crowded round to know how he had come there, where he had been, his eyes went past us, as though this world could no longer hold him.

"I remember the white hart leaping. Full into the sun he rose, as though he was going to take wings and soar. I never saw where he went. A ship came gliding suddenly down the stream, between us and that vision of the stag. It came to rest against the bank, right at our feet. And that was a strange steering, because there wasn't a sign of helmsman or crew on deck.

"Well, you know Arthur. Would you expect him to say no to an adventure? I cautioned him. The signs were plain enough. There was no stopping him. For loyalty, I followed him aboard, against my judgment. Accolon didn't need persuading. Like a boy caught up in a fairy tale, he was, running his hands over every bit of that ship, as though he couldn't believe his luck. I tell you, no palace in all Logres was ever so richly hung with silks or gleaming with pearls or perfumed with precious woods like that vessel. I was close at Arthur's back when he stepped down into that marvellous cabin and we saw them crowding all around us."

"Warriors?" Gawain shouted. "An ambush?"

"Ghosts?" whispered Mordred.

"Women. Maidens? Yet that's too pale a word for what these seemed . . ."

"As far beyond your dreams as the ship was beyond this palace?" I breathed.

My father's eyes came back from the distance then and found not mine but Morgan's. "Beyond your dreams perhaps, son, or Arthur's. Not mine."

Guinevere hissed.

"They dined us on fairy food and wined us with flagons that made young Accolon's eyes even wider with wonder. We weren't going to resist when they led us off to separate cabins. And yet . . . The pillow they laid me on was soft as swansdown. I must have slept before my head pressed it flat. I woke here, in Camelot. And there will always be an ache in me for what I almost had, but could not, there or here."

Urien looked a long while at my mother when he said that. Her cheeks deepened and her fingers tensed, but she smiled for him. Enchanting, my mother's smile.

"And where is Arthur now?" Guinevere's voice came small and cold.

"I followed him as far as I could. That's all I know."

"Don't be afraid, Guinevere," said Mordred softly. "We will all defend you."

Arthur did not come back next day. Nor did Accolon of Gaul.

"He wants Excalibur."

The echo of her voice dropped from the hollows between the rafters. My mother was standing with her back to me. Beyond the dark blue sweep of her gown I saw the gleam of the hero-sword, laid ceremonially. It was half drawn, the blade catching reflected blue in its own chased metal, the scabbard partly withdrawing from it.

She spun swiftly at my footsteps. Her eyes blazed emeralds. "Listen well, Uwain. I put before you this case.

"Two brothers, Sir Damas and Sir Ontzlake. Damas is the elder. The greater part of the family estate, of course, falls to him. But there is a legacy for Ontzlake, some treasure, lands. Or should have been. His brother uses his greater power to keep Ontzlake from what his father intended. The younger has lost almost all the land that was his. What little is left, he defends valiantly. The common people love him, but they give Sir Damas an evil reputation. Ontzlake has offered to fight his elder brother in open combat, to prove before Heaven his right to the land that was his. But Sir Damas will not take his challenge. He knows Sir Ontzlake is the better knight. Yet Ontzlake is so sure of his right, he has offered to fight any champion Damas names."

"Well, he can't lose, if his cause is just, can he? Heaven must be on his side."

She looked at me oddly. "You believe that?"

"Deny it, and the laws of chivalry are as fragile as eggshells. Heaven would be mocked. Might would be right. The bully takes all."

"Damas has sought a champion all this year. No one will fight for him. He has taken to seizing every passing knight and throwing them into his dungeon. Still not one has consented to take up arms in his name. Many have died in that prison, rather than side with dishonour."

"So should every true knight in Arthur's land."

"And what would Arthur himself do, if he were there?"

"Arthur is the prince of chivalry, with the cross on his shoulder. Arthur *made* the Round Table fellowship. Arthur . . ."

"Arthur is in that prison."

"In . . . prison? . . . Arthur?"

"In Damas's dungeon."

"Then what are we waiting for? Let's get the whole Round Table to horse and . . ."

"He wants Excalibur."

I felt the shock leach blood from my heart.

She put her finger to her lips, and laid it on mine. "Soft. There are lessons here. A king that has to be rescued from humiliation is no true hero, is he? Arthur would not thank you for such salvation. He will fight his own way out of any corner. He thinks he cannot be beaten."

"He can't be beaten while he has Excalibur. He's always led us to victory in the true cause . . ." I felt my words slipping away from me, slowing. "And . . . this cause is false . . . *Arthur* has agreed to fight for Damas, against Ontzlake? Champion wrong against the right?"

"Power against the powerless, yes."

"The King of the Round Table?"

"Damas does not, of course, realize who this champion is."

Thoughts of denial whirled through my head.

"And you . . . keep . . . Excalibur."

She was lifting the sword. Rubies glinted as she turned. I saw the weapon in all its splendour, laid across her hands as she held it out to me.

"Take it."

For an awful moment, my heart was in my throat. I was Morgan's son, her eldest son. That is an ancient image. Even before we knew Mary and the Christ Child, my people sang of Modron the Mother and Mabon her Son. My mother's ancestors once ruled Britain, long before Arthur and the Pendragons. I thought she meant much more than she did.

"Give this to Arthur."

I was only her messenger boy.

"You're going to let Arthur be Damas's champion?"

"No one there knows he is anything but a knight errant."

"For injustice? With Excalibur?" I would not touch the weapon now. It was the pure symbol of chivalry. "If he held this . . ."

"Do you still believe he can never be beaten? Ontzlake must lose?"

"Arthur never loses."

"You are his sworn knight. Your king wants it. Deliver it to him."

My mother's eyes stared steadily at me. My heart skipped like a shocked hare. Doors opened dizzily in my mind. A castle so far away from Camelot no one knew Arthur's face.

"*How do you know*?"

Very warm, maternal, her smile, as though I had pleased her.

"Damas has a damsel wiser than he is."

"You are allowing Arthur Excalibur for this?"

"I give my brother only what he has earned."

I should have refused. I could have split from the Round Table and Camelot there and then. But the spell held me. All this time, my brain had been whirling with treachery, chivalry, disbelief, yet my hands were longing for something else. I could not hold temptation down. I took that sword from her.

The thrill. To hold this prince of weapons. The Hero-King's sword. It came into my hands with all the legendary power of past battles, by which Arthur our king had kept Logres safe. This blade had guarded the weak, repelled invaders, felled traitors, avenged wrongs. I held it now.

If it were mine, I would wield it in a higher cause than this. King Arthur became a little smaller in my mind.

When I lifted my burning eyes, Morgan was watching me.

"You are all alike. You swore undying loyalty to him. You are still Arthur's man. Give him his weapon."

She was right. None of us would ever question King Arthur to his face. The sword hung lighter than I remembered, as I carried it out of Morgan's keeping.

"Do not forget what makes it whole," she said quietly, as I reached the door.

But of course I had. I slipped the healing scabbard on, sorry to see the rich-wrought blade, thrice-hammered steel, disappearing into that shadowy groove. None of us ever thinks it will be us who will lie wounded, bleeding, vulnerable, pleading for help. Arthur did not.

It was a long drear way to Damas's castle. I might have been in danger myself, approaching it, a lone knight. But what was there to be nervous about? I had Excalibur in my keeping, hadn't I? I was bound to be safe.

And Arthur had settled the matter with Damas, anyway. He was not the man to starve to death in a dungeon, whatever the fight he was offered.

Perhaps it was as well I was in lands where the faces of the fellowship of the Round Table were unfamiliar, even King Arthur's.

They were setting up lists in the meadow. Good and evil would battle it out in a holiday atmosphere. Half the countryside was running about setting the scene.

No mumming this. This sword I had to deliver would cut through skin, slice flesh, let out life-blood. Damas's champion was bound to defeat poor Ontzlake.

I halted where the track came out of the trees on to the field. I drew the weapon of legend, leaning to balance it across my horse's neck. My breath came slow and difficult as I stared at it. Was this my mother's mission for me? Excalibur, for this?

I straightened and looked ahead. That long straight of grass, where the horses would thunder together. Hope soared like a skylark. Perhaps the lances would settle it at the first shock. Ontzlake would unhorse his opponent. Arthur would lie stunned, speechless, before he had a chance to draw this sword. Right would be vindicated by Heaven. It would all be over.

But if he rose . . . leapt lithely to his feet and drew the weapon I was giving him . . .?

My hands closed hard round the hilt. Cold crept through my palms and wrists and arms, ran through shoulders and rib-cage, stabbed my heart. I felt an awful orphaning. Was this the same sword, the glory that had once fused my hands with its fire so that I could scarcely let it go? I almost dropped it.

A damsel came running across the grass before any herald could sing out my name. A finger on her own lips and then on mine. "Say nothing. Just give it to him for whom it was meant."

"You know my mother's mind?"

"Morgan is the wisest woman in Logres."

"So I once thought."

Wise? My mother? To make me give this death-dealing weapon to my king?

"You don't need me any further. Take it yourself."

"May he not suspect me? How should I have Excalibur in my hands? But you are his nephew. He will trust you."

I knew it was wrong. The deed, this weapon. Yet I put it into Arthur's hand.

She led him in to see me. They had brought him up to a private chamber. He looked gaunt, though he had been locked in Damas's dungeon only a little while. When he saw who had come, he raged like a chained hawk.

"You, Uwain? Is this some mischief of your mother's? Some sermon she's sent me? How did you know I was here? My name is not to be revealed until I've won."

"My mother sends you what is yours by right."

I uncovered the sword.

The old grin split his beard. "Excalibur? Oh, my beauty!" Like a boy to his beloved.

"And this, to complete the gift."

He took the scabbard casually, dropped it on a bench. The ebony snakes disappeared in the shadows. The weapon hilt blazed in the sunlight from the window. I left him lovingly stroking the blade. At the door, I met a squire carrying armour in, grey, anonymous.

The noise was growing outside. I wanted to run. I knew what I had done. I had been loyal to my king, yet not to my oath. I had betrayed a true knight. Excalibur was no longer what I thought it was. I could not understand what my mother was doing.

Sunlight struck me full in the face. The crowd thronged thickly. The day had turned nearly to noon. The tiered seats were filling fast with the nobility.

I pushed through the press, hurrying to bury myself blind in the forest. As I left the lists behind, I lifted my raging face to Heaven.

"What are you going to do about this?"

Out of the flawless blue sky a shiver of thunder mocked me.

My stride slowed. How could I pretend this was not happening, go back to Camelot, not knowing? Like a thrashing pike pulled in a net, the tournament dragged me to it. I stood, crushed against the barrier. I was as much an unfettered prisoner as those knights let out of Damas's dungeon now, to watch the fight all but one had refused.

There was no way anyone could recognize the King of Logres when he rode into view. An unnamed knight, closely armoured. The acclaim for him was ragged. If he won, he could free those prisoners, but he would rob Ontzlake of his birthright.

Opposite him, to ringing cheers, a slighter figure, similarly shielded.

I flashed my eyes to the stand, where the lord Damas stood to preside over his own fate. A younger man stood defiantly beside Damas, his smile engaging, if a trifle weary. I watched him lower himself cautiously on to his seat, then struggle to stand again, as if there was no position which would not pain him. The damsel was back at my elbow.

"Sir Ontzlake could have outfought any champion Damas found black-hearted enough to take his cause. But when the challenge came, the good knight was already wounded through both thighs. So the two brothers must watch their trial decided by others."

My eyes went back to Arthur's slender opponent. "Then who is Ontzlake's champion?"

She looked at me sideways. "Your mother didn't tell you?"

"No."

The trumpet sang. The herald challenged, "Do you both agree to abide by the laws of chivalry?"

"We do so swear," their voices boomed.

"And what are the laws of chivalry now?" I asked the damsel. "Will the worth of the two men behind those helmets decide the issue, in Heaven's eyes? Or the virtue or vice of the cause they champion?"

"We must fight our own battles," she said. "All of us." And she looked up very straight into my face.

They crashed together. It was an impact awesome enough to hurt our eardrums. Immediately, both horses and riders went down. The two heroes were swiftly on their feet, swords out. One big, broad-shouldered, a mighty oak of a man, hidden within the husk of his armour. The other slimmer, suppler, lighter on his feet. The hilts of both weapons were covered by mailed fists. Impossible for anyone watching to recognize Excalibur.

They fought ferociously, no mercy showing. Blood began to spray. Soon it was coating armour with a changed heraldry. Arthur's was the redder by far. He began to stagger at the knees. The crowd cheered.

"How can this be happening?" I shouted at the damsel. "Is this your witchcraft? I gave him Excalibur. He can't lose."

"He took the unjust cause."

"But he's the better man."

"Is he?"

I was silent, watching the lighter knight skipping about the lists, dealing those terrible blows to my king. And it came into my head that I could still save my uncle. I could step into the lists, snatch a herald's horn. Proclaim to all the world that this was Arthur, King of all the Britons. What knight would dare to lift a sword to harm him further?

I took an uncertain step towards the entrance, and fell back.

Arthur would hate me for it. Always afterwards he would be a lesser hero. Arthur would never sue for mercy. He would never yield.

Damas's damsel tilted up her face at me. Her lips curved. "Leave this to the women."

There was a stirring in the stand. My eyes went back to where the brothers Damas and Ontzlake watched, contesting the division of their father's land, fiercely proud. The elder was too cowardly to risk this fight; the younger too damaged. A lady was gliding into the place behind them, slipping like water in her shimmering blue-green gown, changing between the colour of Arthur and Morgan's eyes. Her hair rippled, sunlit. I saw her start of dismay. She had not expected to see Damas's champion so bloodied and bowed.

And slowly I understood, staring at the changeable current of her features, who had come slipping back to us in Arthur's hour of danger. Nimue the Lake Maiden, whom we had not seen at Camelot since she lured Merlin away from us.

"She is a traitor to Arthur." I growled out the words, so loud that heads turned towards us. "Nimue is dangerous."

"Wait," said the damsel, as though Arthur's life were not leaking out upon the sand.

Three times, the challenger summoned the bigger man to surrender, in Ontzlake's name. Three times, the helmeted voice of Arthur refused in scorn. I was sick and terrified. I had given him the wrong sword. I knew that now. Excalibur had left him. Honour had left him. Victory had left him. But he was still a fearsome fighter. Whatever weak weapon he held in his hands, he was doing a deal of damage with it. The other knight's armour was dyed too.

My uncle raised his sword two-handed and struck down. The blow should have sheared the other's brain-pan. But the blade broke. Only a splintered stump stood in his shocked grasp. Reprieved, the challenger rushed in. Across the lists, a movement caught my eye again. Nimue had raised her hand high over her head. I saw the signs she made. Power poured from her fingers.

"Yield," yelled the younger knight.

"I don't know that word."

"In the name of justice."

With a roar, Arthur rushed in, his shield thrust before him, all his staggering weight forcing the slighter man back. He laid about him lustily with the jagged stump. He must know now Excalibur was the wreck of the weapon of heroism, or that I had given him no true sword.

I had armed Arthur. The blood was leaving my own heart as fast as his. I had handed my king a false weapon. My mother had given it to me.

A false weapon for a false king fighting a false cause. And I knew how she must be weeping for that now.

Then Nimue dropped her hand.

As though connected across that space of sunlight, her finger to his, the slender unknown knight let slip his still-whole weapon. It tumbled on the sandy sward and the sun caught the jewels of its hilt. The rubies winked up at us. I lunged forward and checked again. I did not need to vault into the lists and bend over it. I already knew. Excalibur had left Arthur. The fairy weapon lifted from the lake had flown to the side of justice. I had given my uncle only a counterfeit of kingship, a mockery of a hero's honour.

I thought I understood. My mouth was open to howl the death of Arthur. My dream of the Round Table was destroyed.

But with the desperation that will not admit defeat, Arthur darted for the dropped sword. Even as he grabbed it up, he knew it for his own. His yell of anguish shook the stands. With blood sluicing down his sides, he grasped the scabbard I had equipped him with, that could have no healing in it. He tore it from his thigh and sent it hurtling over our heads, empty, useless. But still he could not claim his true one back. It was buckled to the other's side.

Arthur would win this battle. But he could still be killed.

Yet, with his ebbing strength, Excalibur was enough to fell an unweaponed man.

"Yield." We knew by his planted foot what his laboured breath must be gasping.

Still he paused, before the desperate denial of a true knight in a rightful cause. Mercy did not last long. Arthur ripped off the young man's helmet and threatened the bared neck with his blade.

The whole host hushed. Ragged and laboured, the big man's question rasped, as he wiped the sweat and blood from his vision with a weary fist. "Who are you, lad? Haven't I seen you somewhere before?"

The answer was faint on the breeze. "I was proud to call myself a knight of the Round Table. I am Sir Accolon of Gaul, sworn for the honour of King Arthur to die defending the right. I cannot yield to you."

The sun shimmered on the trembling blade of Excalibur as it lowered to the ground.

"How did you get this sword?"

"From the keeping of the wisest and fairest woman in the world. Morgan le Fay."

"Then you are both traitors to my crown." Arthur's hands fumbled with the latches of his stained helmet. When he drew it off, he shook out his still-bright hair. I, who have taken many a gash in jousts, drew my breath in fear. Drops of running blood flew like off like spume. What showed of his face beneath that shocking tide was ghastly white. "You have almost killed your king."

Accolon turned his offered neck, rolled his head upright. His groan trembled through the hollow silence of the lists.

"Arthur? Then, I've fought you for what I thought you stood for. And if I had married your sister, I would have been a better king."

I growled myself at that. The howls of rage against rebellion and treachery were mounting like storm waves on a lake.

Arthur leaned heavily on his recaptured sword and grinned. "So we learn now where treason lies, and lechery, dishonour, murder. With the woman I worshipped more than my own wife."

It was time I left. As I hurried for my horse, heralds behind me were summoning Damas and Ontzlake on to the lists to hear the King's orders. I checked to listen. The ground rocked with the cheering as Arthur gave out his verdict. All the prisoners to be freed. Ontzlake to be made a knight of the Round Table, his legacy fully restored. Damas to be dishonoured by the gift every year of a lady's palfrey in place of his knight's courser.

My heart burned with the rush of returning blood. It was all right, after all. Arthur was the just judge. Arthur was still the honourable hero. He had Excalibur in his fist again. Arthur had won.

Laughing for joy, I looked back at the stands where ladies were waving their favours and blowing him kisses. Arthur was giving me back my dream.

Nimue had gone, vanished like water in the sun.

And then I realized. I was Morgan's son. I must vanish too.

"They're both still alive? You swear it?" My mother's face stared white from within curtains of black hair.

"Arthur nearly died. I handed a false weapon to my true lord. You cheated me."

"*I* cheated you?"

"Arthur won this trial. He must have known he would. He's a better knight than any of us, isn't he? Justice has been done, in the end. Could Accolon have achieved that, if he'd won?"

Tears were sliding down the furrows of her face. "Accolon acted like a hero of the Round Table. He championed the weak. But Arthur took the bully's side. Yes, I sent Accolon Excalibur, or Arthur would have killed him with the sword of chivalry."

"He may have done that yet. They both looked desperately wounded."

"I gave Accolon the scabbard of healing too."

"Not for long, I think, now Arthur knows."

Her voice was a whispered scream. "Accolon was defending the side of right."

"You should have been there, then. Nimue was."

My father's voice, loyal, certain, rang from the doorway behind me. "Arthur is the King. What he does is right."

Morgan was staring speechlessly at Urien.

I woke out of a nightmare of bleeding spears, headless knights. Alison, Morgan's maid, was clawing at my shoulder.

"Uwain, Uwain! Wake up, for mercy's sake."

I snapped upright. "Arthur's recovered? He's back? Does he want my head?"

Around me, my cousins rolled and groaned. Gawain opened a sparkling eye to the candle flame. "What have you been up to,

Uwain? Arthur will be here soon. You'll never keep him down. Shout if you need any help."

"I only want Uwain." Alison spoke too sharp, too frightened.

Mordred watched us from under the edge of the blanket, silent, a dark shine in his gaze.

She dragged me through slumbering rooms to the quarters where my parents slept privately, not far from Guinevere's chambers. We both of us yelled when her candle lit the doorway.

Till then, the room must have been in total darkness. But Morgan stood, her shadow rearing up the wall, my father's sword raised high in both her hands, over the bed where Urien lay half-smiling in his sleep. Dark snakes of hair tangled over her shoulders, her arms were moon-shafts. Yet for all the slight delicacy of her body, something in the way her fingers curled round the hilt of Urien's weapon was very like the grip of Arthur's gauntlets round Excalibur, raised over Accolon's neck.

I lunged to grab her arms. "No! What has Father ever done to deserve this? He loves both you and Arthur."

She twisted her face, furrowed with shadows, though her cheeks were dry.

"Were there not three men who hunted you close, when you ran as the white stag? Arthur, Urien, Accolon. I had the choice. It could have been Urien I chose to champion the cause of right. To gamble for dignity or death. I brought your father back to my bed. I saved his life. And Accolon may die because of it. I was the wise woman. I set that test. But Arthur always wins."

She let fall my father's weapon, clattering on the floor. Urien stirred, rolled over, smiled more broadly. Weeping now, Morgan went down on her knees and took his grey head in her arms.

"I shall never make you see, shall I? You love Arthur too blindly. While I am condemned to go through life with my eyes open, and love him still."

I snatched up my father's sword. "You would have killed him!"

Kneeling, she turned her grief-streaked face up to me, still cradling Urien's head. Her whisper hissed, "Have you still learned nothing? Did you think you could exchange an ideal king for a flawless queen? There are no stainless heroes. Arthur is human. And I am not the wisest woman in the world. You will exonerate Arthur. Will the world forgive me?"

I heard my man's voice say what I must, harsh. "If you had struck but the slightest blow against my father, I should have taken this sword from your hands and struck off your head."

"And who will you strike for the hurt that is done to me?"

I had no answer. I was a knight of the Round Table.

Arthur sent her the corpse.

It came to Camelot on a horse-drawn bier. The slight, shattered remains of the young man who had dared death, fought the lord of chivalry by the rules of the Round Table, and lost. Well, he was bound to. The sword I delivered had done some damage, with Arthur behind it. But it was the last blow from Excalibur which had forced the blood to spout from Accolon's ears and nose and mouth. He had no chance.

Yet Excalibur had done grim work in those pale hands before he lost it. There was a message from the abbey where nuns were keeping the wounded Arthur prisoner in bed. I took it from the groom.

"*Tell my sister I am returning her present. I have my true sword and scabbard now. I shall keep them for myself.*"

Morgan only let her eyes scream.

When I saw her cloaked and booted for riding before the birds had hardly begun to sing, I pulled my own boots on. She swept into Guinevere's bedchamber ahead of me.

"Let me leave court at once. I have business to attend to."

"To find some quiet country place and mourn the murder of your sweetheart, away from your husband?"

"It was a fair joust, by the rules of heraldry. Arthur won."

"Do you love Arthur so little you cannot wait till he is healed and home?"

"Do you love Arthur so little you are not running to his sickbed?"

"Arthur is in no danger now he has his scabbard back. He will get better, whatever I do."

"Yes, he will be better without you."

"I'll never understand you, Morgan. I thought you loved Arthur. You really would have killed him, wouldn't you?"

"Love is not a game. You have never understood that. But Arthur will."

Guinevere sat up. "Get out, whatever your business is. Camelot will be sunnier without you. I release you from my court."

Poor Guinevere. A little petulant power. Too much power over young men.

Gawain passed us, rubbing sleep from his eyes. "Where are you off so early? Did I miss plans for a hunt?"

"Stay where you are. Guinevere needs entertaining. I am only escorting my mother."

It was not true. I had unfinished business.

We rode out into the grey murk of a winter morning. I did not need to ask where Morgan was going. I had questioned the groom for her.

"The nuns have an abbey two miles from Damas's castle. Mother . . ."

She turned green eyes full on me. "Don't say it. Arthur defends the body of this land. I guard its spirit."

I hung my head. "I really believed he was the king we all dreamed of."

"Was that Arthur's fault?" she snapped back.

"Where are you keeping him?" she demanded of the nun at the gate.

"The King has been very ill. You must ask our abbess."

"You are speaking to Morgan the Wise. His sister."

The abbess came scurrying, her skirt swishing clean-swept cobbles. "The poor lad's sleeping soundly, God be praised. He's had a rough three days. I'm allowing no one in until he wakes."

"I shall see that my brother sleeps sounder still. Let no one disturb us."

"Mother!"

Morgan swept past. Even the abbess was silenced. What could I do but hurry in my mother's wake?

He was too lusty a knight for the nuns' infirmary. They had given over their guesthouse to him. A fire flamed softly.

Morgan dismissed the nurse with a flick of her fingers.

Arthur lay sleeping, wan and white. A serpent pattern of gold and black and rubies twined through his hand. Yet it was not the scabbard of healing he had clutched in his extremity. It was Excalibur, naked.

"Look at that. What does it tell you about us?" She knelt by the bed and rested her head beside Arthur, as if it was too heavy to bear.

"Come away, Mother. Let the nuns heal him."

"He will hurt himself."

She rose. I was shocked to see her old now, weary. The fairy scabbard lay discarded among wrinkled blankets. My mother's hand hovered over the bed, over the blade she could never have prised from Arthur's fist, moved to the underprized sheath. She picked it up. Black serpents twined through her hands like the golden snakes through Arthur's. Red, unsleeping eyes watched both of them. She twisted the sheath over, sighed.

"These too were made to sleep together. But he has never wanted it." And there was a mountain more grief in her voice than her lament for Accolon.

I made my decision then. "Give it to me."

Such small words for such a step.

She wheeled, so sharply that I thought Arthur would wake.

"You!"

"You said Arthur was only mortal, didn't you? Let him stay so."

I whipped the scabbard under my cloak and marched out of that monastery with the firm tread of a warrior. Under that cloak, I was shaking.

We called our escort and rode fast for the forest. It was different this time. What I carried now, I had taken knowingly. At the edge of the woods I turned and saw pursuit behind us.

"Arthur's woken up."

"Too late."

We galloped hard, the sound smothered in the felt of fallen leaves. But our horses had come a weary two days' way from Camelot. Theirs were fresh. Deep in the wood, the ground sank soft to a muddy mere. Old trees had tumbled sideways, rotting softly. Fungus bloomed pale along the boughs. Moss hung in rags. The footing was treacherous. Morgan stopped and slipped from her horse. I dismounted beside her. The mud rose up my boots, rooting me into the earth like the red alder.

"Here?" I asked.

Her scared eyes searched mine. "He is our king. You are his knight, his nephew."

I must not let my gaze fall. "Arthur is not a god. He will not live for ever."

"He might have." Her hand caressed the scabbard longingly, as many times I have seen Arthur stroke the sword. "Go, then," she whispered. "He does not want you."

And yet she could not tear her hand away.

At last I tugged it gently from her grasp. She let it leave her.

Perilously, I hoisted that scabbard high over my head, pushing myself deeper into the bog beneath. I flung it from me.

"Sleep, until his sword flies to join you," I heard Morgan's cry.

The hollow sheath, one half of Arthur's greatness, arched into the sky, lanced through the dark air, dropped with a soft suck that swiftly swallowed it down. Pain bit my belly.

"Let his blade stay bare and cold, without it," my mother said.

I hauled myself back into the saddle, daubed with slime, and leaned to hoist her up. I could hear horses coming hard.

The ground grew firmer soon. Boulders guarded a valley up into the hills.

"Stop," she ordered our escort.

"Are you mad? He'll fight us for this." But we all obeyed her.

Her men and maids sat silent, watching her. She lifted her left hand a little, moved three fingers. No more. I felt a stillness settle over me. Stoniness stiffened my limbs, set my face. I could not move my eyeballs. All I saw was the side of the valley opposite and the edge of Alison's elbow. Both were grey, rigid. Yet with ears of rock I could heard them coming.

I do not know how he could sit a horse, wounded as he was. Arthur was white and wild, as I had never seen him before. Ontzlake rode in pain too, from those wounded thighs. But they would bind Morgan, burn her. Arthur had never cared as she meant him to for the scabbard, but he cared mightily that she had taken it from him.

No, I, his nephew Uwain, I took it.

The echo of horse-hooves stilled. "My lord, look at this. Don't these stones appear to you like . . .? Very like . . ." Ontzlake crossed himself.

Arthur was staring just past me, to where my mother must be sitting astride her horse. A savage laugh forced itself across his suffering features. "You robbed me. You have a heart of stone. So God has had a fitting vengeance on you."

His look went lingering over all of us. It came to me. His eyes changed.

"*Uwain*? This witch's kitten, are you? Will all my sisters' sons turn traitor? I could have sworn you loved me."

And so I do, Arthur. So does she. So do all of us. You are not a god, but we would have you one.

I could not move my lips. I could not make my granite eyes plead for me.

They turned away to the abbey. A few moments later, we rode silently on. My mother pressed swiftly for the north, to bar her gates against Arthur's anger.

And I? I crept back to Camelot. I could not help myself. I was a knight of Arthur's Round Table. The magic of that fellowship was stronger than I could break.

Arthur's eyes widened when he saw me enter his hall. Guinevere gasped. I had a glimpse of Gawain's incredulous grin and the secret smile of Mordred. The King's hands gripped the dragon arms of his chair as he levered himself forward.

It was Alison's arrival that saved me.

"Is there no end to that woman's insolence? Will she infest Camelot with her whole household? Her son, her maid? Will she send her hawk next to defy me?"

But when Alison unfolded my mother's act of penitence for Arthur's delight, all Camelot was awestruck. Morgan had made him a robe rare enough to impress an emperor. Amethyst velvet edged with softest ermine, the whole shimmering surface richly stitched with her own embroidery. Alison held the mantle up to dazzle him. Ambition fired Arthur's eyes. He reached for it.

But in through the door opposite rushed the Lake Maiden, Nimue, like a stream in spate. Even out of breath, she could smile sweetly. She poured a trickle of whispers into the King's ear. Arthur's face reddened with fury.

"Alison." His voice rang heavy and hot as hammered iron. "Show me how Morgan's mantle would look, were I to wear it. Put it on yourself."

"No, sire." She started back. "This is a mantle for a king. It wasn't meant for someone like me."

"And I say, wear it."

Arthur's men forced it on her, though she screamed and fought like a cat. As the lining lapped itself about her shoulders, she shuddered. The guards leaped away from the blast of her hot breath. She struggled to throw the heavy magnificence off, but its weight was dragging her down. We watched as, huddled within its glory, she shrivelled, slumped, sank to the ground. From under the edge of ermine her breath smoked out a whisper.

"This is your king's cloak. Honour on the outside. Inside is . . ." She was dead.

Arthur rounded furiously on Urien. "Your wife! Is there no

way of stopping her till she destroys me? Why does she hate me so?"

My father's pained eyes looked back at his brother-in-law. "Hate *you*? Morgan!"

"She gave my sword to Accolon. Excalibur! She would have killed you next, you fool."

I shuddered. But the only witness left was me. Alison would tell no one now.

My start betrayed me. The King's wrath had found its target.

"You dare come back? My sister's son? My false knight? What of that sacred bond between nephew and uncle now? Hey? You, Sir Uwain, armed me with a false sword. You robbed me of my scabbard." He took a stride towards me, till he was halted by the horror of Alison at his feet. "Get out of Camelot before I kill you. I never want to see you at my Round Table again."

I could not bear it. I went down on my knees to my uncle. I offered him my sword. "Then behead me with my own blade, sire. I would rather lose my life here than be banished from the fame of this fellowship. I am your true knight still."

"You? You're as false as every gift your mother sends me."

"Morgan is a wise woman." I could barely whisper those words. "She loves your honour more than she loves your body." I dared not look at my father then. We both knew how much that meant.

"I do not want to set eyes on you or her."

He hurt himself more than he knew. Gawain sprang forward in a swirl of golden hair, to haul me to my feet. The sun always shone out of Gawain's eyes for Arthur, the way it never did from mine.

"You've expelled two nephews, then. If Uwain is banished, I go with him."

"By all that's good, Gawain, what did I ever do to harm *you*? My sister's son."

"We are both, Uncle, as you so rightly say, your sisters' sons. You robbed my mother and Morgan of a father, the night you were got. Had you really forgotten that your father killed him, and stole their mother? Come on, lad. Leave him to guard the thing he loves."

I thought he meant Excalibur. But Gawain grinned to where Guinevere sat pale and shocked in a shaft of winter sunlight. My cousin Mordred was leaning solicitously over her.

"I think Mordred may take care of this for us."

Sir Villiars in EARTHWORKS

Patrick McCormack

Sir Villiars is a minor knight in the Arthurian canon, but he was known as Villiars the Valiant. Patrick McCormack (b. 1958), an antiquarian bookdealer and author of the Arthurian novel Albion *(1997), was curious as to why such an obscure knight should have such a proud epithet. Here's the answer.*

The afternoon sun was a watery ring at his back as he rode down through the wind-stunted woods, the gelding's hooves slipping and sliding on drifts of dead leaves. Villiars ducked beneath the branches or fended them off with his left hand, his right fully occupied with guiding the long lance around the undergrowth. His excitement grew when he saw the menhir he had been told about, half hidden amid the thin trees, marking the limit of the wilds and the beginning of settled land.

Villiars brought Briar to a halt, propped his lance against the pillar and eased himself from the saddle, wincing as the damp undertunic chafed against raw thighs. Everything he owned had been soaked by the relentless rain of the high moors. His armour was in desperate need of treatment: the mail rings were rusting solid and the breast-plate was pitted with dark craters.

He rubbed ruefully at the stains, then wiped his fingers clean on the tall stone. It too was pitted with craters, and it seemed to him he could feel shapes in the rough surface, patterns in the grain of the rock, though no pattern was visible to the naked eye. Shrugging, he turned to look at the coomb below.

The thickly wooded sides were brown and gold in the weak autumn sun, while the bottom was a tangle of marsh and alder trees. Along one slope, skirting the worst of the bog, curved a thin tongue of pasture. Once he entered the coomb he would be committed, and after a week or more of riding across the vast openness of the moors he was wary of enclosed spaces.

Besides, if the tin-miners he had met on the moor were to be believed, an adventure would befall him once he passed the standing stone, though what form the adventure would take they had not said.

Villiars drew a deep breath and led Briar beyond the menhir.

At once the quality of light altered. The coomb seemed both darker and closer. He stopped, glanced over his shoulder. The sun had vanished, blotted by thick black clouds, and the mist was roiling down behind him. Even as he watched the trees through which he had ridden were vanishing one by one.

He remounted and set the lance upright in its proper place at his side, the butt lodged on the stirrup. The ground was broken and uneven, terraced into lynchets by years of ploughing, and the grass under the gelding's hooves was long and dark.

There was no bird song, no sound of little creatures scrabbling in the undergrowth. Villiars paused, uneasy, a hollow sensation in his throat.

Droplets of moisture gathered on his armour as the mist rolled into the coomb. The air was damp and heavy. Briar's breath steamed and sank slowly away. He could hear the trees dripping into the marsh on his right, and turned his head to stare into the tangle of black branches green with moss.

When he straightened he almost dropped his lance with shock. A moment ago the pasture had been empty, muddy and forlorn in the failing light. Now three knights were spread across the narrow space, perhaps a hundred yards away, anonymous in their visored helmets, their horses prancing and snorting impatiently.

Two of them wore armour in the new Italian style, he noted enviously, remembering his own second- or third-hand harness. The heavy shoulder-plates made them seem unnaturally broad, but even at this distance he had to admire the smoothly elegant curves of their rounded outlines, knowing that he himself must present a picture of mismatched bits and pieces.

The third knight, on a black charger, was quite different, thin and elongated like an insect. This Gothic figure urged his mount forward a few paces, at the same time raising and lowering his lance in unmistakable challenge.

Villiars pulled his mail hood over his hair, then reached behind him to free the flat-topped cylinder of his great helm (which had been his grandsire's) from its case on the saddle. He lowered it over his head with shaking hands. His vision reduced to the narrow slits, he felt his own hot damp breath blowing back into his face. With an effort he brought his breathing under control and adjusted his seat in the saddle, Briar shifting eagerly beneath him.

Although it could not have been later than mid-afternoon it seemed like dusk. To his mind it was far too dark for jousting, and had he been acquainted with his opponent he would have suggested they delay until the morning. But these strangers might interpret any such move as cowardice.

The lance was heavy and awkward in his hands. He muttered instructions to himself: sit loose, easy in the saddle, not too firm on the lance (or every tiny movement would be magnified by the time it reached the point), remember to fling the weight forward before the impact – all of them things he knew full well, had spent years learning and practising.

His opponent's spear dipped a final time, and suddenly the black horse was trotting through the mist.

Villiars swallowed, his mouth dry, brought Briar forward in reply. The tip of his lance wavered: he hugged his elbow tight to his body then realized this was a mistake, found himself unable to release the butt, which seemed welded to his ribs.

Briar was running along the right-hand side of the lynchet, so that the knights would pass shield to shield. The other was nearer now: Villiars could see the characteristic points and fluting on the Gothic armour, the gleam of brass edging the different pieces, the grotesque helmet with its visor hooked like a falcon's beak.

The point of his lance was trembling all over the place. Everything was going wrong and happening far too quickly. Flustered, he sobbed aloud as the other loomed closer and closer, the black horse's teeth bared in a grin which Villiars had no doubt would be echoed by its rider inside the bird helm. Since he had no desire to kill the man, Villiars settled on the other's shield as his target, knowing it would be designed in the modern style to catch and hold his point, to prevent it from sliding off to some more vulnerable spot.

He had time to think in an instant of blind panic *Sweet Jesu, he's coming for my head*, and to realize that he had forgotten to lean forward and that his own spear was still waving and dipping uselessly.

Then they met.

The Gothic knight dropped his aim at the last moment. The lance struck squarely in the centre of Villiars's shield. Villiars was flung back against the high cantle of his saddle, and he heard the girth break beneath him.

He was a bubble floating in a vast sea of grey, flying slowly through everlasting space.

The ground was surprisingly soft, though the impact knocked both wind and sense from him. The rings of the mailshirt cut into his shoulders despite the protection of the padded tunic, and a wet cold began to seep through him. He felt rather than heard the thunder of hooves receding into the distance.

As falls went it was not a bad one. He sat up, waited for the dizziness to subside, and checked himself for broken bones. His feet were entangled in the stirrups – when the girth burst he must have flown over Briar's tail with the saddle still firmly clamped between his thighs – and it took him a while to work his way free.

He was sitting on the ground with the stirrup leathers neatly folded over the saddle beside him when he heard the sound of hooves returning. The black charger loomed through the mist and stopped a few yards away, plumes of vapour blowing from either nostril. From its back the Gothic knight stared down at him, then raised one gauntleted hand in query, palm uppermost.

Villiars scrambled to his feet, swayed as the world swam about him, and drew his sword. The Gothic knight regarded him a little longer, as if assessing the chances of Villiars falling over by himself, then swung from the saddle in a single motion.

"Good sir, will you not tell me your name?" said Villiars, disconcerted by the other's silence.

The bizarre falcon helmet turned to one side, and Villiars half-expected to see a single round eye peering at him. But it was the other knights that had caught the stranger's attention, and now they came cantering across the pasture like marshals in the lists hastening to see if the combat could continue.

The Gothic knight drew his sword, the silver steel rasping on the wood of the scabbard, and launched himself at Villiars.

The flurry of blows was so fast Villiars had no time to do anything other than defend himself. A chunk flew from his shield, and a moment later a jagged split opened from the top almost as far as his arm. Before he could discard the remnants, the silver sword caught him in the ribs, sent him reeling back over the edge of the lynchet.

It was not a long drop, and he managed to keep his feet if not his balance. His opponent was on him before he could recover, relentlessly battering him about the head with the flat of the blade until his ears were ringing. The attack shifted abruptly to his arms and torso in a series of strikes that left deep gouges in the rusting steel plates and drove the mail rings into his flesh.

His humiliation seemed unending. In desperation he launched a counter-attack, a feeble swing the stranger easily warded aside: Villiars's sword slid from the other's shield and buried itself in the soft earth. A mailed foot stamped, the sword broke, and Villiars fell forward onto the hilt as the silver blade smote his helm.

He woke to dusk and bitter cold, lay shivering uncontrollably in his thin undershirt. Beside him was the great helm which had been his grandfather's, gashed beyond repair, and not far away was the wreckage of his shield. In one hand he clutched the hilt of his sword; the broken blade was embedded in the mud under his body. Everything else had gone.

He tried to stand, and promptly fell, bleeding afresh in half a dozen places. Each movement brought a wave of pain, yet he knew he must either move or die here as the chill crept deeper into his bones. Little by little he dragged himself across the rough ground, carrying the broken sword though it sliced his fingers, making blindly for the cover of the alders and brambles around the stream at the bottom of the coomb.

He had lost all he owned, and with it all his hope. The knights had stripped him of his possessions, as was their right, but without his armour and his horse he was finished. They had even taken his dagger, leaving him weaponless apart from the shards of his sword.

The younger son of an impoverished knight, he was a poor man. The horse and armour represented all his wealth, his entire patrimony. Lacking them, he was nothing. It had been his dream that he might through skill at arms win a seat at the Round Table – or if not that (for to aspire to one of the 150 sieges was to aspire to the highest honour in the land) then perhaps by performing some great deed he might win the hand of an heiress, or a grant of land.

His dream was ended, and he stood revealed as a failure, shamed at his first serious encounter, unworthy of his knighthood.

The darkness was gathering fast. He crawled along the bank of the stream, forcing a path between the dying brambles, until he came to a dense thicket of blackthorn. There he made himself a lair, burrowing into cover like any wounded animal, and curled into a ball to wait out the night.

Sleep eluded him.

He was here because, riding over the high moors in a misery of foul weather on his quest for a quest, he had come upon a series of neat rectangular pits stretching across the hillside like a giant's footsteps.

He had turned Briar's head to follow the holes, travelling uphill since he could see the line petered out in the wet ground at the bottom of the slope. As he neared the crest Villiars thought he heard voices mingled with the rush of wind and rain, but when he listened again he could hear nothing.

The full force of the gale struck them at the top of the hill. Man and mount bowed their bodies and turned their heads, the one mimicking the other like some monstrous centaur, arching their backs to the wind. Villiars blinked the rain from his eyes and stared down at the raw devastation below, trying to make sense of what he was seeing.

The valley was filled with parallel banks of bare black earth studded with grey gravel. At first he thought it must be some kind of fortification, then common-sense told him nobody would build a castle at the bottom of a valley, and especially not one with banks extending up the far slope. He looked again, and saw a reservoir of water pent behind an earthen wall, fed by a watercourse snaking along the contours of the hill opposite. Figures armed with staves were attacking the base of the wall, while others stood on one of the banks, waving their arms in argument.

Even as he watched the dam was breached and a swirl of water flooded between two of the banks. The figures leapt into the stream and began jumping up and down, or pounding at the water with a variety of tools, their cries carrying to him where he sat bemused on a fidgeting horse.

Frowning, Villiars dug in his heels and sent Briar down the hill. The flow of water was slowing now, but the activity seemed to have become even more frantic. As he came closer he saw it was not the stream itself the workers were pounding but what lay underneath, the loose gravel and silt, turned by more than merely the force of the water. They must have dug first, then let the stream flow over the fresh delvings.

And the lighter stuff, he realized with unaccustomed clarity, would wash away down the slope and finish as part of the banks, while the heavier stuff would be left behind – which was why all this desperate pounding on the part of the workers, to separate the two before the flood died to a trickle.

Pleased at this insight, he hailed the nearest group.

"You are miners!" he called triumphantly.

A red slab of a face swung in his direction, dark hair plastered to the skull by mingled rain and sweat. Wind-chapped lips moved in reply:

"No, boy, we do but seek old Piers' needle, which he dropped hereabouts a sennight since."

Another gave a high-pitched laugh. "He's to be married on the morrow, do you see, and he needs his needle does Piers, if he's to pierce his bride."

Villiars had not been called boy since he became a knight. He glared at the first speaker, tempted to deliver a rebuke with the flat of his blade. The slab face scowled back with pebble eyes, then one lid drooped in a wink.

"What do you want, sir knight?" The words came breathlessly, the stout legs never pausing in their stride.

"I seek adventure, some noble task to perform."

"Adventure? A task? Come down here with me and I'll venture to task you."

With a shock he saw that what he had taken for a man was in fact a woman, and without thinking he backed the gelding a few paces, blushing.

"What, do you fear me?" The ugly face split into a huge grin. "I have more than most, and your lance looks long, if not overthick." She reached inside her shapeless garment, pulled out a flabby breast, veined and seamed as the scarred valley itself, and waved the hairy nipple in his direction. "Dismount, and mount a different ride."

"Madam, I may not." He swung Briar in a semi-circle, ignoring the raucous laughter of the other miners.

"All knights fear women," she announced to her companions, tucking herself back into her clothes. She frowned. "If you want a task, sir knight, I shall set you one."

She closed her eyes and recited in a very different tone of voice:

"Ride north till you come to the edge of the moor. Below you will see a broad and fertile valley, with a river running to a long ridge where it disappears into a gorge. On the southern side of the gorge is an ancient earthwork, and there, three years ago, our comrades went prospecting at the invitation of the local lord. You will descend from the moor by a narrow coomb, its entrance marked with a single standing stone. Beware, sir knight, for once you pass that stone it will be too late to turn back, yet it may well be that you will wish you had."

He stared at her blankly.

"He does not understand," said the miner with the high-pitched voice. "Our comrades are lost, sir knight, and she tasks you with finding them."

"Is it not a noble enough quest?" demanded a third. "To search for commoners like ourselves . . ." He spat into the dirty water.

"No, no," Villiars said hastily. "But why have you not sought them yourselves? How far is this standing stone?"

"Half a day's ride," said the woman. "But we have been busy, child, pulling the white metal from the ground. We have no time for quests if our families are to eat."

He left them then, their laughter ringing in his ears as Briar stolidly picked a route between the banks of gravel and sludge. The miners must have shifted tons and tons of waste, in the process turning what would once have been a peaceful moorland coomb into a scene of utter devastation. When he glanced back a while later they had lit fires, presumably to warm themselves after paddling in the near-freezing water, and he thought to himself that Hell must look like that, a dark desolation with a few flickering flames.

Or perhaps this is Hell, he thought, huddled in the thicket. It may be unknightly to worry about money, and if you have a sound horse and a serviceable harness perhaps it does not matter too much. But if you have nothing . . .

This morning I had everything. This morning I was a knight embarked upon a great adventure.

He burrowed deeper into the mulch of dead leaves and fell into a shivering half-doze, dreaming of gigantic serpents writhing beneath the skin of the earth, of a mighty dragon impaled by the roots of the standing stone striving to be free to join its kindred.

The night passed slowly and painfully. Towards dawn he was roused from a vision of the slab-faced woman digging into the living body of a massive worm (the great cave of the exposed ribs; the gobbets of flesh flying from her shovel) by a crashing in the undergrowth.

He sat upright, reaching for the hilt of his sword, forgetting it was broken and useless, his mind filled with images of serpents and dragons. He waited while the noises came nearer, relentless in their approach, branches snapping and dead leaves crunching as some huge weight dragging itself through the wood. The sounds stopped on the edge of the thicket.

A horse nickered.

Villiars crawled out of the blackthorn and there was Briar waiting patiently, eyes gleaming in the dark, the saddle blanket a misshapen hump on his back.

It took Villiars three attempts to mount without stirrups. Eventually he managed to haul himself onto the blanket (the pieces of his sword still clutched in his left hand), where he slouched exhausted over the horse's neck. Briar began to move, and Villiars adjusted to the gelding's sway with his eyes closed, letting the horse take him where it would.

They followed the stream, Briar's hooves plashing in the marsh, Villiars lulled by the smell and feel of his faithful companion, and around them the alder woods slowly came to life as the sky lightened, until Villiars opened his eyes and saw that it was morning, and that the birds were singing.

"Wood smoke!" he said aloud, startling himself.

He took the reins in his hands and eased the gelding away from the water (which had broadened from a trickle to a muddy stream), picking a path between the trees, following the tantalizing scent of smoke.

They came to the edge of the woods and there was the village, a small collection of thatched huts surrounded by fallow fields, with a rough road running through it. Even from a distance it seemed neglected, and as they drew nearer Villiars saw that it was a loveless place, the kind he remembered from his childhood during the bad times which followed the death of King Uther.

Another wave of pain and sickness hit him, and he allowed Briar to carry him across the fields (the morning mist curling around the horse's legs), onto the road and so up into the village, where people were beginning to stir.

The horse stopped in the middle of the street. Villiars pushed himself upright on the blanket, aware he must make an odd sight in his torn and bloodstained shirt with mud all over him, and opened his mouth to speak.

The words never came. Instead he stared at the silent villagers, and they in turn stared at him. They were dressed in rags, gaunt and aged beyond their years like victims of famine, and their faces were filled with shame and fear, and anger too, though whether at themselves or at him he could not say.

It seemed to Villiars that they stayed thus for a long time, he biting his lip not to plead for help, for he could see that they had no help left to give, and they gazing back as if waiting for some sign to release them, like men and women committed to a reluctant penance.

His eyes roved across them and he noted, even in his lightheaded state, that there were no children among them, though one of the women was hugely pregnant, that in the whole crowd (which seemed to be continually growing although he never saw anybody move) there was not a single person who looked anything less than full grown, however thin and starved.

At length a man haler than the others stepped forward to take Briar's reins, and as if released by his action the villagers melted away, disappearing while Villiars's attention was elsewhere. The man did not speak, but led the gelding and its burden farther along the road, out through the far side of the village, Villiars clinging to consciousness as desperately as he clung to Briar's back, and the hair of the man's head was thick and grey like a badger's pelt.

So they came to a small castle, little more than a square keep with a curtain wall. The battlements were chipped and broken with blocks of fallen stone lying at their foot, and ivy had eaten out much of the mortar. The gates were open, slouched against the wall, and nobody challenged them when they made their way into the courtyard.

The man caught Villiars as he slid from Briar's back, caught him in powerful arms that half-carried him across the cobbles to the stone steps leading up into the tower. Faintly he heard the sound of bolts being drawn above him, and of a great door swinging on rusty hinges.

Villiars forced his head up, focused on the top of the steps with the last of his strength. Framed in the doorway was an old man with a girl standing behind him, and as Villiars let everything slide away into the warm dark his last coherent thought was: the aged knight and his daughter – now I know which story I am in.

"On your mother's side you must be a second cousin once removed to King Ban of Benwick," said Sir Ovran, tapping the book on his lap with a gnarled finger. "That would make Sir Lancelot your third cousin. He is of course a little older than you – five years, or thereabouts – but is unusual to find the generations so evenly balanced."

Villiars struggled to feign polite interest. Sir Ovran was obsessed with genealogy, and Villiars, still recovering from his wounds, was a captive audience.

"They say Sir Lancelot is the greatest knight now living," continued Sir Ovran. "Or at least, they did. It is a while now since we had any news of the outside world." He sighed.

"My kinsman Lancelot is still the mightiest of Arthur's knights," Villiars said proudly. "Unbeaten in the fight, yet the gentlest of men in his dealings with others."

"You know him well?"

"Not well, but he was kind to me when I first came to Camelot, and he allowed me to attach myself to his retinue."

"You yourself are one of Arthur's knights?"

Villiars smiled ruefully. "No, sir, I have not that honour. The Round Table has but 150 seats, and only the best in the realm may fill them."

Sir Ovran closed the book and hauled himself to his feet. In his youth he must have been a big man, larger than Villiars who was himself not small, but age and a swelling of the joints had bent him half double. Villiars found him formidable.

"What made you leave Camelot?"

The question caught him unawares. "Sir Kay," he answered truthfully, which was not at all the response he had intended to give.

"Sir Kay?" said a lighter voice.

"Lady Althea." Villiars fought to rise in the bed, but she waved him back.

"Rest, sir knight, rest." She strode across the room and stood beside her father. "Sir Kay made you leave Camelot?"

Villiars could feel himself blushing. He held his breath for a moment, an old trick somebody had once told him would stop the colour spreading.

"I came to the court young and eager, convinced I was as good as any knight now living." He shrugged, winced as the movement caught his bruises. "Soon I realized I would never be a Lancelot or Lamorak, nor even one of the lesser knights." He smiled at the memory. "They were all as far above me as eagles above a kestrel. I became a hanger-on, a member of Lancelot's following, which would have been well enough in times of great strife when a lord might need a following, but in these more peaceful days I was merely another mouth to feed."

"You have no lands of your own?" demanded Sir Ovran.

"None. I am a younger son, and the family estates are small. I stayed for two years, learning what I could from my betters, hoping to distinguish myself in some joust or tourney. Then one day I overheard Sir Kay the Steward complaining to Sir Lucan the Butler about the number of dependents – parasites, was the word he used – at the court.

"I was ashamed. For two years I had accomplished nothing, except to live on the bounty of others. I determined to leave Camelot and seek an adventure. Either I would win sufficient renown to be worthy of a seat at the Round Table, or, if I failed, I would abandon my hopes and take service with some lesser lord."

"There is of course a third alternative," said Sir Ovran. "You might die in the attempt."

"Then my problems would be over," Villiars said quietly.

"And now?" Althea asked curiously. "What will you do now?"

He looked from father to daughter. "What can I do? With your permission I will impose upon your hospitality until I am fit to ride, then take my leave to find what the world holds for a knight with no armour and a broken sword."

Sir Ovran said gruffly: "It may not be as simple as you think. I doubt that you can leave."

For the first time Villiars wondered whether this castle was the safe haven it seemed. "What do you mean?"

The old man fiddled with his moustache, sat heavily on the stool beside the bed. Althea took up position behind her father and began to knead his shoulders with blunt fingers.

"Three years ago a group of miners sought permission to delve for tin and copper. I granted it, thinking their efforts might prove a useful source of revenue. They moved to the foot of the valley, where the river enters a deep gorge, and started their digging on the site of an ancient earthwork, a serpentine fortress which lies coiled on one shoulder of the gorge."

"And?" prompted Villiars.

"And a lone survivor returned, dying from terrible injuries, prattling of demons from Hell at the beck of a woman." Sir Ovran put his head in his hands.

Althea continued the tale. "My brother gathered our men and went to investigate." She paused, added: "None came back." Her face was bleak, and he saw how she would look when she was old. "We sent messengers for help, but they were unable to leave the valley."

"Unable to leave?"

"They found themselves lost on familiar paths, turned around so they were travelling in the wrong direction." She laughed without humour. "I did not believe, either, until I tried it for myself."

Villiars frowned, trying to understand. "But I came in. Down off the moors, past a standing stone."

She nodded. "You are not the first. I doubt you will be the last. Certain individuals can enter; large parties, we suspect, simply do not notice the valley. Three times over the years other knights have come, men of Arthur's court, proud in their fine armour on their strong steeds."

"What befell them?" he asked, knowing the answer.

She snorted scornfully. "They were challenged, unhorsed, defeated. Then they were not so proud, though none of them were so honest as you have been."

A warm glow spread through him at the sight of her smile. She was not a pretty woman, not by the conventions of Camelot (there was far too much character in her face), but the longer he looked the more attractive he found her. Her eyes were especially striking: ice blue and very penetrating.

"They were brought here to recover, then tried again." She grimaced.

"They failed," Sir Ovran said heavily. "Sir Baldwin died in the attempt. Sir Astomar the Scot and Sir Eustace of Wentland survived, to their great misfortune."

"How so?"

Sir Ovran gestured despairingly. "They serve her now. They were the knights in Italian armour who supported her champion."

"And her champion? Who is he?"

The answer was written all over them.

"She is an enchantress, this woman from the hill, and she holds men in her thrall," said Sir Ovran. "When Caradoc my son went forth to discover what had befallen the miners he wore his new suit of armour, made for him in the Gothic style by the artificers of Winchester."

"We have not seen my brother since." Althea's voice was cold and hard. "But each of the knights who came here, wounded and stripped of their harness, told the same tale. They were overcome by a champion in Gothic armour, who uttered not a word as he smote them hither and thither."

"Your brother was a great warrior?"

Althea cocked an eyebrow at her father. He laid a hand on hers, heaved himself to his feet. "Caradoc was good," he said, "but I could have taken him in my youth. I watched the three knights at their practice before they left, and I would have reckoned Baldwin his equal, Eustace his inferior, and Astomar his master."

The old man limped from the chamber like a puppet with a broken string, leaving the two of them alone.

"I am sorry," Villiars said inadequately.

"So am I. Did you know them?"

"Them?" His thoughts were elsewhere. "Oh, the knights. I have heard of them. Astomar has a high reputation. He is a friend to Sir Gawain, the King's nephew. Eustace I have tilted against, and would account my better. Baldwin I never knew, though people speak well of him."

"They were arrogant men. They deserved what befell them."

"They offended you?"

"What offended me was their assumption that I was a prize. 'Free the valley from the Enchantress and win the old man's daughter,' they thought. Each bargained with my father; each believed himself brought here by God or fate to be the hero of a romance."

Once again Villiars felt himself blushing, and held his breath.

"To fight her is to die, or worse, become her slave," she added grimly.

He released his breath. "What is the alternative?"

"To live." Althea turned to him, almost eagerly. "The cycle could be broken. The Enchantress feeds off the combat: it is like a game to her. Perhaps if one of her victims refused to play his role . . ."

"How do you know? Have you seen her yourself?"

She shook her head. "The peasants talk. And I use my imagination, put myself in her place."

"Do they say whence she came?" he asked curiously.

"They say she has always been here, sleeping in the fortress, and the tin-miners wakened her from her dream of the land. They say she is old as the hills themselves, and that what drives her is her desire to live forever."

Villiars frowned. "How unnatural." He considered it a while longer. "How childish. What would be the purpose?"

"Life everlasting? It does not tempt you?" She seemed surprised.

He shuddered. "Was it not the nature of the curse upon the Wandering Jew, that he must remain alive until Our Lord came again? I see no blessing in living beyond one's span."

She moved to the arrowslit window, leant upon the sill and plucked a leaf from the ivy crowding the embrasure.

"What will you do?" she asked.

He sighed. "What can I do? I have neither sword nor armour. You tell me I may not leave." He fought against the pillows and the weakness of his body, dragged himself upright in the bed. "How did the others manage?"

"My father lent them arms."

"Would he do the same for me?"

She crumpled the leaf between her fingers. "Probably. But you admit Astomar and Eustace are your betters, while Caradoc has already defeated you. What chance do you think you have?"

"Very little, from the sound of it."

"Why not stay here? Refuse to play her game."

He was tempted. Implicit in the suggestion was the offer of herself. (He ignored the obvious contradiction between her behaviour towards him and what she had said of his predecessors.) She was the kind of woman who appealed to him, strong willed and independent, and he could imagine living out his life with her at his side. In many ways she was precisely what he had been seeking when he left Camelot: an heiress with lands of her own. (Always provided her brother did not return, said a small worm of doubt deep inside him.)

"Think on it," she said. "You need not decide until you are well again."

Villiars recovered quickly. Within a few days he was able to negotiate the stairs to the courtyard, and not long after that he walked down into the village, which was further than he remembered.

Almost unconsciously he had slipped into the habit of thinking of things as if they were already his: thus, studying the castle, he had noted the ivy clinging to the walls and wondered how much damage it had done the mortar, had counted the number of stones missing from the battlements and guessed how much labour would be needed to replace them.

It was the same with the village. Limping along the road, he found himself surveying the green and mossy thatch with a landlord's disapproving eye. "Poorly housed peasants produce poor crops," was one of his father's aphorisms, drilled into Villiars and his brother from their earliest childhood. These cottages were tumbledown hovels, and from what he recalled seeing through the mist of his wound fever the inhabitants were as lacklustre as their dwellings.

One would need to change that, he mused, hunting for a place he could sit and rest before the return journey. The easiest way would be to follow his father's advice and start with the cottages, try to instil some sense of pride in the villagers.

A mounting-block grew from the wall of a larger building, beside firmly closed wooden doors. Villiars perched on the cold stone, wondering where the people had gone. It was another dull, misty day, and he found it strange that they should all be out working in the fields at this time of year. Faint sounds of hammering came from behind the double doors, which meant the smith at least was about his business, but it seemed odd there were no children. Where he had grown up the sight of a stranger would have brought them running from whatever tasks their elders had set them. A baby began to cry in one of the cottages, but even as he pricked up his ears to listen, gladdened by this sign of normality, it stopped so abruptly he wondered whether he had not imagined it.

The cold was eating through his borrowed clothing. He slid from the mounting-block and tried the doors. They opened at the first touch and he limped through them into a place of fiery light.

"There you are!" boomed a voice. "Leave the doors ajar, sir knight, if you would be so kind."

Villiars blinked, did as the voice bade him.

The smith paused in his work. "Sit! I must complete this piece while the iron is hot." He pointed with his hammer to a bench in one corner.

Bemused, Villiars forced his aching legs to carry him across the forge, where he sat obediently and waited for the smith to finish. Something about him seemed familiar, and when the man straightened Villiars saw his hair was thick and grey, like a badger's pelt.

"You!" he gasped.

The smith laid his tools aside. "Me," he said with a chuckle. "I had begun to doubt you would ever come to reclaim your blade."

"My blade?" repeated Villiars, feeling stupid.

"Your sword. It was broken when you arrived." The smith wiped his hands on a rag. "You will need it when you ride to seek your revenge."

"My revenge?"

The smith tossed the rag aside. "His wits are addled," he remarked to the air. "The Enchantress and her knights," he explained patiently, as to a child. "You will need your sword to face them."

Villiars glanced about uneasily. Mistaking his purpose, the smith said: "It's all right. We may speak freely, without fear of her hearing us. I have some small magics of my own. This forge is safe from eavesdroppers – of any kind."

"I . . . I must thank you for leading me to the castle. My name is Villiars . . ." His voice trailed away uncertainly.

The smith nodded. "And mine is Matho. There is no need for thanks. The locals are too cowed to aid a stranger, particularly one who has fought against the Enchantress's men and lost."

"You are not local, then?"

Matho laughed mirthlessly, teeth white against the sweat-streaked darkness of his face. "No. I came here a while ago, and like you I cannot leave. Not even smithcraft is proof against a magic that turns the land back upon itself. I have been waiting for you."

"For me?"

"For you, or one like you." The smith regarded him steadily until Villiars dropped his eyes and looked away. "The others were no good to me. Arrogant men, all three."

"Sir Baldwin, Sir Astomar, and Sir Eustace?"

"Is that how they were named?" The smith was indifferent. "One was killed, the other two became her slaves. They were weak once stripped of their pride."

"But . . ." He swallowed, started again. "The lady Althea, Sir Ovran's daughter. She said the way to break the cycle was to refuse to fight."

Matho frowned. "Does Arthur refuse to fight? I thought you aspired to the highest honour in the realm, a seat at the Round Table."

Villiars shook his head wearily. "I am not worthy," he whispered, tears pricking his eyes at the memory of his humiliation.

The smith snorted. "A single setback and you despair? I had taken you for a valiant man." He smiled crookedly, as if at some private joke, shrugged. "You are a knight, you will do as you wish. But had I known I would not have wasted my time on this."

He spun and reached from the wall, where it was hanging among a collection of tools, a sword. He tossed it underarm to Villiars, who sat staring with his mouth agape as it fell through the air, glittering in the red glow of the forge fire. At the last moment Villiars came to life and caught it by the hilt.

"Where? What?"

"It is yours."

The hilt was his own, no doubt about that, but the blade he did not recognize. His had been a crude weapon of dark iron, effective enough in the grasp of a strong man but exhausting to wield for any length of time. This blade was of polished blue-grey steel, with a fuller's groove running its length to lessen the weight, the whole cunningly shaped to give great strength to point and edge. It was a sword of the kind he had seen and envied in the hands of the best knights, a blade of which even Lancelot or Gawain might have been proud.

"This is mine?" he said in wonder. He swung it through the air, and it sang to him.

"With this I might stand against them," he murmured. And all his dreams came crashing into his mind: of knighthood and an honoured place amongst the paladins of Arthur's Table on the one hand; and of the Lady Althea and a peaceful life as Lord of this valley on the other.

"It is only the old metal retempered and reforged," the smith said mildly. "Not an enchanted sword like the one they say is borne by Arthur. It will not win your battles for you."

"No," he said thoughtfully, and swung again, thrusting and slashing at shadow opponents in the firelight. Suddenly he stopped. "How did you know I wanted to become one of Arthur's knights?"

The smith flung back his head and roared with laughter. "What else would you desire? Why else would you be out seeking adventure?" He turned to the bellows, began pumping. "The Enchantress's magic is subtle. Do not let her woo you from your course."

Villiars waited a while, but it was obvious he had been dismissed.

His legs seemed stronger now. He strode through the smithy doors with the naked sword in his hand, and surveyed the empty street. Even if he did decide to stay here with Althea, the problem of the Enchantress would remain. Perhaps one could reach some kind of accommodation with her, a mutual agreement to ignore each other's existence. After all, he thought to himself, sooner or later a real champion – Lancelot, Tristan, Gawain, whoever – is bound to stumble on the valley and put an end to her. In the meantime, everybody keeps solemnly implying that she is terrible, but frankly there is no sign of any great harm she has wrought.

Apart from Althea's brother and the other knights, he added hastily. That's a bad business.

And those tin-miners, he thought as he strolled along the street. Hard on them too. But the peasants, she has left them alone. All they are suffering from is neglect. They need a strong guiding hand, somebody to take them under his wing and encourage them. What does it matter if they cannot leave the valley?

From one of the cottages he had passed came the thin cry of a baby. A flurry of wind brought dead leaves swirling about him, so that for a moment he was blind. Behind him he heard the clop of horses' hooves. The air was unnaturally cold on his skin as he turned, still brushing brittle debris from his face.

Two knights rode towards him, lances held upright so the long poles towered above them like masts. One wore a russet surcoat and one yellow, but otherwise there was nothing to choose between them in their identical armour, smooth and featureless with exaggerated shoulder defences. They came on at a steady pace, their visors down, giving no indication they had noticed him standing in the roadway.

Before they reached him they stopped and dismounted, the one in yellow taking charge of the spears and horses. The other beat upon the door of a cottage with a gauntleted fist, and when it was not instantly opened leaned back and used his mailed foot. A woman shrieked.

Villiars started forward. The yellow knight propped the lances against the wall and raised his hand in warning, bidding Villiars stay. Puzzled, he hesitated, clutching his sword, while the russet knight forced his way into the cottage.

A great screaming and wailing came from within, and the sound of blows. Villiars waited, unsure, assessing the odds – two knights in full armour and he without so much as a shield – knowing he should act but unable to move.

The russet knight strode from the cottage, something small and loudly squealling tucked under one arm.

Villiars gaped, found his voice. "Hold!" he shouted, and the horses started as he ran forward.

The yellow knight turned to meet him, drawing his sword. The other did not even falter, but mounted with the baby still clamped beneath one metal arm, bent to regain his lance, wheeled the horse around, and rode away down the street without a backward glance.

Villiars roared and flung himself at the yellow knight, the new blade light and easy in his hand. He dodged a swing that would have separated his head from his body, cut twice at his opponent's ribs, feinted left, danced right, dropped into a crouch and whirled the sword into the back of the other's knee.

The yellow knight staggered, his leg crumpling beneath him. Villiars straightened and struck, turning the blade at the last moment so the flat smote his opponent across the shoulders. The yellow knight fell into the wall and subsided with a clang of armour.

Breathless and disbelieving, Villiars stared down at him. He was vaguely aware of doors opening, of people coming into the street, of sobbing and crying and soft murmuring, but he could not tear his gaze from the heap huddled in the gutter. A little blood leaked from behind the knee, but other than that he could see no signs of injury.

"Well done, sir knight," said Matho.

"What made him fall down?" he said in wonder.

"You must have struck harder than you thought." The smith knelt and unfastened the helmet, pulled it loose with a grunt.

"Sweet Jesu!" exclaimed Villiars, and crossed himself.

The face was lined and worn, the cheeks gaunt, the hair thin and lifeless.

"Like the victim of a famine," marvelled Villiars. "Or an ancient who has lived far beyond his allotted span."

"Do you know him?" Matho began to remove the rest of the armour.

"Know him?" Villiars shook his head, peered more closely. "Why, yes! This is Sir Eustace of Wentland, a man no more than a handful of years my senior." He helped the smith to ease the armour from the withered body. "Is he alive?"

"Barely."

"He is a husk." He gathered Sir Eustace in his arms. "There is no weight to him."

"I think this one was almost used up. That was why she wanted you alive, to replace him." The smith took the body from him, handed it to one of the crowd. "Take him to my forge. Make him comfortable, but keep watch on him."

"Used up," mused Villiars while the peasant effortlessly carried the shrunken form away. Two years ago Sir Eustace had been a big, powerful man in the prime of life. "Will he recover?"

"He may, if he is freed from the enchantment."

Villiars regarded the smith suspiciously. "You are very knowledgeable, Master Matho."

"I have travelled much." The dark eyes met his. "Trust me, sir knight, for I am all that is left in this valley untainted by her wiles."

"All?" he said, looking round at the sobbing and wailing crowd, and remembering with a stab of horror what had driven him to fight.

"All," the smith repeated firmly, inclining his head in the direction of the castle.

Althea rode down the track, mounted on a red roan mare and trailing a fully saddled Briar on a leading rein. At the sight of her the crowd was suddenly silenced. They melted away, disappearing into their cottages with hardly a murmur, even those whose child had been stolen. Villiars was so startled at their reaction that he made no reply when Althea hailed him, and not until she had halted and slid from the mare did he manage to sketch a bow.

"I thought you might have wandered too far and be glad of a ride home," she said.

Beside him Matho slid back into the shadows of the wall. Althea ignored his presence.

"Will you not return with me?" She stepped closer to Villiars – too close, he thought uncomfortably – and one foot kicked the helmet lying in the gutter.

"What's this?" she exclaimed, stooping and raising the helmet. "One of her knights was here?" She held the helmet at arm's length, twisting it in her hands, then her gaze fell upon the rest of the harness. "And left all his armour behind?"

"Two of them were here, madam," Villiars said, his voice harsher than he intended. "The other escaped, having stolen a newborn child."

"Her tithe." Althea nodded, seeming unconcerned. "She claims all the newborn babes."

Villiars blinked, opened his mouth to speak, closed it again.

"There is nothing we can do," she said. "You will come to

accept it, when you have been here a while longer." The faintest smile flickered around her lips.

He shuddered, bent and dragged Sir Eustace's armour out into the open, began to sort through it.

"What are you doing?"

"Arming myself. We were of a size, once."

The breast and back-plates fitted well enough. The fauld and tasset were loose – Sir Eustace had been renowned as a great trencherman – but a little judicious padding solved the problem. One poleyn was cracked and misshapen where he had struck at Sir Eustace's knee; Matho, who had been silently assisting, pursed his lips in dismissal, and Villiars discarded it. The gauntlets were too small, but the helmet slid snugly over his head.

"Where are you going?" demanded Althea, her face flushed.

"To make an end to this foulness," he said curtly.

"You will be killed."

He paused in adjusting the couter at his left elbow. Matho continued to fiddle with the strap, ignoring Althea as thoroughly as she had throughout ignored him.

"Madam, I do not fear to die." Villiars had spoken for effect, but once the words were out of his mouth he realized they were true. There were many things he did fear – great pain, mutilation, dishonour, most of all being enslaved and sucked dry like poor Eustace – but death was not among them.

"I beg you!" she said, and to his embarrassment she knelt in the dirt of the road.

"I must," he answered. A terrible cold anger filled him at the thought of the knight in the russet surcoat carrying off the child. He turned to Matho. "The baby. Is that how she prolongs her life?"

"One of the ways," grunted the smith.

"I have heard of such things," he said grimly. He took the lance from the wall where Sir Eustace had left it and vaulted onto Briar's back.

"She will make you her slave!" wailed Althea.

He frowned, kicked Briar into a fast trot down the street in the direction taken by the russet knight. He could hear her calling behind him, calling and shrieking imprecations in tones ever more desperate as the distance between them widened.

The weather had changed since his arrival in the village. The sun had fought free of the clouds and burned away the grey mists, which he took as a good omen. Now he could see the full extent of the valley: the water meadows abutting the line of trees that must mark the course of the river; the coppices of hazel and birch; the patchwork field systems, some lying fallow, others put to winter-wheat, divided by strips of grass or partly laid hedges. Like the castle and village, the land showed signs of neglect, but nothing a good master could not mend.

The sound of hooves pursued him and he swung in the saddle, expecting to see Althea on her red roan. Instead he saw Matho riding Eustace's horse, and reined in to await him.

"Every knight should have a squire," said the smith.

"The lady Althea?"

Matho laughed scornfully. "She does not speak to the likes of me. She is gone back to the castle."

They jogged a while in silence, the range of hills through which plunged the gorge looming ever larger.

"I had not thought she would be so uncaring," Villiars remarked.

"Why should she care about a peasant's child?" growled Matho.

"Self-interest, if naught else." Villiars played with the reins, flicking the slack from hand to hand until Briar flinched in protest. "There are no youngsters in the village."

"No," agreed Matho. "And worse, the woman who bore that babe was probably the last left capable of having children. The rest are too old. She took them all."

Villiars did not have to ask who he meant. "Without children there will be nobody to till the fields in a few years' time." He shrugged. "In her own interests Althea should protect the villagers."

"Is that why you are here?"

Aware of the smith watching him curiously, Villiars considered his reply. "I left Camelot in search of some great feat of arms which would make my reputation." He laughed bitterly. "The meeting with the Gothic knight put paid to that. I lack the necessary skill with lance and sword."

"Yet you brought down the yellow knight whilst you yourself were unarmoured," Matho pointed out gently.

"He was a sick man."

"Not while he was inside his armour."

Startled, Villiars looked down at the borrowed breast-plate. "You do not think . . .?"

"No, you are safe enough. If there were any danger, it would have made itself felt by now."

Villiars swallowed uneasily. To take his mind off the possibility that the armour was ensorcelled, and to avoid further examination of his motives (which lay coiled one within the other, selfish and altruistic, wound together so tightly even he could not disentangle them) he said:

"Have you seen her, this Enchantress?"

Matho frowned. By now they had reached the mouth of the gorge. They splashed across the river and climbed the hill on the far side, threading through light woodland, the horses grunting and panting.

"I am not certain," the smith said carefully after a long pause. "Not certain at all."

As they climbed the view unfolded like a flower coming into bloom. The valley lay revealed, the shape of its woods and fields spread out at their feet, and beyond was the brown and golden splendour of the moors. Along the horizon were lines of clouds mimicking the lines of the hills, doubling and redoubling their humps and hollows, blue and grey and golden like the distant land itself.

"Now," said Matho. Villiars tore his gaze from the cloudscapes and looked at his surroundings.

They had come to a plateau a little below the true summit of the hill. To their left the ground fell sharply away into the gorge, a tree-choked mass with white water racing at the bottom. Ahead of them was a ditch crossed by a causeway, which on the far side became a track between high banks. Atop the banks was a palisade of newly cut logs with the bark still peeling. Crowning every third or fourth post was a bleached white skull. Some were sheep or cattle, with the horns attached; others were horse or deer. A few were unmistakably human.

Villiars drew in his breath. "What is this?"

"The lair of the Enchantress." Matho pulled back his borrowed mount and motioned for the knight to go first. "Be ready."

There was no gate, only the causeway over the ditch. Villiars lowered his visor, readied his shield and spear, and urged Briar forward at a walk. The earthen hedges loomed high, the palisades with their burdens blocking the light. The track curved between the banks, narrowing almost imperceptibly as it went. As the riders travelled deeper into the fortress the skulls grew older and more battered, the lower jaws fallen away or altogether lost, the bones green with mould.

"Somebody comes!" shouted Matho.

The warning seemed to come from a great distance. Villiars acted without thinking, couching his lance and bringing Briar to a canter. Around the corner galloped the russet knight, lance lowered. Briar increased speed in response, pacing away, and Villiars had all the time he needed to hug the spear tight under his elbow and fling his weight forward at the moment of impact. The russet knight flew backwards and disappeared. Villiars let Briar gallop on around the corner, then gently reined him to a trot, surprised at how easy it had been.

When he returned Matho had dismounted and was bending over his motionless opponent.

"Stunned, like the other," called the smith, drawing off the man's helmet.

Villiars raised his visor and peered down at the face. It too was gaunt and aged beyond its years. "Sir Astomar the Scot," he said sadly. "A noble knight, and friend to Sir Gawain of Orkney. A man much my superior."

"Not on this day's showing," grunted Matho. He produced some cord, bound Astomar's hands and feet. "He can await us here."

They rode on, following the curving track as it wound ever tighter about an unseen centre, nerves on edge, expecting a second attack at any moment. They made three circuits without incident, each shorter than the last, and then they came to a deep crater in the inner bank and a gap in the palisade.

Villiars halted, peered at the hole. For an instant he was back on the moorland hillside, the rain lashing his face, staring at a line of rectangular hollows.

"Tin-miners," he said.

Matho was studying the palisade. "Lend me the lance." He held out his hand and Villiars passed it over.

The smith leant forward on his horse's neck, using the long spear as a probe. The tip went through the nearest stake, vanished as if he had struck with sufficient force to bury it deep in the wood.

"Illusion." The smith laughed. "Illusion, by God!"

He turned his horse and rode straight at the steep bank. It was the most extraordinary sight Villiars had ever seen. The horse floundered up the slope, baulking at what was being asked, then suddenly gained confidence. It seemed to be wading through the earth, buried up to its hocks, though it continued to move freely.

When it came to the fence it simply disappeared head first, taking Matho with it, swallowed like a ghost.

Villiars licked dry lips and followed.

The smith was waiting for him on the far side. "Your lance," he said, and handed it back.

The knight took it without speaking.

"Don't you understand?" said Matho. "This is illusion, all of it. We are seeing this place as it was hundreds and hundreds of years ago. None of this is real. The reality is grassy hummocks, banks worn down by time and the elements to low mounds. We do not need to tread her path when we can go directly to the centre of things."

"Wait!" cried Villiars before Matho could charge through the next bank. "What is – was – this place? It is no fortification. These passages make no sense."

Matho narrowed his eyes, pointed at the rows of skulls grinning down at them. "A charnel house?" He kicked the horse up the bank.

Again Villiars followed, half-fearing that this time the barricade would prove solid after all. Three more banks they crossed, one of which was marred by another prospector's pit, and then they came out into a bright and windswept space, much larger than Villiars would have thought possible at the heart of all those coils.

"An arena," murmured Matho as Briar slithered down the final slope and came to rest beside him. "And there's your opponent."

The Gothic knight waited on the far side of the circle, tall and attenuated, the armour seeming more fantastical than ever now Villiars was seeing it in full daylight. The great black stallion pawed the ground like a bull about to charge, and the grotesque figure dipped its lance in challenge.

Villiars swallowed nervously, lowered his visor and adjusted his shield.

"Beware the fallen pillar in the middle," said Matho.

He would not have noticed without the warning, so absolute was his concentration on the insectile form facing him, but a long stone lay toppled in the centre of the ring. He trotted Briar a few yards around the perimeter and took up a new position. The wind whistled in his helm, made his eyes water. His hands were red and swollen with cold, clumsy on the lance and reins. There was a familiar hollow in his throat. In the back of his mind a voice screamed: "I can't do this!"

It was too late. The Gothic knight had begun his charge.

Villiars's world narrowed to what was visible through the slit of the visor. The ground juddered beneath Briar's hooves. He could see the dark sods kicked up by the black charger, could see the light flashing on the brass-edged fluting of the other's armour. His lance steadied on a point just above the triangle of the Gothic knight's shield, and he did not allow his attention to be distracted from his target as they raced together.

The impact was tremendous. He felt his lance shiver and shatter into pieces at the same moment as the other's point struck his shield, sent him reeling back in the saddle. Somehow he kept his seat, left side numb, feet out of the stirrups, swaying and bouncing helplessly while Briar slowed to a trot and thence a walk.

The Gothic knight had also broken his lance. He signalled they should dismount and continue the combat on foot. Villiars slipped from the saddle and tossed the reins over Briar's head, advanced towards his opponent, who came forward to meet him by the fallen stone.

They drew their swords and fought. The Gothic knight launched a whirlwind attack which made Villiars give ground, buffeting him with his shield, the silver blade darting back and forth till it seemed to be coming from all sides at once. Then Villiars rallied and struck at the falcon helm, landing a lucky blow that momentarily dazed its wearer. Seizing his chance, Villiars drove the Gothic knight back against the menhir, crowding him, hacking at shield and flanks.

Suddenly the Gothic knight slipped under his sword, danced away from the stone, leaving him flailing the air. Thus they continued, the advantage going to first one then the other, until both were reeling, sobbing for breath. Now they fought without finesse, pushing and jostling, and the grass around them was speckled with their blood.

"Remember the child!" shouted Matho.

Through his exhaustion Villiars heard. He knew he could not last much longer. His legs, which had gained a miraculous new strength ever since the smith had handed him the sword, were failing. His lungs were burning and his arms were tired, his sight was blurred by the sweat dripping from his brow.

Into his mind came a vision of the King, and the King's dream of a just realm where the rich and powerful would not prey upon the weak and poor, a realm where children would not be ripped from their mother's arms.

"Arthur!" he cried, and with the last of his strength struck down upon the other's helm. The casque split in twain and the Gothic knight fell against the long table of the stone, sword flying from his hand.

"Now, witch, your champion is defeated!" Villiars bellowed in triumph. "Show yourself!" He pulled off his helmet and shook free his sweat-matted hair, sucking in the air like a drowning man.

There was nothing except the cold wind blowing across the trampled grass.

"Where is she?" he said, turning angrily to Matho, who stood holding the reins of his horse.

The smith pointed. For a moment Villiars did not understand. He stared about the embanked arena, at the black charger and faithful Briar, at the empty grass rippling in the wind. Then he followed the direction of Matho's finger and saw.

"Althea!"

She stirred, touched her skull with blunt fingers, opened ice-blue eyes. They pierced him through, alien and disturbing. He felt the sword slipping from numb fingers to lie forgotten in the grass, fought the urge to run to her and gather her in his arms, to tend her wounds, to kneel before her and beg forgiveness for having been so blind and stupid. Now he understood Matho's cryptic remark about being uncertain whether or not he had seen the Enchantress. Now he understood her attempt to dissuade him from pursuing his futile quest, his feeble essay at self-aggrandisement, for what does it profit a man to seek a transitory reputation if it be at the cost of such as her, a being as far above him as he above the crawling things that live under stones?

"Well, sir knight. You have defeated me." Her voice was different, deeper and stronger though no less feminine.

"Lady, lady," he stammered. "I did not know."

She eased herself up onto the stone. "You had thought me a man? The Sir Caradoc of whom my puppet Ovran spoke?" She laughed scornfully. "There was a Caradoc once, long ago on the chalk downs of the east, but he is dust now."

"Do not listen, lad," shouted Matho, running forward. "Remember the children. Remember the other knights."

She made a gesture with the fingers of one hand. "Be still, smith." The words hissed across the space between them, and Matho came to a sudden stop.

"On your knees." Her voice was cold and distant.

Villiars could see Matho fighting the compulsion. His whole body stiffened, shook with tremor after tremor. Gradually the smith sank to his knees, his face purple with effort, the great veins beating at his temples.

"Join me, Sir Villiars, and we will rule this valley." Again the blue eyes pierced him, held him. "You could live forever."

"Like Astomar and Eustace?"

"No." She smiled. "You are stronger than they. Why do you think I tried to avoid this confrontation?"

He was tempted, sorely tempted. In the light of her eyes his ambitions seemed petty, pointless, utterly selfish. He had done what he had done not for the good of others but for himself, to further his own career. A peasant child was nothing to him – plenty more where that one came from – and what did he care if in ten or twenty years time the valley was deserted. To live forever, that would be a thing: to watch kings and empires rise and fall . . .

"Arthur," choked the smith.

She swung furiously and made another gesture. Matho fell onto his face and was still.

Villiars struggled against a tightness in his head that made it hard to think. "Arthur," he murmured, and a pang of guilt went through him. He had failed Arthur.

Althea laughed. "Arthur does not want you. You are able enough, but you are not a Lancelot or Gawain."

"No, no." He shook his head desperately, both in denial of her words and to clear it of the tightness. "He does want me. He needs ordinary people like me, not just the great knights, the heroes. Otherwise the Round Table would be . . ."

His tongue seemed cloven to the roof of his mouth. The thought slipped away from him, was lost in the overpowering light of her eyes. She was so much wiser than he, and fair to behold, lying languorously on the couch of stone.

"What, as fodder for his wars? And his jousts?" She laughed merrily. "I suppose there must be somebody for the big men to knock down."

"You are wrong. Arthur is not like that. Arthur is – good."

Even to his own ears it sounded weak.

"Villiars, Villiars," she chided pityingly. "You are naïve, my friend. This Arthur of yours, this noble king. What is he but a man who slept with his own half-sister, got her with child? If he were anybody except the King you would recoil from him in disgust. And his followers – do they not say one should judge a ruler by his servants? Look at Merlin, fathered by an incubus, leching in his dotage after a girl young enough to be his granddaughter. Or bitter-tongued Kay, hating his superiors and despising his inferiors."

"You are wrong," he repeated blindly.

"Am I?" Her lips quirked in a mocking smile. "I tell you this, Villiars. If you return to Camelot, you will never again fight as you have this day. You will be a bystander, a makeweight. Others will win great renown by their prowess, but not you. And the Round Table itself, for which you will have sacrificed your chance of glory, will fail at the end, tear itself apart. You will be forced to choose sides, to turn against this Arthur whose name you keep bleating."

"You lie," he said. Pain lanced through his head.

"Do I?" she hissed. "Then look, and tell me that the vision I send is not a true one."

There before him in the air they hung, scenes in which people moved and fought and loved, and as he watched he knew that she had not lied, that these visions were true.

He saw a man creeping to a lady's chamber, and the two of them locked in close embrace upon a bed, and he knew he watched the noble Sir Lancelot, the best knight in all the world, caught in sordid adultery with Guinevere the Queen.

He saw the court divide into factions: the Orkneys around Gawain; the Cornish around Tristan; the Welsh around Pellinore and Lamorak; and he himself gathered with the kin of Lancelot. He saw knight set upon knight, three or four to one under the cover of darkness, and murder done. He saw the quarrels and the rivalries, the way one group vied with another until the high aims of the Round Table were mired and forgotten. Through it all moved a younger man with a look of Arthur about him, dropping a word here and a hint there, stirring trouble, fanning hatreds.

He saw Lancelot's great castle Joyous Gard under siege, and himself within the walls while Arthur and his knights stood without, and he saw Lancelot and Gawain locked in combat before the gate. He saw Guinevere weeping; the kingdom in flames; great armies marching; the last battle and Arthur's fall . . .

Villiars closed his eyes.

"Do you believe?" asked the Enchantress, her voice throbbing and insistent. "What you have seen is the future, the true future. In fire and blood it will end, brother turned on brother and the fellowship of the Round Table dissolved as if it had never been."

"Yes, I believe you," he said heavily, the tears wet on his cheeks. "It will end in civil war, and Arthur will fail."

"Then join me. Abandon your childish dreams and join me."

For a long moment he stood before her with his shoulders slumped, despair written in every line of his body. He bowed his head and took a pace towards her, and though his eyes were still tight shut he knew she smiled.

He spun and seized the sword from the long grass, struck down at that hateful face, felt the blade jar on bone, heard the scream rising on the whirring air, struck again and again till all was bloody ruin on the granite.

Then he dropped the sword, knelt beside the stone that was now her bier and let the tears flow freely.

After a while he was roused by a touch on his shoulder.

"Sir Villiars the Valiant," said Matho. The baby was cradled in his arms.

"What?" the knight said blankly, his gaze travelling over the child without registering it.

"That is how they will call you when you take your seat at the Round Table." Matho moved, and the sleeping baby spluttered a protest. "I too have some small gift of foretelling."

"Do not speak to me of what will come, smith." Villiar's voice was harsh. "I have seen the future, and it is the death of all we love."

"Yet you defied her," Matho said gently, jogging the baby up and down.

He grimaced. "Better to die than live as she did, preying upon the weak and seducing good knights from their duty."

"Is there no hope then?"

Villiars hauled himself stiffly to his feet. The arena had changed. The palisade with its grisly skulls was gone, and the steep banks with their clean-cut sides had dwindled to a series of soft mounds and hummocks. With a start he saw the slab-faced woman who had set him on his quest, flanked by two more miners, standing where the bank had been, gazing at the body on the stone. They gave no sign of recognition, and he could not find the strength to ask how they had come there.

He turned to Matho. "She must be buried under the stone."

The smith inclined his head towards the watching figures. "They will see to it."

"Good." Villiars stared unseeing at the baby sleeping against Matho's broad chest. "Is there hope? Very little, I say. Arthur will fall, and his Table will fall with him. The realm of Logres will be lost, and the barbarians will conquer all Britain."

"She showed you this?"

"Yes."

"But still you withstood her?"

Villiars wiped the sword clean, limped to his horse and pulled himself into the saddle. Behind him Matho waited, cradling the child.

"She showed me that everyone in whom I trusted was living a lie, that everything in which I believed was false. Our honour is a sham, our nobility a pretence, our chivalry a fraud."

Villiars gathered the reins, his eyes searching Matho's face while the gelding fretted impatiently.

"She thought that would be enough to convert me to her cause. And yet what, truly, did it mean? No more than this, which in my heart of hearts I already knew: that we are all poor sinful men and women. She missed the point, which is not that Arthur and his knights are better than other mortals, but that they strive to create a world in which other mortals may be better than they."

He smiled suddenly. "She called me naïve, and indeed I am a simple man. Yet even in my simplicity I could tell she was not showing me the whole truth. You see, in those visions of the end I saw myself, and others who are dear to me. And we were old, Master Matho, we were old. We have a lifetime before the disaster, and it may be that something will be saved from the ruins, even if it is only a garbled tale of knights riding round the countryside righting wrongs at random."

Without waiting for the smith he set Briar at the low bank, brushing past the watching figures, and went to release Sir Astomar.

Later he would wonder about many things: the slab-faced woman who had sent him from one great earthwork to another; Matho the smith and his small magics; standing stones and dragons beneath the skin of the earth. He would wonder how random his righting of this particular wrong had been, whether he had not been chosen and guided to fulfil a purpose.

He did not know that the visions which presently burned in his mind would soon fade and lose their urgency (though their aftertaste would remain with him the rest of his life). He did not know that both Eustace and Astomar would live to relate how he had freed them from vile enchantment, and that Matho would stand with him before Arthur to testify to what he had done.

He did not care that among a company of men far famed for their courage he alone would be called the Valiant, in memory of the time when he had endured what was beyond endurance and seen the shadow of their destiny.

All he knew was that he was wearier than he had ever been in his life, and that this day had seen the death of something beautiful and splendid, something irreplaceable, something which would not come again.

Sir Kay in
THE TRIAL OF SIR KAY

Cherith Baldry

Cherith Baldry (b. 1947), a former teacher and librarian, has a special fascination for Sir Kay and has written several stories about him. Kay, along with Bedivere and Gawain, is amongst the earliest of Arthur's champions and, in those early tales, Kay was a dynamic hero. It is only in the later French romances that he becomes a grumpy, surly individual, his attitude soured because he was denied the kingship in favour of his foster-brother Arthur. Cherith Baldry has tried to redeem Kay's character, particularly in the following story where Kay undergoes his greatest test.

Cherith Baldry is best known for her children's books, particularly the Saga of the Six Worlds, starting with The Book and the Phoenix *(1989; published in America as* Cradoc's Quest*), which is set on a distant binary star system whose settlers have long since forgotten Earth.*

That year, Arthur held his All Hallows' Court at Carlisle. Sir Gawain of Orkney, as he waited in the great hall for the serving of the midday meal, was well aware of the King's reasons, and not convinced in his own mind that they were good ones.

The northern kings had never paid homage willingly, had never been friendly to Arthur, who had come among them with goodwill, hoping to know them better and to gain their confidence. Gawain, seeing the way in which the members of the various retinues were eyeing each other, thought the Court was more likely to end in murder.

Meanwhile, he was waiting restlessly upon Arthur's custom of hearing of a marvel or an adventure before he would begin the meal.

"Kay," he said to his neighbour at the table, "when you're in charge, at Camelot, how do you manage to have everything running so smoothly, with all this waiting about?"

"Practice," Sir Kay replied laconically.

Sir Gareth, Gawain's brother, leant eagerly across the table.

"Tell me," he said, "do you ever . . . well, go out looking?" Kay's mouth twitched.

"You aren't supposed to ask that," he said.

Gareth laughed delightedly, and the sound attracted the attention of the group of men next to them, strangers, who all wore the livery of the same lord.

"Arthur's men?" one of them asked.

He was a young man, with greasy red curls, his thick-set body already running to fat; for all that, he looked and sounded dangerous. Gawain bowed his head with infinite courtesy.

"Yes," he said. "Sir Gawain of Orkney, at your service, gentlemen. My brother, Sir Gareth. Sir Kay, King Arthur's seneschal."

The young man's eyes narrowed as he looked at Kay.

"Sir Kay," he said. "We've heard of you, Sir Kay. Your fame has spread even this far, hasn't it?" Gawain felt Kay stiffen, but he said nothing, and sat with his eyes fixed on the tablecloth. The young man leant forward.

"We've heard how you're one of the first knights of Arthur's court – when it comes to running away."

Kay reached to where his sword would have been. Gawain's hand clamped hard around his wrist.

"Don't!" he whispered urgently. "They're looking for a quarrel. If we strike the first blow, Arthur will be blamed for it."

Kay nodded almost imperceptibly. He had gone white, and his lips were compressed. Across the table, Gareth, warned by the shake of his brother's head, bit back an angry protest. The red-haired young man smiled.

"You might be some use back in Camelot," he said. "For scraping bowls or counting loaves of bread. But up here – no use at all. I wonder Arthur goes to the trouble of bringing you."

Gawain's grip on Kay's wrist must have been painful, but when he saw Kay's eyes, hot and desperate, he wondered how much longer he could go on keeping him silent. Kay had already endured more insult than any man should be asked to bear; for the fiery Kay, the effort at self-control was truly heroic.

To Gawain's great relief, before anyone else could speak, there was a stir at the door of the hall, and a voice shouting for silence. In the arched opening appeared a lady, veiled in a dark cloak, and riding a white mule. As the noise in the hall died down, she dismounted, entered, and advanced into the clear space between the tables. She raised slender hands to put back the hood of her cloak; Gawain saw how beautiful she was.

"My lord King!" Her voice was clear and confident. "I beg you, grant my request."

Arthur signed for her to continue.

"Good," Gawain thought. "Perhaps now he'll fulfil his custom and we can all eat. Give that lout something to think about besides baiting Kay."

At his side he felt Kay begin to relax, and released the grip on his wrist. The lady was explaining how a strange knight had challenged her father, who was too ill to meet him.

"I ask for a champion from your court, my lord," she said. "Everyone knows that the knights of King Arthur are the finest in the world."

There was some murmuring at that, but the King looked pleased.

"Of course," he said, and glanced round the tables. "Who will go with the lady?" he asked. "Lancelot? Gawain, perhaps . . ." Instantly, Kay was on his feet.

"My lord, please let me go."

As Arthur looked at him, there was a flicker of surprise in his face, immediately suppressed; Gawain knew that Kay would not have missed it. Urgently, he repeated,

"Please, my lord!"

The King hesitated for a moment longer, and then nodded.

"Very well, Kay. Thank you. You had better make ready to go."

Kay withdrew from the table without a word to his friends, or a glance towards the man who had insulted him. Gawain saw him pause for a few words with the lady, and then leave the hall; she sank in a low curtsy to the King, and followed.

Gawain watched her go, frowning a little. He felt uneasy; he felt even more uneasy when he saw the gloating look on the face of the red-haired man. Was it just coincidence, Gawain asked himself, that he had ridiculed Kay, accused him of cowardice and incompetence, and even questioned his right to a place at Arthur's table, just before the opportunity had come for Kay to prove to everyone that he was wrong?

When the servants were bringing in the first course of the meal, and everyone had begun to forget the incident, Gawain leant across the table to Gareth.

"I don't like this," he said.

"You don't think Kay is a coward, do you?" Gareth said indignantly. Gawain smiled; Gareth had a strong protective streak towards Kay.

"No, of course not," he said. "But this – it's too pat, too easy. Almost as if it was arranged. I don't think Kay is going to find what he expects to find. Gareth," he went on softly, "suppose we follow them? At a discreet distance?"

"A very discreet distance," Gareth agreed. "If Kay finds out, he'll kill us!"

They withdrew quietly from the hall, sent a squire to fetch their swords, and had their horses saddled. It was still early on a cold, misty afternoon. They followed the white road that wound down the hill, away from the fortress, in the direction the gate guard told them had been taken by Kay and the lady.

The road crossed a stretch of moorland and then plunged into the forest of Inglewood, a dark barrier in the distance, its outlines blurred by the fine mist. Nothing moved between the forest and the castle; the world was utterly empty.

Gawain let his horse move at an easy trot. Kay would be held up by the pace of the lady's mule, and Gawain had no wish to catch him, at least, not before he had a better idea of what was happening. His earlier misgivings about the court returned with doubled force.

Riding beside him, Gareth was whistling softly, tunelessly, a suppressed tension in the sound. He shifted restlessly in the saddle, as if he would rather have been spurring his horse into a wild gallop.

"What is all this?" he said at last, as if he could not keep the words in any longer. "If it's a trap, who laid it?"

Gawain shrugged.

"Take your choice," he said. "Any of the northern kings who fought against Arthur in the old days. They paid homage in the end, but they've been grumbling away quietly ever since. Carados of Scotland, Brandegoris of Strangore, Nentres of Garlot . . . They're all here, with their attendant lords and their retinues." Affectionately he remembered Sir Kay's acid comments as he prepared to feed and lodge the unwelcome guests in the days leading up to the court. "If I'm right," he added, "one of them at least is making plans against Arthur. And I wish I knew what they are."

Almost imperceptibly, Sir Gareth was increasing the pace. Gawain could see him growing more worried with every step the horses took.

"Do they mean to kill Kay?" he said. "Are they waiting for him, in the forest?"

Gawain reached over and laid a hand on his arm, steadying him.

"It won't be as simple as that," he said. "What would be the point of murdering Kay? He's in danger, I'm sure of it, but not of that kind."

The forest lay across their path like a dark wave. Gawain wondered whether Kay had already been overwhelmed in it. Gareth shivered.

"Inglewood is an accursed place," he said.

Gawain murmured agreement. There was no shortage of stories about the evil things that harboured in the forest; he had encountered some of the evil himself. But he knew that whatever waited there now for Kay did not belong to Inglewood, but had been taken there by Arthur's enemies.

Not until Gawain and Gareth were approaching the borders of Inglewood was there movement on the road. A horse broke out from the trees, riderless, wild, its reins broken.

"Kay's horse!" Gareth exclaimed.

The horse went careering off across the moorland, and they did not try to catch it. Gawain pressed forward now, with Gareth close behind him, his uneasiness sharpened to a desperate anxiety.

It was darker beneath the trees, quieter, the horses' hooves muffled by fallen leaves. Gawain called Kay's name, but there was no reply. They moved more slowly, scanning the trees on either side in case they should miss some clue to what had happened, but when it came, it would have been impossible to miss.

The undergrowth was broken down, trampled over a wide circle that included the road. There was a sharp tang of bruised grasses in the air.

"Someone fought here!" Gareth said. Gawain dismounted.

"Kay!" he called again.

There was still no reply. He began to search, back and forth, across the circle, while Gareth walked his horse on as far as the next bend in the road.

Gawain began to dread what he was going to find. He could feel the fear, tight in his throat. He blamed himself for holding back, for the sake of Kay's honour and self-respect, when his life was in danger.

At last he found Kay lying on the edge of the trampled circle, under a tree. In the failing light, his dark tunic blended into the shadows. He was sprawled on his face. Kneeling beside him, Gawain could make out an ugly, ragged gash in his side, a spear head and a few inches of splintered shaft still jutting from the wound. The dead leaves where he lay were clotted with blood.

Shaking, Gawain turned him over. His face was pale, streaked with blood. His eyes were closed. At first Gawain thought he was dead, but blood was still oozing from the wound, and when Gawain drew his sword and held the bright blade close to Kay's lips, it was stained by the faint exhalation of his breath. Gawain straightened up.

"Gareth!" he called. "Gareth, come here!"

Sir Kay was lying half sunk among the pillows, his face white as the linen, beneath tumbled dark hair. The short winter day had drawn to an end; a single lamp burned beside the bed.

Watching, Gawain saw Kay's eyes flutter open, dark and unfocused. Gently he raised his friend's head and held a cup of water to his lips. Kay drank; gradually his eyes lost that terrifying vacancy.

"Gawain?" he whispered.

"Yes; I'm here."

"Then why. . .?"

The wisp of sound died away. Gawain set the cup aside and let Kay lie back again. Kay was frowning in a vague perplexity.

"There was a knight . . ."

"You don't have to talk," Gawain said.

A flicker of impatience crossed Kay's face. He began to turn his head restlessly from side to side, catching at memory.

"She – the lady – she was taking me to her father's manor." The voice was uneven, but growing gradually stronger. "The road led through the edge of Inglewood. The knight was there . . . waiting, under the trees. He challenged me, and then – " He caught his breath. "Gawain, the lady! Where is she?"

Impossible to lie to him. Gawain shook his head.

"I don't know. You were alone when we found you. They're out looking – "

"Oh, merciful God!" The words were sobbed out. "I pledged my word. . . Gawain, I must get up."

He was struggling to rise, pushing aside the blankets and furs; pain washed over him like a great wave, leaving him limp and gasping. Gawain eased him back on to his pillows, where he lay trembling.

"You're hurt; lie still," Gawain said.

Kay's eyes sought for his, keenly intelligent now; even the pain of his wound could not dull the knowledge of how disastrously he had failed.

"You need not stay," he said, and turned his head away.

For answer, Gawain reached out and took his hand. For a minute, feebly, Kay tried to free himself from the patient clasp, and then gave in. Gawain went on sitting there, in silence, listening to the buffeting of the wind outside. Kay was drifting away from consciousness again, his eyes half closed. Then footsteps sounded outside; the door was flung back, and Kay roused again at the noise.

"Dear God, Gareth!" Gawain said irritably. "Can't you do anything quietly?"

His brother closed the door carefully behind him. He was panting as if he had run up the stairs. He brought a gust of the cold outdoors with him; fine rain misted on his hair and the fur on his cloak. There was a wild look about him that quickened all Gawain's apprehensions.

"What is it?" he asked.

"Is there news?" Kay's weakness made his urgency all the more painful. "The lady – is she found?"

"Yes, found," Gareth replied. "At home in her father's castle."

Kay let out a shuddering sigh, and Gawain murmured a prayer of thankfulness, while still wondering why Gareth should look so distraught.

"Tell us," he said.

"It was getting dark," Gareth began, "and I'd given up the search. I started to make my way back, and when I got to the road, I came up with a knight riding this way, and I asked him if he'd seen her." He had been speaking swiftly; now his voice faltered a little. "He said he was her father."

"I thought her father was ill," Gawain interposed. All his suspicions were alive again, at this first evidence of a lie. Or were they supposed to believe that the lady's father had miraculously recovered?

Gareth knelt down beside Kay, and put a hand on his shoulder.

"Kay, listen . . . I don't believe this, and I don't think anyone else will believe it, either. But he said – he said he rode out to meet her, and found her in the forest with a knight – Kay, I'm sorry – a knight who had raped her, and he fought with him, and then took his daughter home and was coming to the King to ask for justice. I told him – "

Again Gareth broke off, as Kay, who had listened to him with a fierce, unwavering attention, suddenly gave way, all strength leached out of him, his eyes closing, his head slipping to one side.

"Dear God, I've killed him!" Gareth exclaimed, beginning to chafe Kay's hands frantically.

Gawain turned aside to pour a little wine into a cup.

"You're a fool, Gareth," he said. "You didn't need to tell him, not yet, at least, not until – "

"No." It was Kay who interrupted, very weak, but struggling back to consciousness. "No, I want to know, or how can I – ?" He pressed a hand to his lips. "What am I going to do?"

Gawain heard only a cry of desperation, but Gareth chose to answer the question.

"The usual thing would be to challenge him," he said. "Let him prove what he accuses you of, if he dares. But as it is – "

"Kay can't fight him like this," Gawain said.

"I can if I have to."

His mouth was set; Kay at his most obstinate. Gawain almost smiled.

"Dear Kay, I don't think you could walk as far as that door, much less fight. But it doesn't matter. You don't have to. Appoint a champion in your place. I'll do it for you. I'll be glad to."

Kay was staring at him. He said, "Oh, no. I won't involve you in my trouble, Gawain."

Gareth, who by now was sitting on the side of the bed, smiled down at him, and gathered Kay's hands into his own.

"Let me do it, then. There's nothing to worry about. Gawain

or I could get the better of him in five minutes. Or you could ask Lancelot," he went on, growing enthusiastic. "Lancelot wouldn't even need five minutes. One look from Lancelot . . . Oh, Kay, dear Sir Kay, don't!"

His voice changed to distress as Kay turned his head aside, tears spilling over uncontrollably.

"I was never kind to you," Kay gasped out. "And you haven't even asked me, either of you . . ."

For a moment they were both bent over him, comforting, reassuring, trying to call him back from the dark places he had chosen. Gawain could not help knowing that Kay's sharp tongue had made him unpopular; there were plenty of people in the court who would believe, or pretend to believe, the charge against him. But for himself, it was absurd to imagine that Kay would rape the lady he had given his word to serve. Kay's integrity might not be the conventional chivalry of Arthur's court, but it was very real and deep rooted.

At last, Kay won his battle for self-control, though the effort was beginning to exhaust him.

"I won't let you fight for me," he said, the old irascibility creeping back into his voice. "Even if you defeat this man, even if you kill him, you won't kill the lie. People will still think I did this – this foul . . ." Disgust choked off his words.

"The King will never believe it," Gareth said.

Kay's hands clenched. Gawain knew that Gareth, without realizing it, had pierced to the heart of Kay's fears.

"If he does believe it," Kay said, with such desolation that Gawain thought his heart would break, "then I don't care what happens to me."

Once Kay had gone to sleep, Gawain brought a fur rug and a blanket, and settled himself beside his bed. In the middle of the night, he was roused by Kay crying out.

"Arthur! Oh, Arthur – no!"

He was tossing in an evil dream; his face was flushed, his body at fever heat. When Gawain gave him a drink, he half woke and muttered something incoherent. Gawain brought a bowl of water and bathed his forehead until he sank into a quieter sleep. In the early morning, when Gareth came to relieve him, Gawain went to see the King.

Arthur kept him waiting. The anteroom was crowded with the followers of the northern kings, and when Gawain entered there was some whispering, and sidelong, hostile glances. Gawain ignored it all, and went to sit in the window-seat, uncomfortably feeling their eyes boring into his back.

At length he was called into the King's private room, and saw to his infinite relief that Arthur had dismissed his servants, so that they could talk alone. Arthur was pacing, the tawny lion, deceptively weary and slow-moving, but he motioned Gawain to a seat.

"My lord, I want to talk about Kay."

Arthur nodded; he must have realized that. "You've been with him, haven't you?" he asked. "I'm glad of that." He sounded as if he was having difficulty in admitting it. "I'm glad he isn't alone."

"It's you he wants, my lord."

The great head swung round towards him; Gawain could almost see sparks flying off the red-gold hair. The amber eyes shone.

"Gawain, one of my men is accused of a foul crime, and if I don't see that justice is done, we'll have the whole of Britain in flames. You saw them out there? Just waiting for an excuse."

He paced again. Gawain eyed him, and tentatively asked the one question that he had to ask.

"My lord – you surely don't believe it?"

Arthur stood still, his back to Gawain. Gawain found that he was terrified of seeing his face when he turned. But the King remained motionless, and the answer when it came was unexpectedly mild.

"I've known Kay all my life. I know exactly what he's capable of. And rape isn't on the list. But he stands accused. I can't ignore that. I can't prove that this man – the girl's father – is lying, and of course I couldn't be so uncivilized as to expect to speak to the girl herself! And I don't suppose we'll ever know for certain which of my enemies planned it all." He gave a short, humourless laugh. "Of course, Gawain, you can see it was planned – everything that happened yesterday – to trap Kay."

He moved over to the window and stood looking out. Gawain felt the pressure of his power, hemmed in and restricted, and knew that it would break out but for the conscious effort of his will. He himself understood now what the plot had been, but the understanding had come too late to help Kay, or to point a way for Arthur out of the thicket that ensnared them both.

"He was used," Arthur went on. He smiled sadly. "It's easy enough, God knows, to work out how Kay will react. And he's so perfect for their purpose! He's High Seneschal, but that goes with my favour. Of himself, he's not particularly wealthy or powerful. And not a dangerous man – they might have thought twice before they played their games with Lancelot, or even with you. But Kay was brought up as my brother. The one man I might be expected to protect. And if I do so – then what has it meant, all this talk of law and justice in my kingdom? Worth less than the dust on the wind! They will rebel, Gawain, if I make the slightest mistake."

He stood with his hands against the window embrasure. Gawain waited, expecting to be dismissed, but when Arthur turned back to him, it was to ask,

"How badly hurt is Kay?"

"The wound itself wouldn't kill him, my lord." Gawain was choosing his words carefully. "But he needs rest, and instead he's fretting himself into a fever." He hesitated and then went on, "He's afraid you will believe him guilty."

Arthur slammed his fist against the wall, and stood rigid, his eyes closed. Gawain, shaken by the swift uncoiling of passion, would not have been surprised to see the wall start to crumble. Very quietly, Arthur said,

"I am the King. I may not – "

"It isn't the King he wants."

If Gawain had thought about it, he would never have dared to interrupt. But the words were out, and Arthur was looking at him with a sudden daunting intensity. Then he drew a deep breath, and relaxed.

"Very well," he said. "Come."

He scoured through the anteroom like the wind off an icefield; following, Gawain heard the babble of speculation breaking out behind him. Too late to worry about what he had set in motion; was it, after all, the first stirrings of war?

In Kay's room, he and Gareth were talking quietly; they broke off as Arthur entered. Gawain saw Kay's eyes dilate. His voice quivered with a desperate urgency.

"Arthur, my lord – you should not have come . . ."

Standing by the door, Gawain could not see Arthur's face, but he could hear the warmth, strong and vibrant, as he said, "Brother, you're talking nonsense. Now tell me what really happened, and then we can decide what we're going to do."

Not knowing whether he wanted to smile or weep, Gawain beckoned Gareth out of the room, and closed the door softly behind him.

* * *

When Gawain returned, the King had gone. Kay lay still; he looked up as Gawain came in, and smiled peacefully.

"Is everything all right?" Gawain asked.

"Oh, yes," Kay murmured.

His tranquillity was a complex, precarious balance between opposing demands. Gawain wanted to ask what the King had said, but he was reluctant to intrude on Kay's privacy. He was beginning to speak when Kay interrupted him.

"I have agreed to a trial by ordeal."

"What?"

Gawain strode round the bed, bent over Kay and seized his hands urgently.

"Kay, that's barbaric! Surely Arthur didn't ask you – "

"No, I suggested it." Kay sighed faintly. "Gawain, you know that if Arthur ignores the law to protect me, he will lose his hold on the kingdom. How can I ask him to go to war for my sake? This castle is seething with men who were his enemies, and will be again, given the slightest excuse."

"And one of them planned this," Gawain said.

Kay gave him a twisted smile.

"And I fell in with his plans. Oh, I know how I let them use me. I'm not proud of myself, Gawain. So it's only right that I should do this."

Gawain sat back and looked at him. He thought of Kay – practical, logical Kay – submitting himself to the crude torment of a trial by ordeal. His mind shied away from the picture. And yet God should protect the innocent. Did that mean, Gawain wondered, that his faith was not strong enough, or simply that he refused to believe in a God who could connive in such savagery? He asked the question that was sticking in his throat.

"What must you do?"

"I don't know. Arthur will consult with the other kings, and the Bishop. It doesn't matter. I'm not afraid." He had a strange, distant look, as if he was drifting too far away for Gawain to reach him. "You know, Gawain," he went on, almost dreamily, "I don't think this wound is going to heal. If I fail the ordeal, there isn't a great deal more that Arthur can do to me." He closed his eyes and then opened them again. "No, there is one thing that frightens me. I'm afraid that my strength will give way, so that I can't do what they ask of me."

Gawain felt as if an aching wound had opened in his throat. Quietly, he asked, "Do you want me to help you?" The question pierced Kay's hard-won serenity, threatening to shatter it.

"You would . . .?" He was staring, his eyes brilliant, knowing what a bitter thing Gawain was offering for the sake of friendship. "No," he whispered. "I won't have you tainted along with me."

Gawain bent and kissed his forehead.

"You're not," he said. "And I'll be there. Go to sleep."

By the time the summons came from the King, Kay had rested, and found from somewhere the strength to get out of bed and dress. The rules of the ordeal asked for him to be barefoot, bare-headed, and wearing a white penitential garment. Kay had chosen a robe of stiff, figured silk, belted and fastened with pearl and silver; he looked magnificent, and about as penitent as a wild hawk.

It was a sombre day, cloudy and raw with cold. The King and his court, the visiting kings and their retinues, the Bishop and his acolytes, had assembled outside the castle. They looked like a great, restless flower border, blazing against the grey walls. The shifting mass of colour, the murmuring of many voices, all grew still as Kay approached.

Gawain slipped into his place near the King, beside Gareth. Not far away, at the bottom of a gentle slope, a long strip had been cut out of the turf, to make a shallow pit of burning charcoal; a sullen pall of smoke hovered a few inches above it.

"They want him to walk across that," Gareth said, revulsion vibrating in his voice. "Gawain, can't you stop it?" Gawain dared not look at him.

"If we try," he said, "we'll have a war on our hands."

The Bishop was waiting at the King's right hand, and on his left was a tall, grey-haired man whom Gawain had not seen before.

"The lady's father," Gareth told him.

Sir Kay stood before them, head held high. He should have knelt; Gawain knew perfectly well that if he had tried he would probably not have got up again, but the impression he gave was of overwhelming arrogance.

Arthur had a strange, shuttered look, as if his spirit was somewhere else. He said something in a low voice to Kay, and then the Bishop spoke, as if he was instructing Kay what to do; Gawain caught only the last few words.

". . . and we trust that God will defend the right."

"You are to be congratulated, my lord," Kay said, "on the strength of your faith." He paused for a moment, eyes snapping out a challenge, and then went on, his voice raised so that everyone could hear it. "I swear before you, my lord King, and before Christ, that I am innocent of this charge against me."

Turning, not hesitating, he began to walk towards the pit. Gawain watched with a sick apprehension, nothing coherent in his mind any longer. Beside him, he heard Gareth murmuring a prayer. Then a few paces from the pit Kay's firm step faltered; he pressed a hand to his side and Gawain saw a scarlet blotch beginning to spread against the silvery white of his robe. The wound had broken open. Kay hesitated, took another two or three steps, stumbling now, and then crumpled to the ground a pace or two away from the edge of the pit.

There was a stir among the crowd. Somebody close to Gawain said, "Oh, beautifully done!" Remembering his promise, Gawain started forward, not knowing what he meant to do, but before he reached Kay, his friend struggled on to hands and knees, dragged himself the last few feet, and collapsed on his face among the smouldering coals. Flame sprang up around him.

"Dear God!" Gawain sobbed out.

Unthinking, he flung himself into the pit, grabbed at Kay's shoulders and began to lift him, before his senses broke through his desperation and he began to understand.

He knelt on the coals, with Kay in his arms. There was no heat. Around them, flames rose in a golden wall, a shimmering calyx of fire.

Kay's face and hands were unhurt; the charcoal had not even smudged the white robe. Beginning to revive now, he was blinking in confusion, as fear gave way to awe. In silence, in light, the world was changed.

Gawain could feel a quivering through all Kay's body as he reached out towards the wall of flame. Fire leapt to his fingertips, and Kay half-flinched as if he expected it to burn, but it folded on itself and Kay held it in cupped palms like water, or the sacrament. The fire and the rose lived between his hands.

Gawain faced him across the burning beauty and saw tears tracking down Kay's face like streams of gold.

"No," he whispered. "This cannot be for me. I am not worthy."

Wonder and anguish were battling together in his eyes. Gawain saw the pride and the defensiveness stripped away to reveal the core of the man – the love and loyalty to Arthur that he had somehow lost the power to express. While others laid their high deeds at the feet of their king, Kay's hands were empty of all except pain and disgrace. So he offered that, having nothing else, and shrank to find it so wondrously transfigured.

"I cannot . . ." His voice was the same rough whisper. "God forgive me, I cannot . . . my mind will break."

He turned and hid his face against Gawain's shoulder, shutting out the radiance, locked into his own self-loathing.

Gawain was never sure how long they crouched there, clinging together, under the inexorable weight of light. Outside, it might have been no more than a few seconds; within the fire, time had burnt away, and there was only eternity. He was not sure when he noticed that the scarlet stain on Kay's robe had disappeared.

"Kay – " he began, and could not go on.

Kay stirred, and saw what his friend saw. He sat up, a hand at his side where the spear had driven home.

"It is . . . healed."

His eyes met Gawain's again, forced at last to an acceptance that bit as painfully as the wound.

"Be at peace," Gawain said gently, and Kay, shaking his head as if he still had to assert that peace was not for him, sighed an assent.

Around them, the sheet of flame began to sink, to break up, as the world pressed in again. Gawain rose to his feet, pulling Kay with him, and urged him back on to the turf as heat begin to rise from the pit. For a moment he still supported him, feeling him unsteady, the last shreds of transcendence still clinging to him.

"Kay," Gawain said urgently. "Where will you go from here? What will Sir Kay be after this?"

Kay passed a hand shakily across his eyes. "I . . . do not know."

But there was an alertness in the hawk's face, a resolve that Gawain had not seen there before. He was Kay still – and Gawain had no wish for him ever to change – but he was poised now, as if he set his feet on the road that would one day lead him back to the light.

Outside the castle walls, flakes of colour were breaking away from the mass of courtiers, as people hurried down to meet them. Among them, Gawain knew, was the man who had been prepared to trap and ruin Kay so that he could clear a way to Arthur. Probably they would never be able to give that man a name. Gawain could not feel that it mattered any more. He was punished enough in Kay's vindication. Gawain wondered whether he would be able to sleep, or pray.

Gareth was the first to reach the two knights where they still stood beside the pit of coals.

"The King wants to see you," he announced, flinging an arm across Kay's shoulders.

Kay drew a long breath, his hand at his throat, and glanced back at the pit.

"I'd rather walk across there again," he said. Hurriedly, half ashamed, he added, "For God's sake, stay with me."

"You don't need to ask," Gawain said, with a pang of pure joy that he had asked. God was very good, he thought, and there was more than one kind of miracle.

Together, in the few seconds before the crowd engulfed them, they began to walk up the slope to meet the King.

Sir Meraugis in MERAUGIS AND MEDWINA

Seamus Cullen

Meraugis was a child of rape between Mark and his niece Labiane. The child was abandoned in the woods and raised by a forester but grew up to become one of the Knights of the Round Table. His tale is retold here by Seamus Cullen (b. 1927), the pseudonym of a retired US advertising executive who now lives in Ireland. He is best known for his erotic fantasy, Astra and Flondrix *(1976), and his Arabian fantasies* A Noose of Light *(1986) and* The Sultan's Turret *(1986).*

The young boy looked down and trembled. How had it happened? The dead knight's helm had been thrown to one side and his head was . . . gone. Another shudder went through him as he looked about, wondering if the killer were near by, watching him. He wasn't afraid, just deeply sad and disturbed by his discovery.

The boy was tall and quite strong for merely fourteen years of age. And extremely serious of mien. His long, reddish-brown hair swung from side to side as he went to work without further hesitation. When he had the dead knight free of the regal armour, he dug a grave with the long, heavy sword. His lips were grim; what a shameful use for so fine a sword, he thought, but he can hardly be left unburied. Wolves and worse would find the body.

When the shallow grave was covered over and stamped down, he foraged for branches and leaves; soon, it was impossible to detect anything unusual about the forest's floor.

A soft neighing spun him about. A huge white horse entered the partial clearing, saddled, bridled and caparisoned in a manner fit for a prince. The lad stood his ground, not wishing to startle the horse . . . as the horse had surely startled him. At last, he held out his hand and the noble animal came to him. Only then he noticed a long and apparently heavy jousting lance caught in the rest, the point making a fine trail.

Nicknamed Hoot by his guardian when he was very young, the lad could hardly remember another name. He could just remember a great castle; he thought he remembered his mother but he wasn't sure. That sort of thinking hurt his head and he focused again on the armour and weapons. He knew without trying it on that the harness was too large for him. But he was still growing. Hide it, put it on the horse and . . . then he saw the long cape rolled up behind the saddle. When he had the armour packed neatly in the cape and slung up over the pommel, he cleaned the sword with grass and leaves and returned it to the studded leather scabbard. He felt very self-conscious as he fastened the knight's swordbelt around his waist. "Well, he whispered to the horse, how else shall I carry it, then?" The horse shook his head. "See, you don't know either."

Very warily, Hoot mounted and guided the horse through the thick woods. What would he do if he took a trail and was accosted by knights, even a bailiff? He'd be hanged for sure. Once this plunder of his was safe inside his secret cave, he could breathe freely again. As he rode along, stroking the horse's neck and luxurious mane, he wondered what his guardian, Bron, would say to all this. He'd say the whole lot had to be returned . . . Yes, but to whom? Bron would know. Bron knows everything. Many whispered about Bron being a wizard, but he was a good wizard, he harms no one, he never casts evil spells.

He didn't see the two men until they sprang from the undergrowth. The horse screamed and reared, beginning a caracole, but the boy turned the reins to face forward.

"What have we here?" one ruffian asked the other. "A thief, no doubt. And we'd best relieve him of his plunder afore the sheriff does. The sheriff'd hang 'im. We'll just give him a good thrashing and . . ."

Hoot had the heavy lance free and brought the hilt down on

top of the man's head before he could finish his threats. The other scuttled into the trees and ran as fast as he could. Hoot didn't wait to see if the one on the ground would revive.

"Is that the entire story?" Bron asked after he had examined horse and armour thoroughly.

"Yes, Bron, the whole story." Hoot hesitated. "Please, may we keep it all?"

"Please, may we keep it all?" his guardian mocked.

"You are mocking me, Uncle." The lad suppressed a sniffle. Knights don't sniffle.

"Just like you used to mock the owls when you were a baby . . . but you did it so well they used to fly into the cave to see who the new owl might be. That's why we named you Hoot, or don't you remember?"

"But, Uncle . . ."

"Don't 'but Uncle' me. I'm more the only father you've ever known. Your unnatural natural father would have slaughtered you, had he found you." At this moment a tall and and stately woman walked out of the cave; a large shaggy hound bounded after her, changed direction and leapt up on Hoot, licking his face. "Only for Elaine here, spiriting you out of Tintagel Castle, that foul, black-hearted King Mark would have cut your throat."

"Shhh," the woman named Elaine cautioned Bron, "there is no need to go through all that again. And stop calling the boy Hoot. His rightful name is Meraugis. And one day he'll be a knight like his cousin Tristram . . ."

There was a strangled cry from the youth.

"It is not Tristram's horse and armour, be that what you're thinking," Bron assured him, laying an affectionate hand on his arm. The boy sighed with relief.

Elaine would brook no evasions: the story had to be told again. When the lad came to the part about the missing head, she went white and held her hand over her mouth.

"Bron," she whispered, "this is the sort of thing Mark would do . . ."

"This was a mighty and good knight, my dear, Mark doesn't have the courage to attack a true knight."

"I agree," she answered, "but he does have the wickedness to send others to do it for him. And not by fair means, but foul."

"You mean, Mother, he was not killed in fair combat?" Although Elaine had fled with the baby and brought him to Bron's high cave for protection, even marrying Bron to help cement the family, the boy tended to call Bron "Uncle" and Elaine "Mother."

"Jesu, I thank you for this young man's innocence and purity," she said softly, raising her eyes to heaven and making the sign of the cross. "Son, King Mark is capable of such foul deeds. People flee Cornwall every day to be free of his vicious machinations."

"Elaine, the boy wants to keep what he found. You know how dangerous that could be."

"In another year or so, how would we be able to provide him with all he needs to seek his knighthood? And here Providence has led him to the very spot. Surely, it is a divine sign, you as a powerful wizard should know that." Elaine smiled pure sunshine upon her mate.

"The smile that melts iron hearts," he muttered. "Son, take it all to the hidden cave and store it well. As for the horse, I don't know how we shall feed him or keep his presence hidden. Unharnessed, we can always say he found us, do you see?"

Over the next eighteen months, young Meraugis did rise from sapling to tree, growing taller than the stately Elaine and even stronger than Bron. Every day he could, he would ride the great white horse up the hill and down into a narrow ravine where the secret cave was. By now, the armour fitted him perfectly and he could wield the great sword tellingly with either hand. Bron could not teach him much so to a great extent, he was self-taught. In addition to being ambidextrous he had a natural inclination toward physical activities and an instinct with weaponry which Bron said was, in its own way, sheer wizardry. The poor man did his best with an old sword of his father's. Simply, Meraugis was tireless and Bron was not.

Meraugis painstakingly fashioned a cross-section of oak in imitation of a shield. Day after day, as this heavy object hung down from an overhead branch, the eager youth mounted up on Lion, the white horse, in full armour both, and levelled the lance at the target. Bron warned him to adjust his thinking. There was a difference between a stationary target and another horseman riding down on one full tilt.

One evening, when he returned to their dwelling, Elaine said she could use his help with preparing their supper. When he brought the water back from the stream, she handed him a knife and asked him to cut thickish strips from the haunch of venison on the table.

As they both worked, she told him a story which brought tears of sadness and fury to his eyes. She and Bron had decided he should reach a man's estate before they told him this story. This truly terrible story. Yes, Meraugis was the son of a king, but what a king! King Mark was the most reviled man in his own kingdom and despised as a cowardly knight and an evil, murderous monster elsewhere.

Why he suddenly decided to rape his innocent and helpless young niece, Labiane, no one would ever fathom. He was a beast in the shape of a man. Labiane conceived, of course, and very soon thereafter, the fiend murdered her. At that time, Elaine was a widow, her husband, Sir Beaumont, slain in a joust with Sir Palomides. Shortly after, her own baby son died of a fever. When she heard King Mark was about to slaughter Labiane's baby, she fled the castle with the baby, nursing him as her own.

This was not an isolated example. Some while before, King Mark's brother, Sir Baudwin, had fought off an invasion to save Mark's kingdom. Mark accused Baudwin of vainglory and stuck a dagger into him. His wife, Anglides, and young son were forced to flee as Mark could not bear that either of them should live. She brought little but the blood-soaked shirt and doublet her husband had been wearing when foully done to death by his own brother, King Mark. She and young Alisander were welcomed by the Constable of Arundel where they were granted sanctuary. Alisander was made knight and swore an oath on his father's blood-stained clothes to avenge his death.

"Then Alisander is my cousin, my first cousin," Meraugis said softly, trying to undo the terrible knot of emotion gripping his insides.

"Yes, my dear, as is Sir Tristram de Liones, who is Mark's nephew also."

"One day I must find this cousin that we may ride together to rid the world of such a man as my father." He clutched Elaine's hand with his bloody one. "Was she beautiful, she who was my natural mother?" He paused as Elaine fixed him with a shrewd glance. "I mean, as beautiful as you, Mother?"

"May the good Lord guard over that flattering tongue of yours," she prayed. "Maidens will not be safe with you about." Unadmonished he waited, still gripping her hand. "Yes," Elaine conceded, "she was as lovely a young girl as ever you will see. And so young, a mere sixteen at the time. Such a tragedy."

That night, young Meraugis was plagued with horrible nightmares. He saw lines of young men and women standing up outside a castle, their hands tied behind their backs. A man with jet-black hair and beard marched up and down before them, scowling and muttering foul oaths. Every minute or so, he would come closer, select one of the prisoners, then strike with his dagger. He saw his mother – he could not be sure was it Elaine or Labiane – fleeing through a dark forest with him as a baby in her arms. Behind her, dark riders smashed through the thick growth, striking at it with their swords. Pursuing hounds made more noise than the Questing Beast.

A hand shaking his shoulder woke him with a cry. "What were you dreaming about?" demanded Bron, his face reflecting storm clouds. Meraugis told him about the nightmares. Bron walked to the cave entrance and pulled back the heavy coverings, hung like curtains. The moon was full and bright, but it was not benign. Something in the night was disturbed and disturbing.

"Those dreams of yours are like beacon fires. The monsters of the night are now seeking the source of such violent imaginings, such fiendish creations." Bron stopped and listened, straining his neck as though he could send his ears out into the night. Then he started sniffing.

"I'm sure of it! Out there somewhere, and not too far away, there is a werewolf. And he is circling, coming closer." Bron turned abruptly and half-ran to the interior, to return in a moment with a large urn which he placed in the cave entrance; he quickly closed the draping covers.

"What was that?" Meraugis asked sleepily.

"A little something werewolves do not savour, Son." Bron left again and was back in no time with a small goblet. "Here, drink this down and it will calm you. It might even induce some pleasant dreams."

"How do you detect a werewolf by just sniffing?" the youth asked, between gulps of the strong potion.

"This is no ordinary werewolf. We are not sure why she did it, but a certain Sir Marrok was changed into a werewolf . . . by his wife. He'll not invade us now . . . that is, if you have some pleasant dreams for a change."

Meraugis was asleep even before Bron reached his quarters further back in the cave. He was now riding Lion in full harness for battle; he came upon a wondrous clearing he had never seen before. He gazed about, trying to pick up landmarks in the distance. Instinctively, he knew it was that bit further west than he had ever travelled before. This is not like a dream, he told himself, this is so clear and natural it is more akin to having entered another world.

The trees and grass sparkled and yet they were dry. It was not dew. He dismounted and decided to rest. He led Lion to the small river flowing past the clearing. With agile fingers, he undid his armour and was soon out of it and his shirt and doublet and the rest and plunging into the cool water. It revived him immediately and when he got out of the stream he stretched out on the soft grass to dry off. He was very self-conscious about lying there naked, but he knew he'd get a warning from Lion if anyone tried to approach.

Before he knew it, he was asleep. But as though someone or something had sprinkled fairy dust into his eyes. In his dream he was having a dream and that was most peculiar. Then he was half-sitting, his back against a young birch tree, and walking slowly toward him was the most beautiful girl he had ever seen or dreamt about, and she was leading a pure white unicorn. She told him not to be concerned of his nakedness, for his innocence protected him like an invisible shield. As soon as she spoke, his modesty evaporated. When she drew near enough to touch him, she knelt in the grass and spread her gown about her. The unicorn came close as well, then bent its forelegs to kneel next the maiden.

The girl began stroking the unicorn's single horn which shimmered with a coating of silvery powder. As she gathered up this stardust on her fingers, she began to rub it over his entire body. In a whisper, she informed him it was one of the most potent forms of magic known, for what could be more magical than the fabled unicorn? Isn't that true? she asked the unicorn; it nodded sagely. It will protect you from harm, make you strong in battle and pure of heart. You will survive where others perish. You will be made knight by the hand you most desire. And you shall gain great honour and worship through your deeds and purity.

He woke suddenly, a cry stifled in his throat. He was in his bed, it was still totally dark and he was shaking uncontrollably, his whole body filled with unbearable longing for something he could not define. He felt it, it was tangible, he knew something wonderful had been ripped out of his grasp . . . but what? He knew he'd been somewhere wonderful but he couldn't remember a thing.

Bron watched the young man carefully don his armour, taking pains with each detail of harnessing. Elaine was watching Meraugis just as intently from the shadows inside the cave entrance. She had pressed her face against Bron's breast during the night; although she did not make a sound, he felt the sobbing going through his heart like thrusts of a dagger. They were only the lad's foster parents, why were they so forlorn? he asked, as though a guardian angel were standing there. Because, answered the guardian angel, he is the only child you have or ever will, why should you not love him as your very own.

"You should have a squire," Bron said testily, as though it might be his own fault.

"Father, I will have enough to feed myself and old Lion here, never mind some spoilt lesser noble incapable of feeding himself from the forests and meadows . . . Yes, and the occasional barn or hen coop."

"Well, then, a varlet. Someone to carry your spear, boy, a knight does not do that for himself, who will take you seriously?" Bron cleared his throat nervously. He chastised himself: you are chattering foolishly because you cannot bear to say goodbye. By the rood, man, give him a good example of fortitude!

"Father, listen. I cannot afford even a varlet now. But when I am made knight by my good and noble cousin, Sir Tristram, lads will be vying with each other to follow me and carry both spear and helm." Meraugis turned toward the cave. "Mother? Where are you? I must be off whilst the sun still rests on the rim of the world."

"Patience. That very world will be empty enough when the trees close ranks behind you." She came out with a simple white linen square tied up by the four corners. "I've put you up some bread and cheese and some of the rabbit left from supper. Yes, and a small flagon of mead. Only a small amount at a time, mind."

Meraugis was so preoccupied keeping his emotions in check he hardly noticed the route Lion took through the woods. After some while the occasional warmth of sunshine on the back of his head told him they were heading unerringly westward. The horse is a mind-reader, just like my true father, Bron. He thinks we will find my miraculous dream. What if it is the nightmare? he had asked Bron. The quiet sage inclined his head for a moment, before saying: More likely it will be both, so you must be prepared. It was then his father revealed what he had been holding between his cupped hands. A very strange medallion, the like of which

Meraugis had never seen before. It is from Egypt, said Bron, and it dates back to long before the flight of the Hebrews. It is said that Isis, the Egyptian goddess, wore it to turn aside the forces of evil. With these words, Bron produced a stout silver chain which he attached to the jewelled medallion before hanging it about the youth's neck.

"Well, Lion, you seem as determined as Bron. Why should I argue?" He rattled the long lance feutered in its rest and laughed. The laugh was echoed by birds. They chirped vigorously, speeding horse and rider along. And there was intermittent buzzing all about, every insect in the bright morning trying to outdo all the rest. And the eager, would-be knight began to doze. Never quite fully asleep, he teetered between the two worlds, aware of both but unaware of the passage of time. He became fully conscious abruptly when Lion stopped without warning.

It was the clearing! There could be no doubt about it, every detail of his dream flowed back. Aloud, he cried: "But where is she?" As suddenly, he felt so foolish, crying out to the wilderness. Birds echoed his cry. A moment later, he slipped from the saddle, removing it and Lion's armour. He removed the bridle as Lion never failed to answer a special call, but only from his master.

When the young man had bathed and refreshed himself in the very stream of his dream, he stretched out. Would she come? He must feign sleep as she might be too shy to approach him awake. He closed his eyes and waited, the great sword naked as he and resting on the grass at his side, his fingers wrapped about the handle, close to the crossguard. He could hear Lion munching grass at the riverbank. All was so peaceful, so tranquil, he told himself just before slipping into a deep sleep.

When the girl of his dreams came softly to the clearing, Lion jerked his head up and bared his teeth, about to trumpet a warning. The girl made a gesture with her hand and the last thing Lion remembered was the gorgeous white mare by the girl's side. Absolutely gorgeous, and wearing a long, spiral horn, just one, in the middle of her brow.

The girl drew close to the naked sleeping youth. She gestured again, assuring that he would not wake before she wished him to. That dream she had sent him was the most powerful one her magic flower had ever produced. The strange woman who came to see her that afternoon. Just walked into the private garden of her father's castle. She produced that certain white flower and told me it was like the one she brought when I was born. *The man destined to be my mate must find me,* she said; *and with men, you cannot leave this up to their whims or devices. Send him the dream I will describe to you.*

The girl shook her head impatiently. This is no time to dwell on such things, there is work to be done. From inside the bodice of her simple white dress she drew a drawstring pouch made of soft rabbitskin. She opened it wide and softly called the unicorn to her. Obediently, the fabulous beast bent her head and drew her horn delicately across the sword blade just where the girl held the open pouch. Bright silver dust sparkled as it descended; it was like a snowstorm in miniature. When the pouch contained enough of the magical substance, the girl leaned across and kissed the unicorn's brow tenderly. The legendary beast nuzzled the girl's cheek, then sped off silently, vanishing among the trees.

Next, the nymph-like creature took some of the sparkling, translucent powder and rubbed it into the medallion resting on Meraugis's chest. Power, yes, my beloved; she formed the words soundlessly with her lips only. But more powerful needst be . . . for your safety and mine. Little is there more powerful than powdered unicorn horn, but only when freely given. When she had similarly rubbed down the blade of his sword, she tied the drawstring and fastened it securely to the silver chain supporting his medallion.

"Will you sleep all day, my bold champion?" she cried aloud.

Meraugis sat bolt upright, blinking and shaking his head. He opened his mouth to ask who she was but suddenly became aware of his naked body. He swept his clothing off the ground and ran into the woods. He heard the girl's laughter follow him. He was almost furious, then he realized it was not malice but simple mirth. Indeed, how funny he must have looked, taking flight like a startled hare.

There was a deep crimson colour running upwards from his throat when he returned. She patted the ground, indicating he should sit.

"I see by the parcel you have brought food with you. Lovingly packed by your mother, no doubt. We shall have some, and when you are calm again we shall declare ourselves to one another."

She didn't ask, he noticed, simply directing with the air of a queen . . . not that he'd ever met a queen, though he always fancied his adoptive mother was very close to that rank. His mother had enclosed a simple goblet and she allowed him to put the smallest amount of mead in, then insisted he fill the cup with water.

All right, she would begin. Her father was the Lord Earl of

Sarandon, his castle but an hour's walk from here. Her mother died long ago and her father was away – he was forever going to tournaments, to increase his fame and worship, as was his wont. She had attendants, to be sure, but she was sixteen now, a full-grown woman, and would be ruled by no one, not even her own father. His eyes were wide with surprise as she said that. When she was born, she continued, a strange woman in a long black cloak which swept across the stone floor walked directly into her mother's chamber. None of the servants had stopped her. She had a hood drawn far over her head. Of course, she had all this from her mother when she was a few years old.

The mysterious woman told her mother the child was very special, her birth had been foretold and she was to be known as Medwina La Fleur Blanche. Why? her mother had demanded wrathfully. This is why, came the answer. From under her cloak she produced a strange white flower with a scent so strong it filled the room intoxicatingly, causing her mother's eyes to glaze over and her body to become paralyzed. Later, her mother had the impression that this witch, or whatever she was, perhaps a sorceress, had rubbed the white flower over the infant's entire face and body, reciting incantations in a tongue her mother had never heard spoken before. She also had the impression, her mother related, that the woman whispered the name of the flower in the baby's ear.

After a few moments of silence, Meraugis asked: "And what is this flower called, as it has such strange magical powers?"

"If ever I let the name be spoken, those powers shall vanish . . . for me," she answered.

"How do you know this? Did the mystery woman whisper that in your baby ear as well?"

"In fact, I saw her again . . . for the first time in all these years. Once more she passed through the castle unchallenged. She brought me a white flower and told me it was the moment to create a spell. She told me the likely places deep in the forest where I might find this flower. It grows singly and there might not be another for leagues. They are night-blooming, especially under a full moon. Werewolves know of them and avoid them rigorously as the perfume can destroy their sense of smell."

He smiled openly for the first time. "You worked your spell on me, did you not? You sent me a delicious dream, one that drove me mad to come here and find you, don't deny it. My father, Bron . . . he is a powerful wizard and he told me my nightmares were luring a werewolf to us and your dreams were sent to lure me away, that is what he told me and Bron is never wrong."

"Did you enjoy the dream?" she asked demurely, gazing up at him from beneath lowered lashes.

"Oh, yes," he answered shyly, "but it was different. I mean, different from what happened today."

"How so, my beloved?" she asked, startling him with that word "beloved".

"Well, in the dream you arrived with a fabulous creature. Bron told me it was a unicorn and very few are vouchsafed a glimpse of one of those."

"The unicorn was here . . . you were asleep." She clapped her hands and Lion woke neighing. He galloped across the clearing to the exact spot where the creature had disappeared. There, he sniffed and whinnied rather piteously.

"Your horse knows more than you do," she told him without malice. "But then, he fell in love with her just before I sent him to sleep."

"Are you a witch . . . a sorceress?" he asked, his throat dry, the sound strained.

"No, just a determined young woman who was destined to enjoy the powers of a miraculous flower. Yes, and destined to help make you into a knight of great renown and worship so that I will be proud to be your wife." She laughed and grasped his hand between her two small ones. "Isn't that what you've always wanted? A sword which could not be defeated and a wife so lovely she could not be matched in all the land, throughout all the many kingdoms?"

He ignored the wife part. "And where shall I find a sword which cannot be defeated, which certainly means a magical one?"

"You already have one, my dear. Look at the blade." He did and it glowed with a deep mysterious light which had never been there before. In fact, it had always been rather dull and lacklustre.

"Now look at your medallion – I suppose your father the wizard gave you that Egyptian trinket – and you'll see it sparkles as well." She watched him jump when he saw the pouch next to the medallion. He opened it slightly and quickly closed it.

"It's that stuff, the stuff I saw in the dream, the stuff that comes off the unicorn's . . ."

"Stop calling it 'stuff'!" she cried vexedly. "Only because I have the power of the white flower can I approach a unicorn. Also, because of the white flower, I cannot take any of that powerful magic dust for myself. But I can take it for you, so show some appreciation. . . Stuff, indeed!"

"I'm sorry." He rose and walked to the stream, threw himself on his stomach and pressed his face into the water, drinking deeply. When he returned, she was smiling, the storm clouds gone.

"Sit down and kiss me, then plight your troth. In full recognition that we are each destined for the other. Forever and ever." She patted the ground as close to herself as possible.

"Did you – er – well, you know, how in the dream you – you know, I mean, you took that stu – that marvellous powder and you – you know, don't make me say it, Medwina."

"You mean, rub it all over you?" she asked with raised eyebrow. "Most certainly not. There are things you can do in a dream that are simply not proper anywhere else." She patted the ground again. "Be a good boy and do as I asked, then tell me all about you."

The knight rose up in his stirrups and shouted across the field. "Are you or are you not Sir Tristram?"

Meraugis looked at the shield facing him, but it bore no escutcheon, a black, featureless shield. The squire was busy disciplining his rebelious mount. One more rather ominous looking knight sat his horse some distance away. Meraugis answered he was not Sir Tristram. The challenger asked, who then? Politely, Meraugis said he was not at liberty to divulge that; however, he was prepared to joust.

He stole a quick glance to one side. There she sat, fully regaled as a squire in the clothes she took from her father's castle. Also bearing many other items of equipment, to say nothing of the fine horse she sat and a large purse of gold and silver coins. She sat that horse astride, in the manner of a male. If she were exposed as a woman, he would be ridiculed, proscribed, perhaps exiled, never to earn his knighthood. How had he been so weak? How had he allowed. . .? The knight facing him had taken lance from his squire.

Each turned his horse and rode to the border of the field before turning again, then going into a gallop, rushing at each other like maddened boars. The clang of their impact was horrendous. Meraugis retained his seat, the other did not. Nor did he rise from the ground. Before the squire could turn his horse to succor his master, the other knight spurred his horse forward.

"A mighty fall, O knight of mystery. Meseems I have come upon your glittering harness before. A sworn enemy of King Mark, am

I right? It was assumed you were either dead through Mark's treachery, or had taken the coward's ship to foreign shores. You may have bested poor Sir Ector, but you shall have more to contend with here . . . with Sir Palomides. Make you ready!"

As before, they came rushing at each other causing the wind to moan at their passing. Each had true placing of the lance and both were mightily unhorsed. As quickly, both were on their feet, dressing their shields and drawing their swords. The clanging of metal sent the birds in wild flight, stags bounding madly and each caused tremendous buffeting and soreness to the other until turning, Meraugis brought himself between the sun and his opponent, at which moment his sword blazed like a thousand torches compacted into one. To Sir Palomides, his opponent, the whole field simply disappeared. When the blow struck his helm, he collapsed on the ground, blood seeping out over armour and grass.

Medwina and Sir Ector's squire came quickly and undid the helm. It was a bloody wound to the scalp, but not a fatal one.

"Do you yield then, sir knight?" Meraugis asked. Palomides nodded as best he could, still not recovered enough to master speech.

"Treat him well," Meraugis ordered of the squire attending. He looked across the meadow and saw Sir Ector sitting up, helm off, rubbing his tortured head. "When he can travel, there is a small monastery but a league to the east. They are well versed in healing there."

Meraugis remounted and rode off, his squire catching him, bearing his shield and lance. When the trees had closed behind them, he turned and removed his helm.

"Do you realize just what could happen if you were exposed . . .?"

"Meraugis, do you love me?" Her tone brooked no evasion.

His eyes remained troubled and he drew Lion in, stopping to turn in his saddle. "Yes, I love you, but what does that have to do with . . .?"

"Gratitude?" she supplied. "You have just met two knights of great renown. Although a paynim, Sir Palomides has the respect of most knights and certainly, as well, King Arthur's court. You just defeated them both. Don't you realize your 'magic sword' so blinded Palomides he couldn't even see you to smite you? Why don't you just say, 'Thank you, my dearest one, what would I do without you and the great powers you bestowed upon me?'"

Not long thereafter, they espied a tattered yeoman running toward them, shouting and waving his feathered cap in the air. Breathless, he told them he and his company had been attacked by a giant. From a distance, in their march toward Camelot, they had seen two horses tethered to a tree. One of the men had sworn he recognized Sir Launcelot's horse and another was as sure the second belonged to Sir Tristram. When they arrived in front of a nearby cave, the most horrible giant issued forth, a great club in one hand and a battle axe in the other.

The end of the man's story was never heard by Meraugis and Medwina as the ground became a blur beneath the horses' galloping hooves. They tied the steeds near the other horses to help calm them. Inside the cave, all seemed gloomy after the bright sunlight.

"Go no further until our eyes are adjusted to the gloom," he whispered softly. As he did, a bright light appeared before them. Against the far wall, a bright fire blazed and, seated in chairs one either side of the fire, were Sir Tristram and Sir Launcelot. They were not tied, yet they did not rise. They sat, staring straight ahead, not blinking, ignoring totally their would-be rescuers.

"They are either drugged or under a powerful enchantment," Medwina breathed in Meraugis's ear. "And we have no spells to overcome their plight either way."

"We'll simply carry them out, drag them out and tie them to their horses and . . ."

". . . and have them as ornamental statues for the rest of their lives?" she asked sweetly. "We must break the spell!"

"But how?" he demanded more loudly now.

"Yesss . . . how?" a voice queried from the gloom to one side. "Soon, you shall join your friends . . . that is, if you do not die first." A black object detached itself from the darkness of the cave wall, taking a few lithe and stealthy steps toward them on all fours. Then the apparition rose on its hind legs and roared, nearly splitting the couple's eardrums.

"It's the werewolf," Medwina declared, "the very one from your bad dreams, I wot."

"Stay back," he answered, "I'll defend you." There was an insane laugh from the now circling werewolf, mocking the crouching youth, his great sword slicing the air before him rhythmically, enticingly, catching the firelight on its blade and beaming it blindingly toward the foul beast.

Medwina realized the werewolf was immune to such powers; then she saw its eyes blink rapidly as a particularly strong beam struck them. Only partially, she told herself. She slipped up behind her beloved and untied the rabbitskin pouch from about his neck. Still hidden behind her lover's back, she emptied a small amount of unicorn dust into the palm of her hand. Then she waited.

Just as she anticipated, the beast attacked, screeching so loudly the howling sound made the walls reverberate. Just as the clawlike hands began to close about the youth's throat, she blew the dust into the werewolf's eyes. Its hands flew back, covering its face.

"Strike off his head . . . NOW!" She pushed him forward, the sword arced, hissing like a serpent and the head went rolling on the floor, still howling. The body did not collapse, but the claws again reached blindly for her beloved's throat.

"Skewer the head with your sword and thrust it into the fire, quickly," she ordered. "Leave the body to me."

It took all of Meraugis's strength to hold the violent head in the flames. Now, the beast swung around and stalked Medwina La Fleur Blanche. She saw a faint, ghost-like impression of the werewolf's head form in the flickering light. And the phantom head was sniffing, sniffing her out without need of nose, eyes or ears.

Reaching down inside her tunic, Medwina La Fleur Blanche drew out the long-stemmed white magical flower given her by the unknown godmother. She thrust it toward the phantom head. Shadowy teeth, long and ugly, longer than a wolf's, snapped the flower off and spat it at her. She felt the stem stiffen in her hand, becoming harder than steel. She looked down and it glowed like silver. Without a second thought, she thrust the flower stem straight through the beast's heart. The body collapsed and melted. From the fire, a small ball of flame rolled across the cave floor. When it reached the puddle of blackness, all that was left of the werewolf's body, there was a loud explosion: everything vanished.

"How did you do that?" he asked Medwina, the sound of awe in his voice.

"You'd have to ask my mysterious godmother, I believe. Now, let's get them to horse and away from here." Before Medwina reached Sir Tristram, she saw his eyes blink tentatively. Yes, she exulted, the spell is wearing off.

"And where do you think you're going?" a voice like one hundred drums boomed from the cave entrance. They spun about and saw a giant nearly doubled over in order to get through. When he straightened, he had to stoop again to clear the ceiling.

Medwina La Fleur Blanche remained motionless beside the still inert figure of Tristram. She noted his sword lying on the floor next to the seat. When she looked up, she saw the fiery brilliance of her dearheart's sword snapping about like shafts of lightning. The giant merely closed his eyes and swung wildly with his club in one direction, then sweeping before him with the battle axe. He so filled the area between the four prisoners and the exit, escape was well-nigh impossible.

"Circle," she hissed. Meraugis heard her and began to edge about carefully. Just then, he took his first glancing blow from the club and went down on one knee, shaking stars out of his eye sockets.

"Up, up, circle more," she cried out. He did and she began to see the giant's back. As soon as the huge monster's eyes were turned the other way, she didn't hesitate an instant, but picked up Sir Tristram's heavy sword and edged her way around the wall. She took a deep breath, ran forward and slashed with both hands and all her might, severing the giant's legs at the knees.

"There, you bully, now you can battle someone your own size!"

The shock of being on his knee stumps, looking directly into the youth's eyes, then hearing that voice behind him caused the giant to swing his head about. Meraugis lost no time, smiting mightily, removing head from trunk.

"Ho, Launcelot, awake!" Sir Tristram shouted, rising shakily to his feet.

"Ho, varlet, halt!" Medwina shouted just as loudly, dropping the sword and racing out of the cave in pursuit of something none of the others had seen. In truth, she had to change clothing quickly without being detected.

Only moments later, a beautiful young woman entered the cave, dressed in white; she remained poised on her toes for a moment, scanning the three faces before her, ignoring the unsightly giant in three sections on the floor. She ran directly to Meraugis.

"My champion," she warbled dramatically, clinging to her hero, "you have broken the spell and saved my life. I am yours forever and ever."

Everyone spoke at once. Tristram insisted. They would go directly to Camelot, Meraugis would be knighted by King Arthur, Launcelot and himself; three blades resting on head and shoulders, and the wedding would follow immediately. Sir Launcelot agreed, for in sooth, was young Meraugis not Tristram's cousin?

* * *

When Meraugis and Medwina La Fleur Blanche entered the great Hall, Arthur, Guenever and a host of the Knights of the Round Table were waiting to greet them. A cushion was placed on the floor in front of the dais where the two thrones rested. On one knee, Meraugis bent his head respectfully. As the three swords touched his shoulders and head, a great cheer went up.

"Now," said the Queen, "all we need is for someone to give the bride away, for she comes among us as an orphan."

"Such a lovely lass I never did see," said one knight, raising his hand.

"Medwina La Fleur Blanche, will you accept Sir Merton, the Earl of Sarandon?"

"What name did she say?" Sir Merton asked of the man beside him.

"Didn't hear it, but she is indeed most pretty," he answered.

"Medwina, is that not your father?" Meraugis whispered to his bride-to-be.

"Of course, but he hasn't seen me in so long, no wonder he would not recognize me. Which reminds me. An adventure here or there, fine. But you are not knight-erranting endlessly, understand?"

"But what would I do at home?"

"Don't you understand our destiny? We shall raise some of the best knights ever seen in this world. Now that *is* a worthy cause."

Before he could answer that most unsettling statement, the couple were called to stand before the King who would join them together. Horns blared and the musicians went at it with gusto.

Sir Mador in
THE FIGHT FOR THE QUEEN

Leonora Lang

Leonora Alleyne Lang was the wife of Andrew Lang (1844–1912), the writer and folklorist who was best known for his long series of coloured Fairy Books. *Lang is often regarded as the author of many of the stories in his anthologies, but most were written by his wife and her circle of friends. The following story, which comes from* The Book of Romance *(1902), concerns an incident after the Grail Quest where the death of Sir Patrise finds Guinevere accused of murder.*

After the quest of the Holy Graal had been fulfilled, the few Knights that had been left alive returned to the Round Table, and there was great joy in the Court. To do them honour the Queen made them a dinner; and there were four and twenty knights present, and among them Sir Patrise of Ireland, and Sir Gawaine and his brethren, the King's nephews, which were Sir Agrawaine, Sir Gaheris, Sir Gareth, and Sir Mordred. Now it was the custom of Sir Gawaine daily at dinner and supper to eat all manner of fruit, and especially pears and apples, and this the Queen knew, and set fruit of all sorts before him. And there was present at the dinner one Sir Pinel le Savage, who hated Sir Gawaine because he and his brethren had slain Sir Lamorak du

Galis, cousin to Sir Pinel; so he put poison into some of the apples, hoping that Sir Gawaine would eat one and die. But by ill fortune it befell that the good knight Sir Patrise took a poisoned apple, and in a few moments he lay dead and stark in his seat. At this sight all the knights leapt to their feet, but said nothing, for they bethought them that Queen Guenevere had made them the dinner, and feared that she had poisoned the fruit.

"My lady, the Queen," said Sir Gawaine, who was the first to speak, "this fruit was brought for me, for all know how well I love it; therefore, madam, the shame of this ill deed is yours." The Queen stood still, pale and trembling, but kept silence, and next spoke Sir Mador de la Porte.

"This shall not be ended so," said he, "for I have lost a noble knight of my blood, and I will be avenged of the person who has wrought this evil." And he turned to the Queen and said "Madam, it is you who have brought about the death of my cousin Sir Patrise!" The knights round listened in silence, for they too thought Sir Mador spake truth. And the Queen still said nothing, but fell to weeping bitterly, till King Arthur heard and came to look into the matter. And when they told him of their trouble his heart was heavy within him.

"Fair lords," said the King at last, "I grieve for this ill deed; but I cannot meddle therein, or do battle for my wife, for I have to judge justly. Sure I am that this deed is none of hers, therefore many a good knight will stand her champion that she be not burned to death in a wrong quarrel. And, Sir Mador, hold not your head so high, but fix the day of battle, when you shall find a knight to answer you, or else it were great shame to all my court."

"My gracious lord," said Sir Mador, "you must hold me excused. But though you are a king you are also a knight, and must obey the laws of knighthood. Therefore I beseech your forgiveness if I declare that none of the four and twenty knights here present will fight that battle. What say you, my lords?" Then the knights answered that they could not hold the Queen guiltless, for as the dinner was made by her either she or her servants must have done this thing.

"Alas!" said the Queen, "no evil was in my heart when I prepared this feast, for never have I done such foul deeds."

"My lord the King," cried Sir Mador, "I require of you, as you are a just king, to fix a day that I may get ready for the fight!"

"Well," answered the King, "on the fifteenth day from this come on horseback to the meadow that is by Westminster. And if it happens that there be a knight to fight with you, strike as hard as you will, God will speed the right. But if no knight is there, then must my queen be burned, and a fire shall be made in the meadow."

"I am answered," said Sir Mador, and he and the rest of the knights departed.

When the King and Queen were left alone he asked her what had brought all this about. "God help me, that I know not," said the Queen, "nor how it was done."

"Where is Sir Lancelot?" said King Arthur, looking round. "If he were here he would not grudge to do battle for you."

"Sir," replied the Queen, "I know not where he is, but his brother and his kinsmen think he is not in this realm."

"I grieve for that," said the King," for he would soon stop this strife. But I counsel you, ask Sir Bors, and he will not refuse you. For well I see that none of the four and twenty knights who were with you at dinner will be your champion, and none will say well of you, but men will speak evil of you at the court."

"Alas!" sighed the Queen, "I do indeed miss Sir Lancelot, for he would soon ease my heart."

"What ails you?" asked the King, "that you cannot keep Sir Lancelot at your side, for well you know that he who Sir Lancelot fights for has the best knight in the world for his champion. Now go your way, and command Sir Bors to do battle with you for Sir Lancelot's sake." So the Queen departed from the King, and sent for Sir Bors into her chamber, and when he came she besought his help.

"Madam," said he, "what can I do? for I may not meddle in this matter lest the knights who were at the dinner have me in suspicion, for I was there also. It is now, madam, that you miss Sir Lancelot, whom you have driven away, as he would have done battle for you were you right or wrong, and I wonder how for shame's sake you can ask me, knowing how I love and honour him."

"Alas," said the Queen, "I throw myself on your grace," and she went down on her knees and besought Sir Bors to have mercy on her, "else I shall have a shameful death, and one I have never deserved." At that King Arthur came in, and found her kneeling before Sir Bors. "Madam! you do me great dishonour," said Sir Bors, raising her up.

"Ah, gentle knight," cried the King, "have mercy on my queen, for I am sure that they speak falsely. And I require by the love of Sir Lancelot that you do battle for her instead of him."

"My lord," answered Sir Bors, "you require of me the hardest thing that ever anyone asked of me, for well you know that if I fight for the Queen I shall anger all my companions of the Round Table; but I will not say nay, my lord, for Sir Lancelot's sake and for your sake! On that day I will be the Queen's champion, unless a better knight is found to do battle for her."

"Will you promise me this?" asked the King.

"Yes," answered Sir Bors, "I will not fail you nor her, unless there should come a better knight than I, then he shall have the battle." Then the King and Queen rejoiced greatly, and thanked Sir Bors with all their hearts.

So Sir Bors departed and rode unto Sir Lancelot, who was with the hermit Sir Brasias, and told him of this adventure. "Ah," said Sir Lancelot, "this has befallen as I would have it, and therefore I pray you make ready to do battle, but delay the fight as long as you can that I may appear. For I am sure that Sir Mador is a hot knight, and the longer he waits the more impatient he will be for the combat."

"Sir," answered Sir Bors, "let me deal with him. Doubt not you shall have all your will." And he rode away, and came again to the Court.

It was soon noised about that Sir Bors would be the Queen's champion, and many knights were displeased with him; but there were a few who held the Queen to be innocent. Sir Bors spoke unto them all and said, "It were shameful, my fair lords, if we suffered the most noble queen in the world to be disgraced openly, not only for her sake, but for the King's." But they answered him: "As for our lord King Arthur, we love him and honour him as much as you; but as for Queen Guenevere, we love her not, for she is the destroyer of good knights."

"Fair lords," said Sir Bors, "you shall not speak such words, for never yet have I heard that she was the destroyer of good knights. But at all times, as far as I ever knew, she maintained them and gave them many gifts. And therefore it were a shame to us all if we suffered our noble King's wife to be put to death, and I will not suffer it. So much I will say, that the Queen is not guilty of Sir Patrise's death; for she owed him no ill-will, and bade him and us to the dinner for no evil purpose, which will be proved hereafter. And in any case there was foul dealing among us."

"We may believe your words," said some of the knights, but others held that he spoke falsely.

The days passed quickly by until the evening before the battle, when the Queen sent for Sir Bors and asked him if he was ready to keep his promise.

"Truly, madam," answered he, "I shall not fail you, unless a better knight than I am come to do battle for you. Then, Madam, I am discharged of my promise."

"Shall I tell this to my lord Arthur?" said the Queen.

"If it pleases you, madam," answered Sir Bors. So the Queen went to the King, and told him what Sir Bors had said, and the King bade her to be comforted, as Sir Bors was one of the best knights of the Round Table.

The next morning the King and Queen, and all manner of knights, rode into the meadow of Westminster, where the battle was to be; and the Queen was put into the Guard of the High Constable, and a stout iron stake was planted, and a great fire made about it, at which the Queen should be burned if Sir Mador de la Porte won the fight. For it was the custom in those days that neither fear nor favour, love nor kinship, should hinder right judgment. Then came Sir Mador de la Porte, and made oath before the King that the Queen had done to death his cousin Sir Patrise, and he would prove it on her knight's body, let who would say the contrary. Sir Bors likewise made answer that Queen Guenevere had done no wrong, and that he would make good with his two hands. "Then get you ready," said Sir Mador. "Sir Mador," answered Sir Bors, "I know you for a good knight, but I trust to be able to withstand your malice; and I have promised King Arthur and my lady the Queen that I will do battle for her to the uttermost, unless there come forth a better knight than I am."

"Is that all?" asked Sir Mador; "but you must either fight now or own that you are beaten."

"Take your horse," said Sir Bors, "for I shall not tarry long," and Sir Mador forthwith rode into the field with his shield on his shoulder, and his spear in his hand, and he went up and down crying unto King Arthur, "Bid your champion come forth if he dare." At that Sir Bors was ashamed, and took his horse, and rode to the end of the lists. But from a wood hard by appeared a knight riding fast on a white horse, bearing a shield full of strange devices. When he reached Sir Bors he drew rein and said, "Fair knight, be not displeased, but this battle must be to a better knight than you. For I have come a great journey to fight this fight, as I promised when I spoke with you last, and I thank you heartily for your goodwill." So Sir Bors went to King Arthur and told him that a knight had come who wished to do battle for the Queen. "What knight is he?" asked the King.

"That I know not," said Sir Bors; "but he made a covenant with me to be here this day, and now I am discharged," said Sir Bors.

Then the King called to that knight and asked him if he would fight for the Queen. "For that purpose I came hither," replied he, "and therefore, sir King, delay me no longer, for as soon as I have ended this battle I must go hence, as I have many matters elsewhere. And I would have you know that it is a dishonour to all the knights of the Round Table to let so noble a lady and so courteous a queen as Queen Guenevere be shamed amongst you."

The knights who were standing round looked at each other at these words, and wondered much what man this was who took the battle upon him, for none knew him save Sir Bors.

"Sir," said Sir Mador de la Porte unto the King, "let me know the name of him with whom I have to do." But the King answered nothing, and made a sign for the fight to begin. They rode to the end of the lists, and couched their spears and rushed together with all their force, and Sir Mador's spear broke in pieces. But the other knight's spear held firm, and he pressed on Sir Mador's horse till it fell backward with a great fall. Sir Mador sprang from his horse, and, placing his shield before him, drew his sword, and bade his foe dismount from his horse also, and do battle with him on foot, which the unkown knight did. For an hour they fought thus, as Sir Mador was a strong man, and had proved himself the victor in many combats. At last the knight smote Sir Mador grovelling to his knees, and the knight stepped forward to have struck him flat upon the ground. Therewith Sir Mador suddenly rose, and smote the knight upon the thigh, so that the blood ran out fiercely. But when the knight felt himself wounded, and saw his blood, he let Sir Mador rise to his feet, and then he gave him such a buffet on the helm that this time Sir Mador fell his length on the earth, and the knight sprang to him, to unloose his helm. At this Sir Mador prayed for his life, acknowledging that he was overcome, and confessed that the Queen's innocence had been proved. "I will only grant you your life," said the knight, "if you will proclaim publicly that you have foully slandered the Queen, and that you make no mention, on the tomb of Sir Patrise, that ever Queen Guenevere consented to his murder." "All that will I do," said Sir Mador, and some knights took him up, and carried him away to heal his wounds. And the other knight went straight to the foot of the steps where sat King Arthur, and there the Queen had just come, and the King and the Queen kissed each other before all the people. When King Arthur saw the knight standing there he stooped down to him and thanked him, and so likewise did the Queen; and they prayed him to put off his helmet, and commanded wine to be brought, and when he unlaced his helmet to drink they knew him to be Sir Lancelot du Lake. Then Arthur took the Queen's hand and led her to Sir Lancelot and said, "Sir, I give you the most heartfelt thanks of the great deed you have done this day for me and my queen."

"My lord," answered Sir Lancelot, "you know well that I ought of right ever to fight your battles, and those of my lady the Queen. For it was you who gave me the high honour of knighthood, and that same day my lady the Queen did me a great service, else I should have been put to shame before all men. Because in my hastiness I lost my sword, and my lady the Queen found it and gave it to me when I had sore need of it. And therefore, my lord Arthur, I promised her that day that I would be her knight in right or in wrong."

"I owe you great thanks," said the King, "and some time I hope to repay you." The Queen, beholding Sir Lancelot, wept tears of joy for her deliverance, and felt bowed to the ground with sorrow at the thought of what he had done for her, when she had sent him away with unkind words. Then all the knights of the Round Table and his kinsmen drew near to him and welcomed him, and there was great mirth in the court.

Sir Fergus in
MY MOTHER, THE HAG

Brian Stableford

Although this story is about Sir Fergus he never appears in it. It's really about the effect that Fergus had on those about him, in particular Fergus's encounter with the "hairy hag" of Dunnottar. Fergus of Galloway *was one of the many interpretations of Arthurian legends that sprang up during the popularity of the medium in the twelfth and thirteenth centuries. It was written by the Norman Guillaume le Clerc, perhaps around the year 1209, almost certainly at the request of Alan of Galloway in memory of his great-grandfather, the real Fergus of Galloway who died in 1161. He was a descendant of the Celtic lords of Galloway and rebelled against the increasingly anglicized kings of Scotland. Guillaume immortalized him as one of Arthur's knights.*

Brian Stableford (b. 1948) is a renowned writer of science fiction and fantasy, with over fifty books to his credit. They include The Empire of Fear *(1988),* The Werewolves of London *(1990),* The Angel of Pain *(1991),* Young Blood *(1992) and* Serpent's Blood *(1995).*

As my mother reluctantly submitted to the ravages of old age her memories of the past became increasingly vague. She even had trouble remembering me, although I had always been a very dutiful son. I suppose I was too insignificant to be well remembered, because I was the least talented of of all our kind. That has always been the curse of the *vargr*-folk; as each generation spent its magic, wantonly or not, there was so much less to pass on to the next. Had I been born a mere hundred years later I'd have been no more than human.

By the time she died even my mother was only a *little* more than human, but old age is more than the creeping assault of wrinkles and brittle bones; it transforms the mind as well as the body. As her memories of the past faded by degrees into the mists of might-have-been, her knowledge of the future became increasingly distinct. Not that this provided any great or enduring advantage to either of us, alas. Had her powers of anticipation become more complete and far-ranging she might have assembled a worthwhile legacy to hand down to me, but as they became more specific they became ever more narrowly focused on the manner of her death and the motives of her murderer – and that only served to trouble us both.

She had known the exact moment of her death for centuries, of course, and she had always known the name of her killer, but it was only in the last few decades of her life that the whole history of her destroyer became clear to her. Fate has a tendency to insult as well as to injure those who rebel against its dictates – as the *vargr*-folk did, it seems, by the mere fact of their existence.

When I was very young, my mother was still capable of talking about her destiny with a measure of philosophical indifference. "A violent death is the best way to go," she used to say, cheerfully. "It's quick, and it means you don't have to start rotting until you're actually dead. And if you have to die by the sword, it might as well be the sword of a hero. Fergus of Galloway will be a hero among heroes, a paragon of all the virtues, conspicuous even in such an august company as the knights of the Round Table!"

I heard a good deal about Fergus in those days. I heard about his vanquishing of the Black Knight and the nasty dwarf that was the Black Knight's companion. I heard about his mighty exploits at the siege of Roxburgh – which he could not have contrived, of course, without the glorious shield which he stole from my mother – and his punishment of Sir Kay in the great tourney at Camelot.

I protested, as I was bound to do. "How can you sing the praises of the man who will kill you?" I demanded. "And how can you rejoice that the shining shield which ought to be *my* inheritance will be the means of his winning fame, fortune and the hand of the lady Galiene?"

"Even *vargr*-folk must die," she told me, "and it is useless to blame the instrument for the necessity. As for your inheritance, the shield is not mine to dispose of as I wish. It is Fate's, and its disposition is Written."

I came to hate the words Written and Fate, pronounced as if they were somehow finer than all others. What I am doing now is, of course, not Writing but only writing.

The first note of doubt didn't creep into my mother's tales of her forthcoming demise until I was half-grown, and it was a tentative anxiety at first.

"Of course," she would add to her description of Fergus's triumphs in Arthur's great tourney, pensively, "Arthur won't be Charlemagne, let alone Alexander the Great. He'll only be a *local* king – but he'll be very well thought of, for all that. There will always be some who'll think of him as *the* King. A few will yearn for his return – and that of his glorious company of knights – long after he's faded into the mists of might-have-been. Nor will Fergus be the most famous of Arthur's knights, in spite of the best efforts of his biographer Guillaume le Clerc. Lancelot will outshine him in memory, and Gawain, and Perceval too. Even the name of the blackguard Kay will be better known."

My mother's infection with doubt served to redouble my complaints and protests. "It's not *right*," I was wont to wail. "Whatever Arthur is or is not, this liege-man of his must be reckoned a perfect monster. What kind of knight is it that slays a mother and makes an orphan of her loving child? How can that possibly be reckoned *chivalrous*?"

"In actual fact," she would reply, with scrupulous fairness, "the ten commandments of chivalry will not contain any specific injunction against doing injury to members of the female sex, although maidens and mothers of the meek variety will obtain protection under commandment three, which instructs a knight to serve as the defender of the weak. Unfortunately, the *vargr*-folk are dealt with – *en masse* as it were – by commandment six, which exhorts knights to make war against the Infidel *without cessation and without mercy*. You and I, sweet child, are not to be numbered among the people of the book, and we thus constitute fair game, even in our breeding season."

Those were relatively quiet days, although my mother could still be reckoned a seductress. However quiet she consented to become, though, she was *never* meek. When there was no one to love but a man she condescended to love men, but she always did so fervently. It always seemed to me that they loved her all the more in consequence, and ought on that account to have prized her – and all others of her vivid kind – far above their own insipid kin. That, alas, was not their way.

There is something in the strongest of mere men which cannot abide strength in others, although that does not stop them thinking very highly of themselves and naming themselves heroes. Their unreasoning hatred of the *vargr*-folk – and, for that matter, of all things exotic – is but a reflection of their pride in themselves; because they have no magic of their own they are hell-bent on destroying those who have. If I have outlived all others of my kind it is not because my death was never Written, but because my magic is so slight and unobtrusive.

By the time I was on the threshold of puberty I knew from my mother's accounts of him that Fergus of Galloway would think even more highly of himself than most men, even in an age of vanity rampant. How I hated him! I had fervour of my own, you see, although it was never the equal of my mother's. These days, I'm more tolerant of the company of men than I was then, but I've always preferred the company of honest vipers.

The ability to enjoy the company of vipers was then and still remains my only magic. It was a mean inheritance from one so talented as my mother, but I never blamed her for it, nor felt the lack of any greater sorcery. The one inheritance whose Fated loss distressed me was that fabulous shining shield whose glow was every promise, every glamour, every glory.

I was very glad when my mother began to speak of her future murderer less tolerantly. I stopped being glad when I realized that growing doubts and anxieties about the eventual configuration of her legend had begun to cast a shadow over her life and make her permanently sad. It was a shadow which grew and deepened with her increasing decrepitude. The more she remembered about what was Written and what was yet to be written, the more she found to regret – and the more she found to regret, the faster her beauty and her power faded.

"In terms of his actions and ambitions," she told me, the day after I brought home the baby dragon which was doomed to die with her while hardly more than an infant, "Fergus of Galloway will be a knight without compare. Unfortunately, his posthumous reputation will be clouded by the carelessness or mischievousness of his biographer, Guillaume le Clerc."

"In what way clouded?" I asked, more out of politeness than concern. I was momentarily distracted by the lovely dragon, whose misfortunate future had not yet been revealed to me.

"Many readers will think the tale of Fergus mere imitation of Chrétien de Troyes' much better-known account of the life of Perceval," she told me. "Some will deem the imitation tongue-in-cheek and suspect it of irony."

I didn't understand the notion of irony then, although I understand it well enough now. I couldn't see that it mattered overmuch how distant future generations of *men* would judge the reputation of her nemesis; the *real* tragedy, it seemed to me, was that there would be none of the *vargr*-folk left in the world to know the truth and curse the name of Fergus of Galloway.

"I don't mind dying," my mother said, repeating it as if it were a ritual spell. "Everyone must die, although I confess that I can't understand the alacrity with which humans rush to their deaths, slaying others as they go. A thousand years and one isn't a long life, by sensible standards, but it's perfectly adequate. I don't even object to the fact that men will rejoice at my passing, for I freely admit that we are of a different kind, whose mere existence stands in the way of their determined progress. What I do object to is the thought that the record of my demise – my only epitaph, in their tradition – will come to be considered a kind of jest, an item of parody. Whatever else I am, and whatever else I may be deemed when I am lost in the mists of might-have-been, I am *not* an item of parody. If I must be reckoned as a mythical monster or a figment of a fever-dream, so be it – but I'd far rather be a nightmare than a nonsense."

"You'll never be either, Mother dear," I told her, trying to soothe her with gallantry. "For as long as your name is known, you'll have the reputation of a *femme fatale*."

She was sufficiently fond of me then to ruffle my hair by way of thanks, albeit in a slightly rueful fashion.

"My name will *not* be known," she told me, plaintively. "I shall be known only as the hag of Dunnottar."

I had never thought to ask her before – perhaps subconscious fear had made me avoid the question – but I asked her then, for he first time, what Fate had in store for me.

"Not everything is Written," she told me, "and not everything that is Written can be known. All I know of your future is that it will be long in extent – but that your name will never be recorded, unless you can record it for yourself."

"But what will your accursed Guillaume le Clerc say about me?" I demanded. "How will Fergus of Galloway prevent me from saving you when he comes to steal the shield?"

She looked at me tenderly while I cradled the tiny dragon. "Guillaume will say not a word," she told me, sorrowfully. "When Fergus comes you will not be here, and he will never suspect your existence. Your lovely pet will challenge him, but *all* serpents are easy meat for men like him, who will drive dragons and a dozen other kinds to dark extinction."

What a deadly phrase! To the likes of Fergus of Galloway my friends, my companions in magic and my brothers in blood were *easy meat*! The insult so offended me that it seemed hardly worth the bother to notice that my very existence would go unrecorded by those who would make legends of the appalling Fergus and his master Arthur.

When disappointment had finally driven out the last trace of her cheerful equanimity, my mother lost the ability to accept the compliments I gave her and insisted on construing them as ironic taunts. Had I schooled my tongue more cleverly she might have liked me a little better and remembered me a little longer, but I couldn't help voicing my own opinions as to the manner in which she ought to have been remembered.

I was, after all, a dutiful son.

On the last occasion when I tried to flatter my mother with the assertion that it was her beauty and her charm that ought to be recorded in history she scolded me for a fool.

"What will be will be," she informed me bitterly, "and they will call me hag! *Hideous* and *shaggy* are the words that vile clerk will use to record the knight's impressions as he gallops towards the causeway where he will slay me. I will have long, plaited whiskers and my misshapen teeth will be discoloured. *Fiend* I will be called, and *demon*. I will be charged with lunatic self-confidence in delivering the first stroke of my scythe, and idiotic recklessness in embedding its point so deeply in a marble pillar that I cannot pull it out again. Thus will my ugliness become a kind of comedy, and poor Fergus a petty prefiguration of Quixote, the greatest of all buffoons!"

"*Poor* Fergus!" I retorted, unwisely. "*Poor* Fergus, is it, who will cut off your hands at the wrists before driving the long blade of his sword into your belly and up through your vital organs? *Poor* Fergus, is it, who will carry away our fabulous shining shield so that he may use its glamour to liberate his Galiene and to unhorse Lancelot himself in the joust? *Accursed* Fergus I will call him – thrice-damned Fergus if there is any justice in the world beyond the world."

"There *is* no world beyond the world," she told me, with dire contempt. "For all the patience of Fate and all the work she has invested in her Writing, the mists of might-yet-be are as infinite and as inescapable as the mists of might-have-been."

She would not condescend to hate her killer! She was perfectly ready to loathe and despise the imbecile cleric charged by fashion to record his exploits for a world over-hungry for mirages of gallantry, but she would not curse the man himself.

I know now that I ought to have let the matter rest. Indeed, I ought to have done my utmost to *lay* it to rest. I ought to have distracted my beloved mother from her growing preoccupation with the legend of her passing.

I did try, but she became so obsessed that the only way to distract her from the subject of Fergus of Galloway and the literary treachery of Guillaume le Clerc was to ask her about other writings to come.

"They will be many," she assured me, "but vague. Fancy will be pile upon fancy, until gaudy confusion covers the last fugitive remnants of actual memory. Even the fate of Arthur is unclear, although I cannot tell whether it is as yet un-Written or merely doomed to be unwritten. He will fall out with his bastard Mordred, that much is clear. They will meet on a field of battle but Arthur, being Arthur, will try to make peace. Then the mist will descend – both an actual mist and a mist of uncertainty, for in the writings of men the literal and the metaphorical are very confused. The battle will be fought, it seems, although there is a blur on the future page which prevents my seeing precisely how or why. Afterwards . . . well, even men will call that afterwards a Dark Age."

"And will Fergus of Galloway fall in that battle?" I wanted to know. "How will he meet *his* death?"

"I cannot tell," she said, the words weighing heavily upon her. "For all my antiquity and all my sorcery, I cannot tell."

It seems to me now that I might have done more to save my mother's memories from the void of oblivion had I only spoken to her of happier times with the same insistence and precision that she employed in speaking of times to come. I dare say that had I only known how, and taken trouble to cultivate the art, I might even have helped her to think better of me. It is true that I had only the one magical talent, and that a rather vulgar one – there has always been something slightly suspect about kinship with serpents – but I had other virtues. At the end of the day, I *was* a dutiful son, in spite of all my errors.

If I had only had the gift of lightening her spirits, I might have helped my mother to think more about my future than her own. I have now reached the point in my life at which I know nothing at all about what lies before me, except for the moment and manner of my death, because I have run to the end of the little that my mother was able to tell me. Sometimes, I wonder whether that is because she *really* could not remember me well enough to look any further into my future, or whether she simply could not bear to tell me what she foresaw. On balance, I would rather it were the latter; I think I could bear to face a future full of horrors more easily than I can live with the apprehension that my mother did not love me at all.

For whatever reason, there came a time when I could not divert my mother from contemplation of her doom, and how it would be weighed in the fraudulent scales of human estimation. I should not have become angry with her, but I did. I even taunted her myself, when it all became too much to bear.

"If your future offends you, Mother dearest," I howled at her, as if I might secure my place in her memory simply by raising my voice, "then have the courage to defy it! Given that foresight has revealed to you every mocking detail of the rubbishy record that Guillaume le Clerc will make of your presence on this earth, you ought to be able to use what you know! If you know where and when this Fergus of Galloway will be born, slay him in his cradle. If you know the names of his enemies and when they will strike at him, go to them in advance and give them better weapons. If you know that he must have your precious shield no matter what, refuse to defend it. Are we not *vargr*-folk, when all is said and done – and are not the *vargr*-folk rebels, even against God Almighty?"

"You do not understand, my darling fool of the family," she informed me. "Fate is Fate, and has the means to cheat all those who rebel against it. What will be written truthfully is Written already, and the best that any creature of fate can ever obtain is to obscure a part of the lesser writing with the mists of might-have-been. There is little consolation in that, I assure you. If the ultimate result of all our rebellions is to relegate our best achievements to the realm of misremembered fantasy, we will become less than nothing in the thrust of history. It is better to be an item of parody than *that*."

"Perhaps I should be glad that I don't understand," I said. "Perhaps, because I don't understand, I can go to Galloway and strangle the infant Fergus in his cradle. Perhaps, because I don't understand, I can stand with you on the causeway when you meet him, and cut him in two before he severs your wrists. Perhaps . . ."

"No," she said, with a softness infinitely more powerful than wrath, "you cannot. Lack of understanding always weakens; it never empowers. Better to understand, and accept, that you cannot alter any of these things. You cannot alter that which is already Written. Whatever work you do, it must be done in the margins of Fate's pages; only there can creatures of our kind hope to have an effect on the great tide of the world's becoming. We are *vargr*-folk, you see: vampires and shapeshifters, giants and dwarfs, keepers of dragons and makers of wonders, miraculous children of the eternal she-wolf. There have been those among us who spoke all the tongues that birds and beasts know, and even knew the languages of stones, but only humans *write*. That is why, in spite of all their imperfections, they are the darlings of Fate."

"One day, Mother dearest," I told her, still the rebel even while I wept, "*I* will write. If I must become human to do it, I will write. And before then, however I may and however I might, I will avenge you. If it is not Written how and where and when Fergus of Galloway will die, I will be there to carve his blood-stained hands from his arms, and laugh at his helplessness."

I think that was the last time she ever reached out to touch my head. She did not ruffle my hair, as she had done when I was smaller, but she touched my brow with tenderness.

Perhaps she was saying goodbye to my fading memory, although she must have known that I would be with her for years to come, and had centuries still to live.

"That would be no vengeance," she said to me. "Poor Fergus is as much a slave of history as any other man. To take an eye for an eye or a hand for a hand is a human way of counting, of which even they will become ashamed in time. Our kind is not adapted to take vengeance; we know too much of what will be, and the only plans that we may make are those which will help to precipitate the Written actuality from the mists of might-yet-be. What satisfaction can there be in serving as a jealous instrument of Fate? In any case, poor Fergus is nothing but a symptom and a symbol of a phase in moral progress; you might as well strike out against the Round Table, against chivalry itself."

I know, now, that my mother was telling me – as best she could, in the near-delirium of her decrepitude – to desist. What she wanted me to do was to become a little wiser, a little more understanding. What she wanted me to do was to cease to think of such ignoble matters as *vengeance*. Perhaps she had forgotten that I was the fool of the family, or mistaken the magnitude of my foolishness.

I misconstrued her words. Perhaps I did so deliberately; I honestly cannot tell. I too am plagued by the mists of might-have-been, and I am not what I once was. I write, but in order to do that I have had to give up even the meagre portion of magic that I once had.

I took my mother at her word. I left Fergus of Galloway alone. I did not attempt to strangle him in his cradle, and I never tried to strike his hands from his body as he struck my mother's from hers.

Instead, I struck out at the Round Table itself, and against chivalry itself. *You might as well*, my mother said, and so I did.

I did it in the only way I could, according to her account. I struck from the margins of Fate's forewritten page, unsuspected even by those who can read *between* the lines of the tale that Fate is busy writing. I can say, with a confidence born of experience, that there *is* satisfaction in serving as a jealous instrument of fate; what came to pass was already Written, but nowhere was it Written that I should be the one to do it, nor was it ever recorded by human hand that I was the one who did – but it is written *now*.

You have never heard my name. Even those of you who have read the tale of my mother's death in that vile mock-romance by Guillaume le Clerc, learning thereby to love and laugh at *poor* Fergus of Galloway, will not have suspected my existence, until now. You *will* have read, of course, in your beloved Malory, how Arthur's army met Mordred's on that dismal field of battle, and how they agreed between themselves that they would not fight, and that both companies would withdraw – so long as no man on either side should draw a sword.

You will have read, too, that it was a striking viper which caused a single knight to draw his weapon, precipitating the conflict which brought about the death of Arthur, the end of chivalry and the last deep fall of Darkness.

Was that a tragedy, do you think? Was it a terrible accident of Fate?

No, it was not. It was *payment*, for what Fergus of Galloway did to my mother, the so-called hag of Dunnottar. It was *payment* for all that was done by every knight that ever slew a dragon, or ever made war on the precious *vargr*-folk.

I shall not write my name here, for I would rather remain the nothing that your writings have made of me; by that means I add insult to injury and am glad to do it. Know, though, that the *vargr*-folk were possessed of power as well as glory, and that even the last and least of their line had magic enough to carve nightmares from the mists of might-have-been.

Arthur *might* have been more than a local king, had he been given freer rein; chivalry *might* have been more than a farcical fraud, if it had only found more fertile soil in which to flourish. Such hopes as those evaporated into the mists which rose as Arthur's final battle began – the battle which my mother – my mother, *the hag* – had foreseen but dimly as an event which never would be written or explained *in full*.

By the time my mother died she was, I will admit, a hag of sorts – but she had been a true temptress and worthy daughter of Lilith for centuries before that, and I would have that fact known. She should not be reckoned any less because she spent her own legacy so fully that her son had but a single magical talent, and that a meagre one.

As you now know, a great deal may be accomplished by a dutiful son who knows the language of vipers, if only he picks his moment carefully enough.

[Note: The story of Fergus of Galloway's encounter with the "hairy hag" of Dunnottar is recorded in lines 4093–4203 of the Frescoln manuscript of Guillaume le Clerc's Fergus, *rendered into English in pp.66–68 of D. D. R. Owen's Everyman translation of 1991. The ten commandments of chivalry to which the notional author refers were formulated and numbered by Léon Gautier in chapter II of* Chivalry *(1884; translated into English 1891). The most notable not-quite-full account of Arthur's last battle, to which the notional author also refers, is of course to be found in chapter iv of book XXI of Malory's* Morte d'Arthur. *The notion of the* vargr*-folk, which here refers collectively to all the supernatural beings of legend, owes its origin to a double meaning pointed out by Sabine Baring-Gould in chapter IV of* The Book of Werewolves *(1865), which equates* vargr *with "restless" as well as with "wolf".]*

Sir Artegall in THE DRAGON OF CAMLANN

Darrell Schweitzer

Artegall is another of the early companions of Arthur, known from the earliest Arthurian writings. He is sometimes identified as the first Earl of Warwick, and is perhaps associated with another hero of early English romance, Guy of Warwick. In Arthurian legend he is one of the few survivors of Camlann. Darrell Schweitzer (b. 1952) considers this survival in rather more mystical terms. Schweitzer is a prolific American critic, editor and writer, mostly of fantasy, including the novels The Shattered Goddess *(1982),* The White Isle *(1990) and* The Mask of the Sorcerer *(1995), and the short story volumes* We are all Legends *(1981),* Tom O'Bedlam's Night Out *(1985) and* Transients and Other Disquieting Stories *(1993).*

"I hope to God everything will be settled this day, once and for all," said my older brother Constantine, that same one who later became king of the Britons.

I rode by his side as the armies arrayed themselves on the field of Camlann.

"Whether by fighting or by truce?"

"Either way. Over. Done. Damn it all."

He spurred his horse and galloped toward his own company, then drew rein, turned, and came halfway back, standing in his stirrups to shout, "Oh Artegall, I almost forgot! There was a message from Mother this morning! For you! She says take care of Valentinus!"

He waved. I think he was laughing as he turned again and went to join his men.

I cursed. I actually smote my mailed hand with mailed fist, making a loud crack.

It figured. Constantine and I were sons of a great lord, of Cador of Cornwall. We were mighty men. Great deeds were expected of us, and already Constantine had won fame. His exploits were celebrated by the singers. But me? What was the message for Artegall? *Take care of your baby brother*. Don't let the little darling come to harm. He's such a sweet boy. Well, maybe so, but I didn't think he would make much of a knight. He was too young, thirteen, short and slender, his voice still soft; and never before out of Cornwall, innocent to the world, horribly incongruous here, *now*, when everything *was* likely to be settled in a single day and a lot of brave men would be in Hell by suppertime.

Such were my own dark thoughts as I assumed my own position, at the far end of Arthur's right flank, facing Mordred's left.

And the dear boy Valentinus came riding up to me.

"Isn't it *exciting*, Artegall? Isn't it? Look at all the knights!"

He wasn't my brother anyway, but a foundling, deposited on our doorstep by some stray knight or holy hermit perhaps, or, as was sometimes whispered, by an agency less holy, one more mystery of our rocky, shadowed land.

But he was my squire, and I was stuck with him.

"Isn't it grand?" he jabbered again, standing up in his stirrups for a better look. "Oh! There's the King's standard. And Sir Mordred's."

I turned to look.

"So they are."

At that moment, the last hope of Britain hung in the balance. Already there had been fighting, at Dover and elsewhere, when Arthur returned from France in all his wrath, the unfinished campaign against Lancelot left behind him. Heroes were already dead, including Sir Gawain. I wept for him, and for the others. This was no childish game. It wasn't exciting. It wasn't grand. Men who had fought and feasted as brothers, knights of the

Round Table, were at one another's throats. God, yes, I wanted it to be over too, but I was so very afraid of how it would have to be resolved.

But as those standards stood together, as the final parley was held, there was still a chance for peace.

I couldn't explain any of this to Valentinus, who would probably be sorry to miss the fun of a good battle.

"You're a bloodthirsty little barbarian," I said to him suddenly.

"Huh?" He sat down in his saddle.

"You don't have the slightest idea of what any of this means, do you?"

He looked at me as if I'd suddenly grown an extra head, like a giant in a story. "Of course I do! A battle is a time for a knight to win *glory*!"

Then suddenly there was no time to explain anything. You've heard how in the midst of the parley, a serpent made to strike one of the knights. (On whose side? Does it matter?) The knight drew his sword to defend himself, and at the sight of flashing steel *everybody* rushed forward with a great roar –

I don't know. I was in another part of the field. It might even be true. Certainly there was a roar, as the fighting rippled toward us, as the two armies came together like waves closing over a spot where a stone has been hurled into the sea.

Nobody had time to give any orders. Arrows whizzed like bees. One struck Valentinus's shield and he let out a surprised yelp. I twisted in my saddle to see that he wasn't hurt and yelled, "Stay close, boy! Stay close!"

It was all a rage, a rush, a muddle, thundering chaos. Nobody made a proper charge. There wasn't room for that. Long lances were useless, the ground too rough for horses to get up speed. I remember the great mass of mounted men, pressed close together, coming at us. We closed together against them. I struck here, there, as I thrust and parried, as my sword hacked through shields and mail, clove breast-plates, shattered skulls. Men shouted; horses screamed; men died as their mounts stumbled and the riders plunged beneath the mass.

Once again I heard a shrill, wordless cry, and turned again, afraid that I had lost Valentinus after just a few minutes. *A child! A child! What a damned stupid place for a child*! And I fought my way toward him, like a swimmer against a tide, and just as I reached him the whole mass of our army went tumbling backward into a deep, wooded ravine.

Trumpets blasted. Shouting rebels rushed upon us, like a tide, yes, a tide of death, closing over us one last time; a wave of flailing steel that bore me out of my saddle and landed me among sharp stones with a crash.

But I was not badly hurt. I caught hold of a man, pulled him out of his saddle, raised myself, lost hold of the horse again, but at least I was standing, and the wave had passed over me, the armies losing all definition, the Battle of the Ditch degenerating into an incoherent mass of struggling men and horses.

I caught a glimpse of Valentinus again, his helmet gone, his yellow hair flying wild, his pale face smeared with blood, his eyes filled with a panic that bordered on lunacy. He was swinging his mace with both hands, like a bat, because it was too heavy for him. I'd told him over and over not to do that. It leaves your guts open, to be skewered on the next available spear.

He went down and I fought my way to him, my mind quite far from any thoughts of glory. I grabbed somebody by the collar and yanked him up, and beheld a dark, snarling face. Was this a knight I had once feasted with? I struck the head off. Blood exploded over me.

Then I had hold of Valentinus, who wriggled like a hooked fish while three skin-clad Saxon mercenaries came at us all at once. The only thing I could do was swing the boy like a club, his feet flailing into their faces; then I rolled one of them off my shoulder and caught him under the chin with a vicious jab of my spiked elbow.

That was when the marvels truly began, I think, the delirium, the miracles; the *silence*, where time itself ceased to flow and arrows hung motionless in the air. It seemed that the sky darkened, that it was already night, but instead of stars the sky was filled with fiercely burning torches, which flickered down through the treetops.

And the forest spoke with a vast sigh, as shadows rushed out from the trees and washed over me; and I was very cold, my body gone numb, drifting on a great wave of blood and darkness, like a twig in a whirlpool. Valentinus was still with me. I felt him struggle, then cling to me. I too was struggling, drowning, and it seemed that the earth opened up.

A mouth appeared in the side of the hill, and it spoke to me, saying, "Artegall, you who would serve King Arthur, enter freely and of your own will."

But I'm not sure how freely I did anything. I can't remember. Maybe I replied something. There was absolute darkness. Then a lantern floated before me, flickering and sputtering, its fire burning blue. Strange knights rode beside me, in slow, pantomime motion. Perhaps I was borne on a bier of some sort. I saw the knights, clad all in glimmering green, their horses like things of dust and shadow given shape by some magic; and at times there were no knights at all, but animals and birds, ravens circling and shrieking, foxes and bears and stags running before me, led by an exquisitely white hart, which was not a hart at all, but a lady mounted on a white mare, clad in the blue of the morning sky, with the sunlight in her hair.

I cried out in amazement that she must be the Queen of Heaven, but she only laughed, and her laughter was like a winter wind rattling icy branches.

Valentinus was nearby somewhere, shrieking and gibbering.

And the mouth of the hillside closed over us and swallowed us up, and there was only darkness and silence and the smell of damp earth.

Some while later I awoke in twilight, on a hillside, looking out over a landscape that was all shadows, shot through with blues and greens, the colors and shapes shifting like the deep sea when faintly struck by sunlight.

Lights danced around me like fireflies; and grew larger, resolving into shrouded human figures, into animals and birds, then fading into a faintly luminous smoke. The air filled with exquisite music no earthly instrument or hand could have produced.

Glowing faces floated in the air like wind-borne leaves, human faces or nearly so, their mouths forming words I couldn't make out.

Valentinus stirred beside me. He sat up and stared in amazement, while groping about, for his mace I suppose, though to what purpose I neither knew nor cared.

Now the lights assumed shapes again; and I beheld the supernally beautiful queen and all her train, her knights mounted on horses of wind and dust, her courtiers hollow behind, like incomplete shapes of gossamer filled with a faint breeze and given a semblance of life. When they turned just so, their open backs revealed, they were almost invisible.

"Where *are* we?" Valentinus whispered.

As his knight, I was responsible for his education. Like a schoolmaster, I demanded, "Where do you think?"

As the phantom train drew around us and the Queen came

forward, the boy said, "I think only that our souls are in gravest peril."

That was a wise and careful answer. Were I his schoolmaster, I would have commended him. But I wasn't. I lost all control. I leapt to my feet and harangued the boy, the Queen, anyone and everyone, the very sky itself with its alien stars.

"We don't have *time* for any of this! Not *now*!"

Valentinus let out a yelp as if I'd struck him. He grabbed my hand, to restrain me from who knew what.

He probably thought I'd gone mad when I turned my back on the beautiful lady and her knights as if Valentinus and I were alone, and continued my discourse.

"Don't you *see*? Don't you *understand*? Isn't it all so terribly *customary*? Where are we? On the border marches of death, if not in the grave itself. What's going on? We're having an *adventure*. There will probably be a *quest*. All very grand, the sort of thing to tell to the Christmas court when everybody's at the table swilling themselves silly and it comes time to review the year's chivalrous accomplishments. But we haven't time for any of that, Valentinus. Truly. Arthur may be *dying*. He needs us *now*. Sure, we may illuminate our souls and gain wisdom in the course of a fine adventure, but what's the use if there's no Camelot left and Arthur's head is on a pike and Mordred sells the country directly to Hell? Well? Well? Answer me that."

The boy could only gape. It was the Queen who spoke, and the sound of her voice made my whole body go chill and numb.

"Artegall, son of Cador, I find you deficient in courtesy."

I turned and bowed to her.

"I crave your pardon, then, lady. The passion of the moment got the better of me."

She laughed, and her courtiers laughed also. The sound was like a wind rattling icy branches.

"Artegall, you are a knight of the Round Table and therefore bound by certain oaths, one of which is never to refuse a lady a favor. Isn't that so?"

"You know that it is."

"Very well then. There is a dragon to be slain, a most terrible beast, which impedes the execution of all my designs."

"Lady," I said, bowing once more, trembling as I did so, not so much for any concern about my soul or my reputation or any chivalrous obligation I might be trying to evade, but simply for fear of what might be happening to Arthur. "Gladly will I undertake this task for you, as any knight would, be he of the Round Table or otherwise, for what man can possibly refuse such a beautiful lady? But I ask a favor of *you*. Can't it *wait*? My king is fighting for his life. The last I saw of the battle, it didn't look good. Please. Wait. If this makes me less than a perfect knight, so be it. Let me come back and serve you afterward."

Her manner grew more firm, and she did not laugh.

"No, I cannot wait. I charge you now. But remember that time in this land is not the same as it is in yours, so perhaps none at all will pass on the battlefield."

I bowed my head. "Very well, then. I shall undertake this quest."

Valentinus stood up beside me and declared, "I too will undertake it, for I am this knight's squire and – "

His voice broke into a shrill squeak. I never thought him more ridiculous than at that moment. I wanted to swat him for his presumption, for speaking out of turn in front of a queen, if nothing else.

But the Queen smiled on us both, and the anger left me.

Then the wind bore us up into the darkness, and for some time the fairy knights rode beside us on their horses of air and dust. Then they were gone and we found ourselves alone in a rocky tunnel. We climbed toward the night sky and the familiar stars and finally emerged onto a battlefield, where black birds circled by starlight and wounded men cried for succor. Here and there, robbers came to rob the dead and dispatch the dying.

I threw my sword down, cursing, and I probably would have blasphemed had not Valentinus caught me by the hand and said, "Hold! Remember that quests come from God for his own purposes! It's not for us to understand!"

"That's something you read in a damned, pretty book, in some damned, pretty story. Who the Hell cares? We've been betrayed. It's all over. Arthur's dead and we weren't even there to die with him!"

I fell to my knees and the tears streamed down my face like blood.

Valentinus knelt beside me and pressed my sword back into my hands. "You don't know that. Our side might have won."

"I rather doubt it," I said sourly.

"Still you must hope – "

My reply was incredibly foul.

"Take up your sword," said Valentinus, "remember your courtesy, and let us fight the dragon together."

I didn't even swat him for his ridiculous presumption. Here he was instructing *me*. The problem was, he was right. A knight accepts death gladly, but he does not despair.

The boy stood up. He'd acquired a spear and shield from somewhere. He looked all the proud warrior. I sat back and gazed up at him and sighed.

"You think this is a game, don't you?"

"No! Look! There's the dragon!"

I leapt to my feet and looked to where he pointed, and I too beheld the dragon, as huge as a cloud rising up over the horizon, blotting out the stars.

"Come on then," I said, and like a couple of lunatics chasing after the Moon, we pursued the dragon throughout the night, shouting war-cries to draw its attention, waving our weapons, banging on our shields. But ever it remained vast and remote, like a shadow that had fallen on the whole world as we straggled across the battlefield and along roads strewn with corpses, past burnt castles and towns.

We did not catch it, nor ever drew near, though we heard always the thunder of its voice, like the sound of water rushing into a great cataract.

At last the dawn came. We both fell down exhausted, in tears, knowing that we had failed. The sun began to rise. It dazzled our eyes, but then we found ourselves once more in twilight, on the purple hillside in Faerie – for I did not doubt the place – and the Queen and her court gathered around us once more.

"You have not fulfilled your quest, Sir Artegall," she said.

"I'm not done trying."

"Even so, I grant you a respite. Come and feast and make merry with us."

"I cannot make merry because my king is in peril, but I will come with you, because I cannot refuse a lady, as you are well aware."

"I am indeed," she said, and she laughed again, that exquisite and infuriating laughter. I wanted nothing more than to draw my sword and strike off her head, chivalry be damned; but somehow I controlled myself.

Besides, I was supposed to be educating this stupid boy, and that would hardly set a good example.

Knighthood, as I had told him a hundred times, is not glory, not gratification, but sacrifice. It is doing what you *don't* want to do because it has to be done.

So we entered into a wondrous hall, filled with many marvels, where the floor was of black glass and the stars of the Earth's night sky swam like glowing fish beneath it. Wizards in brilliant robes, all blue and golden and scarlet, with wands in their hands, leaned over to study the stars and learn what was to come upon the Earth. Every so often one of them would dip his wand through the glass, as if into the water of a still pond; and the glass would ripple faintly; and the wizard would draw his wand out again, all aglow with unearthly fire; and holding the burning wand aloft, the wizard would rise into the air, to vanish into the darkness above. I looked up to see the specks of firelight wink out, one by one, like stars eclipsed by a slow-moving cloud.

In that hall I saw a fountain that spewed gold, a bronze head that prophesied; there were books that turned their own pages and spoke. An island of glass swam in a lake of blood, somehow encompassed within that place, where distance and time were not as human senses knew them, and I seemed to be walking forever without crossing any distance, and sometimes distances shifted in ways I cannot describe, and I seemed to walk a hundred miles in a single step.

Pipers played on silver stairs. The lords and ladies danced to the music, whirling like leaves and dust in a great storm.

The lady bade Valentinus and myself to sit beside her at a high table atop a dais, and a repast was served: the most succulent meats and fruits the eye has ever beheld.

The boy reached for an apple. I caught hold of his wrist.

"Do *not*. I charge you upon your life. If you take even one bite, you become of this place, and you won't be able to leave."

Wide-eyed and afraid, Valentinus drew his hand away.

The Queen looked on, whether amused or angered that we did not eat, I could not say. Her face was an unreadable mystery.

It was a greater agony to just sit there, watching the dancers, watching the wizards work great illusions, watching the centaurs dance or the fairy-folk dance, *wasting time* – a far greater agony that any wound I'd ever suffered in battle, far worse than anything a torturer could devise. Here was the iron resolve of knighthood tested.

It was time for sacrifice.

"Lady! Great Queen! Let me go *now* and fight the dragon and get this over with! Please!"

She looked at me once more with her inscrutable gaze.

"Do you really think you can?"

"Yes, if I can get close. Or die trying!"

"Then go at once."

She clapped her hands. The hall vanished. There was an instant of darkness, a sound of thunder; and I found myself in a pit of fire, where the very stones burned and ran molten and the sky was filled with smoke and red flame.

Valentinus huddled beside me. We both covered our dazzled eyes with our shields, but then a gentle voice spoke and someone pulled my shield away.

"Brave Artegall. Brave Valentinus. Fear not. The fire cannot burn you, not yet."

I lowered my shield and in time I could see again. I let out a cry, first of joy, then of terror, for I was face-to-face with an old friend, with Sir Gawain, but I knew that Sir Gawain had died for Arthur at Dover when the war against Mordred began. Indeed, I could see on his face the terrible wound that had killed him.

"I'm looking for a dragon – " I amazed myself as I blurted that out.

"I know where it is to be found."

So we followed him through the land of fire, across a battlefield where dying men lay all aflame, screaming in their agony, while robbers robbed them, for all that they likewise burned, and screamed; where cities and castles burned; where fiery champions crashed into one another on the roads, their spears and shields shattering, their steeds crumbling into ash.

"Artegall!" my squire shouted above the universal roar of burning, tugging on my belt for attention. "Are we in Hell?"

"On its border, I think. But this is where we have to go."

He clung to my belt as we both bent against fiery wind, as cinders and hot stones bounced off my shield, as we climbed a mountain that streamed with liquid fire; as we followed Sir Gawain into a castle made of half-molten gold where there were precious stones set into the walls and men screamed and burst into flame and died even as they tried to pry the stones out of the walls. Others fought among themselves over what they had stolen, oblivious to their own pain.

Truly this was like Hell, but there were no demons here, only men, tormenting themselves.

In the great hall of that castle, we discovered even more treasure, heaps inestimable and undreamed of, deadly to the touch.

There, too, stood a great mirror.

"Here is your dragon," said Sir Gawain. "Go on. Slay it."

I raised my sword to strike the mirror, but as I did so the knight reflected therein raised his visor and I saw my own face. I paused only an instant, and in that instant the face was transformed into that of a dragon more terrible than may ever be described. Its voice was a human one, like thousands of men shouting all at once, in lust and anger and agony.

Yet I fought it, there, in the place of fire, as the monster burst out of the mirror, huge and covered with golden scales too bright to look upon, a mountain of fire and living metal and molten earth, its black, smoking wings spread to cover the whole world. I fought against its great claws and gnashing teeth. I knelt behind my shield against the fury of its breath. Valentinus hurled his spear down the dragon's throat, but that was of no consequence, any more than was my sword. I struck once more every blow I had ever struck in every battle I had ever known. Madness and hurt and furious memory swirled together like lurid paints stirred in a pot.

I fought for King Arthur, raging that I should be here and not at his side when he needed me most. I fought to get this damned quest over with and get back to Camlann, even if all I'd ever do there was get hit by the first stray arrow or be run down by a riderless horse.

No, I told myself. No. I cannot die *here*.

Thus I fought the dragon in an endless, timeless moment, throughout eternity; but to no use, for my weapons could not pierce its armor, even those few times when I could get through the flames close enough to strike.

Valentinus fought bravely beside me. I will give him credit for that.

He fought, just as uselessly as I.

In the end I could only stand up and weep as the dragon snatched the sword out of my hand; it swatted me about for a time, as a cat does tormenting a mouse; then I was in its crushing jaws, looking up in despairing amazement at the enormous, golden tooth which protruded from my chest like a spear; for the dragon had impaled me, and I hung there dangling, pierced to the heart, impossibly still alive.

"Arthur!" I cried out. "I'm sorry!"

I dreamed then a terrible dream that went on forever, that Sir Gawain led me through a forest of pikes standing in the earth. On each was the head of a knight I knew, all of them alive, their eyes filled with fire as if their faces were furnace doors with little eye-holes cut in them. They mocked me, saying, "You didn't do very well, did you Artegall? You deserted your king when he needed you the most."

I tried to argue with them, pushing through the pikes, searching for Arthur. I didn't find him. I should have taken hope from that. But the search was as endless as the number of the slain at Camlann, and I took only despair.

When I awoke again, hurt full sore from many wounds and burnt with fire, but somehow not dead, I opened my eyes on the pale blue sky of an earthly dawn. There was mist all about, slowly thinning.

The world swayed, rose, fell.

It took me a while to realize that I was on a boat.

The Queen I had seen before leaned over me where I lay. She touched my burnt face with her soft hand, and the pain went away. But now a glamour had fallen from her, and I could never have mistaken her for the Queen of Heaven. This was a beautiful woman, truly, but a woman I knew, whom I had seen before. She was Morgan le Fay.

"You are my master's enemy." I tried to rise, but she gently pushed me back.

"I hated Arthur because I loved him, and loved him because I hated him. It's all a muddle, a mystery, but it's too late for that, Sir Artegall. Alas, the battle of Camlann is over. Most of the knights are dead. Mordred, too, is dead, and Arthur lies near death, from a blow Mordred dealt him."

Then I could only weep from the uttermost depths of my despair, knowing I had failed in all things. I was like Job, but without his faith; and I would have cursed God, had not Valentinus intervened.

"Artegall," he said, his voice more steady and grave than I had ever heard it before, "did you riddle the meaning of our adventure?"

"I don't have time for riddles . . ."

I rolled over and beheld him where he sat at a table. A feast had been set before him. As I watched, he ate of an apple. But I saw too that this was not the first bite he had taken. And I saw that he was dressed in a gown of purest white, and there was not a wound or a burn or a streak of dirt on him.

I had lost him too. Everything.

He put down the apple.

"I have discovered the meaning," he said.

"And what makes you so smart?"

"While you were resting, I ate of the Apple of Knowledge and of the flesh of the Salmon of Wisdom. This latter is a most marvellous fish, which lives in a pool in the Forest of Broceliande. No matter how many times men partake of it, it remains whole, and swimming in Broceliande."

"That's funny. I thought it was Scotland."

I was losing my reason. I was babbling. I wept all the more.

"Why do you weep, Artegall?"

"If you're so knowing and so wise, it should be clear enough."

"I know that Queen Morgan seeks, at the very last, to aid King Arthur, to carry him in this boat to Avalon, where he may be healed. But first the dragon must be slain, which blocks her way, the dragon of pride, of avarice, of the wrath of men. Only then may she come to Arthur. That is the meaning of the riddle."

"But the dragon is still in the full vigor of its health. So we haven't accomplished very much, have we? I haven't even managed to keep you out of trouble . . ."

Once more I wept.

"Artegall," said Valentinus slowly, "you always told me that knighthood means sacrifice, not glory. You would gladly have sacrificed yourself for Arthur, wouldn't you?"

"You know I would."

"Even so, I sacrificed myself. I ate of the apple, freely, for Arthur's sake."

"But the dragon still lives – "

"I know how to kill it, at least for a time. I am sure it will return, for the world is filled with wrath and pride, and no one in it may be free of sin. I have made myself *not* of this world, and now the task is mine."

"This is how my knighthood ends," I said, falling back, sobbing inconsolably, "bested by a boy."

Queen Morgan's attendants raised me up, and I watched as Valentinus walked upon the water of a misty lake. He wore no armor, only the diaphanous white robe, and the sunlight seemed to shine through him at times, making him almost invisible. His bare feet spread ripples from his path. He blew on a tiny silver horn, and the waters parted and the dragon rose up in all its fierceness.

Mindlessly, I fumbled for my sword. Morgan le Fay stayed my hand.

The dragon opened its terrible jaws. Its teeth gleamed, silver, then golden, like swords in the sunrise. Yet Valentinus walked between those teeth, into the great mouth, which closed over him.

Then the dragon sank down, leaving only bubbling foam behind.

And the Queen held up a magic glass, in which I could watch the boy's progress. He wriggled in the dark, through the endless labyrinth of the dragon's guts, never faltering from his course, until he reached the very centre, where he cut out the dragon's heart and stilled its thunder.

And he returned, walking across the lake out of the mist, holding up the steaming heart. Then the boy was beside me once more, not bloody, but transfigured, like an angel, his face so bright that I could not look on him.

Yet I had the presence of mind to tell him to kneel. With my eyes closed, I got out my sword, and groping gently with the blade, I touched him on one shoulder.

"I'm sorry. I'm the only one here to do this and I'm afraid I don't really have the authority." I touched him on the other shoulder and said, "Nevertheless, arise Sir Valentinus, knight of the Round Table."

"And that's it," I said to Morgan le Fay, somewhat later. "My knighthood is at an end. What use am I now?"

"Of much use," said she, "for you are a knight of great worship, if flawed like all men; for in your travails you sought only to serve Arthur and protect Valentinus, never desiring glory or fame for yourself. That is why the fires burnt you only a little and did not consume you. That is why even the dragon's tooth did not kill you."

"But what use?"

The rest may well have been a dream. So might have been the whole adventure, dreamed in delirium as I lay stunned in the ditch at Camlann. Men say that Arthur died there, that he impaled Mordred on his spear even as Mordred struck him a terrible blow with his sword, piercing him unto the brainpan. Maybe. I didn't see. I was in another part of the field.

But I can tell you that a smaller boat came alongside Morgan le Fay's vessel, and in it was King Arthur, his face and armor all covered with blood, for he was wounded unto death, yet a little alive. The women there, even Queen Morgan, wept as they saw his terrible wound. I touched it. I tried to raise Arthur's head up when he was too weak to raise it himself.

His blood burned me. It made that white scar on my hand, *there*.

He opened his eyes. I think he recognized me. He tried to speak, but blood poured from his mouth.

Some men say that Arthur was carried to Avalon and is not dead. That may be so, but I cannot bear witness, for I was too much of the earth, never having partaken of the Apple of Knowledge or the Salmon of Wisdom; and when the Queen's boat passed into the mist again, I was not on it, but found myself knee-deep in water.

I waded ashore, and there met Sir Bedivere, one of the very few knights left alive. He told me how he had hurled Excalibur into the lake.

That was his story. I told him mine.

Who is to say which stories are true? These things are riddles, to be told again and again until the meaning comes clear.

In this way, humbly, patiently, we serve Arthur.

Sir Modred in UALLANNACH

Parke Godwin

In the Arthurian legend Mordred or Modred is portrayed as the ultimate villain, the traitor who usurped Arthur's kingdom and who died with Arthur in the final battle of Camlann. Others view Mordred more sympathetically. Parke Godwin (b. 1929) is renowned for his Arthurian novels Firelord *(1980) and* Beloved Exile *(1984). When he was writing Mordred he was conscious that he could not allow Mordred the full development of character that was needed because, for the most part, he remained off stage. Several years later Godwin returned to Mordred to allow him his voice in "Uallannach", a word that Godwin himself concocted to mean "love" in the language of faerie.*

> *"I don't know what I expected of Modred. Something more human, a little glad of life, but when all your life has been running and fighting, perhaps glad has no meaning. For this I yearned so many years? . . . This cold, purposeful, malignant, girl-pretty serpent of a son who'd cut my throat and walk away whistling."*
>
> *– Arthur of Britain, Firelord*

Be Modred Belrix, son of Gern-y-fhain Morgana of Reindeer fhain, most beautiful of all Prydn women, whose presence was greater than that of all other gerns.

No – I must use your Briton-speech for tale-speaking. Must say *I* and *you* and *mine* and *yours*. Tallfolk need such words, lacking the closeness and sharing of my people, the Prydn. You call us "Faerie" – a poor sound like all your words, so weak you must use five to make one of our meanings that come from the first days of the world. Like *Dronnarron*. If I tell you it means "the good green time that was," you know it only as the blind man who puts his hand to a stone and thinks he knows the mountain.

Like *uallannach*, which means love to endure forever. Shape it with care on your lips. For that love and hate come from the same heart and hurt, the same word bitten off like the end of a thread or a life means hatred to last as long. My mother's search was for *Dronnarron*, mine for *uallannach*. To find one, to satisfy the other.

I was always soft clay to the shaping hand of Morgana, molt bronze in her sure mold. Every drop of me set in the lines of her purpose, but one betrayed Morgana in seeing beyond her vision to the folly and hopelessness of it all. Following Morgana, our Prydn had become a power north of the Roman Wall, rich in gold, flocks and child-wealth. Now Morgana would go to her third husband, Artos, my father, who led all of Britain-fhain. She would ask of him a gift of land to be ours forever. I knew it was madness and years too late.

Briton-men have always thought my father – their great Arthur – was got on a Cornish woman by Uther. Like most of their beliefs, only half true. Uther was his father, his mother the wife of a Cornish lord but of Prydn birth, born to a woman of Reindeer fhain in a year of famine and placed as changeling in a Roman cradle. When Artos came into manhood, Morgana put a binding spell on him to make him love her. But magic can turn in the hand of the fool. My mother it was who lost her heart, loved Artos all her life. As I loved her and hated him.

Artos comes for the end now. I see the dust his horses raise as they follow the bait I laid for them, a trail of Orkney blood from far south of the Wall to this place Britons call Camlann. The end will be soon, so I will speak of beginnings.

This Samhain past I saw Artos Belrix for the first time, since he left Morgana before I was born. First sight, but ai! did I not know him all my life? Was not his shadow, as hers, over me from the first? Did beg Morgana not to rade south into Britain-land. She promised only caution, even when Artos said she might come only with her own family. There were five of us: Morgana, myself, her husbands

Cunedag and Urgus, and my young uncle, Drost. We were brought by Artos' trusted companions, Bedwyr and Gareth. They showed respect to Morgana, but I did not trust them overmuch.

I first beheld Artos in his great rath at Camelot. Mother had eyes only for him, so I let mine be everywhere. This Camelot might only seem less of an enemy than Pictland. The tallfolk lords in the hall wore clothes of fine wool and rich linen, worked in fashions and colors I would not have thought possible, but the men carried swords and even the women little knives in their girdles. Were not so different from Picts, then, only cleaner.

Artos and his *adhaltrach* Gwenhwyfar sat on raised chairs at the end of the great hall. He left her and came down to Morgana. Now my eyes were all for him, as she had stuffed my ears with him, him, *him* since the day I left her body.

I tried to read him like the land before me, for threat and places to hide, and could see at first no danger in him. A big man, even for tallfolk, with hair like the light of Lugh-Sun at midsummer. Nothing of Prydn about him except the marks of Reindeer on his cheeks. I felt a strength in him. Will not take that from Artos before I kill him. A strength and a spirit like that of my uncle Drost, of gentleness and laughter. That could be false, as Prydn can crouch still on open moor and look like stone. Agrivaine's Orkneymen are learning that before they die.

Belrix put his hands in respect to my mother's belly, and all I could think was: *did leave her*. He spoke in our tongue. Morgana, whose presence was always a robe of dignity about her, in the blink of an eye became a child, hurling her arms about Artos's neck while he swung her up like a child before she remembered that dignity and presented me to my father.

"Greet thy wealth, husband."

I hated him. Did leave her.

Not only the sign of Reindeer cut on his cheeks, but his eyes. They were Prydn; not blue or brown like tallfolk, but the gray of ours, and set *so* in his face. Truly he was born of a Prydn mother, she who was left in a Roman cradle in a hungry year.

But did leave my mother. *Do not search for thyself in my face, Artos. Be not there.*

Morgana bade me speak to him. "Father," I managed, though the warmth did not come with the word. He searched my face and drew aside my sheepskin vest to study the scars on my chest.

"Thee's fought," said the great, golden Belrix. "Who scarred thee?"

This one was my blood, then. This one made me. "Venicones," I answered. "Dead ones."

I saw in his eyes something that hoped and was disappointed because I turned it away. There is softness in you, I thought, but none in me. We have turned on the hunters and hunt them now. We have burned them, killed their flocks, taken their child-wealth to grow as Prydn. They call us demons, which is Roman-tongue for "small gods." That pleases me, for we were in this island since Mabh and the Time of the Ice. Bow to a small god, Artos Belrix.

"Now greet the second wife of Belrix," Morgana commanded me. I obeyed, thinking she gave too much presence to tallfolk. Mother had changed much in her last seasons, but her word was rule. I approached Gwenhwyfar, seeing the fear and disgust she tried to conceal. She wore the sign of the Christ-man, a cross of iron. She is of the Parisii who believe Prydn are reborn spirits of the evil dead who cannot look on or touch iron. Although she knows many ways and tongues, Gwenhwyfar cannot blot this lie from her mind. I speak her fair, little as I know of Briton-tongue, and read what can be seen in her white face.

Yes, there is courage and strength in Gwenhwyfar, and a hate strong as mine. Yet, like Belrix, she seems to be searching me for something she wishes to find. Only a flicker, a flash of color like the finch swooping low over heather, then gone.

"You are unclean," that look tells me.

I stretch my hands to her stomach – she shrinks back from me – and say, "May *adhaltrach* have many years and child-wealth."

I think of that as the Orkney horsemen draw closer across the moor. They have killed their own kind in treachery. How neatly their hot blood will work with the cold in mine, the *uallannach*. Morgana is murdered. For that murder, I rade south of the Wall as she never would. No longer do I take children to raise as she did but leave them hacked where they fall. Like wielding a sword in gorse, will hew a space about me, will kill all I can find.

These Orkney lords are the men of Prince Agrivaine and a gift to me. We were stalking Agrivaine's brother Gawain, who rested carelessly on the open moor. I planned to kill them while they slept (as my mother was slaughtered in Camelot) but Agrivaine came and did our killing for us even as we watched. He trampled his own brother and all with him. Prydn do not kill each other like this. Do have no word for it, only wonder that *we* are called devils.

One of Gawain's men was not killed. After the murderers left, he staggered up, dragged the great body of Gawain to horse, and moved off toward the south. *Then* I saw my vengeance for Morgana. Artos was not far away, still at his peace meeting with Gwenhwyfar and the Parisii. Do not wonder that I know this; wherever Prydn ride, we take pains to know who else is there and why. This helps to keep us alive.

Gawain was oath-brother to Artos. When some of my Prdyn wanted to finish the one survivor, I said no. "He will take this deed to Artos, who will follow Agrivaine with all his *combrogi*-men after him. Agrivaine is our bait. The game comes to us."

When Agrivaine's band pauses to rest, the horses spent, we wait the night through. Before the moon goes down, one of the Orkney shakes off his cloak and rises to make water. My arrow takes him in the heart, and he falls without a sound. When the others find him, they know they are stalked. Time is precious. They must leave the dead to the ravens and ride on.

It is easy to hide from tallfolk. You do not know the meaning of stillness or how to look and really see. When we take two more of Agrivaine's men in daylight, he dashes here and there about the moor to find us. Fool: we are in plain sight, but he cannot see. Artos will; must find a different plan for Artos.

Yes . . . he is following. Will drop more bait for the Bear of Britain, kill him and spit on him as he dies. I swear this by all Morgana was to me. Follow, Father. Greet for the last time your child-wealth out of her body.

I wait. The ravens wheel in the sky.

She was the first and one enduring love I ever knew. My earliest memory was the sound of her voice and the sweet warmth of her breast against my mouth. My first remembered sight should have been a firelit rath and fhain gathered about the firepit. Not so, a different fire, a burning Votadini village and Morgana lifting me to horse, Prydn folk shouting to each other, amazed by their victory. Someone screaming. My mother splashed with tallfolk blood. No Prydn child born in the same winter as me can recall a season when we were not killing and running, or when the summer raths were not full of tallfolk children growing up as our own. Nor a time when we were hungry. Because of Morgana, there was always plenty.

Life was not always so for us. As I grew, Cunedag and Urgus told me of the old life. We lived in a shameful peace with tallfolk and took that miserable portion they left with us. Taixali, Venicones and Votadini had the good lowland pastures and left us the rocky hills. My mother changed that. Never was change so needed.

"Artos knew truth," she told me many times. "Prydn must find a new path."

Morgana's meaning will not be easy for you to understand, but if there be one picture to show the difference between Prydn and tallfolk, it is in how we see and touch the earth. Each tallfolk tribe claims to own so much of the land. To us, the word for earth is "Mother." There is no word for owning in our tongue. Prydn were the first in Britain. Mabh herself, greatest of all gerns before Morgana, cut Britain from the larger lands to the east to make it an island, but no Prydn has ever taken one piece of Mother over another and called it his. The tale-speaking of Mabh is given each Lughnassadh by the gerns to their folk before moving on to winter pasture. Twice in each round of seasons, Prydn moved with their flocks, scornful of the way the later, bigger people rooted in one place and scratched at the earth to coax food from it. Until all the places were "owned" by tallfolk and there were more of them than Prydn because, somehow, more of their child-wealth lived through their first year. This was so tens of seasons before my birth. Artos and Morgana were the first among Prydn to see how we were losing, that we could die out of the land unless there was change.

Change needs youth and strength. First daughters became gerns, but Morgana's elder sister Dorelei was a spirit of love and peace, more concerned with children than change. The spirit of prickly gorse and fire was Morgana. She could not forget that tallfolk killed her first husband, Melga. That her first child died before it ever walked, too weak from hunger to stave off the evil that covered the poor bairn with sores. That there was no "future" for us.

I must use the Roman word. Since the beginning of the world, time has been a circle for us, while you tallfolk see it as a straight line like the marks you make with your ploughs. What part of a circle is greater than the rest, what season more important than others when each has its place and unchanging tasks for us? For Prydn, there is now. Where you say years, we say tens of seasons, how many being no great matter. Nevertheless, Morgana bent her circle to a straight line. When Artos came, she knew she touched the future, as one grasps a knife in the dark, unseen but sure in the hand.

Dorelei's second child died at birth, a hard blow to fhain. On the same day, Artos left Morgana for his Briton-home and old life. Left her with myself not born yet. Treachery, but would Morgana turn on him for that? No, never against Artos Belrix. In the first days when I was young, when none of her shining black hair had yet dulled to ash, when she rode like a small god to burn tallfolk villages in sight of the Wall, Morgana would never cross into the Briton-fhain of her husband. "Husband" she called him ever until the day Britons murdered her. That firm it was in her mind. That foolish.

Then sweet Dorelei herself was killed by Votadini cattle herders for nothing except hatred. Our sheep had wandered down into a glen where the Votadini herd was grazing. Dorelei went to cull them out. The Votadini made a great noise and flapping of arms to frighten and mill the stupid cattle. Dorelei was trampled under them.

For more sport, the herders left her body on the hill below our rath. Her husbands, Nectan and Bredei, were sick with grief and the blind need to kill. Only Morgana knew what to do. As they placed Dorelei's broken body in the barrow, my mother saw how future and change must and would come to be. Born in the waning of the moon, Morgana always knew she could bring evil when she wished. If she wished it then, Artos Belrix, if she washed sacred pebbles in the blood from her own flow and offered them in the stone circle on nights of no moon with dark prayers and no sound else but wolves and wind – whose the blame? Dorelei was not the whole of her rage, only the final blow.

See another picture: a man walks the same path every day and always stubs his toe on a certain stone. Tens of seasons he walks and stumbles and curses the stone for being there but never thinks to clear it from the path.

Then comes a day when nothing goes well for him. He stubs his toe too hard and knows it will be the last time. With all his anger in his hands, he claws out the stone and flings it shattering against a greater one. So with Morgana. She tried to live in peace with tallfolk as her mother Cradda did, but saw the folly of it when Dorelei died.

"Be nae peace atwixt fire and water," she told me many times.

"Ai, what did thee then?" I would urge, most eager listener.

"Did go among the other fhains and speak before them. I was Gern-y-fhain now since first daughter died and Cradda was old and sick and without heart for war."

Mother was only twenty Bel-teins old then. She took me as a swaddled bairn and urged the other fhains to make war with her. The choice was plain, she told them, quick war or slow death. Since Morgana was of the blood of Mabh, the others gerns gave respect to her presence but remained cautious. They spoke of Salmon fhain in seasons past who turned from Prydn ways to follow the Jesu-Christ. They tried friendship and sharing with tallfolk and were spat upon. They also tried war – and where was Salmon now?

"Where any of us next season?" Morgana answered them. "Salmon struck with no plan, but they knew change must come. Must change to live. Who will rade with me against the Votadini? One village at first, then more and more until they fly before us or pay gold to be spared."

If my mother had much courage, there was much folly in the mix. Far away, where the farthest hill met sky, Morgana saw her aim, her *Dronnarron*. When that Prydn folk grew strong enough, she would take me to Artos in his Camelot. He would greet her like a true queen, give us land and help protect it.

"May husband do less for first wife?" Morgana reasoned.

A few fhains joined her, enough to start. One morning, before Lugh-Sun rose, they struck the Votadini village whose men had murdered Dorelei. They were burning and dying before they woke. I remember the flame and stain of smoke against sky, and Morgana pointed with a reddened knife . . .

"As Mabh marked the stones in the first days," she cried to her victory-stunned folk, "so we put our sign on Lugh's own sky."

But quickly: must speed away before more tallfolk came, burdened with treasure, flocks and bawling Votadini children. You think it strange to take children? Ask the great King Artos how precious children are and how many, like his own mother, were left in tallfolk cradles only that they might not starve. I have two bairn myself. This will not happen to them.

"Have left enough child-wealth," Morgana vowed, and for once I agreed with her. "Will take back now."

So we ran out of Votadini land with fat sheep, gold and squalling bairn. So it began as other fhains came to join us. Asking was done. Now we took.

Can fool a man's eye but not a horse's nose. Their horses feed on oats, ours on open graze. Horses can smell the difference, so must keep downwind of them as we stalk Agrivaine and take pieces of him. Artos knows fhain-smell. I want him to know I have done this. When Agrivaine sends two men ahead to nose us out, we are not there but behind them. The Orkney column hurries on, Artos' dust clear to our sight in chase. Come not too swiftly, Father, nor too late. Agrivaine will cross Wall today. We will be waiting for him, but first a little more bait to keep you coming on.

The Orkneymen are alert, eyes everywhere. Those in the rear see a single Prydn rider on a low hill. As they watch, the rider dashes for what little cover the hill can give, but they see his horse go down. The rider stumbles to his feet, but they can see the man is hurt.

They argue among themselves, eager for revenge. After him, then? No time. But we *have* him. Aye, and how many more waiting? No matter there, the thrust-out arms tell us: small Faerie horse cannot outrun ours. We want vengeance.

Three of them wheel out of the line and bolt toward the rise as the others press on. When they top the hill, there is the hurt Faerie not far beyond, trying to mount his horse near a patch of gorse and dark rocks. They come down swiftly, swords swinging, separating to hit him from both sides –

The gorse rustles, the rocks move.

When we have dragged the bodies together, I take one of their long swords and cut Reindeer marks in the earth to either side of them. Artos will know it a greeting and challenge. As I cut the signs, I think of him and my mother, how she talked always of him, made his looked-for approval the measure of our success when we were already beyond hope.

"Do rade toward a new day," she told me proudly before we journeyed to Camelot. *But I knew, Mother. No day we neared, only rode deeper into night. Why would you, wise in all other things, never see the truth?*

Uallannach.

"Must ride, Modred," my war-brothers urge me now. "Artos Belrix comes."

I look off to the north. "And Agrivaine?"

He will cross Wall at the nearest possible place, near Camlann. We will cross west of that where soldiers are fewer. Like Morgana, I let my men see only my strength. I speak of "tomorrow" as she always did, though for tens of seasons I have seen only falling night and tasted the bitter truth that my mother always placed my need for her behind her love for Artos.

This is what comes of leaving the magic of our own circles for the straight lines of tallfolk, to think in the shape of "yesterday" and "tomorrow" and "next year." After Camelot there were only yesterdays. I could have told Morgana. I *tried* to tell her . . .

I grew toward the day when fhain scars were cut in my cheeks, not in quiet crannog or rath but running with Morgana's warband that swelled with each season. Must always move swiftly. The sick and weak were left behind now, a thing unthinkable before. By my tenth Bel-tein, Morgana had fought and defeated villages of every tribe north of Wall. Our raths were not scattered or hidden but clustered thick where we pleased, our flocks grazed where the grass led them. Even Taixali moved their herds aside and came with gold to be left alone.

"Tens and tens of Prydn," Mother boasted to me by the fire. "As I did tell Artos I would do. Was a braw man, Modred. Let me tell thee of his coming and the magic I made them . . ."

As if I needed to hear it yet once more. *Always* Artos in her heart, where I would be. We grew rich with gold and still she would not cross Wall to take one sheep or bit of gold from fat Parisii or Brigantes, because they were *his* folk. When I had seen my sixteenth Bel-tein, I was first husband to Eddaina, a woman of Wolf fhain, but all followed after Reindeer now, old custom forgotten. Instead of my going to Eddaina's fhain, she and our own child-wealth rode with Morgana.

As she grew older, Mother seemed cooler and more cautious, more given to mulling a thing in her mind than acting in the same breath that bore it. Many of the older gerns went back to their own raths, sick at heart from years of war. Those who stayed frowned on the younger of us for whom killing was the way of life, most so the tallfolk changelings ever quick to prove themselves all Prydn in their hearts.

I must say it: did always love Morgana more than my wife, looked to *her* to be proud of my deeds. Came to her with my wounds, counted for her the tallfolk dead by my hand. Honed myself like knife on stone to an anger and determination like hers. Became a bronze mirror where she could see herself in me. Did this make her love me as I needed or turn her gaze by so much as a hair from that other mirror? Let me tell you, tallfolk.

There are some things that men share apart from women, and be times when no man will be ruled by any woman, not even a mother. When my first child was born, I wanted to shout to earth and sky how well I did. Five of us young men were riding near Wall and drinking strong *uisge*. I would bring Eddaina and my son a gift of Briton-gold, and Morgana would not stop me. I was drunk and reckless. Gifts were not all of my thought then. Somehow I needed to take something from Artos. We slipped across Wall into Cair Ligualid and out again with a few trinkets from this house or that, but harmed no one. That far against Morgana's rule I would not dare.

Was far too much anyway. My mother heard of it, came cursing into my rath and pulled me from the sheepskin where I lay with my wife. Eddaina made to touch Morgana's belly in respect, but my mother only thrust her aside and dragged me by the hair from the rath to cry my shame to all Prydn.

"This fool, this worthless son of my body would ruin all we have labored for. Has *stolen*" – she used the dirty tallfolk word – "in the land of my husband, Artos Belrix. For this, he will nae ride at my side but like a child at the rear until he learns to heed gern-law."

Then, before all the people, Morgana struck me across the face. Not the blow that stung but the injustice, the wrong of it. When Morgana was angry, the gray of her eyes went dark as the smoke from the fires of all our slaughters, and her face seemed cut from stone.

"Be nae man like thy father but a child, Modred. A killing child!"

And who did teach me to kill?

"*Thee* the wealth I shall show thy father and these thy gifts to him?"

"Not my father!" I stormed back at her. "I will nae call him that."

"But thee will," Morgana said, as always with no thought to any wish but her own. "I see more now than when we started."

Do you so? I raged in my heart. Do you see what is before you as I do? You love this Artos who lay with you a few seasons, but do you see me? Why so much of your love to him? Have I not ridden with you since the cold Brigid-feast of my birth? Was it Artos who burned and killed for thee, brought you his wounds to heal and deeds to praise, helped make your name a fear among Picts? Who has honored thee before his own wife? Look at *me*, Morgana. I am the one who loves thee, not him who left even before I came from your body.

So I thought but dared not say it. From that moment, cold even for my long cold life as second to *him* in her eyes, I stood apart from Morgana. Loving her no less, I saw her girl-sick with foolish love for something that never was or could be. Raging in silence, I could not lie with Eddaina for days or take pleasure in anything but hate. Love is pain, but did say *uallannach* has a tangle of meanings.

More seasons passed. Morgana began to speak of an end to running and fighting and of her nearing vision. She was now the strongest gern among Prydn, with hundreds behind her, most of our people yet alive in Pictland, and no one tallfolk tribe could muster as many to fight as we could to crush them. Before last Samhain – and it was truly my mother's last – she called to her all the loyal gerns and their wisest men and women, and told of her vision.

"Now we are a power in the land and a pride," Morgana said. "We will go into Britain and meet with third husband Artos at Camelot rath. Will show him his wealth, Modred, and ask him as Britain-gern to give us back *Dronnarron.*"

Oh, Mother, I despaired. Where is there such a place for us? Only my love keeps me from running from your folly as I have run all my life at your word. I cannot leave you any more than hand can leave arm, but heart can war against head. You are a fool.

That day she wore her richest torc and the blue cloak taken from a slain chief of the Vacomagii. She sat with her back straight and legs crossed on her stone in the position of gern-speaking, that we knew her words were law.

"I go as wife to husband, gern to gern, with respect. Let all hear that. With respect. Nae one village, man or woman, sheep, cow, rath or smallest coin will thee touch while we rade to Camelot. Gerns, tell it to thy young men and women. Do love my people, but whosoever breaks my word to Artos will die. Die and nae be barrowed but left for raven and wolf, their names forgotten in rath and crannog."

Speaking so, Morgana turned her greying head slowly about, holding every eye that met hers, lingering on me that I know she would not set me above this rule.

"We will go."

Seeing clear truth, I was sick with fear for my mother who could not. Morgana had grown too used to winning to think she could lose. She saw only Artos, not how far from the hills she would lead us, or that, even if Artos still loved her, he would be the only one in Britain. Twenty years we have made fires of tallfolk houses and rivers of their blood. Could not look for them to love us for it or give us place among them.

Yet, mad as it was, Morgana's dream had the strength of *uisge* in the mind. Drinking, one could forget the *uisge* could leave the head aching and the belly poisoned.

"Could such a thing be for us?" Eddaina pondered when we sat alone by our fire, and the wealth asleep. "Do thee believe?"

I had only cold truth for answer. "Have made war all my life."

"And I, husband."

"Truly. Cunedag and Urgus tell me of the old days, but what do any of us know of peace?"

Eddaina looked into the fire. I could not read her thoughts then. "This Britain-rade be madness. Do want to believe, but . . ."

Eddaina spoke for many Prydn who had no more heart for this new thing than I did. They wanted to believe but could not. The elders said little about the rade, more resigned to it than promised. Yet I could hear in what they did not say the lingering wish for the dream to come true. Young mothers like Eddaina thought first of their child-wealth, trusted no tallfolk, but yearned toward such a place, a *Dronnarron* where their wealth could prosper without the wound-scars and halt legs from broken bones most of us carried. Hanging between belief and doubt, none would speak of their uncertainty to my mother but let me know in one way or another that I should.

I went to Morgana's rath. Entering, I knew that I would only be shouting into the wind. All her gold and finery were laid out to be chosen from. Her newest sheepskin vest shone from brushing, and she was driving the brush over her long blue cloak. The rath smelt not of mutton fat or goat's milk, but a sick-sweetness that wrinkled my nose in disgust. A small chest stood open by the firepit. Mother had tried more than one of the scents it held. I remembered the Taixali woman she took it from, who smelled of this when we killed her. I tried not to breathe deeply. Morgana had even reddened her cheeks with this tallfolk folly.

A girl, I thought. A foolish girl gauding herself for first night with a husband. For *him*. She never needed this weak magic before. Such a thing was beneath Prydn women. But for him, for Artos, nothing was too much. Would go to him with the moon about her neck could she fix it on a chain.

She greeted me in an absent manner. For Morgana, I was hardly there. She folded the brushed cloak and, taking a handful of her hair, began to brush it out.

I put my hands to her belly. "My mother be greatest gern since Mabh of the first days. Will hear thy son?"

She nodded assent but went on brushing. A strange, soft mood was on my mother that night. Morgana was far away from me. I squatted by her firepit.

"Mother, this rade thee speak of. I do not trust tallfolk."

"Nor I," said Morgana.

"Then why go among them?"

As often, she treated me now as a child too slow to learn the simplest things. "To see thy father."

"Thee would go to Artos Belrix out of love, out of *uallannach*. Out of the same – would stay for me?"

"Modred?" Her hand paused with the brush. A shadow of concern: "Speak so?"

"I must, Mother. Would nae speak against the Britain-king, but do beg thee. In all my life have never begged one thing of thee." *Only love, and that was never said.* "Forget this rade. Will only harm us."

Morgana only laughed at me. "Fool boy, have spoken as gern."

I tried not to scream at her. "I am a Prydn man. Did follow at thy side when thee bade and in shame at the rear at thy same bidding. That well did thy son learn obedience, but I am no fool. Dost think that magic alone kept us safe all these seasons? Was shrewdness, Gern-y-fhain. Was the truth of swift horses, few Picts and always distant hills where they dare nae come after us. But in Artos' land, tallfolk are thick as flies on dung. One treachery there – just one – and all thee's made would be undone."

"Oh, son," said my mother with a tired shaking of her head. "Thee ken so little of kings and queens. Artos is my husband."

"With another wife," I dared, desperate now. "And thy foolish wealth is thinking indeed of kings and queens before all else."

Did speak with respect then, but with truth as well. Artos' second wife Gwenhwyfar was Parisii, sister to their prince, and both would kill anything north of Wall quicker than deal with them as equals. Did not Gwenhwyfar's father kill Morgana's first husband, Melga? Even if my mother could speak for Artos' heart, what of his new wife? What of the others about him? Bold we had always been, but never attacked without knowing a clear way out. Deep in Britain-land, the door would be barred behind us. If there were treachery, we would all die there, and if Morgana died, what gern with enough presence to hold so many fhains together? All would be finished; could not my mother, so wise in all other things, see the truth of that?

No, she could not, only picked up her brush again, spreading the long strands of black hair to frown at the gray. She seemed to see it for the first time. "This plan was in thy father's heart and mine from the first days. Will be his gift to me. We have changed much. Will change yet more when do have our own land."

"Mother, please." I knelt beside her, grasping her hand. "Do I use the word 'beg' so lightly? Leave this thing."

"No, Modred."

"*Leave* it. What is there in Britain we cannot take for ourselves here?"

"The new day," Morgana said, calm as stone. "Thy father will refuse me nothing."

"Think, Mother. Tens of seasons he has been apart from you."

"In tallfolk counting, little in ours. Artos has not forgotten me. He could not."

I had not noticed until now how gray her hair had become, or how deep the lines under her watchful eyes. She had the look of a hunting wolf like all of us, but in the last two seasons I had seen the small ills she hid from others. Winter and rain stayed longer in her bones. She rode less than before and always with a double sheepskin for saddle. Speaking as gern pained her back which must be held straight while seated cross-legged on the gern stone.

An old wolf who now hoped to kennel with the hounds.

"Modred Belrix." My mother made a picture of the words, dreamed with them. "Thee were made when thy father was chosen lord of summer. Belrix: the Firelord. So be thee named, and to my purpose."

In that purpose I heard the end of Prydn, though Morgana thought it a beginning. Tallfolk drew pictures of the land in different colors that the shape of what they owned was known under one name, like Britain. Within that Britain would be a smaller shape but as clear. Morgana and Artos Belrix would cause the makers of such pictures to give our land a new colour that would be forever a kingdom of our own.

"You are young yet," Morgana said with the scant softness left her. "Will see. Artos will love you as he does me."

I was helpless, miserable. She must not come to harm but would not let me stay her from it. So Morgana scented herself and dreamed of Artos and went to her death.

New day, Mother? Was night already and the false light in your eyes only him.

Men have always said that Artos had a magic to bind their will to his purpose. For all my caution, his manner softened my hate: strong yet gentle as Drost. In his every look to my mother, each touching of her hand, the way he spoke of their few shared memories, there was respect for her presence, love for the woman. In the rath prepared for us, Artos gave place to Morgana and sat in the second place about the fire, one of us. Yet I saw how Morgana warmed to him, glowed under his regard and the sound of his voice. She was like to a dew-fresh girl again.

Artos joked with fhain brothers and listened to their words. He remembered small things about each that they'd forgot, made me remember the small god who was my mother. Will say it before I kill him: *uallannach*. Love or hate. I was filled with him. To stay free of that spell, I studied the tallfolk house we were given, saw how every line of it departed from those we knew – doors, tables, stools, the many gifts to us, more straight than curved, all Roman. Nae, was mad to think Prydn could live so.

And yet I would . . .

When my fhain brothers grew weary and Morgana kissed Artos good night one last time out of tens and went to rest, I spoke alone to him, sterner than I felt, fighting with every breath against the magic that came from him. Losing. I spoke my true doubts of Morgana's dream. With contempt, to *show* this tallfolk that my love was harder won than hers. That he dealt with an equal, perhaps his better. It seemed I labored too far to prove I could hurt him, to let him see only the hardness in me.

And was rewarded with success. That was all Artos saw. He turned back from it. "I want to love you, Modred," my father said, and I could hear that the desire was hardly satisfied. "I will do all I can for fhain."

Losing myself. Lost. I gazed into his face and saw myself in it, and part of me reached out to my father-self. Was evil that magic, stealing through my veins to find a weariness I never guessed until that moment. Listening to Artos's voice, I saw a picture of Eddaina and our wealth driving the flocks to a safe byre that would be ours by right. Sleeping in peace, never more having to rade for new pasture among folk whose respect for us was only that they gave to the wolf pack. *Ours*. I tasted the owning-word and it was good. All my life I killed for Morgana and savored it as salt to my food. Now, under this new magic, I turned away for the small space of one moment from killing, not sickened but gorged, done with it.

I believed his lulling song to a tired mind. When he went to bed with my mother, I lingered awake by the firepit, drinking the gift-wine slowly. Then I lay down by the curtain before the bower they shared, pondering before sleep took me away.

Could it be? Out of my mother's strength, out of my faith that never wavered from that strength, and Artos' magic – could we at last make dream into waking?

The smell of the air and sounds of the night were different here. I closed my eyes with one hand on my knife. Lying so, farthest from any opening, I saved my life, if such could be called a saving.

As always in sleep, I did not know when my spirit left its body to walk. One moment I was thinking of Eddaina and our children sitting outside our own new safe rath, and then did see them there. Running to my wife, my spirit begged with a passion I could never speak in waking.

"Could it be, wife? Could make this place ours?"

"*No.*"

Then it was not Eddaina's face but Belrix's before me. Denying, laughing at me, all the magic ended.

"*Thy life's done, Modred.*"

Not alone Morgana's death cry that woke me but truth like cold water dashed over my closed eyes, opening them. In the barest moment before my mother cried out, I woke and knew it all a lie and saw the tallfolk men coming through the door with swords.

"Mother!"

I tore aside the bower curtain, better able than Belrix to see in the dark. There he was, the sword in his hand, the shape of another man writhing on the floor by the casement.

"Mother!"

And there was Belrix striving to say this was none of his doing, even as I lifted Morgana's shoulders from the dark-stained bed and her head lolled back. I hissed one word at Artos before I struck at him, my flesh hot with Morgana's blood.

"Liar!"

Would have killed him then but for the fox-wariness of a lifetime. *Wait*, it stayed me. *Might kill him but these others will finish thee with no vengeance done. Wait and take many with him.*

I dove through the casement onto the earth, hearing the shouts in the rath behind me, ran to the murderers' horses, leaped one full running. The brute was frightened, already smelling blood; it sprang forward with me flat along its neck, grabbing for the rein. Did use the horse's fear for speed, ran it through dark and sunrise into day, then took another from the byre of a Coritani chieftain. Hid by day, rode by dark and lamed three mounts in all before crossing Wall to the hill where Morgana's folk waited.

Her blood was still on my arms. Would not wash it off until the wind picked it, dried drop by drop, from my flesh. I showed the dark smudges to our people and told them the end of Morgana's dream.

"Will go to Britain as Morgana said." I lunged back and forth before the people, hungry to be at it even then.

"But in no peace. Here, on my arms, is what my mother's peace brought her. Will take tens of them for every drop."

When the older gerns hesitated, I knew that Morgana had driven a spear forever between the old way and the new. To fight Picts was one thing, the gerns argued, all Britain another. Winter was coming; there were flocks and child-wealth to think of. If such a war against Artos were wise, would be as wise in spring when Prydn could live off the land they raded through.

"War be *now*," I commanded. "What gern among you can lead Prydn as my mother could or myself now?"

No, the gerns would not be persuaded. My mother was always too rash, they said, took too much decision to herself. Wolf Gern said what her sister gerns felt.

"Thy mother's dream rested on *uallannach*. Her love for one man. The bravest she was but not most wise. Wolf fhain will rade north among the Atecotti where we can rest the winter in safe crannogs."

But the Prydn young and the fierce changelings scorned this. Born running and fighting like me, they knew or wanted nothing else. They would follow Modred Belrix, the Firelord. The gerns disowned me, but when they were done, full seventy young men and women crossed to my side of the stone circle. The rest rode north.

To my faithful I gave my first speaking as gern. "Let those women whose flow be on them mix their blood with the strongest of poison root and flower. Let the sacred moonstones be boiled in this. When the moon is dark, we will make a killing spell for Artos of Britain and take it to him."

"And shall we take wealth from the cradles as thy mother did?" Eddaina's anxious face showed a troubled spirit. She loved children and used the tallfolk word "future" more than the other women did.

"No," I ruled. "Wealth will slow us when must ride more swiftly than ever."

"And what then for the days to come?" Eddaina argued. "I have no wealth in me, few of these others do."

I could not say she was foolish. I thought only of Morgana who made her very life into a sword: did she not die of one flaw in that blade? One moment in Camelot when even I softened – and came alone out of that place of treachery, all my dearest dead. I could thank Artos for that small mercy, allowing so few of us to Camelot, that my wife and children were not sent to the slaughtering like sheep.

"Thee may take from any cradle what will not weigh thee down," I told Eddaina and the others. "An arm or an ear."

The changelings grinned at this, but Eddaina turned away from me. When we were alone, she spoke to me like an unloved stranger. "Thy own mother said it, Modred. A killing fool."

Lugh-Sun was high over the stone circle when she said it. When Lugh moved the shadows of the stones only a little to the east, Eddaina had taken our children and ridden after Wolf fhain. That was her right. Child-wealth descends through a mother. They belong to her and she to her own fhain. Watching her go, I knew she was not ever the closest thing in my life, nor were the children. Were other women, would be more child-wealth. I could not feel much grief then. My heart was barrowed with Morgana and mourned that love in darkness rather than live in the light. Cut those words on my barrow-stone. They are as close to truth as any.

But we would make Britain weep with us. Our magic would draw Artos to me.

So we rode. We left a trail of death through the land of the Parisii and Brigantes through the winter, and in the spring our magic hit its mark. Artos and Gwenhwyfar had warred against each other. Artos came north to meet with his queen and make peace. I sharpened my knife, rubbed fresh mutton grease into my bow and chose among my best arrows.

Agrivaine and his men lie dead on the moor, the last bait for Artos. My folk have broken from cover, dashing away to the north. A good trick most times, but a fatal mistake today. Over open ground they cannot hope to outrun combrogi horses. If I live through this day, I will go to Wolf fhain, to Eddaina and our children. If not, if we have said farewell until we meet in Tir-Nan-Og, then so have Artos and pale Gwenhwyfar.

The combrogi follow my riders. Only Artos and two others remain. Now the three of them descend from the hilltop toward the field of the dead that the ravens have already found.

One of the dead is your scout, Artos. The man you believe to be him is a changeling in your man's ring-mail and helmet – waiting, his back to you, arrow nocked to the bowstring, until you are too close to miss.

How bright and hot it is as I wait; as you near the killing mark, Artos. There is a hard light over both worlds now, that which I can touch and that within me. Morgana could see tomorrow in it, but I only night falling and falling forever.

Artos finds Agrivaine's body. Moments now. A few more breaths.

How to tell you, Father? That night in Camelot I could have yearned for you and loved you beyond all else with a folly to match my mother's. Even now, as my changeling draws his bow and I sight myself on your broad back, I keen for the three of us, Mother and you and me. For what might have been. What could never be.

Sweating in the heat of Lugh-Sun. A fly buzzes past my ear, hurrying to the carrion feast below.

I could not believe in her dream, though for one moment in Camelot I reached for it and tried. Barred even from that.

Kill him! Now!

Hit.

Artos staggers back with the arrow in his belly. Mine will be next. I draw it as Morgana strung and drew my whole life taut to her purpose, aimed at your heart.

Love makes and takes life.

Holding and – loose!

So *I* touch you, Artos-father. Murderer. Liar. Did leave her. Did leave me.

Uallannach.

[*The Prydn language was pre-Celtic but had borrowed many Gaelic and Brythonic words from Picts, Britons, and early Scots. Modred and Morgana used* adhaltrach *in its original sense, merely a second wife. To the Christianized southern Britons, the word had come to mean an adultress. In Gwenhwyfar's case, the unintended accuracy was fatal to Morgana – Ed.*]

Sir Pelleas in
A FIGURE IN FAERIE TIME

John T. Aquino

We end with a love story. In the Arthurian legends Pelleas is the victim of unrequited love for Ettard until he is enchanted by Nimuë. John Aquino (b. 1949), whose story "The Sad Wizard" was in the second volume of this series, The Camelot Chronicles, *takes this love story through time till its final denouement.*

Pelleas hated himself for what he was telling Gawain.

And Gawain, in spite of his vow of loyalty to other knights of Arthur's Round Table, hated Pelleas for his tale.

Gawain could not believe that a true knight would allow a lady's legions – whom he had already defeated in combat – to take him prisoner, tie him to the belly of his horse, and parade him before the lady. "But you must understand," Pelleas said. "It is the only way that I may see her."

"There is another way," Gawain said, but only to himself. While he was listening to Pelleas, Gawain hoped that his eyes were not showing the disgust he felt. The knight before him had chiselled features that any Roman temple would welcome, blue and steady eyes, and a reputation with women that, until several months before, had rivalled Gawain's. And now, to hear him cry out, "I do not know what drives me to her" – was more than

Gawain could stomach. "It is as if," Pelleas said to hold him his attention, "it is as if I am only acting out what I have done before, that I have no control over my arms or legs – or my soul."

Gawain did not consider what he was about to do betrayal: weakness had no place among true knights of the Round Table; Pelleas must either become strong or die. In some strange way, Gawain might actually be doing Pelleas a favor. As Pelleas was talking about his soul, Gawain was mentally rehearsing his proposal: Pelleas, I will help you have the Lady Ettard. I will take your armor and horse and tell her that I have killed you. In elegy, I will praise you to her, and, when she sees her mistake, her love for you will grow. Then I will send for you.

After three days, there was no message from Gawain. Finally, Pelleas rode out at night on Gawain's horse to the twin castles made of Derry, the site of his multiple humiliations. The moat, fed by a nearby lake, was wide and the drawbridge up. Pelleas stripped himself bare, bringing only his sword, and, with the aid of a stout arm, good aim, a grappling hook, and agile toes, he scaled the face wall.

In the first room he came to he found three knights sleeping in three beds – he did not know their faces but did recognize their boots with which they had often kicked him in derision. In the second room, he found four women lying in four beds – Lady Ettard's apathetic gentlewomen. In the third room, he found one bed, and in it Gawain was lying tightly bound in the arms of Lady Ettard. Her full, blonde hair filled his chest, and, as Pelleas stood and watched, she stroked his face with the back of her hand and purred, "It is a pity you killed Pelleas. He was a passing fair knight. But of all the men alive, I hated him, for I could never be quit of him. Since you have killed him, I will be your woman and do anything I can to please you."

The sight of them both together filled Pelleas' eyes and mind down to his throat and legs. He could not breathe and held the wall to stand. For a knight who had played the fool for a woman, the greater shame was being a fool to a man whom he had trusted with the woman. "Alas," he could only whisper, "that ever a knight should be found so false."

His sword was raised to kill them, but he knew that murder would only make his folly known to the world and that the death of this contented liar and whore would destroy the honor of every knight in Christendom. He waited until they slid to sleep and then, for what it was worth, made sure that they knew he knew. He lay his sword gently across their throats and quietly left.

Pelleas let go of the rope half way down, hoping that the fall would kill him. Battered but breathing, he staggered up and, still naked, stumbled past the moat and Gawain's horse until he came to the lake. Sinking to his knees, he turned his eyes to the sky full of silent, accusatory stars and said aloud, "Arthur! I will not let my shame seep to you. I will not corrupt the high order of the knighthood. To all the knights, I give my goods and only ask that, when I am dead, you cut the heart from my body and carry it to her on a silver dish."

With this request of morbid and vain fancy, which he could only hope would come to Arthur in a dream, Pelleas prepared to die. But he had left his sword on Gawain and Ettard's throats, and Gawain's horse and armor were back at the wall. With no weapons within reach, Pelleas took up two rocks and, finding the driest ground away from the lake, madly piled up the grass into a large mound. He then struck the rocks together until they sparked and fired up the pile into a blazing pyre. Pelleas crossed himself and extended his arms to throw himself into the fire, thinking all the while of how the light from his burning might flash through their window and wake them and how they would find his sword at their throats and, later, his charred remains.

But then, suddenly, the water in the lake rose above the bank and flooded towards him, hitting him from behind and dousing Pelleas and the fire at once.

When he awoke, he was on his back, and straddling him was a woman whose long and sopping black hair hung in his face. "Always with fire," she said to him. "Why do you always use fire?"

"Who – who are you?"

She laughed in a thick and throaty way. "Well, until a while ago, I was a lake, and you were almost a torch. Water and fire have always filled our lives together."

"What lives?" he sputtered. "I have never seen you."

"Oh yes, you have. Many, many times, in many, many lives. I am now Nimuë. When I first met you, across the waters to the south, your name was as it is now, but with one 'l' and a 'us,' reflecting the culture."

Pelleas remembered that he was naked and tried to push this anxious woman off him. "You are mad."

"I am water, I am life, I am time – and yes, I am mad." She

ran her hands across his chest, and her moisture created rivers. "I will help you remember – remember how we met and why you are who you are."

Pelleas became water and was swept through the torrents of time. The current became hotter, his beard grew, and within a wink he was lying on a beach with the round sun over him, turning his skin to brown.

"You are 'Peleus,' a wanderer in the Greece before democracy and Christ," Nimuë said as she still straddled him. "Twice murderer, twice purified, you came to Iolus. You loved the Amazon warrior Hippolyta, who at first shunned you. But you soon desired me and ignored Hippolyta, who had belatedly seen your worth. I was born Thetis, one of the fifty daughters of Nereus, and we dwelt in the depths of the sea. You courted me, in spite of the prophecy that my son would be greater than his father – which certainly cooled the passion of my other suitors, Poseidon and Zeus. But you loved me regardless. And while my kind thought it careless to love a mortal, they admired your worth and bent the rules.

"We were married, but Discord – of all the gods – was not invited, and his anger started the chain of events that led to the bloody, decade war between Troy and Greece, in which our son Achilles fought and outshone you, gentle Peleus. Troy was destroyed by fire, and our mix of water and fire had begun."

"I have read this," the dazed Pelleas murmured.

"And lived it! I was immortal and you were not. But we lived together for thirty of your earth years and loved each other like this each night for 10,000 nights."

On the beach of the ancient land, she leaned down and kissed his mouth and neck and rubbed her cheek against his black beard. The tide poured over them and matched their pounding. In sixth century Britain, she kissed his bare face, as the lake again overflowed and covered them.

"You loved me!" she shouted triumphantly. "Me! And Hippolyta died of grief in Megara!"

Gawain and Ettard were awakened by a commotion outside and felt the sharp blade at their throats. In an instant, Ettard knew the truth. "You have betrayed me and Sir Pelleas both, for you have told me you had slain him and now I know he is alive," she shouted at Gawain, who was still taking in where the sword must have come from. "And if he had behaved toward you with the lack of honor you have shown him, you would be dead now!"

The noise continued from below, and Gawain ran to the window to see that the lake and moat were empty and dry. "We are open to attack," the warder was yelling to no one in particular. Gawain was only too glad to leave Ettard and his shame to work with true men to refortify the castle.

Alone, Ettard sat on the edge of the bed and started to cry out in grief. But before the sound could leave her mouth, three black sparrows flew through the window and rested on the sill. She had never seen such birds before and turned to call Gawain. Standing in the doorway was Nimuë, looking like a shadowed wraith. "You should not have hurt Pelleas," she said.

Pelleas awoke in his own bed. Wet and sweating, the words from his mouth were, "Hippolyta died of grief in Megara."

"Ah, I see you are remembering," said Nimuë, suddenly beside him. She touched his shoulders with both hands and started to gently push her thumbs into the small of his bare back. "You are not surprised to see me, are you? Did you think I was one of your knight's conquests," she said, punning.

"Of this I am sure," he laughed, relaxed with her. "No knight has ever had a woman like you."

"No knight," she said.

"I love you," he said simply. "And evidently have. I remember – "

"Paris, Achilles, Aphrodite – "

"I was going to say that I remembered last night and my vision of the past."

She moved closer and stirred his hair with her close breath. "No vision. You were there."

"And you said that there were many other times?"

"Come," she took his hand. "Get dressed and I will tell you."

They strolled through a passageway of bowing elms. "In the Greece of a thousand years ago, we knew that such trees held the imprisoned souls of mortals or even gods," Nimuë said, tenderly pulling a twig from a branch. "These trees may have kept such souls. But they are long dead. Souls can live forever, but their lives must be renewed through love remembered, through unfinished business, or through magic. These souls were abandoned and died of neglect."

"And I," asked Pelleas, "how was I renewed?"

"Why, through all three," said Nimuë a little surprised at the question. "I made you mine and have renewed your soul a hundred times through my magic, through my love, and because our story is not yet finished."

"Am I born each time?"

"The method is the natural one. I assist nature by directing your soul. It is in keeping with nature that the body be of Peleus' line, which it mostly has been."

"A hundred times!"

"And more – although only a few famously."

"When?" asked the knight, trained to seek glory wherever he could find it. "When famously?"

Nimuë smiled at her love's vanity. "I carried your ashes to this country when I served as faerie escort to Joseph of Arimathea when he brought the Holy Grail of Christ's Blood to England. In Wales, you were born as the child of one of Joseph's sailors, whose mother was Greek. Through their way of speaking in that land, your name became Pwyll, and through your prowess with a sword you grew to be king of the land. I took as my new name Rhiannon and lived in the sea until our time came again. In one of your adventures, you changed places with a demon and lived in his dimension, chastely sleeping with his wife. When you took your own place again, she followed you here, in passionate love with you. But I came out of the sea while you fished, and you were mine. The demon wife returned to her land and died of grief."

"We were married?"

"Yes, and ruled the land from bright beaches to the hills that grazed the stars and treated all of Celtic blood with justice and grace. I used my magic sparingly but kept three birds who could bring the dead to life and those alive to death. Poor dears, I had forgotten all about them – until yesterday. But the magic that hosts them, hosts you."

Their heels crackled as they trod over branches and the shards of rocks that shone like crystals. "How long did we live as Pwyll and Rhiannon?" Pelleas asked her.

"Thirty years again, 10,000 nights. And again your end was linked to fire – invaders from the North swooped down the sleek hills. You brought your warriors to the front to cover the retreat of your subjects and your queen. Unlike many generals, you *led* your troops – and so were in the face of the attack when the fireballs hit, pitched by catapults. I mourned you, but with pride."

"Why always by fire?"

"We are mated through the order of the universe, Pelleas. Of the four elements, air and earth are fixed, water and fire are free. You are fire, you wanderer, you knight errant, and I am water."

"Nimuë." He stopped and pulled her by her long, velvet sleeve to face him. "Is that how you can bring me back, because we are not fixed?"

"Not exactly." She shook her head at his attempts to understand. She let out a short breath, trying to decide how to start. "There is an order that is observed by all faerie kind. Within that order is discretion. But then patterns form, and we follow their flow."

"And why have you always brought me back?"

"Because you feed my spirit, gentle man. I have tasks, and then I have you."

"But I must be born again – "

"And so I wait for you until we meet."

"I see," he said in acceptance but shook his head just the same. They continued walking. The weather had chilled and their breath formed figures. "And what have you been doing while you have been waiting?"

"I had my task – and had a fine time. It is so green here in summer, so full of new life, and in winters the snow and ice freeze the moments in time. From the seas and lakes, I watched Arthur grow and joined the faerie spirits here to help him. It was I who handed him his sword Excalibur from the lake. That chore being done, I came to court in human form and served as student to Merlin."

"But Merlin has been missing many a year. And you – who can keep the dead alive – you were a student?"

"Yes, funny, is it not?"

They walked past a cave whose outer walls were lined with crystal. As they passed, Nimuë heard, but Pelleas did not, a shrill voice cry out, "Nimuë, hear me. Release me!"

"But that was a diversion only," Nimuë spoke above the old magician's voice. "There were local spells that I could learn from him. And yet, Merlin was an arrogant man who finally fulfilled his purpose – as has she."

They stopped as Lady Ettard approached. Her thick hair, which had just the day before covered Gawain's chest, was clotted with grime. Her rich, purple robes were torn from neck to hem. Her grief at her perfidy had joined with Nimuë's enchantment. Lady Ettard joyed at the sight of Pelleas and ran to him on stained velvet slippers.

But Pelleas held up his hand, and the woman stopped so quickly that one of her slippers fell off. "What have you to do with me, woman? You love another, not me."

"I was in error, and it was my folly. I love you."

"More's the pity. But the time is past – "

"Oh, my Pelleas – "

Nimuë moved between them like a knife. "So it has been, and so it is. I told you that you should not have hurt him."

The Lady Ettard trudged away with one foot bare as three black sparrows circled overhead.

The next morning, Gawain's page came to Pelleas' room with sad news. Nimuë would not come, so Pelleas rode on alone to the twin-turreted castle with the empty moat and lake. Gawain was standing stiffly at moat's edge, looking down. Pelleas saw Lady Ettard's twisted shape in the bottom's corner, and from her apparent injuries he assumed that she had jumped from the left tower's top. "Hippolyta died of grief in Megara," Pelleas repeated.

Gawain did not understand and said nothing in return. But Pelleas turned to him and said, "It is a sad state of affairs for true knights to have caused." Again, Gawain said nothing. He simply turned away and mounted and rode toward Camelot. He and Pelleas never spoke again.

As Pelleas returned to Nimuë, for some reason he found himself listening to the clatter of his horse's hooves, which seemed to precede him in echoes, and go on and go ahead of him, down the road and out of sight. "So am I," he whispered. "So am I."

Waiting for him, Nimuë lit a candle to place in the window for Pelleas' return. She watched the flame and then slowly covered it with her moist hand, embracing it, trying to hold it, until finally it sizzled and went out. "You can only be lit just so many times, dear candle, until our time is up," said Nimuë.

That night, as they lay in each other's arms, Nimuë said to Pelleas, "That is the pattern that has developed. You love another, I bring you to me, and the other goes mad and dies. I should probably have stopped it earlier, but I cannot now, it is too late. It is not a bad pattern – "

"Not bad?" said Pelleas. "I do not think I like being a love-sick puppet in these matters."

"You are no puppet," Nimuë chided him. "You are what you are. You are a good man who loves powerful women. The one who is evil to you dies. The one who loves you back, keeps you. It has justice, it has drama. That is not a bad pattern – at least for us."

But Pelleas remained unconvinced. "And some day soon I will die in fire, and then in a hundred years – "

"Or less."

"– I will be born again. And I will remember nothing?"

"Faint, faint glimpses. But savor the now, Pelleas. For I fear our heroic times are passing. After Camelot is ashes – "

"Ashes!"

"Hush, love. I have told you too much. But once it is gone, few glories await. Few Troys, few Camelots. And we will become sketches of ourselves. The day will come when we will have power over little, for that is the way the world will move. Our time will pass, and we will finally part, for we will be subject to the rule. So savor the now."

Nimuë and Pelleas married in a faerie chapel across from Merlin's crystal cave. Sprites and elves danced in a sparkling faerie ring, and their tiny lights could be seen by farmers a hundred miles away north and south. Nimuë even allowed the old magician a brief moment of freedom to give her away, and then unceremoniously returned him to his confinement.

Pelleas retired from the court, and Nimuë and he lived together for many years on a dairy farm outside of Glastonbury. One day, word came that the forces of Mordred had taken Camelot and that Gawain had been killed at Dover when he and Arthur had returned from France. Pelleas found his sword, borrowed a neighbor's horse, and rode to join his liege and friend. He was not on the lists of battle. He just came.

Nimuë said nothing. She no longer said anything when he left.

Her vision power told her all in an instant – three knights lay wounded on a bridge that had treacherously been set ablaze by Mordred's men. Pelleas pulled two to safety – and almost the third before the bridge gave way.

That evening, wading up to her thighs in the smoke and soot of the burned bridge, Nimuë rescued what was left of Pelleas, placing it in a box of cedar. Arthur and Mordred were also dead. Nimuë did not stay to see Camelot set ablaze by marauders. She had seen it before.

Through the years, Pelleas was re-born again and again, and he and Nimuë found each other and loved again. But Nimuë had been right. As generation after generation passed, reason replaced magic in what humanity called its renaissance and enlightenment. There were few times of gigantic passions, and when Pelleas died of fire, they became little more than household accidents.

In the middle of the second millennium from the death of Christ, the magic left England, and, just as the spirits of ancient times left in trees died of neglect, just so faerie spirits in the land perished and were forgotten.

With these departures, there came a time when Pelleas was born again, but Nimuë did not come to him. He died without her magic and died alone.

As the lights and sounds of her world slowly vanished around her, Nimuë sped back to Glastonbury. Just beyond the abbey there, there is a fragrant field full of daffodil and poppy in the spring and summer. With the dregs of her magic, Nimuë rounded the field with two rings, one of fire and one of water. The one was Pelleas' spirit, and the other was hers.

In the month of November in the year 1882, the idea of faeries was revived in England, but only in the form of a musical play. The operetta-team of librettist William S. Gilbert and composer Arthur Sullivan fashioned a work that they called *Iolanthe*. It was their seventh collaboration, and, like the others, it parodied numerous things, including the Germanic operas of Richard Wagner and their battled-horned faerie women from Teutonic mythology. Among the many plot elements was the battle of the Fairy Queen against her passion for a mortal, in this case a Palace Yard sentry named Private Willis. This was expressed in a song entitled "Oh, foolish fay."

The opera was debuted in the newly finished Savoy Theatre on the Strand. It had been built overlooking the Thames on the spot where Nimuë and her faerie band would dance in rings. With its innovation of electric lights, the Savoy would allow *Iolanthe's* fairies to dance with electric-powered lights in their wooden wings.

The diminutive Sullivan and his tall and former barrister partner Gilbert had not been getting on. On opening night, Sullivan conducted the overture with the fresh knowledge that bad investments had brought him into bankruptcy. To distract himself from this bitter news, he tried to bathe himself in his music. But, between the acts, Gilbert and Sullivan exchanged words about the pacing, which Gilbert as author and director thought was too slow for the drama. As the second act of the first performance was about to begin, both abruptly turned their backs on the other – Sullivan to return to the podium, Gilbert to go back to the wings to glare at Sullivan. The audience – of whom there were many dignitaries including royalty, politicians, and the heads of both the London police and fire departments – did not notice that anything was wrong.

The second act was ten minutes old when the Fairy Queen, played by Alice Barnett, approached the sentry.

QUEEN: *Who are you, sir?*
WILLIS: (coming to "attention"): *Private Willis, B Company, 1st Grenadier Guards.*
QUEEN: *You are a very fine fellow, sir.*
WILLIS: *I am generally admired.*
QUEEN: *I can quite understand it.* (To Fairies.) *Now here is a man whose physical attributes are simply godlike. That man has a most extraordinary effect upon me. If I yielded to a natural impulse, I should fall down and worship this man. But I mortify that inclination; I wrestle with it, and it lies beneath my feet! That is how I treat my regard for this man!*

Sullivan's left hand signalled the orchestra to start the song, and he nodded to the Fairy Queen at her cue:

Oh, foolish fay,
Think you, because
His brave array
My bosom thaws,
I'd disobey
Our fairy laws?

Sullivan did not like the lyric, especially the refrain:

Oh, amorous dove,
Type of Ovidius Naso!
This heart of mine
Is soft as thine,
Although I dare not say so.

He was convinced the audience would not understand these words, in spite of every attempt to enunciate them, and so he suddenly picked up the tempo to hurry into the second verse and refrain and get the song over with.

But then, a magic returned to England. Alice Barnett was gone, and in her place was Nimuë, a faerie creature singing of her love for a mortal and her ultimate acceptance of the rule.

On fire that glows
With heat intense
I turn the hose
Of common sense,
And out it goes
At small expense!

Neither Gilbert nor Sullivan recognized the lyric – or the singer. Both turned their eyes in anger at the other.

We must maintain
Our fairy law;
That is the main
On which to draw –
In that we gain
A Captain Shaw!

Nimuë stretched her arms out to Captain Bryn Massey Shaw, head of the London Fire Brigade and a descendant of Peleus of ancient Greece and Pelleas of medieval England:

Oh, Captain Shaw!
Type of true love kept under!
Could thy Brigade
With cold cascade
Quench my great love, I wonder!

And in that moment, summoned by Nimuë, the spirit of Peleus/Pelleas lived again in Captain Shaw. He remembered the 10,000 nights of love with the powerful woman who had loved him for nearly two millennia. He saw the fires of Troy and Camelot and felt her wet hand and warm kisses and true love.

They were one again in that moment, and time flowed like a river through the years. Their spirits touched, although physically Shaw only limply moved from his seat to acknowledge the applause.

"Fire and water," whispered Nimuë, and Pelleas heard her. "Always fire and water. We have become sketches, indeed. Our long moment is passed. But now we are immortal. Our images of fire and water are fixed forever in this play."

Sullivan was sure that Gilbert had inserted the lyric to get a cheap effect from the first-night presence of Captain Shaw. Gilbert thought that it had been Sullivan's doing, he who kowtowed to royalty and the affluent. It would not be long before their partnership would be dissolved, a victim of Nimuë and Pelleas' love. But, that night, both knew that the lyric, which had drawn great applause, would stay in the printed text and the vocal score.

By the time the applause was over, Alice Barnett was back in view. Nimuë was gone, gone from earth forever, and Pelleas was sleeping again, to be reawakened only at the end of time when Nimuë and he would join to the music of the spheres.

Afterword: THE ROAD TO CAMELOT

Parke Godwin talks to Marion Zimmer Bradley

Marion Zimmer Bradley is sitting in my Salvation Army chair, drinking a lemon spritz, a chunky, sturdy woman in black with the frosty blue eyes of an upstate farm woman who's looked at a lot of trouble and weather. We've both done Arthurian books. She's written The Mists of Avalon, *I've done* Firelord. *Neither of us had a conventional view of Camelot or its denizens, and people don't like you messing with their favourite myths. For every reader who waved a flag, another threw a rock. For every kudo, a cheer from the Bronx. Kind of exhilarating. We're talking about the different roads to Camelot. You hang a left at Stonehenge and . . . no, wait. You go right and . . .*

GODWIN: It amazes and amuses me that reviewers will compare a book with another before even considering the work for good or ill on its own merits. We've both been unfavorably compared to White's *Once and Future* . . . though I have more respect for White than you do. It's always bothered me that a reviewer would feel he *has* to compare your book to another – unless it simply makes his job easier. Although your *Mists* was very different from *Firelord*, I have a tremendous respect for your sense of music – like Walton saying hello to Mahler.

BRADLEY: Comparing my work to T.H. White is not even comparing apples and oranges but oranges and floppy disks. White was using whimsy and satire to show that the Arthurian people were very like us – Sir Ector and King Pellinore wearing their old school ties, etc. I detest anachronisms to start with, and when we find Arthur being transformed into various animals, dumped into ant colonies and falcon mews – yes, it's political satire, but I can't see much application to the Matter of Britain.

I was trying to recreate the way in which the Roman Empire restructured the world and then fell apart and was succeeded by chaos. The history and fall of the Roman Empire has always fascinated me. And one of the major influences, both on my life and on this book, was Sigrid Undset's Nobel prize novel *Kristin Lavransdatter*, which goes deeply into the mind of a woman in the Middle Ages – twelfth century. I tried, with Morgaine and the other women, to recreate the daily life and mind-set of a woman of the Dark Ages. I grew up on a farm without any modern conveniences, and know what it's like to spend your whole time keeping people fed and clothed, an endless round of drudgery for the women so that the men can get out and do the really hard work.

I also wanted to evoke the time when the ancient matriarchal religion was making its very last appearance. The Gauls and the Romans had very different ideas of religion, and they were just beginning to reach an uneasy peace when Christianity swept the world and altered the whole equation with a third factor that wouldn't compute. England has always been at the center of every cultural change, because, as an island, it's being subjected to pressure from every direction. In the fifth century, people were coming at England from all over; Angles and Saxons coming across from Europe, Northmen coming down from Scandinavia, everybody pushing into the island. Not even a melting pot, just a huge clashing stew of cultures. You know that originally I was a science fiction writer, and to me, cultural shock, the clash of alien cultures, is the essence of literature and drama.

GODWIN: Me too; we saw the same thing and expressed it in totally different ways. To me, the genius of White was how the book grew from children's whimsy to adult drama. The falcon mews scene is brilliant comedy. Then the portrait of Mordred: White was a homosexual, and his rendering of Mordred as the victim of a devouring bitch-mother is very powerful in a recognizable, human way. And humanity's what I'm writing about, even though you've scored me personally for my anachronisms. I did use modern British idioms. It felt right, especially for the comedy and the strong two-scenes. Gardner did the same thing in *Grendel*. Anouilh, Shaw and Goldman did the same thing with historical themes to illuminate what was important to them. I was painting in Arthur the arc of a man's life, all men, from youth to prime and age, how it all harmonizes.

BRADLEY: Much as I disliked White's *The Sword in the Stone*, I did like and admire his *III Made Knight*, and my view of Lancelot was formed by that book. I didn't know White was homosexual, but when you mentioned it, I thought: of course, I should have known. In the time when he wrote, he couldn't have seen Lancelot as homosexual, but he did portray him as a man with a guilty secret, filled with misery and self-hatred. I tried to retain that view. As the son of the Lady of the Lake, he was a man who'd been terribly intimidated by any strong woman, and this was why he couldn't cope with Morgaine; she was like his mother; a powerful and intense woman. But my view of Lancelot – and White's – is perfectly consistent with Malory. He was a man tormented by conscience. He always had pets among the younger knights; Gareth, for instance. And Tristram. Following them around, doing nice things for them. And how would you better excuse or underline your interest in women than by proclaiming enormous devotion to the one woman you could not have? Even back in my teens, that was the one thing I always saw clearly about Lancelot. Well, of course he was devoted to the Queen, otherwise they'd have married him off to someone else.

GODWIN: And of course the chaste passion for an unattainable lady was the ideal of the twelfth century. It may have covered a multitude of motives. We seem to come closest in our Lancelots. You did him with a guilty secret. Mine was probably not so complex in this respect. It was his ambition to be an Anchorite and an ecstatic. As Guenevere said, "Failing God he found me, and I did a better job than heaven ever could." In Malory he married Elaine through a rather transparent trickery. I don't believe that anyone fumbling into bed in the dark, drunk or sober, would mistake one woman for another . . . but I may be jaded.

BRADLEY: Well, this is what I did, but of course I had Morgaine drug Lancelot so he wouldn't know whether it was Guinevere or Elaine or which woman he had.

GODWIN: For Elaine – I see human passion as a single force that can be channelled one way or another. Elaine could have been God's perfect nun, but she saw Lancelot and a light went on. This same passion went into him; this same force soured her in the disappointment she couldn't transcend for all her holiness, knowing he loved Guenevere.

BRADLEY: I did the same thing with Elaine; she admired Lancelot and didn't want him wasted on a woman who couldn't give him anything – meaning Guinivere. So she was willing to marry him by a trick. But about Lancelot and his own passion: in the end of my book, Lancelot became a priest, which is what he did in Malory. And Morgaine commented after his death, "So far he had gone, in quest of a God who would not mock him." To me the whole book, especially Morgaine and Lancelot, was the story of a quest for direct spiritual experience – not accepting what people tell you about God, but going out and searching for it yourself. That is the whole story of Morgaine's life; searching for the Goddess, both in the world and in herself. Morgaine is in complete contrast to Guinevere, who, like many women in that day, was willing to accept whatever she was told about God, and religion, and the duty of Christian women. She spends her life literally fearing God, but under the influence of the Grail she reaches one moment of transcendence, when she is no longer afraid. Before that, if she had been shoved back into a convent, she would have found it a very welcome shelter from the world. As it was, when she found the moral courage to give up Lancelot, it was a real sacrifice; she no longer wants to shelter from the world. Your Guenevere is very different; like my Morgaine, she is a very strong person, very much of an individual.

GODWIN: Like Morgana, she just took off. Against a vivid Arthur and Morgana, a weak Guenevere would unbalance the book. Your Guinivere is very much like my Yseult, very much acted upon. And, Jesus, could an actress like Rita Tushingham play my Yseult. I always see my stuff as playing rather than being read.

We both painted from passionate conviction on vastly different canvasses. *Firelord* is a male consciousness moving from youth to age across a changing political canvas with personal spirituality and insight and discovery. In *Mists of Avalon*, a female consciousness moves across a changing *spiritual* canvas, matriarchal to patriarchal. For all the difference, we sometimes achieved the same thing. I'll never forget your closing scene with Morgaine in the nunnery, it damned near made me cry. The Catholic Church would probably argue with you from now until I get religion about sneaking the Goddess into Christianity, but you managed it in a marvellous way.

BRADLEY: I come from a basically Christian consciousness, but my training was as an Old Catholic, which is an attempt to recapture the Christian Church before the so-called Church Fathers, Augustine, the Nicene Council, got hold of it and revised it for political reasons. I wrote this book in fear and trembling, afraid all my Christian friends would hate it, and I was surprised and pleased when such Christian laywomen as Madeleine L'Engle approved of what I was doing. They realized I wasn't attacking Christianity but the bigots who infest it. One thing we do know about the ancient religions is that there have always been Goddesses and virgins with child. There's a very famous Coptic Christian image which is now known to have been an Isis with the infant Horus, later worshipped as Mary with the infant Jesus. A book I loved as a child was *The Birth of The Gods* by the Russian author Dmitri Merezhkowskii. It was laid in the time of Crete, and Akhnaton of Egypt, and takes the stand that the pagan gods were given to mankind as a way of teaching him to worship until the "true God" was sent, meaning Christ. All the Mother-of-Goddesses are interchangeable with Mary. Christians tried to create a patriarchal religion without Goddesses, but the human spirit demands a world-mother. This is why Morgaine, seeing the goddess vision in the Christian church, realizes that the Goddess can take care of herself. If men reject her in one form, she will appear in another. All the great shrines where the Virgin has appeared – Guadaloupe, Lourdes, Fatima – are all the sites of old pagan shrines where the Goddess has been appearing long before Mary was ever heard of. She just changes her name.

GODWIN: If you consider Camelot as one of the archetypes of the world, you can't get away from the female image; it's integral. All our legends – Arthur, Oedipus, Hamlet, Orestes – woman is central to all of them. They're the story of the fall of a house or order only in a cautionary sense. Don't mess with the old man's women or the cave will break up.

BRADLEY: Not only that, but don't mess with the old lady. Men come and go, but if the child-bearing women are really unhappy, the tribe won't prosper. Women are always the keepers of culture. Whenever a culture goes masculine, it loses a great deal in terms of beauty. The Romans, a major patriarchal culture, never came to terms with the Gauls or Celts, never could understand that the real rulers were women; the Romans called the chiefs *kings*, but they were simply war leaders. In peacetime it was the women's arts that kept the tribe going. Even metalworking: originally women dealt with metal, because metals were the province of the Goddess of Earth; like vegetables and seeds, they were ripped out of the womb of the Goddess.

GODWIN: It was in this context that I found my justification for Guenevere in *Firelord* and *Beloved Exile* – that she could reconcile so blithely her position as a goddess figure and also as one hell of a trembling deathbed Christian. She lived at a time of interface in history and balanced very easily between tribal fertility goddess and Christian. I'd like to talk a moment about our Morgaine/Morgana who were both pagan but very different. Yours is educated and highly literate – a goddess, as you described. Mine was very much like the northern Picts of the time. Working in the field with British archeologists and adding their observations to my research, I saw the Faerie as neolithic and Bronze Age holdovers who couldn't keep up with the people around them. Like the American Indian, people who advanced so far and stopped. Small and dark as the neolithic Iberians, probably looking a cross between a Lapp and an Eskimo. Your Morgaine was much closer to the mainstream of British life. I found her fascinating.

BRADLEY: I suppose your Morgana is historically more valid than mine, especially since you made her a Pict. But in dealing with the Lady of the Lake, I made her a Druid, and they, of course, were one of the Pythagorean wisdom religions. Morgaine lived in the house of Uther who was Roman, so of course she would have understood Roman – and therefore Greek – literature. Arthur himself, being brought up by Sir Ectorius, would have had a good Roman education. The Druids wrote in Greek characters, long before the Romans came – I cite Lewis Spence for evidence – and thus Morgaine too would have been well-educated. The difference in our Morgaines is fascinating, but so is the similarity – they both have enormous dignity, though yours is a child of earth and mine of civilization. My Morgaine is more like your Guenevere.

GODWIN: Another similarity: our focal characters, whoever, are educated and reflective to serve narrative purpose. I took my authority for Guenevere as an educated woman from the period in which she lived. Beginning with the high place women had in Celtic society, she had at her disposal the entire learning of her time. She and Arthur *thought* in Latin; this gave them a precision of thought and speech. They had a Roman sense of organization. They were professional rulers. They had to be.

BRADLEY: One of the few things we do know about the historical Arthur was that whatever else he did or didn't, he revived Roman culture and probably Roman law. But I made my Guinivere a conventional woman, and of course, influenced by the medieval view, I made her the perfect Christian woman. And probably she could just barely read and write – the Christians didn't think too much learning was good for anyone, especially women. I saw Guinivere as Lancelot's romantic queen, and of course any woman who bought into the romance trips, as Guinivere did, couldn't be anything but a ninny. Your Guenevere is my Morgaine; the educated and intelligent woman who could have, and should have been Arthur's co-queen, and far more intelligent than he ever was. As I saw it, though, they married Arthur off to this little ninny because she had a dowry of a hundred knights; that was how Arthur saw her, though he tried to make her take more responsibility, but that was how Guinivere saw herself. She was intended as a foil for Morgaine; the educated pagan woman against the perfect Christian queen. Are you familiar with the writings of St Jerome and St Augustine? Then you know how they wanted women to behave, and that was just what Guinivere became. My Gwenhwyfar, anyhow.

GODWIN: Jerome and Augustine seemed unpleasant sorts even in their own day – unduly harsh and plain . . . *uncomfortable* in the matter of women. The British Church *and* the British spirit never really came into line with Papal doctrine for centuries after them . . . my concept of Arthur and Guenevere comes wholly from the historical period: late Roman. There is nothing about it, except, arguably, Lancelot's mind-set, that is medieval.

BRADLEY: Well, one thing Malory had in common with the world Arthur lived in; each lived in the collapse of the civilization they had known. Arthur in the fall of Rome, including his extension of it, Malory in the change from Christian hierarchy into the Renaissance. Tennyson, who rewrote the myth in *Idylls of the King*, lived in a day when the Victorian concepts of kingship, personal morality, *noblesse oblige*, were dying all over Europe even as he was trying to honor and perpetuate them. All these writers were writing enormous metaphors, comparing their world and their collapsing values with the great death of Rome and Arthur's attempt to preserve the light for a little while. And we too live in a world we perceive as collapsing around us, and are trying to keep our own light alive. . .

GODWIN: And that, if it does nothing else, gives the bloody moralists tremendous grist for their mill. I've been criticized for completely negating the "Christian drama" of the story. I don't think and have never thought that the Arthurian story was originally any more of a Christian cycle than Little Bo Peep, but a heavy layering of Christian morality over an essentially pagan thing, which I think you might agree with. Expecially the Grail which has always been a pagan symbol. In *Beloved Exile*, the Abbot of Glastonbury adopts the pagan ritual of dipping the censor into the bowl – done in the Church today – and it comes directly from the idea of dipping the male phallus into the bowl/vagina of earth.

BRADLEY: One of the things which evoked for me the high tragedy inherent in *Firelord* was this, too. Our world treats romance as desirable, even, sometimes, sacred. The ancient world, the real world of Arthur, and even Malory's world, held that romance, sexual passion especially, was an enormous intrusion on the orderly progress of society, and almost always a tragedy. And you recognize this, you treat Arthur's passion for Morgana as the disruptive force in Arthur's life, which set in motion the affairs which eventually brought him down. Your Morgana was a very touching figure, but basically tragic, and their passion disrupted his life. Is that how you saw Morgana and Arthur?

GODWIN: Not consciously, but the older I get the more I rely on instinct and less on conscious control. Consciously I saw Morgana as the catalyst that brought the transcendent humanity out of a conventional Roman soldier – or, if you will, patriarchal meets matriarchal, and his growth is the synthesis. I couldn't imagine this vivid a canvas without people filling it with their passion. What I was going for were eternal values. Interesting . . . passion intruding on an orderly life. This is something that never consciously occurred to me as an aesthetic. Passion's always been a part of life to me; a pain in the integral ass sometimes, but never an intrusion.

BRADLEY: And of course you've written a very passionate book, while I felt mine on the level of a spiritual quest. Your Morgana is a wonderful child of Earth, and she brings all the upflooding of primitive passion into Arthur's orderly life. My own Morgaine and Arthur, on the other hand, are actually the victims of political scheming by Viviane, the Lady of the Lake. It is not their own upflooding passions which create tragedy, but their reactions to Viviane's plans, which they see as personal tragedy. To me this is the tragedy of the legend; that by doing exactly what he is supposed to, commanded to do, a man sows the seed of his own downfall. And of course this is the basic legend of the sacrificed god – the theme of the whole book, "What of the King Stag when the young stag is grown?" Arthur is simply another in a whole procession of sacrificed God-Kings.

GODWIN: I touched on this in my use of Merlin. He becomes a chorus to illustrate and comment. I wanted to speak about the women in your book as they happened to me. I loved your Morgaine. I had a rowdy – a word you used for me – affection for Margause. She was a horny old bitch with a healthy appetite for men. Even in the end when the young man refused her politely, Margause would have the guts and common sense to say, as it were, "Well, that's showbiz," because she'd lived such a full life. In regard to men, she was always reaching for a plate of goodies that was always there. One last time she reached and the plate was empty. I think Margause just shrugged and said, "what the hell," and got on with her life. She was a marvellous character . . . I've always had the most love for my own minor characters. Perhaps any author does because the major characters are such work, you get tired of them. In *Firelord*, I adored writing Geraint and Morgana. In *Beloved Exile*, there was Rat. Maybe it's perversity or simply the actor in me that would take someone as unlovely as Rat and strive to make the reader care about her. Don't you agree, the heavy work aside, that minor characters are almost like dessert?

BRADLEY: I suppose it's because the major characters, Arthur, Guenevere, Mordred, really belong to history, but the minor characters – your Rat and Gunnar, my Kevin and Raven and Taliesin – are our own, and we can exercise our own creativity on them. So little has been written about the Lady of the Lake, for instance, that Viviane is, I think, an original character. But every new society rewrites the Matter of Britain in its own way, to explain the legend to their own time. The Arthurian legend is the great epic of the English Language. This explains why Americans, as well as English, are always having a fresh go at it. Malory, in his collapsing society, his constant preoccupation was with a world where the King was next to God, sometimes literally God's regent on Earth, and yet the best knight, Lancelet, was NOT the best Christian, he was a sinner, an adulterer. Malory was just beginning to come to terms with an idea that was almost heretical: that God was not on the side of the right, but on the side of the bigger armies and maybe even on the side with guns. If he had written these ideas about his own king, it would have been heretical and scandalous, so he wrote about a time so distant that he could think without being criticized. In effect he wrote fantasy for the same reason we do – to criticize his own time and distance himself from it. We get along to people like William Morris who of course recreated the legend as a way of showing his time what was passionately important to him, aesthetics, as opposed to Tennyson who was working with the basic Establishment values of personal morality, loyalty to Queen and Empire. In the twentieth century, we get into twentieth century values; and exaggerated wish for facts: *what really happened?* Whether in the debunking vein of Henry Treece in such books as *The Great Captains*, or the more romantic versions of such writers as Rosemary Sutcliffe or Mary Stewart, they are all trying to reconstruct what really happened in the fifth century to give rise to all these legends. This is the twentieth century's passionate preoccupation – to recapture *what really happened*. Until about the twentieth century, history was a didactic thing, telling us how great people had been in the past and how the present generation didn't measure up, and encouraging us to be more like the heroes of the past. And of course, along with an exaggerated passion for facts, the great event of the twentieth century is the rediscovery of the feminine powers. Science, didacticism, materialism and logic, which are very Roman concepts, are finally failing us. They've led us to the brink of nuclear extinction, in the same way that the Roman love of law and order and precision and power led their world into the political mess it was when the barbarians took over. So now we are re-creating the old legends to deal with the re-emergence of these feminine powers; spirituality, mysticism, intuition. Each generation re-creates the legend. A hundred years from now there may be books explaining a space-going society to itself by the Arthurian legend. When we write about Arthur and Morgana and all those people, the important thing is, we are writing about *ourselves* as Morgana and Arthur and Guinivere. This is why, whether Arthur was "real" or not – and of course in the twentieth century we writers are committed to "proving" that he was historical – if Arthur had not been real, we would have had to invent him, just as we have to re-invent him for every generation.

GODWIN: As Gildas more or less re-invented the "golden time" from which his generation had declined, and he had a lachrymose good time lamenting it in bad Latin. I came to the Arthurian legends in 1951 in Bullfinch's *Mythology*. Even then I began to see reality and legend as two hands reaching to touch one another. As you demonstrated, a child of my century, I became fascinated with the question: at what precise point do fantasy and reality meet? And this early interest pervaded my work in *Firelord*. I tried to keep a sense of the interface, painting it with my own colours and feelings. *Faust* became one thing for Chris Marlow, quite another in another time for Goethe. In Malory's Arthur, only the heavies plot and scheme; in my century, and in my own experience with the intelligence establishment, the good guys can't afford lofty morals, but have to be better at the very serious game than the opposite side.

BRADLEY: Well, this is what an artist does. He uses himself for his own background. I said once that in writing about Morgaine, I had in a sense to become Morgaine. I started out writing science fiction, and SF is very like historical fiction; one deals with the past and the other with the future, but it's the same thing; you have to put your head into a completely different space than the one you're living in, whether for Martians or King Arthur.

The basic image of Morgaine in my mind comes from a little girl nine years old reading *Prince Valiant* comics, and seeing this strange, elusive figure slipping around behind the doings of the knights, never coming into the day, being regarded as an evil sorceress – and beginning to wonder. Why, if Malory disapproved of her so much, didn't he just cut her out of the story? And then I started to realize, it must have been that she was so integral to the legend that he couldn't. And I wanted to know what Morgan le Fey had been before the Christians got hold of her. And so, for me, it's this little girl looking at this sorceress – perhaps a psychologist would say a little girl sitting on the sidelines, watching her brothers playing knight, and realizing that the sorceress in the background is really more interesting to her than the knights.

GODWIN: In the end of *Firelord*, the characters step for a moment "outside" the story and realize what's going to happen to them in the eyes of posterity. Very Shavian. The spirit of Ambrosius says to Arthur, "I'm only a fact, but you're going to be a legend. Ought to save *something* of you for the historians." And history itself, as Shaw wrote, will tell lies as usual.